from the Salon *to the* Schoolroom

from the

Salon *to the* Schoolroom

EDUCATING BOURGEOIS GIRLS IN NINETEENTH-CENTURY FRANCE

Rebecca Rogers

THE PENNSYLVANIA STATE UNIVERSITY PRESS
UNIVERSITY PARK, PENNSYLVANIA

This book has been published with the support of the Scientific Council of the University Marc Bloch Strasbourg II and the Conseil Général du Bas Rhin.

Library of Congress Cataloging-in-Publication Data

Rogers, Rebecca, 1959–

From the salon to the schoolroom : educating bourgeois girls in nineteenth-century France / Rebecca Rogers.

p.   cm.

Includes bibliographical references and index.

ISBN 978-0-271-02491-2 (pbk : alk. paper)

1. Women — Education — France — History — 19th century.

2. Women — France — Social conditions — 19th century.

I. Title.

LC2097.R642 2005

371.822'0944'09034 — dc22

2005016965

For my mother,
Jacqueline Rogers,
with whom this adventure began.

CONTENTS

LIST OF ABBREVIATIONS

AD	Archives Départementales
ADC	Archives of the Congrégation de la Doctrine Chrétienne de Nancy (Nancy)
AMD	Archives of the Congrégation de la Mère de Dieu (Paris)
AN	Archives Nationales (Paris)
ASSC	Archives of the Société du Sacré-Coeur (Sacred Heart)
CAOM	Centre d'Archives d'Outre Mer (Aix-en-Provence)
GGA	Gouvernement Général d'Algérie
REF	Revue de l'ensignement des femmes

ACKNOWLEDGMENTS

I imagine I'm not alone in reading the acknowledgments before all else, interested in learning about the author's sense of location within an institutional framework, but above all curious to discover his or her network of colleagues and friends. And then occasionally acknowledgements offer a more personal glimpse into the whole experience of writing a book over many years, a glimpse that goes beyond the ritual thanks to those nearest and dearest and speaks to why the book exists and what it means to the author. But in the end I'm not sure it's possible to put into words what pushes us to devote years of our lives to exploring the lives of those long dead, trying to fit words to their thoughts and experiences, nor can we really express what our community of friends and colleagues has meant during this process. Still, I'll take a stab at it.

I'll begin with the easier institutional acknowledgements. The University of Iowa first welcomed me into an intellectual community and gave me Old Gold summer fellowship money as well as a sabbatical that allowed me to begin work on my "new project," oh so many years ago. The Spencer Foundation and the National Endowment for the Humanities provided summer travel money to explore archives in France. The Minda De Gunzberg Center for European Studies at Harvard gave me a study, stimulating companionship, and access to Widener Library as a visiting scholar in the spring of 1999, when I was in the first stages of writing. The University Marc Bloch in Strasbourg granted me another sabbatical in spring 2004 when I finally finished the manuscript. During that sabbatical, the University of Michigan offered me a position as a visiting professor and provided the sort of intellectual setting which made me grateful to be part of a historical community for whom women and gender count.

Libraries and archives constitute another set of institutions without which this book would not exist. Aside from Widener and the Bibliothèque Nationale de France, many archivists in departmental archives spent time advising me on where best to look for information on girls' schools and hauling out dusty cartons. I have had the good fortune to have been given access to private archives, notably those of the schools of the Legion of Honor, the Congrégation de la Mère de Dieu, the Congrégation de la Doctrine Chrétienne de Nancy, and the Congrégation de Saint-Joseph de Cluny — my gratitude to all those who facilitated this access. Special thanks must go to the Société du Sacré-Coeur and especially Phil Kilroy, who introduced me to Marie Thérèse Carré in Poitiers and Anne Leonard in Rome, and whose friendship and scholarship has been a source of succor to me for years. My first and only experience of convent life came thanks to Phil in the Society's house in the Trastevere in Rome, an experience that made me better appreciate what the life of a scholar nun might entail. Dare I confess that my love of France found a rival in Rome?

People and communities have made all the difference throughout the process of working on this book. Many people have shared their work in progress, have sent me tidbits, listened to me talk, shared my interest in French women and education, and guided me toward references, which have not only added to the bibliography but also made the book far richer. These people include Jim Albisetti, Linda Clark, Ken Cmiel, Suzanne Desan, Mineke van Essen, Dena Goodman, Ralph Gibson, Steve Kaplan, Claude Langlois, Jean-Noël Luc, Margaret MacCurtain, Rene Marion, Karen Offen, Lou Roberts, Susan Whitney, and Michelle Zancarini-Fournel. Several groups have read or heard my work, offered suggestions, and encouraged me to go on. My special thanks to the Bay Area French history group under the aegis of Susanna Barrows, to the Cornell European history group under the aegis of Steve Kaplan, to the group "Espace" and the "Groupe femme" in Strasbourg, and to the Wisconsin French history group. I have had the opportunity to present arguments developed within this book at talks and conferences throughout the world. The feedback offered in such situations, often by scholars who were not French specialists, has been particularly useful and has convinced me there is something to this move toward "global" history. Thanks then to Pierre Caspard in Paris, to Serge Chassagne in Lyons, to Margret Kraul in Germany, to Claudia Opitz in Switzerland, to Macej Serwanski in Poland, to Frances Gouda in Amsterdam, to colleagues at the University of Tel-Aviv in Israel, and to colleagues of Seijo University in Japan. In the United States, Laird Boswell, Whitney Walton, and Tom Broden have recently opened their doors to me and given me hope that an Alsatian-Midwestern connection will continue to offer the opportunity to exchange ideas, fine wine, and companionship. The meetings of the "female adolescence" group in Bielefeld, Germany, and in Columbus, Ohio, are among the best intellectual experiences I've had — special thanks to M. J. Maynes, Birgitta Soland, and Christina Benninghaus for making them happen and letting me be a part of them. My "secret garden" was nourished and replenished in that setting. Thankfully, my intellectual community in Strasbourg has not been limited to the imperial setting of our Palais Universitaire. I've shared laughter, tears, and conversations far beyond the subject of history with a number of people who have made a tremendous difference: Arlette Bothorel, Nicolas Bourguinat, Odile Goerg, Isabelle Laboulais-Lesage, Jean-Yves Marc, Catherine Maurer, Daniel Payot, André Rauch, Anne-Claire Rebreyend. . . . I'm grateful that our intellectual communities include so much more.

The members of the jury for my "these d'habilitation" — Alain Corbin, Nancy Green, Dominique Julia, Jean-Noël Luc, Jean-Luc Pinol, Françoise Thébaud — all took the time to read my manuscript and offer precious criticism. I dreaded the experience of going before a jury at age forty plus; not only did they make the experience (relatively) enjoyable, but they also offered countless suggestions for ways to improve my text, and their work has nourished mine in many ways prior to that experience. Philippe Lejeune and Viviane Isambert Jamati have generously shared their nineteenth-century sources with me, as well as their insights on how to use them and make them speak. Sarah Hanley, Linda Kerber, Rachel Fuchs, John Merriman, Michelle Perrot, and Bonnie Smith have supported my career for many years; I'm deeply grateful that they always seem to be there when I need to put their names down, once again, as potential referees.

A few individuals have taken the time to do more. Dominique Julia took me on as an unknown American graduate student in the early 1980s; he probably didn't suspect that our relationship would become one of the *longue durée*, as I continue to turn to him for advice about performing within a French historical community that I initially had not expected to become a part of. François Debarre has spent countless hours in the archives of the Seine, tracking down birth, marriage, and death certificates of Parisian boarding-school mistresses. I don't know whether to be embarrassed or proud to have communicated my passion for these women to my father-in-law. Jean-Luc Pinol welcomed me into his research group on urban history, introduced me to the pleasures of life in Alsace, notably *vendanges tardives*, and spent many hours with me making maps, only three of which have made it into this manuscript. Sarah Curtis read and commented on several chapters of the manuscript and has shared my interest in nuns for many years; Odile Goerg read one chapter and has spent countless hours listening to me talk about others. Sheryl Kroen read the entire manuscript and offered what I've come to expect: insightful suggestions for making a "bigger" argument, fabulous meals, and the kind of friendship that sustains and encourages. Céline Grasser knows this book better than anyone else, having translated it into French, offered suggestions, helped frame arguments, and passed on bibliographies and books for many years now. Pat Howard-Hudson, Howard Lay, and Mira Velimirović are always there for me. They know what their friendship means to me. Marie Louise Munts, Susan Fox Rogers, and Jacqueline Rogers proofread chunks of the text in an attempt to get rid of all those gallicisms, and have lived with me emotionally from day one, or almost. Thomas Rogers provided an example of how to write and maintain a sense of humor when surrounded by family members;

Alice and Thomas Debarre have always seen their mother at work on this manuscript in various guises. Should I laugh or cry that their vision of the historian is of a person typing on a computer? Olivier Debarre escaped rereading every word of this manuscript because I wrote it in English, but he didn't escape the way its existence has framed vacation plans and invaded family life. Still it's a lot more interesting reading than Abelian varieties, or perhaps that's a question of positioning. All of you know how much your help and support has meant through the years, but it doesn't hurt to acknowledge it now more publicly.

The transition from manuscript to book isn't an easy one, especially in this day and age. Special thanks to Peter Potter at Penn State University Press for taking the time to read my manuscript and for believing that French history still remains of interest in our global world. Anonymous readers, whose reports lit up my year, offered useful suggestions most of which I took. Andrew Lewis copyedited the manuscript with great thoroughness, revealing to me how very French my English has become.

My first book was published in 1992, less than five years after defending my dissertation. I'll leave the reader to calculate the years I've spent on this book; somehow I seem to have left the fast track between then and now. One explanation may lie in my decision to give up competitive running during those years. No more striving to go ever faster or to maintain the pace. The more probable explanation for this slackening of the pace lies in my decision to leave the University of Iowa in 1994 for the University of Strasbourg, a decision that involved far more than packing boxes of books and translating lectures into French. Adapting to the French university environment proved more arduous than I had imagined, despite my intellectual familiarity with the history of the French educational system. Teaching and teaching expectations are wildly different in France, and scholarly resources are conceived along different lines. Although I had easier access to French libraries and archives, I lost the institutional support an American research university offers: an office, research and teaching assistants, summer support, time off for research. As a result, while I continued to scour archives in the summer — to the distress of my family — I had a great deal of difficulty finding the time to sit down and write. Still I have come to appreciate what I received in exchange: first-hand experience of those "lessons in community" I explore in this book. The collective organization of research programs in France brought home in a very visceral sense why we do what we do. Scholarship is about community and speaking together despite different languages, different traditions, and different expectations. It's often been frustrating, and it hasn't always worked, but when it has, I've realized how much this experience of fitting into another national culture has enriched my intellectual and personal life. Fitting in doesn't mean becoming French, of course, and this book reflects how the process of fitting in involves borrowing, exchange, and the occasional jagged edge. I have struggled undoubtedly more than most with the difficulties of finding a voice and of determining an audience for this project, which has been so influenced by my dual national allegiances. I first dived into the study of French education because of my deeply held belief that education and schools have much to tell us about a country, its culture, and its people. As an American woman living in France, education seemed to offer a way to understand the historical roots of cultural differences in gender relations. This book is an attempt to figure out those roots, but it seeks above all to develop the dialogue between American and French historians, who do not always converse easily, particularly when it comes to the study of women.

Introduction

Reflection on the education of nineteenth-century bourgeois girls rarely conjures up images of fire and brimstone. Instead, most readers probably imagine saccharine religious and moral tales, straitlaced teachers, and dull lessons in becoming the accomplished wife and mother. For readers more versed in women's history, the term "domestic ideology" springs to mind, as well as a host of scholarly studies on both the American and British middle classes. But this is a story about French middle-class education. Does that change the images one conjures up?

Readers of French nineteenth-century novels are likely to have quite a different set of images. Think of the education Emma Bovary received in her convent school in Rouen. Initially seduced by the mystical languor of Catholic liturgy, she quickly received more openly erotic stimulation through the laundress who sings love songs and sneaks novels into the convent. As readers of Flaubert's famous novel know, this boarding-school education was poor preparation for the expected duties of a provincial middle-class woman, and it certainly contributed to leading Emma astray. Similarly, George Sand's real-life education at the hands of the Augustines Anglaises in many ways went seriously awry. Although the young Aurore Dupin experienced a period of devout religiosity while in school, she also assumed leadership of the "bad girls," defied the school's rules and regulations, led her classmates in escapades on the roof, and read quantities of strictly forbidden novels. Once liberated from her convent walls, her career as writer, feminist, and adulterous mistress must have shocked and horrified her erstwhile teachers.[1] Balzac's literature is also replete with young women whose boarding-school educations led them to lives in stark contradiction with the principles of bourgeois society. To take but one example, Mme Schontz in *Beatrix* (1841) becomes a wealthy man's mistress, despite — or perhaps because of — her accomplished education at one of the schools of the Legion of Honor. Her mastery of the arts of conversation, painting, drawing, and music made her ineligible for the secluded life of the bourgeois wife.

British fiction adds another layer of images, frequently suggesting the inappropriateness of French girls' education. In Elizabeth Gaskell's *Wives and Daughters*, Cynthia Kirkpatrick finishes up her education at a French boarding school in Boulogne-sur-Mer. She returns to England a coquette, eager to seduce, but incapable of deeper love. Gaskell clearly suggests that the contrast between the serious and thoughtful Molly Gibson and her capricious stepsister, Cynthia, was in part the product of education; Molly's English home education was clearly superior to Cynthia's French education. British authors frequently portrayed French girls and young women in ways that highlighted the general laxness of French girls' education, producing women prone to ostentation and subterfuge. In Charlotte Brontë's novel *Jane Eyre*, for example, the heroine works to correct the flaws in Adèle's character; this daughter of a French opera dancer has a tendency toward flightiness of character "inherited probably from her mother, hardly congenial to an English mind."[2] Such portraits presented French codes and mores as somewhat of a puzzle. Something about French girls' education looks very different from its Anglo-American counterpart—or does it?

Alongside these images it is not difficult to find contrasting ones, although they may be less familiar to the nonspecialist. Think, for example, of those prim and proper bourgeois women whose images people family albums by the second half of the century. Surely their education bore little relationship to the fictional portrayals just described. Or there are the prolific writings of Mathilde Bourdon (1817–88), whose heroines find ultimate fulfillment in domestic settings.[3] What were the recipes that produced such domestic bliss? Countless boarding-school mistresses, like Eugénie Dubois, offered an educational program that they argued would create "sweetness in the home, the joy of your fathers and the pride of your families"—no lessons in artifice and coquetry here.[4] Are these snapshots of French bourgeois existence closer to the stuff of "real" history?

This book seeks to answer that question, suggesting that French girls' education was far more complicated and multifaceted than any single image can suggest. The writer and educator Mme de Genlis summed it up nicely when she wrote:

> The education of a woman can be compared to a complicated machine composed of many counterweights ... the most ingenious and reasoned combinations are required to maintain the perfect equilibrium. One wishes a woman to have grace, instruction and some accomplishments, and one wishes that having acquired the means to seduce and to please, she would have only a moderate desire to please and would never seek to dominate. . . . See what nuances and difficulties there are in the education of a woman!

One is forced to combine opposites, weigh virtues and reduce them carefully to the appropriate degree: what work![5]

Girls needed instruction, but also facility in the decorative arts; they needed to please, without seeking to seduce; above all, education was not the means to acquire authority. By comparing the education of girls to a "complicated machine," de Genlis suggested that it involved fine tuning and subtle touches. In sum, it represented a challenging task for educators. Although not stating it directly, her description did not encompass all girls — she was describing the education of the middle and upper classes in the aftermath of the French Revolution.

The Landscape: Education, Gender, and the French Bourgeoisie

Throughout the nineteenth century the French educational system remained strictly segregated by class. The lower classes sent their children to elementary schools at best. Secondary schooling was reserved for the bourgeoisie and concerned a very small — although increasing — percentage of the population.[6] Secondary education was also strictly segregated by sex: boys could attend a variety of both private and public institutions; and most important, boys' *collèges* and *lycées* prepared them to take the *baccalauréat* examination, which opened doors into university and professional life.[7] Girls, on the other hand, had only private institutions to choose from until 1880 when the state created girls' *collèges* and *lycées*. But even then girls' institutions did not prepare them for the *baccalauréat*. The gendered characteristics of secondary education contributed powerfully toward creating a French bourgeoisie with certain distinctive features: most notably, bourgeois women acquired unusual influence in what has been considered the "private sphere."[8]

This book studies the educating of girls to understand the fashioning of French women's identity in the nineteenth century. What did it mean to be *une bourgeoise*? The simple answer would emphasize motherhood and domesticity; *la bourgeoise* was located in the home as a wife and a mother. Her range of action was limited to the private sphere, her civil identity was merged with that of her husband's, her social worth was measured through her children and the education she offered them. As historians we know this simple answer is inadequate. It fails to register the diversity of ways these women engaged in both public and private life. It ignores how teaching and religious life allowed women to lead different lives and to achieve social and cultural authority outside the family. It obscures the increasing complexity of bourgeois society in the face of economic and urban change. And it does not even begin to address how this vision of domestic womanhood emerged in France. This book seeks to explain how domesticity triumphed as a value among the middle classes while emphasizing how education contributed to this triumph and at the same time undermined it. Most important, I argue that educating for domesticity after the Revolution involved from the beginning the breaking-down of simplistic divisions between public and private. The reconfigured family that emerged from the Revolutionary period played a central role in political debates about citizenship and formed the basis of a new social order. But what place did women hold within this family? The analysis of laws, normative discourses, and civil practices offers one way to grapple with this question.[9] Educational practices offer another. The messages bourgeois girls received in the postrevolutionary period could lead to responsibilities that were not limited to private life.

Contemporary debates testify to the difficulties in determining what women needed to assume domestic responsibilities in a society in flux. In reaction to the cultural authority of salon women, countless authors insisted that women needed only a minimum of intellectual knowledge. Most infamously, Sylvain Maréchal argued against teaching women to read.[10] Although few contemporaries went to such extremes, the association of women with knowledge posed clear problems for many. For the conservative writer and politician Joseph de Maistre, a woman's desire for knowledge betrayed her sex and femininity: "The main flaw in a woman is to desire to be a man, desiring to be knowledgeable testifies to the desire to be a man."[11] Medical and scientific opinion corroborated such attitudes and advocated an education for girls that would not overburden the mind, but rather focused on preparing the future mother.[12] However, other voices, preaching other viewpoints, existed as well, and these voices became more vocal by the second half of the century. Most notably, one finds that of Félix Dupanloup, the bishop of Orléans in the 1860s, who defended the idea of the *femme savante*. He argued, along with more outspoken feminists, that girls needed serious study to fill their domestic role appropriately.[13] Emancipation was not his goal, but his concern for the French family led him to defend serious instruction for girls. How then did schoolteachers respond to this variety of cultural messages? Schools were critical elements in Mme de Genlis's complicated machine. In action they redirected some women along unintended lines, introducing girls to values and lifestyles that bore little relation to domestic discourse even in its more liberal manifestations.

The study of French girls' education goes beyond helping us understand the making of the French middle class, since this education also influenced other societies, both colonial and otherwise. From the beginning education was part of the French civilizing mission, and girls' education was not forgotten in the efforts to spread civilization beyond the borders of France. Religious teaching orders as well as individual laywomen promulgated a French model of girl's education throughout the world. Historians are aware of the widespread ramifications of Jesuit education, but far fewer people have considered how French education for girls played into the cross-cultural interactions of modern society, producing an image of the Frenchwoman that continues to tantalize and fascinate the Western world.[14]

Peopling the Landscape: Characters and Images

This book examines the variety of schools that existed for girls in the nineteenth century, the women who ran them, and the girls who attended them. But I also wish to juxtapose the realities of institutional life with the representations that existed concerning these schools and particularly the women "scholars" who effectively moved bourgeois girls' education from the salon to the schoolroom. Attitudes toward giving women access to reason were forged in the interface between contemporary images and the actual working of thousands of schools.

Most commonly, people imagine middle-class girls being educated within convent schools. Carefully secluded from outside eyes, adolescent girls learned the lessons for domestic existence from nuns, whose knowledge of such matters was second-hand at best. Well-known women writers, in particular George Sand and Daniel Stern, have contributed to this image, painting portraits of their boarding-school existence that do not speak highly of the intellectual training they received at the hands of teaching nuns.[15] These representations, however, are only part of the story. True, many girls did indeed receive cursory educations where religious messages dominated. But many teaching nuns were in fact highly educated women whose efforts to promote serious education for women changed the character of institutional offerings. Obscure figures, such as Aimée Halley, superior general of the Congrégation de la Mère de Dieu, created educational programs in the 1860s that prepared lower middle-class girls for careers in teaching and office work.[16] Similarly, Eugénie Milleret, the founder of the Religieuses de l'Assomption, defended the idea of giving girls a rigorous intellectual curriculum that included Latin and theology.[17] Convent schools varied tremendously, but the general trend over the course of the century was toward providing an increasingly rigorous and more intellectual education for girls than had existed earlier.

Alongside convent schools, thousands of schools run by laywomen proliferated in urban settings. These institutions were heavily religious in character as well, but they were run by another set of incipient "professional women"—boarding-school headmistresses. The information we have on these women is scattered and piecemeal, but I argue their presence in the educational landscape contributed in a fundamental way to constituting a *system* of girls' secondary education. Above all, the variety of these institutions and their sheer number durably modified contemporary representations of girl's education. Boarding-school education became accessible to more than just the happy few, and the lessons of this education contributed to the shaping of bourgeois values.

Conservative pedagogical messages undoubtedly prevailed within these institutions. Girls were urged to become the angels of their homes and thus learned mainly moral lessons without much serious study. Frequently, lessons in domestic arts took priority over those in history, literature, or the sciences. But not all headmistresses adopted this limited "feminine" curriculum. Joséphine Bachellery was one such headmistress, who as the head of a small business — in 1852 she ran a Parisian school with some one hundred students, forty of whom were boarders[18] — actively sought to change the place of women in French society and proposed a program of study that would allow young women to envision lives of greater autonomy. In 1848 she went so far as to argue that "the hour has come to break the bonds that prevent us [women] from savoring certain just and reasonable family rights. It is necessary that we have access to civil and governmental functions."[19] While boarding schools were rarely the site of feminist organizing and proselytizing, they could propose far more radical messages than has been generally acknowledged. The organization and development of girls' secondary education not only helped to forge the French domestic woman but also opened the way to imagining the new woman.

Under the Scenery: Methods and Historiography

This book has emerged within a specific context. My approach to the study of girls' education reflects both my training as a social historian in France and the changes wrought by the insights of gender history and what has come to be known in the United States as the "new cultural history."[20] I have sought throughout this book to juxtapose actual schools and their students with debates within French society at large about women's ability to reason and their place in the social order. This means, more concretely, that I am interested in discourses, institutions, teachers, and students. Like an ethnographer I seek to anchor my analysis of girls' schooling within a specific historical moment and illustrate how social, cultural, and political factors were intertwined. Schools cannot be understood without considering the broader context that determined how they functioned and what they sought to achieve. By the same token, attitudes toward women and their place in society did not exist in isolation from the educators who raised girls, often along lines that failed to conform strictly to normative discourses. If we position women within a particular set of cultural configurations — as family members, students, teachers, and individuals — it becomes more apparent how female educational experiences helped forge new cultural identities. Obviously, the interplay between cultural visions of bourgeois womanhood and the institutional parameters of girls' schooling experiences produced not one, but a variety of models of womanhood.

This is not the first book on French middle-class girls' education; I am greatly indebted to the work of Françoise Mayeur, whose pioneering books on girls' education written in the late 1970s remain the standard references.[21] Over the intervening twenty years, however, historians, including myself, have looked more closely at individual institutions, have gained access to the archives of religious orders, and have begun to explore new private sources, most notably diaries and letters.[22] This wealth of new sources enables me to flesh out the institutional parameters of girls' schooling that Mayeur only suggested. My research in departmental archives has brought to light a hitherto unexplored mass of information concerning lay institutions and their teachers. As a result, I offer a social history of schoolmistresses that does much toward rewriting the educational history of the period prior to 1880.

By highlighting the workings of individual institutions, I propose a more nuanced chronology of change. I note, in particular, a first moment of change in the 1830s and then again in the 1860s, when new debates emerged and new possibilities were offered to middle-class girls. Above all, my work brings to light both an institutional context and a series of ideas about girls' education that should put to rest the argument that girls' secondary education did not emerge in France until the Republican state took action in the 1880s. Girls' secondary education has been largely viewed through the prism of studies concerning the *lycées* and *collèges* that proliferated after the Camille Sée law in 1880. Jo Burr Margadant's beautifully crafted study of the first three generations of *Sèvriennes* and the women who taught in these schools argues that the model of the new *femme professeur* was that of the earlier teaching nun. And yet we still know very little about the teaching nun.[23]

This book does more, however, than challenge the Republican *doxa* concerning girls' education. The influence of women's history, gender history, and cultural history has considerably changed the sorts of questions I ask my historical documents and shifted the focus of the story I want to tell. To be more specific, I am interested in understanding the relationship between discourses about domestic womanhood and the social practices that produced educated women. How did women teachers develop a sense of their professional identity at specific moments and how did this identity influence the messages they transmitted in the classroom? How did students respond to these messages and construct a sense of self within an institutional environment? How do these questions of identity and identity formation change how we understand the rise of the domestic woman? By engaging in these questions relating to professionalization and identity formation, this study argues that teaching was one of the important means by which bourgeois women adapted to, and influenced, the emergence of modern urban society.

This study offers a way to link interpretations of the effect of the Revolutionary period on women's place in French society with studies documenting the rise of the new woman in 1900.[24] In very basic terms, the dominant argument concerning the French Revolution is that women's voices were silenced and their political participation in the Republic squashed, so that the Napoleonic Empire only confirmed in law what Republican ideology had already elaborated—that women belonged in the private sphere, as Republican mothers, not as citizens. My analysis situates me clearly within a new wave of "revisionist" gender historians, who by combining the study of discourses with that of social and cultural practices discern a more subtle reorganization of gender relations that offered women more authority in public than has been generally acknowledged.[25] I argue specifically that schools and teaching offered women a way to bridge the gap between the public and private spheres.[26] The studies in French women's history that implicitly assume the existence of this gap have probably been unduly influenced by American and British studies of domestic ideology.[27] By highlighting what distinguishes the French setting, this book also offers a comparative perspective on the dominant interpretation concerning the relationship between the sexes in the middle classes in Europe.

Studies of the French bourgeoisie have proliferated in the past decade or so, in response to a new cultural orientation in the analysis of class.[28] These cultural approaches are undoubtedly more developed in Anglo-American scholarship than in French, but on both sides of the Atlantic there is a growing interest in understanding the formation of bourgeois identity in terms that go beyond the economic and the political. For historians interested in women, this cultural turn has opened up new ways of understanding how the politics of gender were critical in the making of the French bourgeoisie. The first such study, and one that has durably shaped our understanding of the French domestic woman, is Bonnie Smith's *Ladies of the Leisure Class* (1981). Using the tools and insights of psychologists and anthropologists in particular, she paints a persuasive picture of the *bourgeoise*, whose domestic world followed the rhythms of Catholic rites and ceremonies in stark opposition to the workings of the public arena where her rational, scientifically minded and anticlerical husband performed. Smith's concern to "put into words what women expressed through their system of domestic artifacts" offers a compelling interpretation of the rituals of everyday life that emphasizes how women actively shaped this life, thus opening a way to understand the emergence of conservative feminisms at the turn of the century. Still, Smith traces the emergence of this domestic world to the economic changes that brought major changes to an industrializing northern France: "The transition from mercantile to industrial manufacturing, however, terminated the relationship between home and business, and made for a separation of the sexes and a sharp definition of functions."[29] Women constructed their domestic worlds, but economic changes placed them in this world. Although this vision of the *bourgeoise* has been criticized, and many have drawn attention to the difficulties of generalizing Smith's analysis of a small group of elite women in industrialized northern France, this study remains the dominant interpretation of women from the French middle classes.

The influence of cultural history has pushed historians beyond the worlds of politics, industry, and the home to understand the middle classes and the fashioning of bourgeois identity. Leora Auslander, for example, has analyzed practices of consumption and argues for the role of women in the elaboration of taste with wide-ranging impact not only on the economics and the culture of the bourgeoisie but also on the formation of national identities.[30] Studies of leisure and sociability have examined such cultural practices as visiting spas, keeping pets, collecting art, buying clothes, and doing charitable work. These histories have successfully challenged a vision of bourgeois society that emerged primarily as a result of economic change.[31] Recently, Carol Harrison has studied "emulation" societies and the practices of association that forged a male bourgeois citizenry, which she argues was critical in France's transition from the Old Regime to a modern industrial society.[32] Clearly, the making of the French middle classes was a product of complex interactions, where cultural factors played an important role.

Curiously, however, few studies have placed education at the heart of their reinterpretation of the bourgeoisie and the formation of bourgeois identity. Borrowing from Simone de Beauvoir, Alain Plessis writes, "One is not born bourgeois, one becomes it," but he devotes a mere seven pages to the topic in an essay of some eighty pages.[33] And yet, far more than leisure or consumption, educational practices forged ways of thinking and behaving with wide-ranging consequences for the gendered organization of middle-class society. Indeed, while the bourgeoisie is the object of many new cultural histories of France, gender and women are rarely central, in notable contrast to a long tradition of such scholarship concerning nineteenth-century England and the United States.[34]

Recent studies of masculinity have gone to some effort to address how one becomes a *bourgeois*, although the formation of class identity is not always explicitly the subject of such studies. William Reddy, for example, analyzes what he describes as the "hidden pedagogy of honor" in girls' and boys' education through a study of canonical texts by Cicero, Racine, and Sévigné. His concern to tease out how honor and emotion structured people's outlooks gives him a way to reinterpret the public sphere and reveal a male world of feeling in the first half of the nineteenth century.[35] André Rauch and Gabrielle Houbre have looked more closely at schooling practices in an effort to understand gendered identities. Within boarding schools, boys learned Latin and Greek, but also the lessons in virility that helped to forge the identity of what Rauch characterizes as the "first sex." But boys also corresponded intensely with friends and family and developed a sentimental culture that does much to nuance our vision of what constituted bourgeois masculinity.[36] For their part, girls imbibed religious lessons, learned to sew, embroider, and play the piano, but they also acquired some book knowledge and learned the importance of community. How did these very gendered educational experiences shape French bourgeois society?

The books just mentioned offer ways to understand the construction of French gender identities, but they do not trace changes over a broad period of time. Their focus, moreover, is not specifically on bourgeois society and women's place within it. This book then uses the study of girls' education to shed light on a host of questions that preoccupy social, cultural, and political historians today, questions that revolve around the rise of companionate marriage, the emergence of women professionals, the development of gendered forms of political consciousness, the formation of gendered adolescent identity, and representations of women's relationship to culture. By looking carefully at the messages girls received, at the women who transmitted these messages, and at the institutions that gave girls access to forms of knowledge, this analysis sheds light on the making of a bourgeois society where women were active not just in the home and in the church but also in the intermediate social space of schools, institutions whose impact was far more complex than has been generally acknowledged, and which peppered not only the French urban landscape but also that of colonial and foreign cities.

This book compares the characteristics of French girlhood and womanhood with the better-known British and American models. Does the oft-repeated comparison between cloistered French girls and independent American and British girls bear up under closer examination? How does my analysis of French "learned women" modify the stereotypical image of the sexy and liberated adult French woman? What does a comparative perspective on schooling experiences teach us about distinctly national models of gender relations?

A final remark concerns the spatial metaphors and images that structure the entire book. My interest in both material and metaphoric spaces stems from my effort to understand the realities of the public/private divide within French society. Nineteenth-century writers constantly refer to the concept of public and private spheres, and they unquestioningly positioned women within the latter. The moralist and writer Paulin Limayrac, for example, emphasized that "the domestic hearth is [women's] real nation; public life is for them a sort of foreign soil."[37] Such statements have clearly encouraged many historians to envision the existence of a physical reality behind this division. As a result, bourgeois women have been studied within the home or within the church or else studied as they entered public space, through analyses of the feminist movements. By turning my attention to the organization of institutional space as well as to the relationship of schools to urban space around them, I am explicitly seeking to muddy the boundaries that have been erected around such concepts as "public" and "private." Above all, I am arguing that schools and a certain type of woman professional deserve attention within the landscape of modernity alongside such objects as the new apartment houses, the department store, the wax museum, women shoppers, and women actresses.[38] My consideration of spatial arrangements and spatial practices is part and parcel of my concern to blend studies of representations with more material analyses.

On Roots and Flowers: Theoretical Underpinnings and Narrative Structure

This book is anchored in two academic traditions, two cultural settings, and two languages. My graduate training in Paris at the École des Hautes Études en Sciences Sociales introduced me to the methods of social history and the insights of a socio-cultural approach often associated with Roger Chartier.[39] My focus on cultural prac-tices within schools is very indebted to how he has suggested we approach the study of culture. In this intellectual setting I developed a vision of education and educa-tional institutions that owes much as well to the insights of Michel Foucault, Michel de Certeau, and Pierre Bourdieu.[40] Briefly stated, I follow Foucault in arguing that a disciplinary logic underlay the development of girls' schools, a logic that is particu-larly obvious in the organization of everyday life within institutions. Girls, like boys, experienced the weight of daily rules and regulations that sought to control and nor-malize access to knowledge. Pierre Bourdieu's work on social reproduction and on distinction has also influenced how I understand the role girls' institutions played in French society. For girls, gaining access to schoolrooms often occurred for profoundly conservative reasons, and families frequently sought a certain type of "salon" educa-tion that had far more to do with seeking status than with providing their daughters with a means to achieve independence. And yet, I argue, inspired in part by the work of Michel de Certeau, that these conservative and constraining institutions opened up spaces for cultural experimentation where new social practices and identities were forged. Access to knowledge for girls and access to authority for women teach-ers could, and did, at times lead to forms of emancipation and an ability to criticize and challenge prevailing gender norms.

Many readers will recognize that this vision of girls and women using reason and power to challenge existing representations also owes much to the work of historians of women and gender (who themselves have frequently drawn on the scholarship of the three intellectuals just mentioned). The insights of such scholars as Natalie Zemon Davis, Joan Scott, Leonore Davidoff, Catherine Hall, Martha Vicinus, and Michelle Perrot have stimulated me to place more weight on understanding how the workings of gender altered the disciplinary logic within girls' schools and how the politics of gender played into the structuring of educational offerings and created hierarchies.[41] As Bourdieu has recently argued, the gendered structuring of the edu-cational system has powerfully contributed to "masculine domination," and yet it opened up opportunities for women that are also the subject of this book.[42]

Finally, my interest in landscapes, spatial arrangements, and spatial practices is the result of my encounter with urban history, particularly those works influenced by geographers and anthropologists.[43] This has pushed me to consider more carefully the relationship between schools and urban space and to ask how material space and spatial practices affect individuals and groups. This book investigates how women organized their professional spaces and then examines how they positioned their schools — both concretely and metaphorically — with respect to the outside world. I argue that this sort of analysis offers a way to go beyond the division between public and private space that has so dominated scholarship on the nineteenth century.

What then lies in store for the reader? This book is divided into three main sections, no doubt reflecting in part French rhetorical and argumentative strategies. The first section covers the period from 1800 until 1830 and analyzes postrevolutionary efforts to reconstruct girls' education. Traditionally historians have presented this period as one of political conservatism, marked by, among other things, women's retreat into the home. My purpose here is to show how a focus on educational practices offers a more complex picture. Here, as throughout my book, I juxtapose debates about women's role in French society (in Chapter 1) with an analysis of the teachers and the institutions that emerged at this period (in Chapter 2). Without a doubt, pedagogues emphasized women's responsibilities within the family, but headmistresses instituted cultural practices within schools that appear strangely at odds. By focusing on singular voices, be they students or teachers, I seek to untangle the complicated messages of the postrevolutionary period when no dominant vision of educated womanhood really emerged. Most important for the future, however, women teachers and pedagogues staked out a space for girls' education that was not solely located in the home. When one looks at education, the Revolutionary legacy does not appear unremittingly dark.

The second section considers the period from 1830 until 1870, which represents the apparent triumph of domestic womanhood. Certainly the reigning cultural discourse emphasized, as the poet and deputy Alphonse de Lamartine put it, that "women are destined to the family."[44] Chapter 3 considers then the range of ideological responses to intellectual and learned women. But this period was also one of considerable institutional growth as laywomen and religious orders opened thousands of schools, creating networks of girls' schools within urban centers. This growth also stimulated the first more systematic efforts to establish the contours of this new teaching profession and contributed to the emergence of new professional identities. Chapters 4 and 5, on lay women and teaching nuns, highlight the nature of these identities and demystify the contrast generally established between these two groups of women. More abundant sources about these midcentury schools allow me in Chapter 6 to map the institutional infrastructure and to explore its implications on the adolescent boarders within. Here again the messages are mixed; nonetheless, they clearly point to how education was increasingly a way for girls to stake out new individual identities at odds with the dictates of domesticity.

The final section then moves on to explore how culture and politics were intertwined in discussions about middle-class girls' education and had an influence well beyond the borders of metropolitan France. In Chapter 7, I focus specifically on how girls' education became "politicized" (although I argue throughout that the stakes of girls' education were in fact political from the French Revolution on). By the second half of the century, however, girls' education had become the subject of a very vocal and often acrimonious public debate. As anticlerical Republicans sought to wrest women from the influence of the church in the period between 1865 and 1880, they were forced to reconsider the characteristics of girls' education. The creation of girls' *collèges* and *lycées* was a political decision on the part of the state to offer bourgeois women the opportunity to become the responsible wives of Republican citizens. But state intervention did not radically alter the content of girls' education; on the contrary, the Republican reformers failed to consider how new professional identities had begun to emerge among women of the educated middle classes. As a result, the new institutions were premised on politically and socially conservative values, preparing girls primarily for motherhood. Not surprisingly, the new state-supported secondary system for girls was challenged from the outset.[45] This politicization of girls' education also had a national dimension, which has rarely been explored. The final chapter then considers how French lay and religious women transmitted their vision of educated womanhood to other cultural settings, both in the colonies and in the United States. This analysis highlights how, despite variations, one can indeed discern a French model of girls' education whose influence extended far beyond the French middle classes and whose ramifications can still be felt today.

PART I

Reconstructing Girls' Education *in the* Postrevolutionary Period (1800–1830)

The destruction of religious communities during the French Revolution entailed the disappearance of most girls' schools in the 1790s. As a result, the postrevolutionary period constitutes a critical moment for girls' education as schools were rebuilt and new schools were founded. Their appearance in the cultural landscape occurred precisely at a moment when the reconfiguration of gender relations was the topic of the day. For some of the protagonists in this highly public debate women bore the burden of regenerating the social and familial order, while others accused them of being lackeys of the church or hysterical revolutionaries. Without question, however, contemporaries saw education as key in shaping them for their future role, whatever that might be.

Recent historical scholarship has drawn attention to the revolutionary impact on gender relations. In particular, scholars have deconstructed discourses and representations highlighting how the Revolution and its aftermath excluded women from the public sphere, relegating them to family life.[1] The Napoleonic period consolidated this exclusion in legal terms, since the Civil Code erased married women's civil identity and established paternal authority in the family: women could not serve as guardians or legal witnesses, fathers became the sole guardians of children in the event of a divorce, paternity suits were disallowed.[2] Although historians have noted paradoxes and exceptions, most interpretations see the Revolutionary period as ushering in a misogynistic nineteenth century, where women were increasingly confined to their roles of mother and wife.

This vision of the years between 1789 and the fall of Napoleon in 1815 has recently come under criticism as a number of scholars have pursued empirical studies that bring to light other facets of women's lives. Carla Hesse, in particular, has traced the proliferation of women's writings, noting how the commercial revolution of these years allowed women to take to their pens. Although the Revolution denied women equal rights in political and civil terms, it nonetheless opened up possibilities for women to engage in public political debate and hence contributed to the democratization of cultural life.[3] Similarly Suzanne Desan's work on the family has shown the pitfalls of listening solely to the dominant Revolutionary discourses concerning women.[4] While the Napoleonic Code did indeed restrict women's rights within the family, the First French Republic offered women a degree of autonomy that they seized in order to redefine their relationship both to the family and to the state. And as citizenship and private obligations became structured around the family, women's responsibilities acquired new meaning.

These revisionist interpretations strongly influence the following two chapters. Like Hesse and Desan, I am interested in women's writings and social practices and how these created opportunities for women in the first three decades of the new century.[5] Chapter 1 explores how the writings of pedagogues and women writers shaped the cultural universe of elite and middle-class families. By highlighting the terms of their discussions on what should constitute bourgeois girls' education, I explore the variety of meanings they attributed to the concept of public and private and show the implications of their analysis for women's role in postrevolutionary society. I argue in particular that although no single model of womanhood emerged, these authors contributed in important ways to defining for the future the characteristics and responsibilities of that elusive figure — "the domestic woman." Chapter 2 moves then from discourses to practices to show how educated women from the upper classes of society carved out niches for themselves within schools, granting themselves the authority to define the universe in which young girls were raised. Specifically, I argue that familial strategies and expectations as well as educators' professional ambitions clearly resisted the more confining messages articulated in pedagogical writings, and as a result, many schools failed to conform to the expectations of these writers. As families sought to position themselves in the new order, the characteristics of their daughter's education speak eloquently to their vision of what it meant to be bourgeois. Attention to how young girls internalized both broad cultural messages and specific institutional practices offers a suggestive framework for understanding how cultural identities are forged.

I

Defining Bourgeois Femininity: Voices and Debates

In the postrevolutionary debates about gender relations men's voices have tradition-ally dominated those of women. And yet women were far from silent in these tumul-tuous years, particularly on the subject of education. Women writers and pedagogues responded to the cultural flux of this period by producing writings whose influence lasted throughout much of the century. In their texts, these women authors largely accepted the idea that the Revolutionary period had introduced radical changes in gender relations, notably within the educated classes. Their responses to the chorus of voices that proclaimed women's "natural" inferiority with respect to men granted mothers a degree of authority and influence, which tugged uncomfortably at the more limiting messages of Napoleonic society.

Women's Role in Postrevolutionary Society

Contemporaries struggled with a complicated legacy about women's cultural influence. As salon hostesses, working-class activists, or church-loving counterrevolutionaries, women were very much a part of the revolutionary story. Educated women in par-ticular had to contend with an extensive literature that attributed the decadence and fall of the Old Regime to the influence of court women in general and Queen Marie Antoinette in particular. The scurrilous denunciations of the queen's sexual and financial misdeeds said little about the relationship between women and education, but they did contribute to the idea that it was dangerous to let women assume pub-lic influence and authority.[1]

The Revolutionary Legacy: Women and Private Life

Jean-Jacques Rousseau, the prerevolutionary Genevan philosopher, is most often associated with the vision of domesticated womanhood that developed after 1800.[2] In his famous pedagogical novel, *Émile* (1762), he emphasized how natural differences between the sexes, coupled with their differing places in the social order, entailed a strictly gendered education. Writing partly in response to the pernicious public influence he attributed to aristocratic salon women, he argued that women's place was within the family, while men exerted authority in public.[3] Thus Émile's education emphasized autonomy, independence, and self-control, while his companion Sophie's education was aimed primarily at making her an agreeable and pleasing wife: "Thus the whole education of women ought to be relative to men. To please them, to be useful to them, to make themselves loved and honored by them, to educate them when young."[4] This carefully circumscribed education was a response to the figure of the salon woman with her array of female artifices; Sophie was not to have access to abstract culture or to public life in general. At the same time Rousseau praised certain aspects of "natural" womanhood, such as their presence of mind and their sensitive observations; women's intelligence was practical and intuitive, complementing men's more scientific and speculative reasoning. It followed from this vision of male/female capabilities that girls' education needed to be carefully contained and directed toward women's social role within the family. But within the family, Rousseau granted women unusual authority: "Woman's empire is an empire of sweetness, dexterity, and good-nature. . . . She must reign in her house as a minister in his state, and ensure she is given orders to do what she desires. In this respect the best households are those where women have the most authority; but when she fails to recognize the voice of authority, and when she seeks to usurp her rights and command herself, disorder ensues that can only introduce misery, scandal, and dishonor."[5]

Despite the apparently limiting nature of this vision, contemporaries for the most part noted how Rousseau highlighted women's influence. The pedagogue Riballier in 1779, for example, applied Rousseauean ideas about male education to girls' education, thus developing an argument about the need for reform.[6] As a result, the legacy of Rousseau's educational vision was considerably more complicated than has often been assumed. Certainly, he contributed to the domestication of women, but at the same time he infused this condition with new responsibilities in the transformation of bourgeois morals and the attainment of virtue.

Revolutionary debates about education reinforced the association of womanhood with domesticity. Honoré Gabriel de Riquetti, comte de Mirabeau, followed Rousseau, stating, "Interior life is women's veritable destination . . . indeed, it may be preferable that they never leave the surveillance of their mother."[7] Talleyrand's report on education in September 1791 argued that women did not need more than maternal education after the age of eight, given their position in the social order. The Revolution encouraged, however, more egalitarian visions of male/female relationships that generated efforts to offer girls the same education as boys. The marquis de Condorcet argued most forcefully that both boys and girls had a universal right to public education. He defended in particular coeducation, arguing that only such an egalitarian measure would guarantee liberty and equality within the nation.[8] Other, less well known individuals used debates about the family in the Revolutionary period to develop educational projects that sought to give women more responsibility within emerging civil society, just as the early American republic gave voice to the concept of republican motherhood. While the patriotic aspect of French girls' education vanished in Directory discourse, the Revolution opened new ways of envisioning educated women's relationship to public life that did not completely disappear after 1795.[9] In the end, however, with Napoleon's rise to power, the Empire gave greater weight to claims that women had a natural role within the family that required a certain type of education.

The new importance attributed to the family in the aftermath of the Revolution generated wide-ranging analyses of women's maternal responsibilities where the issue of their access to culture or reason through education played a critical role in defining the limits of feminine influence in the postrevolutionary period.[10] During the Empire, political, economic, and scientific discourses contributed to essentializing the differences between the sexes so that women were in effect banished from public life. As the division between public and private life was established with increasing clarity, so too were the gendered implications of this split. In particular, contemporaries associated reason and creation with the public and masculinity; women were then relegated to the home. Among the most vehement expressions of this vision was that of revolutionary Sylvain Maréchal, who in a provocative essay *Projet d'une loi portant défense d'apprendre à lire aux femmes* (1801) argued, as I mentioned in the introduction, against permitting women to learn to read or write.

Napoleon Bonaparte expressed similar reservations about women's access to intellectual studies both privately and publicly.[11] Like his contemporaries he justified limiting women's access to serious study on the grounds of their putative "natural" as well as cultural inferiority to men: "The weakness of women's brains, the flightiness of their ideas, their destination in the social order, the necessity for inspiring them with a constant and perpetual resignation and a mild and indulgent charity, all that cannot be obtained except by means of religion, a charitable and mild religion."[12] His concern to "contain" women as he wrote in 1802 is clearly reflected in the legislation adopted several years later that made women's inferiority official.

Although more measured in their approach, the Ideologues, who were associated with the journal *La décade philosophique* (1794–1807), also elaborated a vision of French womanhood defined through the figure of the *mère-ménagère*. In their writing, "women's empire" came to be associated with the domestic and moral order, which was rhetorically opposed to the former influence of women in salons.[13] Even as prominent a public figure as Germaine de Staël argued in *De l'Allemagne* that "it is only right to exclude women from public affairs; nothing is more opposed to their natural vocation than all that established relations of rivalry with men."[14] De Staël defended women's access to culture while accepting their natural location within the home. This emphasis on the necessity of confining women to private life appears somewhat paradoxical in the early decades of the nineteenth century, given the public prominence of such literary figures as de Staël herself, the poet Constance de Salm, the novelist Sophie Ristaud Cottin, and the writer and educator of princes, Stéphanie-Félicité Ducrest de Saint-Aubin, comtesse de Genlis.[15] But, as Carla Hesse has shown, this development of women's writings was part and parcel of the commercial revolution of this period that gave women increasing access to a public voice.[16] And among these voices, a certain number argued publicly for the need to develop girls' education.

Women Pedagogues: Defining Women's Empire

The educational essays and treatises of the postrevolutionary period built on an established genre that the authors generally acknowledged openly. The classic statement about women's relationship to private life came from François de Salignac de la Mothe Fénelon's highly influential *De l'éducation des filles* (1687), which urged aristocratic women to regenerate society through their influence in the family, rather than in salons.[17] This theme developed during the Enlightenment debates about the characteristics of civil and political life, as both men and women published treatises and essays proposing a more rigorous conception of upper-class girls' education.[18] These writings, however, apparently had little effect on the actual nature of this education, according to historian Martine Sonnet.[19] Efforts to implement a widespread reform in girls' education received new impetus in the early nineteenth century because of the effects of the Revolutionary period and the disappearance of most existing girls' schools. The women authors I am considering wrote their proposals in a context of considerable institutional void and social turmoil; and since they were themselves of upper-class origin, they inevitably associated their own often traumatic experience of the Revolution with their reflections on girls' education and the role of women in French society.[20] Moreover, as they considered the role of women in postrevolutionary France, they addressed a far broader audience than earlier reformers had, for their interest in reforming the education of girls was part of a desire to refashion both aristocratic and bourgeois family life.

I have focused on the writings of six prominent women thinkers of this period (see Appendix 1). Three of them were aristocrats — the comtesse Françoise Thérèse

Antoinette Le Groing la Maisonneuve (1764–1837), Albertine-Adrienne Necker de Saussure (1766–1841), and Claire-Elise Jeanne Gravier de Vergennes, who published under her married name Claire de Rémusat (1780–1821) — and three of them came from the upper ranks of the bourgeoisie — Jeanne Louise Henriette Campan, born Genest (1752–1822); Elisabeth Charlotte Pauline Guizot, born De Meulan (1773–1827); and Fanny Mongellas, born Burnier (1798–1829). Five of these women lived through the revolutionary years, while Mongellas's text offers the perspective of the generation that emerged from the tumult. Two authors were Protestant, Necker de Saussure and Guizot who converted, the rest Catholic, although only nominally so. Campan, Guizot, and Rémusat had close ties through their families and spouses to the ruling elite after the Revolution. Although they were all educated, their viewpoints on the appropriate education for girls were not identical. On the contrary, the diversity of their perspectives illustrates the variety of responses the Revolution produced.

For some of these women the Revolution disrupted either their lives or those of their families. Le Groing had entered the queen's *chapitre noble et séculier* in 1780; there she studied ancient history and translated Homer, Virgil, and Cicero until forced into exile during the Revolution. Returning to France during the period of the Consulate, she ran a boarding school with her sister and thus had hands-on experience as an educator. Written in 1799, her *Essai sur le genre d'instruction qui paraît le plus analogue à la destination des femmes* attracted the attention of the emperor, who sought to hire her as the superintendent of his schools of the Legion of Honor. Her text is in many ways the least ambitious with respect to girls' education; it concludes, nonetheless, with a reflection on how to prepare girls for a "major reversal in fortune," which points in subtle ways to future developments.[21]

Rémusat was the daughter of a tax official who was executed during the Terror and the grandniece of the comte de Vergennes, the foreign minister of Louis XVI. After her marriage to Augustin de Rémusat at the age of sixteen, she became lady-in-waiting to the empress and thus was well acquainted with Napoleonic court life. She both attended and hosted intellectual salons, cultivating her active and inquiring mind. Unlike Le Groing, who only published one book, Rémusat is also known for her memoirs. Her treatise on girls' education, *Essai sur l'éducation des femmes* (1824), reflects a desire to take stock and to present her enlightened vision of male-female relationships. Since she was not an educator herself, her posthumously published essay is more historical and philosophical in orientation than those of the other writers with teaching experience.[22]

Although of bourgeois origins, Jeanne Campan gravitated to both old and new elite circles. At the age of fifteen, she became a reader for the sister of Louis XV and swiftly earned the honor of becoming a lady-in-waiting to Marie Antoinette. After narrowly escaping execution during the Revolution, she found herself responsible for a sick husband and a young son. This led her to establish a boarding school that catered to the daughters of Directory notables. An astute reader of political currents and the consummate opportunist, she campaigned actively and successfully to become the superintendent of Napoleon's famous Legion of Honor schools in 1805. She wrote her well-known treatise *De l'éducation* (1824) after her fall from grace during the Restoration, as well as a number of other educational texts and her memoirs. Unlike most of the authors considered, she elaborated a pedagogical doctrine that was firmly grounded in her many years of teaching experience.[23]

Pauline de Meulan, the future Mme Guizot, lost her father, like Rémusat, in the Revolution and essentially became responsible for her family. She gave her dowry to her sister and turned to writing to support herself. Publishing notably in Jean-Baptiste Suard's newspaper, *Le publiciste*, she met François Guizot, the future minister of education, in Suard's salon in 1807. He apparently directed her toward writing on more womanly topics, and in the last years of the Empire after their marriage in 1812 they coedited the *Annales de l'éducation*. Her *Éducation domestique ou Lettres de famille sur l'éducation* (1826) clearly represents the couple's liberal values.[24]

For Necker de Saussure and Mongellas, the period after the Revolution wrought changes in their personal lives. Although Necker de Saussure was Swiss, not French, her life was intimately tied to that of France. A member of one of the leading Calvinist families in Geneva, she married Jacques Necker, the nephew of Louis XVI's minister of finance in the 1780s; her cousin by marriage was the famous French author, Germaine de Staël. When Napoleon annexed Geneva in 1797, she joined the group of exiled intellectuals who gathered around de Staël in Coppet, Switzerland.[25] While she and her family did not suffer directly during the Revolution, it did bring a downturn in family affairs that led her to write for money beginning in 1812, which may in part explain why she frequently alludes to women's careers in her three-volume *L'éducation progressive* (1828–38).[26]

Similarly Fanny Mongellas's brief life was marked by revolutionary politics, since her family left Savoy in 1814 when the department ceased to be French. She began writing amateur histories of the French regime while living in the Paris region, where she moved with her doctor husband, but her reflections on the influence of women in society were probably inspired more than the others by anxiety over her own ill health and the consequences her death would have for her family. In a sense, her *De l'influence des femmes sur les moeurs et les destinée des nations, sur leurs familles et la sociéte, et de l'influence des moeurs sur le bonheur de la vie* (1828) was a form of testament to her four-year-old daughter.[27] Unlike the other essays, this text is less pedagogical in its orientation, but its careful attention to the role of women in postrevolutionary society offers an interesting complement to the others.

Circumstances forced all these women to think seriously about their own positions in the new political order. As aristocrats, or women closely affiliated with aristocratic mores, they clearly understood that the Revolution had irrevocably changed French society, and their writings inevitably reflect their awareness that the parameters of upper-class women's lives needed to be redefined. Although the nature of their writings range from the historical and philosophical (Rémusat) to the concrete (Campan), all these women conceded women's general inferiority to men, but at the same time they also emphasized aspects of women's character that gave them a form of moral superiority. Like other women writers of their time, they adopted public voices and even at times assumed very public personae while advocating a specific role for women in private life.[28] The characteristics and contours of what constituted the private were, however, relatively more nuanced and flexible than historians have tended to recognize. Finally, all of these authors were responding as well to Rousseau's vision of womanhood and sought through their arguments to enhance women's responsibilities in a postrevolutionary world.[29]

Rémusat's *Essai sur l'éducation des femmes* develops the classic argument that "man must be formed for the country's institutions; woman must be formed for man, as he has evolved. Our natural state and dignity are as wives and mothers." More specifically, she lauded woman's destiny as wife and mother of citizens, stating that "by nature" women were made for private life.[30] In similar terms Necker de Saussure stated that "woman's special role" was "to render private life more perfect in accordance with the limits imposed by God's law."[31] More prosaically, Campan prefaced her volume *De l'éducation* with a defense of women's need for serious education, given their responsibilities within the family: "Solid instruction must render women capable of appreciating the talents and virtues of their husbands, of preserving their fortune through wise thrift, of sharing their social recognition without silly ostentation, of consoling men in times of disgrace, of training their daughters in all of their sex's virtues and of directing the first years of their sons' lives."[32] Le Groing pragmatically stated, "What society requires of a women can be reduced to the following: that she be loveable and useful in her household." She emphasized, moreover, "Women do not belong to society, they are daughters, wives and mothers, not citizens. Man belongs to the state; woman is all to the family."[33]

These authors emphasized women's roles as wives and mothers while arguing that private life had assumed new importance in the new century; for Rémusat, "domestic life has replaced public life."[34] In rather different terms Necker de Saussure recognized that "while women may have acquired greater liberty and more learning, their social influence has declined" as a result of political changes. For her the loss of public status, however, was no cause for regret, since the sources of women's empire were not natural or inherent: "This type of empire . . . was never more than a form of usurpation, an empire acquired through seduction, maintained by craft." This veiled condemnation of the erstwhile influence of aristocratic courtly women led her to recommend women's confinement to the private sphere as she urged both men and women to invest in private life and seek each other's happiness.[35] In essence both Necker and Rémusat were calling for a private life that included men and women and whose values would extend far beyond the family. Mongellas was less explicit in stating that women belonged to private life, but her judgment that women controlled daily life, conversation, and fashion, while men controlled women's influence through their writings and laws, certainly suggests that she saw women operating within a more circumscribed sphere than men. In her book she insisted that women's control of the fabric of daily life was critical in forming and modifying the character of men, and that when they abandoned this role by pursuing political intrigues, their own influence declined. To influence society effectively, then, women needed to operate within the home.[36] Le Groing was undoubtedly the most conformist in her defense of women's role within the home; still, even she noted that women's education was important to direct "habits and morals."[37]

These authors linked women's role within private life more broadly with the regeneration of society as a whole. They posited a "black" period at the end of the Old Regime when women contributed to the general decadence of French society and politics.[38] Necker de Saussure associated this decadence with how public life invaded private life, while Rémusat more elliptically referred to the negative cumulative effect of "all the elegant corruptions, all the destructive amenities."[39] In order for France to achieve moral strength once again, women needed to play a critical national role within their families. Campan, in particular, associated women's domestic life with national duty: "A true national sentiment must turn women to consider their interior as the sole theater for their glory, and soon public morality would reflect the immense steps taken in the social order toward achieving a better order of things."[40] Interestingly, while these women saw the influence of private life extending into the public, they nonetheless sought to establish clear distinctions between the two; in this effort gender roles and obligations became more sharply delineated.

Pauline Guizot also made it clear that women belonged within the home and therefore their education should not encourage the same liberty and independence as that of boys: "We are destined to exercise independence within such narrowly defined limits that there is no need for education to prepare women for more . . . the house is where we will stay."[41] At the same time she insisted on women's influence within the family: "I believe it is just as useful for women to be able to have their reason prevail as to submit to others."[42] As a result, while women were not given a broad range of action, they were seen as individuals participating in mutual decisions concerning the family. Given the new weight assigned the family in postrevolutionary France, this was not as limiting as it might appear.

On the Appropriate Studies for Women

Women required both religious and intellectual education to exercise their empire within the family. As these authors turned to consider the content of such an education, they made clear that feminine domestic responsibilities required a curriculum that would allow women to exert authority and influence in the regeneration of postrevolutionary society. Religion, in particular, conferred new authority on women even when they themselves were not particularly religiously inclined.[43] All these writers, except Le Groing, agreed that one of the fundamental problems in modern society was the loss of religious sentiment, which resulted in moral and social decline. Le Groing insisted that since religion was primarily a private affair, for women it should be less "learned" than "affectionate," and she recommended the study of religion over philosophy as a way to "transform our unhappiness into joy."[44] For the others, however, religion was a means to bridge the public and the private. For the most overtly pious of these writers, Necker de Saussure, women's natural affinity to religion required they assume a more active role in a private life whose influence implicitly extended into the public sphere. She associated the Christian regeneration of post-revolutionary society with the growth in women's religious and moral influence, while Mongellas stated more succinctly, "Our sexes' empire comes from the insights [of Christianity]."[45] Rémusat argued that one of the destructive legacies of the Revolution was the loss of religious education. In bringing it back she urged girls to move beyond family to society as a whole: "Enlightened and charitable women should unite their efforts in the countryside with those of priests; this sort of salutary enterprise will produce great moral improvement."[46] Guizot also insisted that religion and morals were necessarily linked and that the "idea of God" should expand both boys' and girls' minds.[47] Rather than insist on a certain religious doctrine, the two Protestant writers, Guizot and Necker de Saussure, argued that religious belief was integral to an educated woman's worldview, and that an active life needed the presence of God. The necessary regeneration of "morals" was linked inevitably with the insistence on the need for Christian principles in girls' education and set the terms for the increasingly tight association between women and religion in the nineteenth century. At the same time, as these examples illustrate, this association born within the home was the force pushing women to extend their influence beyond it.

Recognition of the need to educate women in religious principles did not imply, however, a conviction that they also needed intellectual instruction. Indeed, Mme Bernier's award-winning essay in 1803 argued that "women's real science" was moral: "This is the only study that is both necessary and appropriate for them . . . , this science is within their reach, is practical and ubiquitous."[48] Women pedagogues disagreed, however, and in their theoretical and practical writings argued in response to the likes of Rousseau, Napoleon, and Maréchal that women's reason needed developing and strengthening; this was part and parcel of the broader need to reform society.

Developing Reason: Education in the Postrevolutionary Period

In their defense of women's need for reason, these women authors sought to combine the strengthening of women's rational faculties with those of their religious principles in order to combat the dangers of artifice and superficiality so often associated with the female sex. Since the immorality and decadence of Old Regime France was frequently blamed on women, these writers offered a specific antidote — education. Although the content of this education was the subject of debate, they all agreed that regeneration would not occur unless women's intellectual capabilities were developed along with their moral and religious sentiments. Once again, Le Groing appears the most conservative in her attitude toward reason and learning, despite her own considerable intellectual achievements. A brief presentation of her arguments highlights in contrast the modernity of the others' positions.

Le Groing's essay noted the following subjects that all women should know in order to render them "kind and useful": domestic economy, sewing, reading ("perfect knowledge"), writing ("satisfactory knowledge") and mathematics, some notions of history, mythology, natural history and botany, and all that was necessary to nurse. Although one of her chapters is titled "What are the most appropriate studies to perfect women's reason?" she spends little time emphasizing the importance of reason over knowledge. Instead she continually warns against the dangers of overeducation; women should not be "academicians" (she herself was a member of the Société Linnéenne because of her botanical expertise), they should not be "walking libraries," they should not be lawyers, and so on. Despite the limits she placed on girls' education, her treatise reflected her own experience in its concern to prepare women for misfortune. She devoted an entire chapter to considering what "talents" would best serve women in need. Interestingly, she argued that sewing and spinning were more useful than painting and music. At no time did she suggest that teaching might prove a more lucrative way to use the knowledge acquired as a student. Writing some twenty years later, the other women authors were less timid in their proposals and above all more assertive that women had a right to educate their minds for reasons that went beyond being agreeable and useful.

Necker de Saussure, Rémusat, and Guizot most forcefully argued that reason rather than learning was the issue at stake in girls' education. Necker de Saussure's Protestantism probably influenced her when she wrote: "Women, in our opinion, should have a taste and facility for studies rather than a great deal of knowledge."[49] Similarly, Guizot argued it was less important for women to acquire knowledge than "to use what they know like reasonable beings and in conformity with the duties of their position."[50] Although couched in the language of duty, the development of critical reasoning abilities opened the possibility for women to acquire a sense of self that was fashioned by more than familial concerns. That reason could lead to independence was most strongly expressed by Rémusat. She argued that the Revolution had effected a beneficial change, since women, as a result, had greater access to reason. The bulk of her treatise dealt with the need to educate women for autonomy, and she harshly criticized pedagogical methods that introduced rote obedience and an attention to rules. Rather than have girls imbibe precepts, she wrote, they needed to acquire "real principles" so that their moral instincts would be transformed into "reasoned knowledge."[51] Guizot similarly emphasized the need to develop children's reason in general, and girls' in particular. Since marital life required women to participate in discussions about finances and the future of their children, they needed to be able to assert their reason. For women to acquire this empire they needed habits of mind and the ability to think independently, which rote study would never facilitate. Mongellas represented a more conservative viewpoint in her emphasis on forming women's "spirit and heart," but she nonetheless defended reason as well: "A woman needs the enlightenment of reason, fortified by the [maternal] example in order that her passions not lead her away from her religion and duties."[52]

This concern to develop women's reason was clearly a reaction to conservative attitudes that sought to contain women in a more "natural" state, leaving access to culture and learning to men. To some extent Le Groing reflected this viewpoint despite her own intellectual achievements. And yet she was aware that some women, such as herself, required better preparation for life. For the widow or the single woman: "I consider that her mind must be enlightened to the degree that is possible, so that if, in the future, she must deal with her own affairs, she will have the capability of doing so."[53]

So while the rhetoric of these texts appears conservative compared to the egalitarian statements of Condorcet or the more socialist pronouncements of later Saint-Simonian writers, it nonetheless articulated a vision of educated womanhood whose influence carried considerable regenerative power. The more practical consequences of this vision entailed refashioning girls' education through concrete pedagogical proposals. Campan and Necker de Saussure, in particular, were among the best-known writers whose detailed educational programs established the need for relatively rigorous study to develop women's intellect. The comparison of the two texts illustrates how their respective social positions as well as those of the audiences they addressed introduced subtle distinctions. Campan positioned women in the world exerting influence in ways reminiscent of Old Regime society but with a new twist. At heart she sought to form women of the new postrevolutionary elites. Necker de Saussure advocated more clearly women's domestic future; in this fashion, she took part in a broader discourse concerning the regeneration of aristocratic society, which saw domestic life as a haven for both men and women. For these landowning notables public life no longer was the center of their existence.

Campan's De l'éducation (1824)

Campan's treatise, written after twenty years as a school director, presented not a plan of study, but rather a series of suggestions that left ample latitude for improvisation. This absence of precision for the mother-educator may be related to the fact that despite her statement that home education was the best education, her text clearly suggests she had little faith that most mothers could do this well, nor did she really believe that the family was the appropriate context for a girls' intellectual and moral development: "Method and regular schedule are not the only advantages of public over maternal education. Healthy competition [émulation] reigns within schools, which cannot be introduced into private education without changing its nature. In the school it is always accompanied by generous sentiments; in the family it only produces rivalry, jealousy, and sometimes even hatred."[54] As a result, she concluded De l'éducation with a rousing defense of public education for girls, using her own institutions as examples of what this could offer.

In both home and public education, Campan insisted on a number of issues that are clear responses to contemporary criticisms of the superficiality of girls' education. To begin with she was careful to argue for the need to develop the study of religion through sacred history, through the readings of sermons, and through a daily schedule of prayers. She presented the development of religious sentiment in girls less as a natural requirement for women than as a social obligation; society wanted women to be religious, and even men with modern opinions preferred women to be religious.[55] In her view, religious education placed girls in a social context, since it introduced them to the wider world through the acts of charity that begin after the First Communion. Campan's insistence on religious values appears less to reflect intimate conviction than the recognition that such values were a necessary aspect of pedagogical discussion for this period.

Similarly, the emphasis Campan placed on inculcating the principles of domestic economy — although she never uses that expression — shows her concern to educate the "mère-ménagère." In the home, girls were encouraged to learn the value of money by paying for their lessons themselves. Like Le Groing, she also valued the development of sewing skills: "This talent most captures the wisdom of an educational plan and responds most directly to the attacks that are constantly directed against the more developed instruction that young women receive today."[56] Moreover, needlework produced objects for the poor, so that practical work here reinforced the religious message of charity. In her section on public education, she emphasized the aspects of her plan of study that contributed to forming the future mother and wife, undoubtedly because institutional education was frequently criticized for its lack of attention to such prosaic concerns. In schools, she argued, girls must learn to care for their belongings, should sweep their classrooms, and should even learn to cook.

In terms of instructional content, Campan's plan followed a tradition of pedagogical reformers who all asserted the need to offer "solid" studies for the female sex. For young girls, she advocated the study of religious history and geography. Writing, reading, and mathematics also figured in her plan, although the general level of such studies was not made clear. In public schools students should be organized in classes according to their educational levels, and tests should be administered to determine whether students progressed from one class to another.[57] Unlike Rémusat or Necker de Saussure, Campan strongly defended the virtues of memory for strengthening the minds of young women; in this respect she seems less preoccupied with developing a girl's reasoning capacity than with ensuring her ability to appear intelligent in educated circles: "What does it matter if they repeat their lesson word by word, so long as the facts are clearly stated and the precise dates clearly etched in their memory?"[58] Like her contemporaries, she warned against reading novels or even lighter children's fiction, fearing the influence of strong emotions and concerned that such readings would replace more serious ones. While insisting on a girl's need for serious study, Campan was scarcely radical in her suggestions.[59]

Other aspects of her plan, however, were more unusual and suggest a somewhat different vision of women's role in French society than the one that she officially espoused. In particular, she advocated the use of emulation in schools to produce a challenging educational environment. Emulation meant more than the simple desire to imitate. For Campan and her contemporaries, emulation was distinct from competition in that it carried more positive overtones and was considered a stimulus of virtue. Within public life, emulation was seen to promote social cohesion rather than further individual success. While the term was generally used to describe male activities,[60] for Campan it was at the heart of her defense of public education for girls: "Emulation constitutes the strength of public education, it reigns over young minds, it directs them toward all things good and does not alter the generous sentiments of the heart and soul; only in public education does this rivalry not breed jealousy; one learns to share the happiness and the glories of others, and friendship adds as well to the pleasure."[61] Thanks to emulation within schools, girls struggled to be good, to learn their lessons, and to progress in their studies from class to class. Both rewards and punishments formed the stimulus for such behavior, which clearly took its inspiration from boys' schools in general and the Jesuit pedagogical vision, in particular.[62]

In her emphasis on emulation, Campan revealed her underlying intellectual ambitions for girls and women that emerge more clearly in the private writings I examine later. Undoubtedly, this emphasis on intellectual rigor sat oddly with the accompanying discourse on women's role within the family and hinted in these passages at the nondomestic logic underlying her entire educational program.[63]

More obviously, Campan's concern that girls develop worldly talents offers insights into the vitality of a certain image of the cultured woman whose influence extended well beyond the fall of the Old Regime. Despite her statement that singing, dancing, painting, or playing an instrument should not be the focus of a girl's education, she nonetheless devoted two of the four chapters of the *cours d'études* to such subjects, reflecting in part the weight such studies played in contemporary representations of womanhood. She justified such studies by pointing out how "talents spread charm throughout a life, they enliven solitude, add to happiness, console chagrin; but they are useful and sweet only within the home, elsewhere they can be disastrous."[64] Although her text is full of warnings concerning parental pretensions with regard to their daughter's talents, Campan's text frequently suggests how such talents allowed women access to a nondomestic future: to begin with, "talents are a poor woman's wealth" and a precaution against the slings and arrows of outrageous fortune.[65] More generally, her remarks on both dancing and piano playing suggested a worldly more than a domestic future. Girls needed to start such training early (around age seven) in order to acquire "natural" grace in body position and the ability to perform before others without false modesty.

Campan's educational program ultimately aimed at forming intelligent and accomplished women whose position in French society was far from being anchored solely in the home. She sought to form the future wives of the new postrevolutionary elites, women who could manage households, entertain as salon hostesses, and if necessary survive on their own. Writing during the Restoration, she was well aware that elite women continued to play a role in salons. But the young women for whom she was writing were not destined to have political influence, but rather to act as civilizing agents in the consolidation of a new bourgeois order.[66]

Necker de Saussure's L'éducation progressive (1828–38)

Necker de Saussure's program, written in the following decade, at a time when domestic education had become far more widely espoused, differs from Campan's in a number of interesting ways. To begin with, she begins sex-specific education at age ten and proposes a plan of study that extends beyond age twelve to age fifteen when Protestant girls participated in the religious ceremony of the *Sainte Cène*. The actual content of this education was more ambitious in its concern to develop women's reasoning powers. Second, she far more unequivocally advocates home education as the appropriate context for girls' upbringing. Finally, her treatment of training in the arts presents a very different vision of women's destiny, one where salons and balls play a minimal role.[67]

Necker thought girls between the ages of ten and fifteen should limit their intellectual studies to four hours a day, but in these four hours she packed a lot of work. An initial hour of science was expected to include both abstract reasoning, through mathematics and more concrete experiments, and observation, through the study of the natural sciences. A second hour was to be devoted to the study of languages, literature, and grammar, including the study of Latin. She advocated a third hour of history, geography, and the study of the globe in which the emphasis should not be on dates and facts but rather on understanding the ways of God and the progress of humanity. The study of history should develop "poetic imagination," and that of geography "picturesque imagination." Finally, the fourth hour was to serve as reinforcement through memory exercises of the different objects of study. Although this program was intended for more mature girls than those Campan described, it is still striking to note how much more "progressive" and rigorous her suggestions appear; unlike Campan, she emphasized learning over memorization. Still, although Necker de Saussure advocated the study of Latin, which was not normally taught to girls, her plan was clearly less intellectually ambitious than the one the boys followed in *collèges* and *lycées* at the time.[68] Boys studied classical antiquity in far more detail, pursued the study of philosophy, and generally devoted more hours to study than girls would under this plan.[69]

Necker de Saussure envisioned the young girl as a whole with spiritual, bodily, and intellectual needs. In addition to the four hours devoted to the development of women's reason, she then proposed one hour of religion, one and a half hours each for the *beaux arts*, physical education, and sewing and other domestic chores, and finally four and a half hours of freedom to rest, eat, and socialize. Religion formed the basis of her educational vision, which is in accord with her emphasis on women's role in private life. In addition, she emphasized throughout the need to continue learning and to adapt each stage in the educational process to the student's stage in the life cycle. Unlike Campan who acknowledged only the mother as educator, Necker de Saussure also encouraged the father to play a role in his daughter's education, particularly during adolescence as the young woman contemplated her domestic future. What emerges from Necker de Saussure's treatise is an image of the serious domestic woman, who exercises rather than dances, who learns to draw and sing in order to develop her soul, to train her eyes and ears, and to develop her expression, and who cultivates her relations with her family while avoiding the dangers of the world.[70] In her text, *le monde* (society) represents danger and temptation: "Society . . . is all that seduces, all that intoxicates, all that draws thoughts away from God and duties."[71] This perception was strikingly different from Campan's, who states in *De l'éducation*: "I write for society in the hope of being useful; I will not be more austere than it is."[72]

On one level it is tempting to reduce these differences to religious differences between the two authors: the Protestant emphasis on reason, the Catholic preference for memorization; Protestant austerity, Catholic willingness to live in the world. Yet in many ways, Necker de Saussure's pious domestic woman ultimately resonated more widely in Catholic pedagogical literature than Campan's reasoned and accomplished lady. In the end it seems more useful to recognize that within francophone Europe, domesticity, as a vision of womanhood, presented different faces depending on social positioning. Campan wrote implicitly for the new bourgeois elites, while Necker de Saussure represented the point of view of the "new" domesticated aristocracy.[73]

All of these writers about women's role in postrevolutionary society accepted that girls' education needed to reflect changed social and political circumstances. Their approach to education was less philosophical than rooted in a specific historical context. They used examples from the eighteenth century and the Revolution to argue for new orientations and new rigor in the education of girls. In their essays and treatises, these women writers used a vocabulary that emphasized distinctions between public and private life, between the life of the city and that of the family. But this vocabulary represented something different for these women than for us today: when they redefined women's place within private life, they located political, social, and cultural influence within families that defined the characteristics of public life. Rémusat, for example, stated that domestic life was increasingly influencing both men and women. As a result, she infused her call for stronger, more rational education for women with political overtones: "The time for political reforms is that of educational programs."[74]

Necker de Saussure's writings expressed most directly the public power women acquired through their private responsibilities:

> Concerns of general interest occupy men; they defend the entire family, the city, the nation, society. On the contrary, women are responsible for individual interests or those which fall within a more restricted circle.... Poor or rich, married or free, women have influence on private life, the happiness of families depends largely on them. We speak about private life in opposition to *political* life and public functions for we have no intention to restrict women's actions to their household. On the contrary we believe they are destined to produce good widely, but their influence is always along similar lines. They speak to individual souls, their advice concerns the individual and the relations he entertains with those around him.[75]

While carefully distancing women from political influence, she nonetheless empha-sized how the public and private spheres were inextricably intertwined: "As a result there is constant action and reaction between public and private life, and it is this interaction which allows civilizations to progress along two lines. For while outside movement constantly brings new wisdom into families, these families can be exam-ples of the most perfect organization, the least subject to vices of all sorts. In this fashion, a more perfectly understood domestic administration spreads its purifying influence through a thousand different channels into society."[76] Thus while recogniz-ing women's subservience to men in the social and familial hierarchy, she nonetheless urged women to perfect an education that would allow them to regenerate society as a whole. Ultimately she argued that women should not be reduced to silence in soci-ety, because "they have been granted a mission of peace and conciliation, and when their conscience leads them to undertake the holy causes of justice and charity, their influence is often positive. They have that precious tact which, through the utterance of a word, brings back good taste, reason, and humanity."[77]

Writing Stories and Women's Experiences

Pedagogues were not alone in writing about girls' education in the postrevolutionary period. The authors of children's literature, in particular, placed the education of both boys and girls at the hearts of their moral tales, often proposing clear models of behavior for a society in transition. The messages this literature conveyed echoed many of those developed in the educational treatises I have discussed, particularly the concern to specify women's place in society and their new roles following the Revolution. Historians of children's literature have recently drawn our attention to the development of fiction for young girls beginning in 1750 and its widespread circu-lation among educated families.[78] From the outset this literature had international references, which explains the similarity of certain cultural messages in England and France in the early nineteenth century. English authors, such as Maria Edgeworth, were translated into French, and Mme de Genlis's stories were read in English. Ger-man influences were also at work; Berquin modeled his children's journal, *L'ami des enfans*, on the writings of the German Felix Weisse.[79] The work of Isabelle Havelange emphasizes the significant growth of this literature — between 1750 and 1830 the number of books for girls increased fivefold, testifying to the heightened interest in women's education in the late eighteenth and early nineteenth centuries.[80]

   This literature aimed to provide serious amusement: moral stories, plays, dialogues, and fictional letters all sought to offer models of behavior in a less didactic fashion than schoolbooks. The number of such texts grew thanks to the emergence of a few specialized editors, such as Pierre Blanchard, Alexis Eymery, and Eugène Blanchard, as well as the contributions of approximately one hundred other editors. Havelange's analysis of girls' literature (which includes both children's literature and schoolbooks) offers interesting insights into the authors of these works: of the 193 titles she examined, she found seventy-eight (40.4 percent) had women authors, and thirty-eight were anonymous. Although there were slightly fewer women authors than men (forty-six to fifty-five), the women tended to be more productive. Sophie de Renneville, for example, wrote eleven of the books under consideration. The majority of the authors came from the nobility or the upper middle classes, and many of them used writing as a source of income.[81]

Like the amateur women historians recently studied by Bonnie Smith, the women authors of this children's literature lived lives that contradicted the message they increasingly emphasized. By the early nineteenth century, writers concurred in advocating maternal education and emphasized that woman's place was in the home, and yet they themselves lived by the pen and often led quite public lives at court or in salon society.[82] Stéphanie de Genlis (1746–1830), for example, was the official educator of the royal children as well as a prolific author of children's tales. While staking out a public persona as a woman writer, Genlis praised the realm of the private and of sentiment. Revealingly, Sainte-Beuve described her in 1850 as "even more than a woman author, she is a female *teacher*, a female *enseignante*," suggesting that as an author she belonged in the public sphere, but as a woman teacher she dealt with private life.[83]

Most of these authors juxtaposed good and bad girls or women or good and bad behavior in order to highlight what to avoid. From these juxtapositions emerged a relatively complex set of values that encouraged more than simple obedience and submission coupled, of course, with religion. Since the stories' messages varied depending on the age of the reader, my analysis focuses on those that targeted adolescents — the term is at this time anachronistic — and particularly those books which considered the transition from school life to society.[84] The short stories and plays, in particular, emphasize a number of themes that echo the tensions underlined in the earlier discussion of pedagogues (who at times also wrote such literature themselves).

Three themes in particular emerge most clearly. To begin with, this literature overwhelmingly insisted on the importance of instilling a work ethic in young girls, an ethic that associated work with deeper moral values. As a result, these texts present paid women's work as a possible and viable alternative to domestic life, if necessity impelled such a decision. A second general theme concerned the need for girls to "read" their surroundings accurately. In these tales, the young girl is encouraged to scrutinize friendships and to uncover the workings of society; the emphasis is often on seeing accurately in order to discern true motives and to behave then in an honorable fashion.[85] Finally, the main objective of these stories is to help young women learn their place, not just within the family, but also within society, and in this way they transmitted class values.

Authors of girls' fiction sought to amuse and educate their readers—both mothers and daughters—through a variety of narrative strategies. Most frequently, they wrote short stories or plays where the moral and didactic message emerged quickly in a few pages. Such stories lent themselves to an educational use, be it at home or in a school.[86] Some authors preferred, however, to write lengthy stories that required solitary reading; the absence of chapters, for example in Amélie Castel de Courval's *Les jeunes orphelines ou les contes d'une grand-mère* clearly rendered a more pedagogical use of this book difficult. The burgeoning production of this literature testifies to its success.

Work, Play, and Moral Qualities

All of these authors sought to convey the idea that girls and women needed to occupy their time usefully; even activities that seemed like play were to be done seriously in order to instill work habits and cultivate self-discipline. This message emerges clearly in the writings of the enormously productive author Elisabeth Félicie Bayle-Mouillard, who published under the pseudonym of Madame Celnart.[87] In her two-volume book, *La sortie de pension ou la bonne tante*, the reader follows the experiences of Claire Desan, who has just completed her boarding-school education at a school run by the Chanoinesses de Saint-Augustin. Returning home to her recently widowed father, she unwittingly disappoints him with her idle chatter and the superficiality of her knowledge. Her aunt then undertakes her second education, forcing her to recognize that she must continue her studies and cultivate her mind in order to deal with solitude: "The first goal of an education is to preserve us against the weight of boredom and the errors of passions."[88] This book insists, like many others, that a serious education is important for personal reasons, since the young girl then better appreciates the world around her, but it is also a necessary precondition for motherhood. In a more serious book, Bayle-Mouillard noted in the preface that "frivolous occupations almost always bring about the decline of morality and lead, little by little, to the forgetting of duties."[89] Thus serious occupations were presented as an antidote to decadence. This message is often more subtly communicated through examples of older girls who take in hand the education of younger ones. This is the case in Julie Carroy's book, *Étude et récréation ou l'intérieur d'un pensionnat*. Here Zélie, the model student, argues that good education is "the conjunction of sciences which teach us to live in peace with each other, to aid those in need by inspiring in us the courage to instruct those whose means are not equivalent to their desires, to relieve those who are in misery."[90]

The emphasis on work and on pursuing studies in a rational fashion echoed, of course, the messages expressed in Guizot's, Rémusat's, and Necker de Saussure's writings, but it acquired a new urgency in this literature where examples of poorly educated women abounded. Above all, these stories stressed the uncertainty of the future that required girls to consider their education in potentially "useful" terms. In other words, the trauma of the Revolutionary period played itself out in countless tales where the hardworking and talented young girl had to use her abilities to earn a living. Consider, for example, Jean Nicolas Bouilly's story, "Les trois genres," where one daughter (Armande) has learned to draw, the second to play the piano, while the third and youngest pursues a number of activities in a superficial fashion. The family is ruined during the Revolution, and all three daughters are imprisoned. Thanks to small sums of money acquired from the sale of Armande's paintings, the family is able to live in some comfort, and upon their release from prison the youngest daughter has learned the value of studying things seriously. To ensure that the reader got the point, Bouilly prefaced this tale with a criticism of modern education. In his view the latter had a tendency to "touch on everything without ever pursuing anything to perfection or to any useful goal."[91] Mme Campan also offered a similar cautionary tale in her play, Les deux éducations, where she contrasted even more starkly the futile nature of Mlle Brillantine Toutor's education with that of the pious, hard-working and impoverished Aglaé Fournier. Upon completing their studies, Miss Brillantine lived up to her name, leaping into social life with a vengeance, going to balls, and sleeping late in the morning, while Aglaé supported her sisters and herself through her needlework. In the end work and high moral seriousness are rewarded, since it is Aglaé, not Brillantine, who marries a wealthy young man.[92]

Religious values and behavior do not saturate these texts, and in many instances religion is simply not mentioned.[93] The moral values that underlie these tales were more often the concern to develop a work ethic, honesty (to self and others), and only secondarily the values of obedience and submission so often presented as quintessential feminine virtues. Indeed, this literature pushed girls to uncover social realities on their own, through their schooling or life experiences. But independence or autonomy was not the object of these lessons as they were more frequently for boys. In the end the model of feminine identity that is presented is one that sacrifices personal desires and ambitions for the collective, or more frequently, the familial good.

The Dangers of Artifice: Going Beyond Appearances

In all of these tales the emphasis on work and seriousness was overladen with moral or religious messages that urged readers to judge others on the basis of inner worth rather than superficial accomplishments. Bouilly's stories in particular emphasize the need to go beyond appearances. The introduction to his frequently reissued *Conseils à ma fille* develops at some length his concern to cultivate his daughter's natural qualities as well as her ability to judge others for their inner qualities:

I am seeking to turn you into a mistress of the home, to develop your honest gaiety and your natural goodness so that you will be sought after for
these qualities rather than your lively exterior.... Finally, I seek, my dear
Flavie, to direct your heart's movements without ever constraining it, and
to guide you in the choice of a husband; I wish you to find him, not among
the masses of opulent lazy souls, the titled fools, the handsome good-for-
nothings, the pretentious learned men, the mawkish hypocrites and the
insipid lovers, but among direct men with simple manners, who exercise a
profession that is useful to the state, who are used to working, are comfortable with good morals without being enemies of pleasure, who are situated
neither too high nor too low in society.[94]

The ability to see others clearly emerges as a priority in these tales. Campan played
on this concept in Les deux éducations when she has a well-bred mother disguise herself in order to view a prospective daughter-in-law. Miss Brillantine does not pierce
her disguise, while the mother sees through the thin veneer of Brillantine's accomplishments. In story after story a contrast is established between girls who remain
simple, modest, and limited in their cultural ambitions and those girls who aspire to
dazzle others with their wit or their science.[95]

Warnings about the dangers of artifice are often associated in these tales with a
discourse on the decorative arts, echoing in this respect the prescriptions of the
pedagogical literature. Learning to sing, dance, or paint was an important part of
girls' education and could not be dismissed out of hand, but at the same time these
writers were wary of the decorative arts because they were so often associated with
frivolity and superficiality. As one writer put it: "One knows the ways the arts are
taught in boarding schools: everything is sacrificed for effect, and it is not unusual to
see the most brilliant students ignore the very basic principles of the arts they supposedly possess on a level with their masters."[96] Since the mastery of certain arts
could lead the unsuspicious to believe a young woman was something other than she
appeared, their development needed to be carefully circumscribed to avoid developing what one author described as "salon practices."[97] The comtesse Amélie Castel de
Courval, for example, clearly stated the need to teach girls these subjects, but within
the domestic setting: "Women's [talents] must only serve their own amusement;
knowledge of their existence must not leave the family." For this aristocratic woman,
author of some twenty books for young people, the decorative arts are not presented
as a potential source of work, but rather as a form of private amusement.[98] Other
authors more directly criticized the sense of pride that accomplishments at times
instilled in young girls, showing how pride could break up friendships.[99] As these
moralists reminded their readers, the inner worth of individuals should never be
judged by their ability to strum a harp or sketch a portrait.

Like the discourse on luxury and consumption in the eighteenth century, that concerning ornamental talents and artifice reflected general anxiety about the social transformations of the period. This explains in part the number of books that addressed the question of young women's entrance into society. While speaking to young girls they expected to take a place in society, they hesitated between offering them the means to decode fashion and simply warning them about its dangers. Mme Celnart, whose etiquette writings are more widely known, also wrote stories and more pedagogical texts for young girls that highlight the uncertainties contemporaries had about how to prepare bourgeois girls for society.[100] In them she emphasized the importance of cultivating individual taste, rather than simply respecting fashion. For Celnart, fashion's relationship to society paralleled that of etiquette in court society; it represented the ceremonial trappings that guided outward actions and behavior.[101] In her view, a girl needed some knowledge of fashion in order to understand society, and this justified, for example, her lessons on the historical evolution of hairstyles. At the same time, she warned against an excessive concern for fashion.[102]

Fashion, like the decorative arts, was the object of numerous warnings, since high society was represented as a world of appearances where deception frequently reigned. The desire to paint and sing was associated with this concern to be fashionable and condemned when it operated in the social space. In Bouilly's *Conseils à ma fille* the tyranny of fashion is illustrated with a story that highlights the dangers of appearances. In "La robe feuille-morte de Mme Cottin," the author vaunts the modesty of this real-life woman novelist who accompanies three young protégées to a party wearing her simple "dead-leaf dress." The other partygoers mock this woman's apparel, believing that she is a servant, until to their embarrassment they learn their mistake and rue their impolite behavior. The young women learn as a result that one must never judge others by their appearance.[103]

Society is presented as a place where deceptive practices abound, where one must learn the codes, but recognize their superficiality and above all cultivate simplicity, which is equated with honesty and inner virtue. But the value attached to simplicity did not erase subtle class distinctions that education could not eliminate. Curiously, the supposed equality of the boarding-school setting ends in many of these stories at the gate, and friendships formed at school often do not continue. Girls whose families lost their fortunes were taught that social intermingling would cease upon leaving school.[104] As a result, the authors seem to be arguing that female self-fashioning could only go so far: discernment and hard work allowed girls to function in society and support their families in times of need, but even the best of educations could not compensate for social inequalities. This literature then clearly positioned itself within a larger discourse at the time about the place of individuals, and particularly women, in a society whose markings had vanished in the Revolutionary period.

Positioning Girls and Mothers in Postrevolutionary Society

The assumed future for most of the young girls depicted in these stories was within a family setting, a setting that was, however, part and parcel of broader French society. The society young girls read about was one where class and gender differences, overlaid with moral qualifications, were painted in vivid colors so that they would learn how to position themselves with respect to others. The frivolous wealthy student was contrasted with the serious bourgeois student, the fiancé capable of discerning a young woman's true worth was opposed to the one who was fooled by talents, the indulgent father was counterbalanced by the example of the rigorous grandmother. Through examples and counterexamples the young reader was expected to acquire the capacity to judge, to discern, and to exercise her empire as justly as possible within the home. And yet a great number of these stories feature mothers who are absent or sick, and thus unable to provide appropriate examples to their daughters, at a moment when pedagogical literature emphasized the importance of mothers providing examples. In story after story girls are thrust on their own without close guidance to untangle the complicated messages of social life. While aunts or fathers sometimes stand in for the missing mother, at times they prove inadequate to their task. In Bouilly's story "Les nuances de l'âge," for example, Albertine de Rostange loses her mother at age six and is brought up along Rousseauean principles by a doting father. Her educational setting then is the outside world, specifically the port cities where her father works. Raised and surrounded by men, she adopts their easy manners and their style of speaking, thus shocking people who meet her. Ultimately, another mother steps in and warns her that her behavior is inappropriate. Albertine changes her ways and remains ever thankful. The story concludes: "Decency in a woman is like a limpid sea which the least impurity alters; just as there are flowers for each season there are nuances for every age."[105]

A twist on this theme of the absent mother was that of the bad mother who raised her daughter along false principles. Once again a Bouilly short story provides an interesting criticism of maternal mismanagement, a theme that emerges frequently in this sort of literature. In "Le premier pas dans le monde" a lawyer sends his daughter off to a boarding school to counter the influence of her mother, who has raised her to think herself above others. The egalitarian ethos of the school setting is lauded because "[the students], who were all treated equally, only received lessons in modesty, were only surrounded by subjects to emulate, only experienced sentiments of frank and disinterested friendship, and above all, had acquired that invaluable habit of being recognized for what they were worth and not who they were."[106] Unfortunately, the influence of the school setting only improves his daughter's behavior in a superficial way, and upon entering the world she is responsible for a duel where a young man dies; her father then loses public esteem, and she is condemned to caring for her parents for the rest of her life. Bouilly highlights here how thoroughly girls' education had implications for families and families' relation with society.

The absence of appropriate maternal models raises important questions about how gender relations were reconfigured after the Revolution, particularly with the execution of the "bad mother," Marie Antoinette.[107] Naturally, the loss of life associated with the revolutionary struggles and the Napoleonic wars may explain why authors frequently depicted broken families, but one would expect then to have absent fathers more often than absent mothers, and this is not the case. On the contrary, this literature is striking in the extent to which fathers intervene in the educational process and offer the critical lessons that enable girls to navigate more serenely through the seas of experience.[108] It is all the more striking if Lynn Hunt is accurate when she argues that in the new child novels of the late 1790s "children and their struggles to make their way in a shifting world are the center of interest . . . these children . . . are almost always without fathers."[109]

On a symbolic level, postrevolutionary society was undoubtedly in search of new familial models. But these literary representations reflect perhaps a more prosaic and tragic reality: these years of warfare produced a large number of boys and girls who discovered society as orphans.[110] Reconstructing the family in the first decades of the nineteenth century was both a symbolic and a material problem. Not surprisingly, then, representations of the model family were unusual; instead these stories depicted heroines who have to struggle to create such a family. In the context of the cultural reconstruction of the family following the Revolution, authors placed their heroines in situations that force them to confront and to conform to new standards of bourgeois femininity. As a result, this literature shows girls actively having to forge a sense of self and a sense of place in a world that is fragmented and deceptive and where families are not tidy or well defined. On a certain level, these stories render both the family and society problematic; they argue that there is no easy path to virtue in the face of widespread dishonesty and deception. In an uncertain world, neither mothers nor families can be counted on to provide the appropriate education. Girls must cultivate those qualities in themselves which allow them to distinguish reality from the deceptive facade of appearances. Ultimately the emphasis in these tales becomes much more the relationship between girls and the outside world than between girls and their families.

In seeking to understand the place of bourgeois women in postrevolutionary society, historians have too often understood the discourse about public and private spheres in too literal a fashion, imagining distinctions that contemporaries did not perceive. Careful readings of these classic "domestic" writers allow us to see that the postrevolutionary feminine retreat into the home was not so simple; domesticity as a normative vision was interpreted in a variety of fashions by the women who served to define for the future the characteristics of a good education for girls. The texts and stories under consideration highlight women's continued presence outside the home in what some historians have suggested we consider a "social space."[111] This social space included salons within homes, but also such public settings as dances, charities, churches, and other mixed-sex assemblies. Certainly the concept of public and private played an important role in pedagogical writing, but this rhetoric of separate spheres needs to be deconstructed. Like in Great Britain, women adopted Rousseau's message concerning civic virtue and the family to forge a space for themselves within society. By midcentury, the nuances, however, were largely lost, and historians have rushed perhaps too quickly to accept the division of public and private that the Revolution and the Napoleonic Code seemed to reinforce.[112] Moreover, these intellectual constructs pose problems for understanding the role of more social spaces, such as schools.

2

Schools, Schooling, and
the Educational Experience

The Revolution's destruction of educational infrastructures offered women educators an unprecedented opportunity for experimentation even if the economic and military climate were not particularly propitious.[1] The reconstruction of girls' schools was largely the product of private individuals, since the French state took relatively little interest in girls' education, aside from creating the schools of the Legion of Honor. The state created a public secondary system for boys in 1802, the *lycées* and *collèges*, but saw no need for an equivalent system for girls. The women who set up the new private schools were nuns or educated women who had often lost their families in the Revolution and opened both elementary and secondary schools to survive. Those who sought to attract a middle- or upper-class clientele all positioned themselves, consciously or unconsciously, in relation to the recent past and to representations of educated womanhood; their schools played an important role in defining what constituted secondary education for girls after the Revolution. Although their institutions often included lessons in the basics, contemporaries considered them to be secondary schools because of the clientele they attracted and the curriculum they proposed.

This chapter describes the educational landscape for bourgeois and elite girls between 1800 and 1830 as the product of individual educational offerings and, at times, a response to strong local demand, such as in Paris. Although the French state did not intervene in this development, the new institutions were the object of decrees and regulations at the municipal and departmental levels. In the capital, in particular, rulings emerged that defined the characteristics of girls' secondary education for the future. And as these schools came under local control, the first voluntary inspectresses appeared whose reports offer precious insight into the pedagogical practices and everyday workings of these schools. This chapter explores the characteristics of an emerging women's academic culture. How did teachers respond to the multiple messages of the pedagogical literature? How did schooling practices subvert, reinforce, or resist the dominant discourse about domesticity? And finally, of course, what messages did girls internalize in their schooling experience? By looking more carefully at a few widely publicized institutions that attracted the old elites (the schools run by the Société du Sacré-Cœur) and the new Napoleonic elites (the schools of the Legion of Honor), I seek to understand the influence of such schools on the emerging educational landscape, as well as on students' collective imaginings. The cultural borrowings between new and old elites emerge clearly in school programs and practices and help to illustrate how cultural identities were forged and transformed.[2]

The Educational Landscape

Prerevolutionary Paris was covered by a dense network of girls' schools, both lay and religious, that catered to all classes of society. Despite some efforts to establish schools with progressive educational programs as well as Enlightenment calls for serious education, however, the curriculum in most of these schools remained mediocre with a strong emphasis on the arts.[3] Educational historians of the early nineteenth century have tended to argue that showiness rather than substance characterized the new schools as well; boarding schools essentially imitated those of the Old Regime through their emphasis on the decorative arts and ostentatious theatrical productions. Campan herself repeatedly noted that competition between boarding schools resulted in institutions that "combined bad taste with a bad moral tone, thus privileging superficial talents over the education of young French women." Rivalry among institutions in the provinces produced even worse effects, where "in order to have an impressive locale, headmistresses rented theaters."[4] These judgments, however, were clearly self-serving; she sought to emphasize the mediocrity of other institutions in comparison to her own. In the years between 1800 and 1830 girls' schools proliferated, most of them run by laywomen. *Contra* Campan, the diversity of these institutions reveals a wide range in quality of girls' schooling that merits more careful attention.

Institutional Growth: Occupying the Terrain

Girls' boarding schools appeared quickly after the Terror, in part because a legislative void meant that aspiring headmistresses had relatively few requirements to fulfill.[5] Jeanne Campan's famous Institution d'Éducation de Saint-Germain-en-Laye, founded in 1795, was among the first to open its doors.[6] Within a year her school had one hundred students, and by the early nineteenth century she claims to have attracted some three hundred students.[7] Other lay schools proliferated in the early years of the Empire. In 1800 some forty-five "maisons d'éducation" run by women were noted; Goblet's administrative dictionary of Paris lists sixty schools for *demoiselles* in 1808. That same year an official report indicated eleven religious schools (and only eight of these had paying students) in the capital city.[8] Outside Paris, lay schools also opened in the major French cities, and their numbers steadily increased in the 1820s. In Amiens, for example, in the north of France, four *pensionnats de demoiselles* offered girls some form of secondary education; in west-central France Châlons-sur-Loire boasted eight such schools and Poitiers four in 1820; in 1825 in Narbonne in the south there were five boarding schools for girls; and by 1830 in the department of the Bas-Rhin twenty-three such schools had opened since 1800, principally in Strasbourg. Some boarding schools opened even in very small cities, such as Auch in southwestern France, where Mme Gary ran an institution that would form a generation of future teachers. But Paris clearly dominated with the variety of its educational offerings: in 1821 the department of the Seine had 114 lay schools, 90 of which were in the capital, and by 1830 this figure had jumped to 190.[9]

While private lay schools dominated the educational landscape throughout this period, religious teachers were far from absent: old orders, such as the Ursulines or the Bénédictines reemerged and spread throughout France, while many new active congregations were born, most prominently the Société du Sacré-Cœur (1800) and the Congrégation de Sainte-Clotilde (1821) for daughters of the elite.[10] Some of these orders, such as the Dames de Saint-Thomas de Villeneuve or the Augustines Anglaises received legal recognition for their teaching activities as early as 1802, but others functioned in an administrative limbo.[11] A first wave of recognitions occurred between 1810 and 1813 following a law in 1809, and a second wave during the Restoration between 1826 and 1830.[12]

The growth of religious teaching orders was far more visible than that of lay schools, which explains the state's early concern to control them. Given the Empire's centralizing ethos, Napoleon considered organizing these religious orders to form a national network of girls' schools. Although this project never materialized, the reports it generated reveal why he believed it necessary to provide an education for girls, particularly the daughters of his civil servants: he saw education as a means of bolstering loyalty to the Empire. The mothers of future citizens would learn not only how to exercise domestic virtues but would inspire love and respect for the head of state.[13] Education was not the means for women to achieve independence, but rather the key to establishing effective family relationships. In the end the emperor backed away from his initial idea of systematically establishing a network of religious schools for girls throughout France in favor of creating six *maisons d'orphelines* for six hundred orphans of fathers who had received the Legion of Honor.

Ultimately, the Napoleonic state only officially supported one institution for girls, the schools of the Legion of Honor.[14] In 1805 Napoleon announced his intention to offer secondary education through free tuition and board to the daughters of those who had supported the Empire, and he placed the well-known educator Jeanne Campan at the head of the first school, which opened in Ecouen in 1807. A second school opened in Saint-Denis two years later, and by 1813 an additional three schools for orphans had been created, run by a religious order. The size of these institutions — the five schools were intended to accommodate twelve hundred students — and their fame durably marked the educational landscape far beyond the teachers and students actually present, and their existence alone testifies to how this period constituted a critical moment in the development of secondary education for girls.

Rulings and Decrees

Although girls' secondary education was not the object of any legislation, girls' schools were subject to a minimal amount of supervision. Beginning under the First Empire, French officials established certain guidelines in the running of such schools; and although these guidelines and their application remained vague and poorly understood until the mid-1830s, their existence reveals an early effort to introduce professional standards in girls' schooling. In 1801 the prefect of Paris required that schoolmistresses receive authorization from the mayor of the arrondissement before opening a school, that they produce proof of having taken a teaching examination, and that they transmit two certificates of morality and loyalty to the constitution.[15] A decree of 25 pluviose an 12 (15 February 1804) placed all schools over the primary level under the supervision of the prefect. Elsewhere in France, guidelines concerning girls' secondary schools only emerged in the late 1830s and 1840s (see Chapter 4). In Paris, however, as early as 1810, the municipality published a *règlement pour les écoles de filles* that sought to define a reformed lay model of girls' education complete with qualifying examinations and inspectresses to monitor the schools. This ruling set up a placement bureau for teachers' aides (*maîtresses d'études*), defined inspectresses' roles, and established a series of regulations concerning how the school advertised itself to a larger public. More important, schoolmistresses had to take an examination to open a school. This text established the framework for future Parisian decrees.[16]

The move to regulate women teachers testifies to the state's perception that women's influence extended beyond the family; this in turn explains the concern to ensure women teacher's political loyalty to the Empire. The Empire's fall in 1814/15 did not change this perception, if anything, it was reinforced under the Restoration through the Catholic emphasis on the family.[17] On 7 November 1816 the prefect of Paris requested that his mayors seek out those schoolmistresses whose teaching certification indicated that they had pledged loyalty to the "Usurper"; these women were then required to shift their loyalties to the king.[18] In the school of the Legion of Honor at Saint-Denis, a similar anxiety about political loyalties led to the following decision:

"Any teacher, student, or cleaning woman discovered to have conversations that contain outrageous propositions concerning the king or the royal family, or anyone who utters seditious cries, sings, or is found in possession of forbidden objects, such as books or songs . . . will be expelled from the house."[19] Moreover, at this time over half of the teachers at Saint-Denis "resigned." Their personal dossiers suggest that they were dismissed for loyalty to the emperor. The widow Séron, for example, was asked to leave because, as the daughter of a Napoleonic military officer, she had "never heard" of the "august family of Bourbons."[20] The state recognized education for private life could carry political overtones with the potential to disrupt public life.

Efforts to define the new lay institutions along professional lines continued under the Restoration with an initial rule in February 1815 that schoolmistresses could no longer choose the subjects they would be tested on for their teaching certificate. Henceforth, any woman who wanted a diploma to run a boarding school or a primary school would be tested in French grammar, arithmetic, history, and geography; a teachers' aide was expected to know one of these areas in addition to being able to read and write.[21] More significant for the evolution of girls' secondary education in Paris was the ruling of 1821, which for the first time established a clear hierarchy of educational institutions above the primary level; at the lowest level were *écoles secondaires*, followed by *pensions*, and then *institutions*.[22] The prefect appointed a commission of seven people to administer the teaching examination at the Hôtel de Ville. While the head of an *école secondaire* really only needed primary education skills, the head of a *pension* was tested in the history of France and geography, and that of an *institution* was expected to know ancient and modern history and French literature. The new ruling also established a clear administrative procedure for those women seeking to open schools: schoolmistresses had to be twenty-five-years old, and their aides sixteen; an applicant needed to address a petition to the prefect or the mayor of her arrondissement; and three witnesses had to testify to the candidate's character.

Finally, the new rule devoted considerable attention to the responsibilities of the inspectresses: "Public opinion could be alarmed to see girls' boarding schools inspected by men . . . it is essential that women conduct them." The prefect appointed two women for each arrondissement in Paris, and their duties were varied. They checked for proper credentials, inspected sanitary and hygienic provisions, measured the distances between beds, and worried about the location of windows and the presence of students of both sexes. They also ensured that religious practices were properly observed, that the food was ample and healthy, and that punishments and rewards were appropriate. The rule intended to establish a greater uniformity and simplicity among establishments in an effort to eliminate the frivolous and worldly character of the new secular schools. It recommended that inspectresses should encourage the adoption of school uniforms so that "there would be no difference between those who are rich and those who are less so." In a similar vein, the prefect pronounced the end of all games, concerts, dances, and theatrical productions in the school setting. Among schools catering to the rich, the administration sought to encourage those that emphasized domestic accomplishments rather than the arts.

At the same time that the new rule created diplomas and administrative requirements for secondary-school teachers, it also established certain precedents that would plague future efforts to spread girls' secondary education throughout France. The new diplomas were given for a specific department and were not valid elsewhere in France. Although the rule encouraged schoolmistresses to use female rather than male teachers, employing the latter was not prohibited. Given the absence of any training schools for future female teachers, this effectively meant that more difficult subjects remained the exclusive domain of men. Finally, nuns were not required to take examinations, although their schools were subject to inspection.[23]

Ultimately, although lay schools were more prominent in the French urban landscape than religious schools, the latter benefited from a number of both objective and subjective advantages. To begin with, nuns did not have to establish their teaching credentials in order to open a school. This effectively eliminated an important roadblock into the profession. Second, religious women lived in communities that were able to take in more paying boarders than the average lay teacher. Finally, and most important, public attitudes toward having religious women teachers were undeniably favorable in the wake of the Revolution and the concomitant association of women with religion. As a result, they did not have to pursue potential clients as laywomen did.

School Programs and Practices: Defining Bourgeois Girls' Education

The schools that opened in the postrevolutionary years sought to attract a specific clientele through advertisements and prospectuses that defined their educational ethos. In addition, larger schools wrote up educational programs and even at times guidelines for teachers that illustrate how school directors envisioned the educational experience. These two types of sources reveal, not only the ethos of girls' education in this period, but also the skills and talents considered necessary for the bourgeois woman. The results of inspections offer insights then into the expectations of local educational officials, as well as how well normative procedures were followed.

With the exception of the schools of the Legion of Honor, these early institutions received no financial support from the state or the cities and as a result functioned as private businesses whose incomes depended on the number of boarders they attracted.[24] This was particularly true for the lay schools and was one of the reasons motivating Napoleonic officials' concern to encourage religious schools. In 1807 the minister of religion Étienne Portalis argued, perhaps unjustly, that the new lay boarding schools "are generally self-interested enterprises, genuinely commercial speculations . . . they rise and fall according to the private interests of those who found them. During their brief existence they are run by salaried teachers whom the main teacher has hired at a discount. . . . Such boarding schools have no stability and inspire little confidence."[25]

In order to survive financially, school directors needed a critical mass of students, and they needed to attract families who could afford to pay relatively stiff tuition fees. Campan in the 1820s estimated that headmistresses with fewer than fifty students made a profit from the tuition of one student in ten; in larger schools the profit came with every seventh student.[26] Tuitions varied during this period from about 600 francs a year to 1000 francs, and lessons in the arts cost extra, which effectively barred the lower and lower middle classes.[27]

Boarding-school advertisements shed light on how teachers responded to contemporary discussions about bourgeois womanhood. The larger and more expensive institutions all tended to emphasize the educational history of the headmistress or the order. In Auxerre in Burgundy, in 1802 Mme Richard de Saint-Aubin wrote that she was already known "thanks to the eminent students she had trained in Paris."[28] The Ursulines in Paris presented their school thus: "This religious institution, which has been known for two hundred years in Europe and even the colonies, needs only to reappear in France's capital, its erstwhile home, to excite considerable interest in this great city."[29] Those women who had no prior claims to fame tended to emphasize their own "polished education." Hygiene was also highlighted in advertisements and reflected heightened concern about communal living, a concern that continued throughout the century.[30] Mme Richard de Saint-Aubin indicated: "The building that it will occupy combines all one could wish for in such an institution: the space, the distribution, and the cleanliness."[31] Similarly, Mme de Bailleul's advertisement for her Parisian school began by specifying: "This house benefits from excellent air."[32]

The educational content proposed in these institutions varied, of course, but all included a core curriculum in reading, writing, arithmetic, French literature, history, and geography. Mythology also frequently figured in the program, as well as some elementary instruction in the sciences.[33] All emphasized training in the arts — drawing, music, and dance — in addition to sewing, illustrating the ongoing tension between an educational program that aimed to produce good housewives and one that really aimed at producing cultured society women. The emphasis on one or the other of these more feminine accomplishments undoubtedly reflected the anticipated clientele. Mme Masson's boarding school in Dijon highlighted the presence of three teachers who taught sewing, knitting, festoonery, and embroidery, as well as the presence of "all the specialized professors parents may wish to give their children."[34] Clearly, the families she sought to attract were less distinguished than those being courted by a school in Auxerre where lessons in music were particularly prized, including piano, harp, and vocal lessons culminating in the sort of public prize-giving ceremony that would become the object of repeated prohibitions.

Increasingly, however, schools sought to emphasize their moral and familial atmosphere in a clear effort to assuage anxieties about the danger of public education. Mme de Bailleul insisted that in her expensive Parisian boarding school "her intention is that the house never cease to resemble a united family rather than a boarding school."[35] The Ursulines made similar claims in a prospectus that merits quotation at length for how it sought to play several chords at once:

> The goal of these Ladies is to unite in their house the advantages of public with private education. On the one hand, thanks to the means of instruction, students' hearts are formed in virtue, their minds are trained in the useful sciences, they learn innocent talents and even those accomplishments that make their company sweeter and their virtue more amiable. On the other hand, they also experience the *émulation*, the pleasures of collective diversions which one finds in a wisely run institution, those assiduous attentions and that maternal solicitude that they would find in their family; this is how the Ladies will endeavor to fulfill the functions to which they are committed and which are so sweet to fulfill.[36]

Earlier in their prospectus they reinforced the family metaphor by referring to their "pious teachers or rather these second mothers."

What emerges from these different documents is a collective concern to emphasize that girls' education was directed toward forming virtuous and Christian women whose future place was in the family. But the constant reference to the arts, and to the world, make it clear that the family was more or less porous, more or less open to outside influences, and that educators recognized some parents in fact might prefer a more worldly education than the official discourse admitted.

In practice, of course, even small institutions with only ten or fifteen boarders functioned very differently from a family and found it a constant struggle to develop private virtues in a public setting. Inspection reports for schools in Paris indicate both how teachers managed this balancing act and how they perceived girls' education in the early years of the century. The first *dames inspectrices* were volunteers from upper-class families.[37] They visited a wide variety of schools, making little distinction between virtually charitable institutions and upper-class boarding schools or between lay and religious schools. Their concern was not to ensure the quality of instruction offered, but rather to ensure that all schools respected moral values: "Our goal and recompense in this tedious inspection is always to provide good wives and mothers to the state and to families; none of that can be achieved without religion."[38] Their language strikingly illustrates how girls' education in this period linked religion, motherhood, and the state.

Inspectresses found that a majority of the schools in their jurisdiction offered a "good education on all accounts." Their reports focused on the quality of the teachers, the respect for morality — measured especially in terms of the space between beds and the number of students per bed — the sanitary conditions within the institution, the rigor of supervision, and the quality of religious life: "Religion is essential for the preservation of morality, the happiness of families, and the support and consolation of individuals."[39] Mme Thomas, who ran a boarding school on fashionable rue du Faubourg du Roule, earned high praise in 1812 for her "paternal" style of education. She offered her seventy students the opportunity of studying with excellent male teachers but also provided a clean locale with careful surveillance: "Morals and religion were well respected." Small institutions also came in for their share of positive comments: "Marie Edme Martine, attractive setting, clean, well-followed education, good on all accounts, eight students."[40] Interestingly, these upper-class inspectresses virtually never mentioned needlework, which suggests that they did not actually consider this skill essential.

A number of schools, however, attracted criticism when it became apparent that the schoolmistresses were addressing the wrong cultural aspirations. In the scramble to attract a regular clientele, some institutions offered more polish than religion. In 1812, for example, inspectresses indirectly accused Mme Deffault's schools on the chic rue Faubourg Saint-Honoré of suffering from the eighteenth-century taint of "luxury." Her sixty boarders took lessons from male professors who emphasized artistic accomplishments. As a result, students learned little religion and were largely unsupervised. The same women criticized Mlle Sauvan's school for lacking simplicity. Moreover, this teacher encouraged elitist sentiments among students by allowing certain privileged girls to eat their meals separately from the others. Finally, this same report noted the dangers associated with mixing day and boarding pupils. Day students must be kept separate because "they sometimes bring books and letters and always introduce a spirit of insubordination."[41]

By the period of the Restoration, families and the outside world were increasingly the focus of criticism by both inspectors and teachers. Their influence posed problems in the efficient functioning of schools. The more intellectually ambitious religious schools in particular sought to isolate their students from the influence of their families; as a result they instituted stricter rules concerning the number of letters allowed and the right to leave the school. In 1817 an Ursuline boarding school in Brittany, for example, prohibited students from leaving school "for reasons inspired by the genuine interest of families."[42] In 1826 the Société du Sacré-Cœur took similar measures restricting the number of letters students were allowed to write.[43] Paradoxically, training women to be good mothers meant isolating them from their own mothers. Many schoolteachers were far from agreeing with Necker de Saussure that home education was the means to reform society in the aftermath of revolution.

Models and Countermodels: Forming Serious and Christian Women

The paradoxes inherent in forging a cultural model for French women that sought to combine aristocratic graces with the dictates of the new domesticity can perhaps best be illustrated through a comparison of two institutions that served as cultural references throughout the century: the state-supported schools of the Legion of Honor and the schools run by the Société du Sacré-Cœur. The first institution acquired enduring fame through its association with Jeanne Campan and its unique relationship with the state, while the second became one of the most prestigious religious institutions, attracting a wealthy and aristocratic clientele that ensured its visibility in elite circles.

Both institutions positioned themselves within a reformist discourse seeking to provide a solid education for the middle and upper classes that would serve to regenerate French society. Both institutions also developed detailed school programs and rules that provide another lens through which to examine how these institutions sought to define girls' education. Finally, both institutions left copious archives and produced literate graduates whose combined testimony paints a complicated picture of what it meant to form serious and Christian women in the aftermath of the Revolution. Ultimately, the reputation of the Société du Sacré-Cœur has suffered from its association with both the aristocracy and the church; educational historians have tended to discredit its model of education on the basis of such associations and the testimony of a few famous alumnae.[44] The schools of the Legion of Honor, however, have received more favorable historical attention even if contemporaries were not unanimous in their perception that they truly served to educate serious and domestic women. My concern here is to highlight the vision of girls' education that these institutions sought to construct while noting how this vision was altered in practice. More precisely, I will explore the relationships between normative texts, social practices, and emerging representations in the period prior to the revolution of 1830.

Visions and Programs

Napoleon Bonaparte founded the schools of the Legion of Honor with a decree on 15 December 1805 that announced the creation of three boarding schools for three hundred girls; his goal was characteristically immodest: "I won't restrict myself to raising a small number of girls. . . . I will educate four to five hundred girls or none at all, and I will reform society."[45] These schools were reserved for the daughters of his officers and soldiers who had received the Legion of Honor and were to provide free education without regard to social class. The schools at Ecouen and Saint-Denis both had women directors and a lay female teaching staff, while the Congrégation de la Mère de Dieu ran the six *maisons d'orphelines* for six hundred orphans.[46] After the fall of the Empire, Campan, who directed the school in Ecouen, was sent into forced retirement so that only the lay school at Saint-Denis survived, along with two of the religious schools in the Parisian suburbs.

Despite Campan's retirement in 1815, her pedagogical vision largely molded the educational programs that remained in effect at Saint-Denis until the mid-1840s. This vision was noticeably more ambitious and intellectual than the one she described in *De l'éducation*, and as a school director she pushed through a curriculum and established teaching practices that represented a clear challenge both to Rousseau's and Napoleon's views on the domestic woman.[47] With considerable political acumen, she presented her pedagogical objectives in rhetoric that echoed the reigning domestic discourse: "The object of [women's education] must be directed (1) toward domestic virtues; (2) toward French language, math, history, writing and geography so that all students can have the pleasure of educating their daughters themselves. Public education will thus serve maternal education."[48] Publicly, Campan insisted she was preparing women for an exclusively domestic role, but her own career and personal ambition led her to envision far wider possibilities. In particular, she was interested in establishing a program of nationwide public girls' education beyond the schools of the Legion of Honor: "Despite the undeniable success of the plan of study dictated by His Majesty the Emperor [at Ecouen], there will be problems and even intrigues so long as there is no general and definitive organization of girls' education."

Writing to Hortense de Beauharnais, a former student and step-daughter of the emperor, she laid out her proposed reorganization of the contemporary educational scene in Paris and the suburbs. In her concern to "serve the morals of a new generation," she proposed the creation of a system of boarding schools for the middle classes and day schools for the lower classes, with inspectresses to ensure their proper functioning. She specified that all teaching positions in these schools would be reserved for women. Campan placed her own institution at Ecouen at the center of her project, referring to it as "a form of feminine university where the youth of our sex will be raised and from which a normal school of women teachers will develop which will spread not only throughout the French Empire but also in the foreign schools founded in imitation of our French schools." Her own students would become the future teachers of a national system of boarding schools.[49] This ambitious — and self-serving—proposal was never seriously considered, but it does show how Campan associated public educational settings with the development of professional opportunities for women.

The curriculum she developed at Ecouen highlights the intellectual aspirations she held for her students. By 1811 the lay schools had an established program that included the study of literature, ancient, sacred and French history, geography, geometry, and a smattering of natural sciences (especially botany), in addition to more feminine lessons in sewing, hygiene, and cooking.[50] This plan of study differed from the better Old Regime convent schools in the time allotted for literature, geometry, and the sciences. While the rulebook emphasized its concern to form girls for "all that is necessary for a mother to run her interior," more ambitious goals emerge when one considers the list of prescribed textbooks. Legion of Honor students were encouraged to read the Christian orators of the seventeenth century as well as Louis Racine, J. B. Rousseau, Fénelon, Corneille, Jean Racine, and Mme de Sévigné. More recent texts by approved pedagogues of the Empire were also included such as Pierre Blanchard and the abbé Amalric; in addition the list included the catechism of the Concordat, the Napoleonic Code, and a book of biographies of the members of the Legion of Honor. Most striking perhaps is to note the similarity between this list of books and that established for boys in the Napoleonic *lycées* and *collèges*, although, unlike boys, girls were not introduced to Cicero and public rhetoric.[51] Feminine accomplishments naturally figured in the curriculum, with time allotted for the study of drawing, music, and dance.

Campan organized the educational setting with far more rigor than in existing schools. The program consisted of seven classes, each class being visually distinguished by the color of the belt on the school uniform. Students had to take examinations to advance from one class to the next, and these examinations were regularly scheduled twice a year. Existing reports show that these examinations were taken seriously, and many girls were held back when they failed to achieve the required scores.[52] Since the schools were free for most students, girls tended to stay for five to six years, ensuring an intense educational experience. Within the classroom, Campan sought to stimulate good behavior and intellectual achievement through emulation, a concept that structured her analysis of public education in *De l'éducation*. Campan was a strong believer in the pedagogical value of public rewards and punishments, and her rulebook established a wide range of both good and bad points, marks, and ribbons that were distributed on a daily basis. Girls received medals when they got good marks in academic subjects and in sewing; good points were given as well for obedience and for respecting religious duties. In this fashion, the model student combined feminine qualities of obedience and religiosity with more practical and intellectual skills. More significant, however, the systematic introduction of emulation in all aspects of daily life introduced a spirit in girls' schools that resembled that of boys' education. In the end, Campan devised a program that on paper at least endowed domestic women with serious intellectual knowledge as well as the appropriate values and practical skills.

The Société du Sacré-Cœur similarly established an educational program that testifies to religious women's concern to develop girls' reason in order to train Christian domestic women. Unlike the Legion of Honor schools, however, where the rulebook reflected Campan's coherent pedagogical vision, the initial school programs at the Sacré-Cœur more obviously oscillated between different conceptions of what constituted the Christian woman. These oscillations can be attributed no doubt in part to the differing influences at work in their development, but more tellingly they speak to uncertainties that persisted concerning the appropriate education for upper-class girls.

Madeleine Sophie Barat (1779–1865) founded the Société du Sacré-Cœur in 1800 in Amiens with the help and encouragement of the Jesuit priest Joseph Varin.[53] From the beginning, her focus was on providing education for the daughters of the French upper classes: "The Christian education of young women from the elite is the foremost and most important means for the Society to honor the Sacred Heart of Jesus, to whom it is devoted; all the houses of the Order will tend in this direction by opening boarding schools for young girls; day students will not be admitted."[54] Like Campan, the nuns of the Society saw their task in moralizing terms and added strong redemptive overtones to their mission: "The ladies who will be called to help in the education of young women must be vividly convinced of the importance of this work and of its great consequences in the propagation of faith, the honor of religion and the reemergence of good morals and true and solid piety in society." The constitution of the Société acknowledged that their task was to form wives and mothers of families and to do this they advocated the study of religion, "those aspects of profane learning that are necessary and useful for a Christian person to serve God in society," as well as domestic tasks and a minimum of domestic arts.

This balance between religion, profane sciences, domestic economy, and the arts was a tricky one, since emphasis on one or the other introduced inevitable tensions in the proposed model. Between 1800 and 1830 the Society produced four educational plans under the guidance of Jesuit priests, who gave them an unusual degree of intellectual rigor.[55] The need for such rapid revisions in the space of sixteen years speaks both to how growth and success necessitated rethinking and to the difficulties the Society had establishing the appropriate parameters for its curriculum.

In 1804 the curriculum was divided into classes that spanned initially four years; soon a fifth year was added for advanced studies, and in 1852 a sixth class was added for younger students. The educational content resembled that of the schools of the Legion of Honor with studies in the basics as well as history, geography, literature, and mythology. The natural sciences, however, were not taught; studies in arithmetic did not advance to geometry; and geography also was more limited than at the lay schools. The more feminine aspect of the curriculum differed from that of the Legion of Honor in the emphasis on studies of domestic economy, in addition to sewing and the arts. In 1806 these differences were reinforced in the revised plan, which introduced a stronger domestic orientation to the proposed studies. Indeed the plan spent more time detailing the characteristics of domestic economy than any other subject matter, arguing, "domestic economy, which was so in honor with the Greeks and Romans, requires a more elevated and more ample genius than one imagines, because it involves policing a family, which is a small republic; after the study of religion, it is without doubt the most important subject for young students. All in their instruction should tend toward domestic usefulness." This study included teaching girls to keep accounts, introducing them to the cost and quality of cloth, dishes, and pots and pans and giving them ideas for meals and home decoration. The overall inspection of the house was included in the tasks of older students, as well as learning basic concepts in law and business, since the author claimed, "It is inconceivable that women do not play a role in [outside affairs]." This unusual emphasis on learning to run a house, and indeed policing it like a small republic, certainly confirms Margaret Darrow's argument about the rise of a new domesticity in the aristocracy.[56] In addition, the whole tone of the plan deemphasized the need to shine intellectually through its warning about emulation: "[It] can awaken vanity, the subtlest of poisons for girls and the regular source of their misfortunes, their faults and their ridicule." Indeed girls were encouraged to hide their learning, cultivating an attitude that "far from pretending to have knowledge, hides it with as much care as sincerity." At the same time, however, the plan also introduced the study of foreign languages, including Latin (which ceased to figure in the plans that follow), in order to respect parental wishes. This tension between a desire to reform and a concern to attract an upper-class clientele inevitably raises questions about the spirit of girls' studies in these schools; the plans after 1806 placed somewhat less emphasis on their students' future lives as household managers.[57]

Teachers in Action: Schooling Practices

The effort to form serious, Christian women that emerges collectively from the different study plans encountered obstacles in practice that resulted from parental strategies and requests, from the constraints of institutional development, and from teachers' initiatives or limitations. The initial ethos of the Société du Sacré-Cœur, in particular, was in many respects a victim of its success among the upper middle classes and the aristocracy. In 1830 it boasted some twenty-four houses (including five in the United States) and had established a reputation throughout France for the quality of its expensive education.[58] Although Mother Superior Barat was herself from the working class — her father was a cooper — the order attracted wealthy and aristocratic novices, which naturally influenced parents seeking elite educations for their daughters.

The Legion of Honor schools at Ecouen and Saint-Denis attracted students whose fathers came from the mid to upper ranks of the military.[59] As a result, these schools mingled daughters of the solid bourgeoisie with those of both old aristocratic families and the new Napoleonic nobility. While no statistics for the Sacré-Cœur are available, evidence suggests that they catered more exclusively to the upper classes.[60] In both cases, however, it seems that the clientele did not always share the reformist ideals of either Jeanne Campan or Sophie Barat. More generally, it appears that the rulebook only presented a general framework for girls' studies that depended tremendously on the willingness of teachers to carry it out.

The teachers at Ecouen and Saint-Denis in the first two decades came from upper-class families, and many of them already had some pedagogical experience. Mme Fain had run a boarding school prior to the Revolution, and both Mélanie de Boileau and the comtesse Anne-Marie Beaufort d'Hautpoul were known for their writings for children. But this sort of experience was no guarantee that these women intended to promote Campan's pedagogical vision, and she complained frequently of their insubordination. In particular, she considered d'Hautpoul "a person who is inappropriate for our schools. She is a wit [bel esprit], we need pious and learned women."[61] The memoirs of Mme Sophie Durand indicate that both teachers and students sought the sorts of worldly distractions that the rulebook explicitly prohibited: "The teachers and the students were constantly in Paris, I frequently heard people criticizing the school at Ecouen for this."[62] Clearly certain privileged students did not live according to the rulebook and devoted considerable time to preparing their entrance into society. In March 1808 Annette de Mackau wrote home to her father describing mainly her music and drawing lessons, while two years later Nancy Macdonald noted spending most of her days doing a painting for the empress.[63] The notebooks of Eugénie Pascal-Diacre, who was a student at Ecouen from 1811 until 1814, confirm, nonetheless, that students were given a secondary education in the contemporary sense of the term; these contain lessons on the geography of the Roman Empire, on modern literature, on geometry, on English history, and on the history of the late Roman Empire.[64]

Campan's students were indeed more educated than the average bourgeois girl, but the nature of the institution, with its close association to the Napoleonic court, meant that it acquired a curiously nondomestic reputation. On the one hand, it attracted families who sought to ensure their daughters' futures through the patronage of the imperial family.[65] On the other hand, this patronage introduced envy and a sense of rivalry that retrospectively colored the school at Ecouen, in particular, with the taint of worldliness. The comtesse de Bassanville is among the most virulent in her judgment that this education turned girls "into princesses," contrary to the emperor's wishes.[66] In sum, the Napoleonic institution appeared to form women whose range of action and influence spilled out of the private sphere.

The schools of the Société du Sacré-Cœur similarly developed in ways that did not always echo the prescriptions noted in the study plans. To begin with, parents both pressured the nuns to focus on worldly talents and refused to allow their daughters to pursue a full academic curriculum, since the average number of years that students stayed has been estimated at two.[67] Unlike the Legion of Honor schools, parents paid for the education their daughters received, and the cost of these studies — between 600 francs and 900 francs a year in the period before 1830 — undoubtedly contributed to shortening their length.[68] As a result, Sacré-Cœur students frequently did not reach the upper classes, and reports indicate that the lower classes tended to concentrate the mass of students.[69] The comtesse d'Agoult's memoirs concerning the early 1820s confirm the weak level of studies, as well as the mediocre abilities of supposedly advanced students. In an oft-quoted statement, she noted that in her advanced class of girls from ages fifteen to eighteen: "Of five noble demoiselles raised by these noblewomen, only two knew how to spell correctly."[70]

Throughout these early years the schools of the Société du Sacré-Cœur suffered from a number of problems related to their rapid growth. The lack of qualified women teachers was particularly acute for them, since their need was so much greater than that of the Legion of Honor where only one lay school survived the Empire. Barat herself complained of the difficulties of finding qualified and competent teachers.[71] Perhaps more important, with its emphasis on teaching feminine graces and its lavish public prize ceremonies the Society quickly acquired a reputation for offering the trappings of an aristocratic education. This reputation stemmed largely from the example set at the Parisian school, where the headmistress, Eugénie de Gramont, cultivated the school's elite orientation. The daughter of an aristocratic émigré family, Gramont (1788–1846) used her connections among the nobility to attract daughters of the best families in the Faubourg Saint-Germain where her school eventually settled.[72] Repeated criticisms from the mother superior highlight perceived problems with the school's orientation: it opened its doors far too often to distinguished guests and had students perform theatrical plays or charades that struck Barat as particularly inappropriate, given her reformist preoccupations. Their Jesuit adviser Joseph Varin warned: "Too many people see in your Society the wit and the habits of high society."[73] As at the Legion of Honor, students appeared to come and go far too frequently for an institution whose rulebooks expressed considerable reservation about the corrupting influences of the outside world.[74] Not surprisingly, the General Councils of the 1820s increasingly restricted contacts with the outside by limiting the opportunities to leave the school and fixing a limited number of visitors to the schools.[75]

In the 1820s, concern about the nature of studies in the Society's schools prompted Barat to request a general report on the subject by one of her head teachers. In a series of handwritten memoranda, Mère d'Olivier highlighted problems within the existing system and suggested remedies. These documents offer an unusual window into the pedagogical methods and practices of this well-known institution.

As mother superior of the boarding school in Beauvais, northeast of Paris, Marie d'Olivier (1788–1866) had some twenty years teaching experience when she recommended changes in the organization and general ethos of teaching at the Sacré-Cœur.[76] Like Rémusat, Olivier situated her thoughts on education within a historical context, developing at some length the reasons for the current need for reform. Fundamentally, she saw ignorance about religion as the cause for "the excessive disorder of morals," but this ignorance of religion was directly tied to educational issues: the focus on luxury, talents, and "the sciences of calculation," coupled with the general frivolity of studies and the destruction of religious institutions during the Revolution, had produced a situation where change was needed. Rather than posit a golden age of religious education, she argued instead that women had failed to develop the "voice of reason" and as a result exerted a corrupting influence on those around them. Even more emphatically than Barat she insisted women needed not only the "reasoned principles of religion," but also a solid and varied instruction: "Women need to have an embellished mind. They must be able to converse about honest subjects in society. History and literature must not be foreign to them."

In order to promote such a serious educational plan, she insisted that the Society needed good books to put into the hands of their students, since "the taste [for reading] bolsters their home's interior, enlightens their spirit, fortifies their soul, enables them to learn their duties better, and finally, it nourishes their imagination, protecting them from one thousand errors and often from one thousand vices." Nuns from the order should write these books, and the order urgently needed to recruit such talented women to produce books on early modern history, a textbook on literature for the teachers, a book on natural history, and a book on the history of the papacy, which she proposed to write herself. This concern to develop reading and to promote serious habits was echoed in her insistence on the need to create a library for the students that would also contain the sort of light and amusing books that nonetheless instructed girls in important values and virtues. Finally, she proposed the creation of an *Annales des dames chrétiennes ou journal d'éducation*. In the *Annales* she suggested that members present, in an amusing and informative fashion, information about the Society's schools and pedagogical suggestions, as well as more general pieces about "women's duties, their destination, their interests, the dangers to which they are exposed." Her text speaks little of women's ultimate destiny but is more concerned with offering girls a "serious education" and in regenerating society via the affirmation of religious values given the increasingly important influence of women in society.

While this project never took shape and Olivier herself shortly thereafter left the Society, the report in which she articulated the reasons for rethinking girls' education clearly positions her among the postrevolutionary pedagogues discussed earlier and reveals the common interests that motivated both lay and religious women in this period.

This comparison of the Legion of Honor and Sacré-Cœur schools reveals that the characteristics of girls' education were indeed contested and took their inspiration from a variety of sources. Very real cultural tensions existed between representations of learned, worldly and domestic women, and both lay and religious institutions sought to concoct programs that threaded their way through the pitfalls of such tensions. The Jesuit priest Druilhet's lectures to the nuns of the Sacré-Cœur in 1827 provide an excellent example of the balancing act required to form serious Christian women. Warning against the dangers of yielding to the desire for knowledge for its own sake, he nonetheless urged nuns to keep abreast of new knowledge. Contrary to the 1806 plan, he argued for the need to stimulate emulation among the girls, while keeping uppermost the thought that the essential goal of this education was to inspire love for the sacred heart of Jesus. But as he listed common faults in teaching nuns, it was apparent that he recognized, as did Mère d'Olivier, how difficult it was to bolster religion and morals with serious studies in an age when parents wanted agreeable and worldly talents.[77]

In the early decades of the century, the issue of reasserting religious values and of combating worldliness preoccupied reformers the most, but it also resonated in bourgeois and elite circles as both asserted the concern to regenerate society through women's influence within the family. As the discussion of schools and school programs has shown, however, the accompanying insistence on forming serious women opened windows that did not always fit well with the proposed domestic orientation. Indeed the lifestyles and career ambitions of many of these early teachers represented clear counterexamples to the advertisements of their institutions. The contrast between the proclaimed concern to reform girls' education and the realities of schoolgirl culture emerge most clearly when one turns to the girls themselves.

Enter the Girl Students

Students' experiences in the new boarding schools of the early nineteenth century are difficult to pin down, and it is particularly hard to know whether they heard and responded to the reformist messages of pedagogues and writers. Did they perceive education itself or religious values, in particular, as a means to acquire greater influence in society? The sources that might provide answers are few and far between — a few surviving letters and the memoirs of a few students — and so what follows is necessarily fragmentary. Three questions structure this interpretation of these girls' writings about themselves: to begin with, how did girls respond to the religious values and messages that were so important in the reformist rhetoric? Second, what weight did they place on acquiring those ornamental accomplishments whose usefulness and meaning were the object of such discussion? And finally, is it possible to grasp the "imagined families" at work in these women's writings? Or to put it another way, can one see how girls positioned themselves with respect to others and most notably the family? The answers to such questions offer a way, distinct from that of normative discourses, to understand the meaning of girls' education in the postrevolutionary period.

Religious Lessons and Religious Experiences

Religious messages permeated both lay and religious boarding school life, as normative and more personal sources all concur. Within the curriculum, young girls studied the famous sermons of such seventeenth-century churchmen as Massillon, Bourdaloue, and Bossuet; in the lower grades history classes typically focused on religious history, where students learned about the "grandeurs of God and the miracles he has worked for us."[78] Lessons in sacred geography reinforced students' perception of how religion shapes both historical time and the physical world. Rulebooks all allocated a significant portion of the day to activities and lessons associated with religion and the acquisition of religious values. The school day typically began and ended with prayers; at the schools run by the Sacré-Cœur students recited catechism lessons every morning and studied sacred history for the first three of six years of study.[79] During sewing hours and mealtime it was common practice to read a religious text, and in convent schools the presence of religious teachers made concrete the more practical realities of a religious vocation. For boarders, Sundays were devoted to mass and religious rituals, and frequent religious holidays reminded students of how Catholicism structured the school year. Within Catholic schools, the required fasting on Fridays as well as during Lent was a very physical reminder of God's lessons. Finally, many young girls prepared their First Communion in a school setting, reinforcing the religious dimension of the educational experience.[80]

How then did this religious culture affect the students who were raised in such settings? For some, it provoked a religious vocation, but only for a minority. How then can we interpret the impact of this experience? George Sand's and Daniel Stern's personal writings offer some answers, despite the fact they were far from ordinary women, even among an educated elite. The daughter of an aristocratic father and a bourgeois German Protestant mother, Marie de Flavigny, the future Daniel Stern (1805–76) grew up in a cultivated family and traveled widely in France and Germany. She was brought up a Catholic, thanks to her paternal grandmother, but her family was not particularly religious, and she prepared her First Communion deco-rously, "like a well-bred person." Indeed she emphasizes that the rote learning of the catechism did not "provoke the slightest reflection about dogma or doctrine," so that the actual ceremony struck her as "the least significant event of her entire moral life."[81] In 1821, at the age of sixteen, she was placed in the prestigious Parisian Sacré-Cœur school to complete her education, and to preserve her from the dangers of life in high society.

The year that Stern spent in school in Paris left her with strong religious inclina-tions that she explains in large part by the atmosphere of piety and even mystical effusion that permeated the school. Under the combined influence of the teachings of the Jesuit father Varin as well as her admiration and love for one of her teachers, the suggestible young woman grew increasingly devout. Her descriptions of her religious awakening provide an interesting contrast to Marie d'Olivier's vision of the serious Christian woman. As Varin prepared her for her confirmation, she writes: "He avoided my questions, he exhorted me to defy Satan's traps, the desire for knowl-edge and the need to understand; he pushed aside or veiled, through reference to mystery, all those questions I found unacceptable to my good judgment or incom-patible with the pride of my instincts; he threw me at the feet of the crucifix, into the arms of Mary, into what he called the heart of God, where all reason was overcome."[82] Criticizing the absence of real theology or the rational understanding of religious dogma, the mature woman complained that

> our Catholic nourishment was steeped in an indistinguishable insipid flavor, designed to corrupt our taste and weaken our spirit. [They encouraged] a perpetual confusion between history and legend, between doctrine and mir-acle, calculated, it seemed, to trouble our young brains, and to prevent us from acquiring the strength of discernment and the ability for critical think-ing. About our conscience — nothing; about our future duties as wife and mother — nothing; natural history — nothing: nature was Satan.[83]

Although the harshness of this criticism probably reflects Stern's ultimate rejection of this religious message and her "conversion" to the cause of the Social Republic in 1848, it is likely that many girls left school having had similar experiences, where reli-gious fervor took precedence over the development of logical reasoning.

George Sand's autobiographic writings trace a similar awakening to religious life during the three years she spent as a boarder at the convent of the Augustines Anglaises in Paris. Born Aurore Dupin (1804–76), this friend and contemporary of Daniel Stern had a less conventional family background. The daughter of an aristo-cratic military officer and a poor camp follower, she was raised primarily by her mother and grandmother after her father's death when she was four. Placed in a convent school at age thirteen, she spent three relatively happy years quite isolated from her family. Unlike at the Sacred Heart, Sand's teachers were secular men and women, but clearly the nuns influenced her through their regular devotions and the religious teachings they dispensed. Like Stern, her admiration for a relatively young nun, who assumed a special role as adoptive mother, undoubtedly contributed as well to her religious conversion. For an entire year she spent her days in what she describes as "ardent devotion," throwing herself into the dirtiest tasks as a form of penance and spending long hours in the cemetery contemplating the afterlife. Although this period of mystical fervor dissipated in her final year as she adopted a calmer and more reasoned devotional life (in part under the instigation of her adoptive mother), Sand argues in her retrospective writings that religious experiences far outweighed intellectual ones. In both cases, however, these young women entered the convent school having read considerably, but with little formal religious education. As a result, it is not surprising that their introduction to the daily rituals of Catholicism within a convent school had a particularly powerful impact.

These descriptions hardly confirm a heightened concern to teach girls to reason. Was religious and intellectual development always so starkly opposed? Evidence suggests not, although information about lay schools is far sketchier, except at the schools of the Legion of Honor. Under the influence of the intellectually ambitious Campan, it appears that religion did not occupy a central position in girls' socialization. She prided herself on the reasoned piety of her students that eschewed "the false manners of poorly educated women."[84] Student testimonies appear to confirm that religious messages were not at the heart of their experiences. Marie Cappelle, who earned fame in the 1840s for her sensational trial and imprisonment following her husband's death by poisoning, did not have the sort of religious conversion described by Sand or Stern. For her the morning mass was a daily ritual that held little significance. On the other hand, despite criticizing the general educational experience, she still wrote she left the school "genuinely educated."[85] At the ripe old age of eighty-eight Thérèse-Mélanie Martin still remembered the names of the priests at Ecouen but her memoirs do not feature daily prayers, and Sunday is described as a day for walks and letter-writing, not for religious introspection.[86] Similarly, the memoirs of an early teacher at this institution, Sophie Durand, virtually ignore the religious lessons of this institution, although she notes the presence of six chaplains.[87] In Nancy Macdonald's correspondence the texture of religious life emerges somewhat more clearly when she describes her First Communion, but on the whole the religious atmosphere of this model institution certainly appears quite different from that of the convent schools described previously. What then of more modest lay institutions?

The scandal that erupted around the Reboul institution in 1822 offers some insight into these questions about the religious culture in schools, even if this probably represents an unusual case. Ernestine Reboul owned a boarding school in Paris on the rue Montaigne in the fashionable Chaussée d'Antin in 1819 when she accepted as boarders three English girls, the two daughters and a niece of Charles Douglas Loveday. The mother had initially argued, in order to overcome Mme Reboul's hesitation to take in Anglican girls, that she only wanted her two daughters and niece to stay with Mme Reboul for a few months without benefit of education. The girls remained, however, for two years. There they received some lessons in the arts but apparently experienced the sort of Catholic religious experience that encouraged them to abjure their Protestant faith. When the father accused the teachers of proselytizing, Reboul defended herself by arguing that she only agreed to discuss religious issues after two years of the "the most persevering demands" on the part of the girls.[88] While it is difficult to know what exactly happened in this boarding school, it seems clear that the daily culture was sufficiently imbued with Catholic ritual and practices to prove attractive to these young English girls, despite parental opposition.[89]

The published memoirs of writer and essayist Amélie Bosquet certainly suggest that some ostensibly lay institutions were fervently religious in tone during the Restoration. Indeed, the owner of the school she attended, Mlle Chevalier, whom she describes as "a heroine of the holy books," aspired to found a religious order, apparently without success. For the young Amélie this schooling experience was primarily religious, in the most excessive fashion: "Mlle Chevalier didn't see prayer as the sweetness of a caress between the sky and us, but rather as an austere duty toward an all-powerful and severe God. As a result, prayers took up more and more time and the boarding school transformed itself into a convent ... every day we said as many rosaries as a Muslim. We did not remain seated during religious exercises; we were on our knees in two long lines."[90]

A final, more unusual testimony comes from the future actress Frances Kemble, who spent three years in a Protestant boarding school in Paris. Within this school, like those run by nuns, religion permeated everyday life: she attended several masses on Sunday, she recopied sermons by heart, and she experienced the same religious fervor as that described by George Sand. When she heard the Genevan priest Cesar Malan, "it gave me my earliest experience of that dangerous thing, emotional religion, or to speak more properly, religious excitement."[91] Unlike in Catholic schools, however, she read the Bible frequently and even went so far as to declare that acquiring intimate knowledge of the Bible constituted "the greatest benefit I derived from my school training." But these religious lessons were coupled as well with secular studies in French literature and grammar, mythology, history, needlework, and the decorative arts.

Religious messages clearly permeated most boarding-school education, but the tenor and intensity of these messages varied according to the educational ethos of the institution. It is not surprising in many ways that Sand, Stern, and Bosquet stressed the importance of this religiosity during the Restoration when the Catholic Church staged a major comeback from its low ebb during the Revolutionary period. In the concern to conquer souls, the more elite-oriented orders like the Société du Sacré-Cœur or the Chanoinesses de Saint-Augustin undoubtedly emphasized religious values, at times to the detriment of more serious learning. In the more numerous lay schools, however, inspection reports did not overly emphasize religious issues, criticizing more frequently the frivolous character of girls' education. For reformists in this period the challenge to serious Christian women came more from families who sought the trappings of an aristocratic education rather than from the excesses of religious practices.

Performing Girls and the Talents in Girls' Education

The tension between emphasizing serious study and forming agreeable women was at the heart of much pedagogical discussion. How girls experienced this tension is a different issue and one that brings us closer to understanding how they interpreted cultural messages. Two sources offer some insights: the descriptions of prize ceremonies offer one way to explore what qualities received recognition within the school setting, while surviving letters attest to what subjects girls saw fit to report home about. While neither source speaks directly to what sort of future girls envisioned, they both suggest that the schooling experience in the early decades of the century had a very public dimension that encouraged girls to think about themselves operating more in social than in familial spaces. Moreover, families clearly encouraged this social orientation through their concern to have their daughters study the arts. At the same time, however, the importance of prize ceremonies within the new schools encouraged some girls at least to measure themselves against others, introducing an element of individual competition that marked a new departure in girls' educational experiences.

Prize ceremonies existed during the Old Regime, although our knowledge of them is largely restricted to the elaborate productions of the school for noble girls at Saint-Cyr. Founded by Louis XIV and Mme de Maintenon in 1686, the Maison Royale de Saint-Cyr sought to regenerate aristocratic education. In the early years, however, regeneration took a back seat to theatrical displays. In particular, the girls at Saint-Cyr performed Racine's plays *Esther* and *Athalie* before courtly audiences. Mme de Maintenon soon stopped these spectacles, deeming such public performances scarcely fitting for young girls, but the tradition of theatrical presentations nonetheless continued in more elite boarding schools, such as the Abbaye-aux-Bois, up to the Revolution.[92]

Not surprisingly, the new schools that emerged during and after the Revolutionary period initially renewed such practices but within a somewhat different setting that infused traditional practices with new meaning. Most notably, Campan's first school in Saint-Germain-en-Laye performed Racine's play *Esther* several times in the early years of the century. Her elaborate public prize ceremonies attracted widespread attention to her institution and placed the question of girls' education before the public eye.[93] A vivid description of one such ceremony exists for 1802 thanks to the Englishwoman Fanny d'Arblay's detailed letter to Queen Charlotte of England and her daughters. Her foreign perspective, moreover, highlights the more unusual aspects of the whole production. D'Arblay was above all struck by the highly public character of this school-ending ceremony, which included judges who were members of the Institut de France, as well as many high-ranking officials and their families. The presence of such dignitaries reflected in part the student body; First Consul Napoleon's stepdaughter and sisters were among Campan's students, although in 1802 his reserved box remained empty. Given the pomp and circumstance surrounding this occasion, d'Arblay's description of the actual ceremony is somewhat surprising. Not a simple award ceremony for work accomplished over the year, it involved lengthy public exercises where girls were tested on their writing, reading, grammar, geography, history, literature, and politics. As a result, the whole process took up a great deal of time:

> The next trial of skill was in Grammar. A Book — I did not hear its title — was given to one of the young ladies, who was desired to read the first Paragraph, stopping upon every word to declare its part of speech. When she had done, she sat down, and gave the book to her next neighbor, who, in like manner, analysed the following paragraph: and so on till every one had gone through the same task. This took an immense time, and was not very lively.[94]

The spectators naturally wearied during such exercises and got up to stroll and to talk in the garden. According to d'Arblay, "I saw more of *les élégantes* here, than I had yet beheld in France, as the room was almost filled with the rich and gay who first set afloat, or first adopt the modes of the day."[95]

The ceremony then concluded with the distribution of prizes. Characteristically for a girls' institution, the highest prize — a rose — was awarded for behavior, in this case Temper; the entire school, teachers, masters, and students chose the lucky recipient. Campan then rewarded girls with books for their academic or artistic successes. D'Arblay notes, however, that geography, history, and recitation were treated "with greater dignity" than other matters, as the members of the Institut de France spent considerable time commenting on the performances of the students. This emphasis on intellectual achievement characterized Campan's educational vision and tempers what appears at first glance to be an institution pandering to the new consular elites. Indeed, the commentary insists on how the students remained modest and demure during the entire proceeding, "seeming bent only upon their business, not their observers."

This curious mixture of public spectacle, serious examination, and prize-giving serves to emphasize the multiple messages young girls received in their schooling experience. Although Fanny d'Arblay emphasized the modest behavior of the students, a certain number must have been aware that such ceremonies were a prelude to future lives in public. Hortense de Beauharnais, for example, learned to perform first in this setting under Jeanne Campan's protective wing before appearing on a more influential stage as the wife of Louis Bonaparte and the mother of Louis Napoleon, the future Napoleon III. For the lesser-ranking members of this elite, however, the school experience taught them the importance of hard work and set a value on intellectual as well as artistic achievement.

The correspondence of Nancy Macdonald (1792–1870) with her father from 1798 until 1840 offers a unique opportunity to explore how she internalized these messages. The daughter of a high-ranking military officer, Nancy Macdonald was placed at Mme Campan's Institution in Saint-Germain-en-Laye in 1797 and remained there for the following ten years with her younger sister; from 1809 until 1810 she had special status as an older student at the Legion of Honor school in Ecouen. Since her mother had died when she was a young child, her strongest personal relationship was to her father, who paid close attention to her upbringing even as he helped the emperor wage war and climbed the military hierarchy. The letters enable one to glimpse the slow maturation process of a young girl and to trace changes in her attitude about her schooling experience. What emerges as well from this one-way correspondence is that her father encouraged her to study all aspects of Mme Campan's curriculum and wanted her to perform well.

From a very early age Nancy demonstrated a concern to please both Campan and her father through her studies, going so far as to associate her father's meritocratic promotions with her own efforts at school. When she was only six years old, she wrote: "My dear Papa. Accept my compliments for your new rank, it is convincing proof for me that merit never goes without recognition. Following your example, I want to acquire sufficient merit to become the first of my class, I desire this place so intensely so that it will increase my dear papa's love for me and make me deserving of his goodness."[96] Two years later she reported: "I'm working as hard as I can and Madame Campan is very pleased with me. I am able to draw an owl relatively accurately and I am learning geography. I have gotten as far as the subdivisions of the department of Lyonne [sic]. I now play two sonatas.... I'm learning English and how to dance. Finally, my little papa, my report card is very good. My sister works well also."[97] This juxtaposition of her progress in drawing, geography, piano, English, and dance shows she did not establish priorities or clearly distinguish between studies aimed at developing her reason and those which ensured she would behave properly in society.

Throughout the many years she spent in boarding schools she kept her father up to date on her successes. Mediocre results were followed by tears and renewed pledges to do better; in 1803 her sister Adèle insisted in the same vein: "How can you scold your little girls, my dear Papa, they are so nice; they have worked their heart and soul to death just to please you by getting several prizes, they get up at five in the morning to work, all just to satisfy their dear papa."[98] The concern to succeed and to progress in their studies continued into adolescence, as the following breathless addition to a letter indicates. In short staccato sentences and with shaky handwriting, Nancy announces she has received the school's most treasured prize: "Imagine my happiness, my dear papa, I'm opening my letter to announce I have been pronounced the rosebud of the red class. I can't add anything more. My hand is still trembling. I'm crying! I don't know what to do. You can imagine my joy. Oh, Papa, I am so happy. I kiss you and I'm unhappy not to be able to see myself the joy this will bring to you."[99] Nancy's joy and her constant efforts to succeed testifies to Campan's success at instilling a spirit of healthy rivalry in the classroom, a spirit of emulation that pushed girls to perform well in all areas — conduct, academic studies, and the arts. But unlike male successes these rewards had few practical consequences for the future, and Nancy certainly seemed to prize her rewards less for their own sake than for the pleasure they would bring her father.

By 1807 Nancy believed she was in her final year in school and was working hard, but mainly on the piano and on drawing (her father even had a piano delivered to her private room in the school). At this point she was one of the oldest students in the school and was clearly preparing for her entry into society. Her letters reveal an acute awareness of what this society represented and of the connection between society and politics in the First Empire. This comes through most tellingly in letters that urged her father to transfer her from Saint-Germain to Campan's newly opened Legion of Honor school at Ecouen. She worried that "society which is so mean" would think her father was snubbing the government by not putting her there.[100] In the end her father granted her request to transfer to Ecouen, and there she prepared herself in a tranquil setting for the wheelings and dealings surrounding marriage offers and settlements.

Other families whose daughters were educated at Ecouen clearly took a more superficial approach to their daughters' educations, as can be seen in this intriguing letter from a young girl's grandmother: "I am irritated that you have not taken piano again, and I do not understand why; I entreat you my dear friend to apply yourself to your drawing, few women these days know how to draw; in this way if you lose with respect to music, you gain with drawing. It is very good to be learned but still you need to have some of the decorative arts."[101] Writing in a French that is riddled with grammatical and spelling mistakes, this Old Regime woman clearly believed, as many teachers did as well, that drawing and music were more important for the future than intellectual studies. Both George Sand and Daniel Stern deplored the absence of intellectual stimulation in their schools and never mentioned the sort of prize-giving ceremony that existed in other lay institutions. The only performance Sand mentioned was a theatrical production of Molière's *Malade Imaginaire*, which she herself initiated.[102] Stern argued that too much time was spent learning ornamental accomplishments, given the pressure exerted by both parents and teachers who wanted girls to receive the sort of education that would enable them to catch good husbands.[103] Sand was even more critical in her autobiography; in her view, her teachers failed even in this worldly orientation. The absence of lessons in manners and politeness left students unprepared for life in high society. Indeed, her description of convent life was of friendships and escapades, not study and rewards.

The criticisms voiced by George Sand, Daniel Stern, and Amélie Bosquet[104] concerning their frivolous education were, however, written in hindsight, after all three had acquired public renown thanks to their intellects. For all three their boarding-school experiences appear to have had little impact on their trajectories. Stern's memoirs describe her awakening to intellectual stimulation while attending the courses run by the abbé Gaultier. This renowned pedagogue organized day classes for wealthy girls in Paris in 1786; after his death in 1818 these classes continued. Once a week, young girls accompanied by their mothers attended classes, and every Saturday the students received cards for their studies, and at the end of the month an Honors table proclaimed the most successful students. Stern contended that she never afterwards received a prize that produced a comparable impression on her.[105] By promoting emulation, pedagogues such as the abbé Gaultier or Jeanne Campan were able to stimulate behavior that shows postrevolutionary girls' education was not as limited as critics often stated. Admittedly, the religious, worldly or intellectual ambiance within a school varied a great deal, according to at time contradictory visions of what place women should occupy in society. Ultimately, then, what were the messages young girls retained?

Imagined Families

The boarding-school setting encouraged strong relationships between students and between teachers and students, which were part of the learning experience along with religious and academic lessons. The strength of the familial model in postrevolutionary France explains why girls' writing were replete with family metaphors. Headmistresses encouraged the association between schools and families, but schools were not families, and their modes of functioning could not "naturally" produce future wives and mothers. The children's literature of this period, where mothers were often dead, sick, or frivolous, is testimony to how contemporaries recognized that the domestic model was an ideal to be constructed. In these early decades of the nineteenth century, girls were often placed in school precisely because their families were not what they should be: mother and fathers were absent or dead, or the mother did not have the ability or the desire to complete her daughter's education. Nancy Macdonald remained in school for some twelve years because her father was a military officer and her mother was dead; she had no familial model to help her to position herself. Daniel Stern also lost her father in 1819, which in part explains the decision to place her in a school. George Sand entered her convent school with relief because she was fleeing a family where her mother and grandmother fought continually. The girls who attended the schools of the Legion of Honor were very often orphans with no clear picture of what constituted family harmony. Indeed, in the context of the Napoleonic wars, the domestic and familial model of social relations was inevitably problematic. How then did girls use family metaphors within boarding school walls to construct their own "imagined families"?

Within boarding schools, girls often sought out "adoptive mothers" who filled the role their own mothers could not or would not play, as we have seen in the memoirs of George Sand and Daniel Stern.[106] Jeanne Campan, in particular, assumed the position of adoptive mother to a considerable number of girls from the Napoleonic elite, like Annette de Mackau, the daughter of a liberal aristocrat whose wife died when Annette was four. Despite her mother's dying wish that the family never be separated, the father placed his daughter with Campan in Saint-Germain-en-Laye. Her correspondence is replete with maternal and even familial references, since as her brother Armand recognized, "Ever since the age of six, she has served as your mother."[107] Campan's correspondence is testimony to the serious way she performed her adoptive maternal role; she warned her students about the dangers of the world, but at the same time set up meetings for potential suitors, arranged secure positions for her cherished "daughters," and faithfully kept in touch with her former students until her premature death in 1824.

On another level, schoolgirls' writings suggest that students viewed their school community as another "family" where their friends played a critical role in allowing them to establish a sense of belonging. Correspondence, in particular, offered the opportunity to express the intensity of these bonds. Jeannette Henriod, writing to her friend Eugénie Pascal-Diacre after the former's departure from the school at Ecouen, constantly reiterated the strength of the bonds that tied them together. Her letters show as well how friendships structured young girls' lives even after they left boarding school. As she prepared to leave for Besançon where her father was established, she wrote: "Our little society is already chosen. It will be composed of a few students from Ecouen and several young women from Besançon."[108] Similarly, Nancy Macdonald understood through her schooling experience the importance of friendships, which in many ways appear to have filled the gap left by broken familial relationships: "I am distraught. Two boarders have just left, and one of them was the person I was closest to. Now I am without anyone to whom I can give my entire friendship, and I don't know how one can live without friendship. It's what holds me up in moments of great unhappiness. . . . I am excessively sad."[109] Nancy Macdonald associated families and friendships, heeding in this respect the importance placed on true friendships in the didactic fiction analyzed earlier.

Nancy's letters to her father provide the most eloquent testimony to how some girls strove to maintain a sense of family despite the separation entailed by boarding-school life. The intensity of this father-daughter bond is expressed in countless letters where she writes: "My greatest pleasure is in writing you and when you don't get news from me it will be because I cannot write you. I long for your letters. I would like to get them every hour." On 7 January 1808 she protested in passionate and even amorous tones her father's refusal to remove her from Campan's institution:

> I understand the price you are paying to enable me to perfect the education I am receiving, but I would accept all sorts of privations in order not to be separated from my excellent father. . . . I long for the happy moment when we will be united for life. . . . I would like to read your letters all day long. I amused myself the other day by reading all of the old letters I carefully keep. Oh! I felt an inner joy to be with you for such a long time. I felt as if you were next to me and that you were speaking to me. I was very happy then because as I've already said to you and repeat to you now, I will never be completely happy, except with you.[110]

The intensity of her desire to be with her father, in a curiously configured domestic nest, increased as time went by and her friends left the school, and this, despite the continued presence of her sister who was rarely the subject of her letters.

Finally, the Loveday-Reboul case mentioned earlier offers another way to glimpse the strength of family metaphors within the school setting. Emily and Mary Loveday's decision to defy their parents and convert to Catholicism was on a certain level a desire to join another religious family, to seek out new models for behavior in order to make sense of the world. This willful reconstruction of a family bore little resemblance to the vision of the Napoleonic family offered in the Civil Code. In effect, the Lovedays, like most of the other examples, were imagining families of women; in their case religious sentiment played a central role in their new family.

Most school girls during this period left no traces of their experience within school. Nonetheless, the composite testimonies of those who did suggest a wide variety of behaviors in response to messages that were varied as well. Consider, for example, the descriptions of a young English girl, Mary Browne, who attended for a month what was considered the best lay school in Versailles. Her portrait is one of a miserably run institution where the students were filthy and rude, their skins yellow, their hair matted with dirt, their manners vulgar. The lessons inspired a similar condemnation: teachers maintained no discipline, the writing master never looked at her work, the study of the performing arts was a farce, since the pianos hardly sounded, and the dance room was only a corridor without chairs: "We none of us did anything but write and copy one another's writing," Browne reported. Finally, not even religion was respected, as prayers were said hurriedly while teachers mended pens and corrected exercises.[111] Although the school and its students appeared clean and well behaved on the day of the First Communion, Browne certainly took away the impression that French learning, manners, and religion were very superficial indeed. Reputation and appearances, in her eyes, were deceiving.

Whose vision of girls' education then should we believe — the pedagogue's, the headmistresses', the inspectresses', or the students'? Taken together, these sources suggest the realities of girls' education were multiple. Despite the diversity, however, some features of French girls' education deserve to be noted in comparison with the education of British girls at roughly the same period. In both countries, girls' education lay at the heart of an effort to re-Christianize society, and in both, new schools appeared with real intellectual ambitions, offering serious academic programs that required competent teachers.[112] Next to such institutions, however, there were also schools that sought mainly to earn a profit and where the curriculum responded mainly to parental demands, be these to provide ornamental accomplishments or religious lessons. Adèle Boury, who attended both a school run by the Ursulines and a British boarding school, wrote that in England needlework received far greater attention, since the mornings were devoted to this subject.[113] But since schools varied greatly in England, as in France, it is difficult to conclude that this represents a significant national difference. Still, what does appear different is the educational landscape: British parents preferred home education or day schools for their daughters, while the French preferred boarding schools. As a result, French girls' schooling experience represented a far sharper break with the family.

In the 1830s the numbers of girls' secondary schools in France soared, and their objectives became clearer as well with the development of a professional press. But the origins of the system that emerged during the July Monarchy were established, in all its diversity, after the Revolution. The presence within the educational landscape of a few elite institutions created models that made an impact: henceforth, most reformists agreed on the need for girls to have access to reason via a rigorous plan of study, organized in classes, and using emulation as a way to motivate students. The revolutionary heritage for girls' education remains nonetheless a complicated story.

Alongside a discourse that emphasized the relationship between women, religion, and the domestic hearth, a range of practices existed which suggest that revolutionary rhetoric about individual rights had also fallen on feminine ears. In general, however, pedagogues and schoolmistresses had heeded Rousseau's message that the development of girls' education had to go hand in hand with that of domestic values.

PART II

Women, Schools, *and the* Politics of Culture (1830–1880)

During the years between the revolution of 1830 and the creation of a state-supported system of girls' secondary schools in 1880, the number and variety of educational institutions for middle-class girls expanded tremendously. Thousands of laywomen opened boarding schools, and religious orders multiplied the number of schools they ran. The Republicans who created girls' *lycées* and *collèges* vaunted their own efforts by denouncing the educational void that had existed for girls prior to 1880, but their vision is clearly inaccurate. Although the state watched institutional development with a certain lofty detachment until the 1860s, individual men and women established an institutional infrastructure for bourgeois girls whose contours have remained little explored. Certainly contemporaries recognized that schools for girls existed, but whether these schools represented secondary education was a matter of some contention. Indeed, the state legislated girls' secondary schools out of existence in 1853 with a ruling that declared that henceforth all girls' institutions would be considered primary for administrative purposes and subject to the controls of primary schools.

Defining what constituted secondary education for girls was not easy, since girls' schools did not prepare for the *baccalauréat* as did boys' schools; moreover, existing school diplomas did not open doors to either the university or to administrative positions except as schoolteachers. The content of girls' secondary education also varied. Generally considered to encompass more than the rudiments, the issue of what that entailed was obviously open to debate. Many schools claimed to offer a secondary course of instruction and yet their plan of study really approximated the program of the higher primary schools (*écoles primaires supérieures*) that first appeared in 1833. And indeed many "secondary" institutions accepted young students and offered them essentially elementary instruction. What then was secondary about the schools that developed for girls during these years? My argument follows that of contemporary educators in insisting that girls' secondary education was primarily defined through its clientele — secondary schools educated the daughters of the middle and upper classes. As the middle classes expanded, the content of this education evolved to address the perceived needs of an increasingly diverse middle-class clientele.[1]

Our current understanding of the characteristics of bourgeois girls' education in the middle years of the century is still heavily influenced by the effects of the educational wars that have characterized the past two hundred years of French history, despite the intelligently nuanced work of Françoise Mayeur.[2] French Republican historiography systematically vilified religious teachers and orders, and more recent studies have often followed this path, emphasizing the mediocre quality of girls' education.[3] American readers similarly often have a negative impression of girls' education, having read Bonnie Smith's path-breaking book on the bourgeoises from the Nord. Smith's insistence on the Catholic dimension of this education with its emphasis on timeless rituals where "ignorance and darkness meant innocence and true wisdom" in many ways confirms the Republican vision.[4] Prior to the state's (tardy) intervention in the field of secondary education, ignorant nuns raised superstitious girls, who then introduced disharmony in the family through their irrational and unreasoned modes of behavior, or so the story goes.

My intention is not to offer a counternarrative to this dominant historiographic vein, but rather to suggest that the story is considerably more complicated and that many figures, voices, and schools have been left out until now. In particular, the wide array of educational institutions for girls has frequently not been acknowledged. Throughout the century, lay schools for bourgeois girls far outnumbered religious schools but their presence is virtually ignored. Few studies incorporate an understanding of the actual daily workings of religious orders beyond the testimony of George Sand and Daniel Stern writing about the period of the 1820s. Above all, with the notable exception of Mayeur's synthesis, most studies focus on one institution or one particular set of institutions and lose, thereby, the ability to understand how competition among different institutions with different orientations structured educational offerings. The history of education as a whole has a tendency to narrow the range of its investigations in a way that obscures the central role that education plays in a society.[5] Finally, our understanding of French girls' education has undoubtedly been affected by the relative dearth of studies until recently about women's lives and conditions. And yet such information is critical to understanding how educators and reformers positioned themselves at a given time and how this positioning acquired a political dimension.

Before exploring the educational landscape, Chapter 4 considers how visions of bourgeois womanhood evolved during the July Monarchy and notes the emergence of powerful new images of femininity: the *femme nouvelle*, the bluestocking, and the domestic mother. The vituperative condemnation of the woman intellectual reveals the extent to which the association of women with knowledge continued to pose problems in a society that trumpeted the values of domesticity. The following chapters explore two categories of educated women: the professional woman educator and the teaching nun. Both of these figures need to be understood in relationship to each other and to the broader cultural debate about women's place in French society. Anxiety about bluestockings, as well as the impact of professionalizing forces in girls' schooling, help to explain the emergence of a specifically French vision of the female teacher, be she lay or religious. This section concludes by returning to the schools themselves and exploring how the various strands of thinking about bourgeois womanhood expressed themselves in school programs, objectives, and practices. I argue that schools modified the terms of the debate about girls' education through what I term a form of spatial politics. By buying buildings and setting up schools throughout the urban landscape, both nuns and laywomen carved out an institutional space for women whose implications have yet to be explored. Finally, I ask what impact these debates and these schools had on girls' sense of cultural identity. How did the family model of girls' education withstand the pressures of institutional growth and the emergence of a political debate about women's place in society?

3

Debating Women's Place in the Consolidating Bourgeois Order (1830–1848)

> *Why must a woman be ignorant, why can't she be learned without boasting and without being a pedant?*
>
> — George Sand, letter to Mme Maurice Dupin, 18 November 1821

The period from 1830 until 1848 saw the crystallization of a number of themes about women's role in society that were initially debated in the immediate postrevolutionary years, notably the issue of motherhood and granting women access to reason. Compared to the early decades, specifically middle-class education received heightened attention with the consolidation of bourgeois economic and political power after the revolution of 1830. This newly felt authority allowed the middle classes to carve out a cultural vision of French womanhood that progressively distanced itself from earlier preoccupations with the aristocratic model. Its contours congealed by midcentury around the concept of domesticity. Women's association with the home and family was not, of course, new in the 1850s but the impact of a burgeoning publishing market that produced quantities of new educational and more recreational journals and books changed the tenor of the discourse.

Recent work on women and gender in the middle years of the nineteenth century has shown the degree to which gender and familial relations were contested and debated.[1] The implications of these debates were political, given the family's central position in French society and politics. Feminist and religious forces contributed most powerfully to the politicization of domesticity as a cultural mandate for bourgeois women over the course of these years.[2] The feminist challenge to the sexist premises of bourgeois domesticity brought the issue of women's role in society to the forefront at certain critical moments, notably after the revolutions of 1830 and 1848. At the same time, however, the effort to infuse maternity with religious and moral values, paralleling as it did the feminization of religion in France, introduced tensions that played themselves out in very political ways in educational debates concerning women. Paradoxically, as education and its goals became increasingly associated with political positions, those who advocated a domestic educational setting gained cultural ascendancy in explicit opposition to those who advocated aligning girls' education more closely with that of boys'. As a result, one can see during these years a clearer delineation of ideological positions concerning the appropriate relationship between the sexes as the bourgeoisie acquired increasing influence in French society.

This chapter begins with an overview of how girls' education entered political discourse, focusing on the Saint-Simonian-inspired critiques of the 1830s and 1840s. During these same years a moralizing discourse also emerged that served to establish increasingly distinct gender roles, through the relegation of middle-class women to the private sphere. Evidence of the weight of normative domesticity can be traced in the caricatures and mockery made of bluestockings during this period, which illustrate the fears associated with women stepping out of their sphere and acquiring the mental characteristics of men. Finally, the chapter concludes with an examination of how the revolution of 1848 altered the meaning of moral motherhood as feminists reemerged to challenge women's relegation to the private sphere.

Saint-Simonian and Feminist Critiques of Gender Relations

The gender dynamics of Saint-Simonian thought in the late 1820s and early 1830s have recently received renewed attention with the development of women's history.[3] The Saint-Simonians were a group of men and women who professed allegiance to the doctrines of Claude Henri de Rouvroy, comte de Saint-Simon (1760–1825). The latter believed in the notion of progress, which would contribute to human and social regeneration, and he articulated a productivist vision of the future where cooperation among the classes was the key to industrial expansion. After his death, a number of followers, particularly Prosper Enfantin and Saint-Amand Bazard, modified his technocratic orientation and developed the premises of a new religion of humanity. Their belief in an androgynous God, in a world where a couple-pope reigned, radically challenged traditional Christian thought through the high value that it placed on female sentiment. In their doctrine, Saint-Simonians rejected the traditional separation between spirit and matter, rehabilitating in this way the material world and gender roles within it. As historian Claire Moses writes, the "reevaluation of the physical expression of love and a rejection of the Christian concept of original sin [led the Saint-Simonians] to the revaluation and ultimately to the emancipation of women."[4] The Saint-Simonian critique of social, sexual, familial, and religious relations in the 1830s opened the door for more explicitly feminist positions.

The liberating potential of Saint-Simonian thought as it developed around Enfantin attracted mainly working-class women who initially embraced and then had to struggle with the ramifications of a doctrine whose commitment to sexual freedom left many of these women both literally and figuratively holding the baby. The intellectual promise that this doctrine offered had important ramifications beyond Saint-Simonian circles, however, as new journals appeared and debated the gendered implications of liberty and sexual equality in the aftermath of the revolution of 1830. The Saint-Simonian critique allowed both their women followers and interested literate companions to forge out in new directions, creating their own women-run newspapers and clubs that developed a dynamic of their own. Through a feminist press, petitions, and new associations, a number of working- and middle-class women increasingly turned their attention to the problems inherent in the Napoleonic Civil Code that left women subservient in the family and shackled in the working world. For these women activists, the allure of sexual freedom quickly took a back seat to a more urgent call for social and economic reforms that would allow women greater independence both at home and in civil society. At the heart of much of this discussion about women's place in the 1830s and 1840s was the recognition that to combat gender inequalities women needed an education that was more serious and more politically aware.

The Feminist Press and Feminist Voices

The development of the periodic press after the revolution of 1830 gave women an unprecedented opportunity to express their views in public. As they took to their pens, both educated and uneducated women embraced a vision of gender relations where female sentiment and male reason were placed on an equal footing.[5] Women like Jeanne Deroin and Eugénie Niboyet led the way in their criticisms of existing educational opportunities for women arguing that women's sense of inferiority stemmed from their education. Deroin wrote:

> Women's education is directed in such a way as to restrict her moral and intellectual faculties. Efforts are made to persuade her she is inferior to men and to ensure this odious supposition becomes a reality . . . if she has an inquiring mind and studious habits, education crushes in her all that might bring her strength and moral dignity. It seeks to cultivate her frivolous tastes, suggests to her that the gift of charm and the art of pleasing should be her sole aim and the object of her wishes . . . even when she reaches a high level of knowledge and genuine superiority, all careers are blocked for her, her entrance is barred to all public service, *lycées*, university faculties, and educational academies.[6]

While Deroin increasingly devoted her energies to more explicitly political issues, even running for election in 1849 after the Second Republic proclaimed universal manhood suffrage, Eugénie Niboyet placed girls' and women's education at the heart of her efforts to regenerate French society.

Born into a family of Protestant philosophers and scientific men, Eugénie Niboyet defined herself as a *femme de lettres* and participated eloquently in the public debates about women from 1830 until her death in 1882. Over the course of her long career, she worked tirelessly to promote women's emancipation through the creation of newspapers, classes for both educated and poor women, and her activities within the Société de la morale chrétienne. Her initial forays into the public arena reflected her adherence to Saint-Simonian doctrine even if she moved progressively away from the movement. In her paper *Le conseiller des femmes* (1833), she urged women to speak out and championed the need for education. In particular, this paper urged the creation of normal schools for women as well as access to such artistic training schools as the École des Beaux Arts and the Conservatory. Concern for women's professional lives underwrote Niboyet's writing as well as that of Louise Maignaud, who called for women's access to scientific and industrial careers.[7]

Another Saint-Simonian inspired woman's journal, *La tribune des femmes* (initially titled *La femme libre*), similarly took up the issue of the "new woman's" intellectual emancipation in 1833, as the government signed the Guizot law on elementary education.[8] Girls' primary and female normal schools were ignored in this law, provoking a considerable outcry in feminist and Saint-Simonian circles. Feminist journalists wrote urgently about the need to develop girls' education, while the Saint-Simonian Marie Reine Guindorf called for its complete reform.[9]

The criticism of girls' education was by no means restricted, however, to the more radical pronouncements of the Saint-Simonian or explicitly feminist journals. More moderate women's magazines, such as Fanny Richomme's *Journal des femmes* (1832–37) or Madeleine Sirey's *La mère de famille* (1833–36) adopted similar positions. The *Journal des femmes* had as its subtitle "gymnase littéraire," thus declaring its commitment to broadening women's minds: "A strong and constitutional education, as Mme de Rémusat wrote, will give renewed force to those souls that a frivolous education has rendered vain and coquettish."[10] Its first article in 1832 was titled "The progress in instruction for women of the nineteenth century" and reflected the widespread preoccupation with girls' education in these years. Clémence Robert articulated perhaps most clearly the stakes of this education in her eloquent statement: "Knowing represents the fortune of the soul and its liberty; knowing is to possess time and space, to enlarge our limited horizon to all aspects of the universe."[11] In this effort to give girls access to knowledge Richomme published numerous articles in 1833 about existing girls' schools that highlighted the need for reform, while also encouraging women's presence in public courses and at scientific lectures.

In pedagogical circles, as well, girls' education was a topic of the day. The Société des méthodes de l'enseignement sponsored a debate in 1833 on the subject "What are the means to favor and make profitable the great intellectual movement which has emerged among women?"[12] It was before this learned society that Sophie Mazure first proposed the creation of a woman's normal school as an obvious response to the question posed. Like Campan before her, Mazure responded to her own life experiences with a concern to offer women professional opportunities. Born in 1801 into an educated middle-class family, she never married, and like many educated single women of this period she turned to writing for a living and published her first novel under the pen name Francis Dazur in 1833.[13] Encouraged by her friends, she presented her request to the education minister François Guizot, to no effect. Although her call for a normal school received relatively widespread attention both in the national press and women's journals, the government did nothing.[14] The voices that defended an image of the "new woman" in these early years were still a small minority.

Petitions and Demands: "On the Necessity of Women's Instruction"

After 1833 the debate in feminist circles about girls' education moved onto new ground, becoming on the whole more pragmatic and more professional in its criticisms. Feminist journalists and activists put aside their condemnation of the liberal moral economy in favor of more concrete actions to reform the social and economic order. Eugénie Niboyet founded a woman's club known as the Athénée des Dames in Lyons in 1834, which offered courses in social science, political economy, education, science, literature, and morals, as well as access to a library at the cost of twenty francs a year.[15] Other women returned to revolutionary practices and petitioned the government, demanding changes in family, property, and matrimonial law.[16] The feminist journal *La gazette des femmes* (1836–38), in particular, focused its efforts on improving women's civil status, publishing many articles about the law as well as giving public attention to feminist petitions. These petitions sought to modify articles of the Civil Code, to introduce the right to divorce, and to give women access to the legal, medical, and teaching professions.[17] In common with the Saint-Simonians, women who took to their pens in this period clearly linked the improvement of women's status to better educational opportunities.

The very first issue of the *Gazette* included an article by Louise d'Ormoy titled "On the necessity of women's instruction," in which she linked women's education to civil rights: "Not only must women know laws, but they must be able to explain them to their children."[18] Other journalists urged women to acquire university diplomas, informed readers about the best existing schools and pushed the state to open a woman's normal school.[19] While these proposals may appear relatively innocuous in the context of a modernizing society, contemporaries judged them differently. As the discussion surrounding Mazure's petition to open a girls' normal school reveals, advocating women's intellectual emancipation through education was perceived as a very real threat to the "natural" relationship between the sexes and their positions in society.

The romantic poet and future revolutionary figure Alphonse de Lamartine spoke several times in defense of Mazure's petition, but his choice of terms speaks eloquently to anxieties about the implications of girls' education. In an initial plea he argued, "It is not learned women [*savantes*] we need but *substitute* mothers for orphans and moral and well-meaning *female teachers* [*instruiseuses*]."[20] By backing away from the professional connotations of the word *institutrice*, and by contrasting substitute mothers with learned women, his text suggests a singular reluctance to recognize that women teachers did indeed operate within civil society. When the petition reappeared before the Chamber of Deputies in May 1835, he even more cautiously specified the spatial and political limits of this education:

> It is not Mlle Masure's [*sic*] intent, nor my own, to pull women from the sphere of domestic life to transport them to that of public education. Woman is the soul of the family. . . . There is no public education for women; education must be special: public education is only appropriate for those who are destined like ourselves to an active and public life. Women are destined for the family, drawing from it their principle education, from the lessons, the examples, and traditions of the mother. All other systems are false and harmful. Note the corrupted society of the eighteenth century where women emerged from public education. Note today's society where scandal has ceased to be a source of glory and domestic virtues have reestablished their status. Women emerge from domestic education.[21]

By carefully circumscribing the space within which women teachers would operate, Lamartine emptied this demand of its more radical edge. Not surprisingly, then, the Chamber approved the idea and voted to send it back to the minister of education, who failed, however, to act; the state did not create public female normal schools until 1879, forty-five years later.[22]

Calls for women's intellectual emancipation were buoyed as well by pedagogical innovations that radically undermined assumptions about women's innate inferiority. Joseph Jacotot (1770–1840) promulgated in the 1820s a teaching method he termed "universal teaching." Its emphasis on the fundamental equality of male and female intelligence had an obvious appeal for feminists of this period. His method involved getting students to act on their own, following the principle that since "everything is in everything," one should learn one thing and bring it to bear on the rest. In practice, students were expected to learn more on their own without the strict attention to first learning one subject and then another. Although many pedagogues expressed horror at what this iconoclastic method implied, a Société de philosophie panécastique et d'enseignement universel emerged to spread Jacotot's ideas; certain key women educators, such as Joséphine Bachellery, were active in this society.[23]

Since petitions achieved very little, both moderate and more radical educational reformers turned their efforts after the mid-1830s to creating a groundswell of opinion in favor of improving girls' education. The expanding pedagogical press commented on the weaknesses in girls' education, and some journals appeared that focused more particularly on this subject.[24] The short-lived *La tribune de l'enseignement* (October 1838–June 1840) announced in its first issue that teaching was not in harmony with the spirit of the social pact and that women's education in particular needed reform: "People recognize today that maintaining women's inferiority with respect to education has proven a permanent cause of disorder and an obstacle in the progress of civilization."[25] In this journal Joséphine Bachellery, boarding-school mistress and pedagogical reformer, began her public campaign to introduce professional standards in girls' education. Between November 1838 and May 1840 she published a series of letters that illustrate the impact of feminist challenges to dominant perceptions of women's natural inferiority.[26]

She began her series of essays by criticizing the majority of reformers who restricted their view to that of private life. Noting the modernization of contemporary society, she insisted that girls of the middle classes (*classes moyennes*) needed an education that would prepare them for professional lives. Although she claimed detachment from those "burning theories driven by a radical and feverish logic which seeks to overthrow everything without reconstructing," her arguments were considerably more radical than her disclaimer suggested. As a follower of Jacotot, she repeatedly affirmed her belief in the essential equality of intelligence between men and women and offered proposals that would allow women to develop theirs. She argued that people's vocations should not be fixed by either natural or social hierarchies and suggested that education offered the means to rework and challenge sexual and social inequalities.[27] While her proposals were couched in relatively moderate terms, her vision of education in general and women's education in particular was a far cry from the dominant liberal paradigm that accepted and reinforced class divisions through a two-track educational system that left girls' education almost entirely in private hands.[28] Moreover, her suggestions were also distinct from those who spoke in the name of motherhood; women needed vocational education rather than domestic education, she insisted, and she harshly criticized the nature of religious education.[29]

Bachellery's general concern to improve girls' education was not isolated in the more conservative climate of the 1840s, although most writers approached the subject in less radical fashion. Characteristic of this attitude were the articles printed in the first professional journal to address solely girls' education, the moderate and liberal *Revue de l'enseignement des femmes* (REF), which appeared between 1845 and 1848.[30] Although they publicized Bachellery's criticisms of religious education, they were careful to distance themselves from her viewpoint. The REF mainly provided a useful summary of legislation, information on teaching examinations, as well as articles on foreign and French institutions and on famous women educators. Direct challenges to women's inferior position in society and unequal access to public and economic life were left to more adventurous souls.

One such soul was the unusually combative woman of letters, Louise Dauriat, who wrote regularly for the Saint-Simonian *Globe* as well as the *Tribune des femmes*. She is probably best known for petitions she sent to the Chamber of Deputies demanding revisions in the Civil Code, but she also published novels and a *Cours d'histoire religieuse et universelle* (1828), and in 1836 opened a Cours de droit social des femmes. Her forays into the public debate about girls' education occurred in the mid-1840s as she began a high-profile campaign to rid girls' boarding schools of men. Although she argued that men's presence among young girls led to equivocal and potentially scandalous situations, her dominant concern was to give women professional opportunities equivalent to their intellectual capacities. The mayor of the tenth arrondissement viewed her petition favorably recognizing that her "apostolate" consisted "not in liberating womanhood from her duties, but in giving her rights as well, to place her at the same level as man and to call her to share public functions." His "enlightened" position contrasted notably with that of the educational hierarchy who cataloged her as belonging to the "detestable school of George Sand."[31]

Dauriat's campaign about male professors initiated a spate of discussions about girls' education that the *REF* covered in some detail. Increasingly, even moderate voices were linking girls' education to expanding vocational opportunities for women, illustrating in many ways the success of the more pragmatic challenge to gender roles. Among the proposals that emerged at this time was that of the future spiritist leader Hippolyte Léon Denizard Rivail (better known as Allan Kardec), who argued for the need to create a baccalaureat degree for girls. He believed only a nationally recognized diploma would establish girls' secondary education on a more solid footing and open doors to women in commerce, industry, and even the administration.[32] In 1847 the progressive minister of education Narcisse Achille, comte de Salvandy, created a commission to investigate the establishment of state-directed model *collèges* for women.[33] By the late 1840s a range of arguments existed to defend women's access to a more solid and potentially career-oriented education; the revolutionary context then opened the way to putting these ideas into practice. At the same time, however, a far more conservative discourse also paid close attention to women's role and status, offering another way to envision gender relations.

Moralizing the Domestic

Feminists during the July Monarchy sought both to politicize the domestic sphere and to claim a place for women in the broader polity, but their voices were a minority. This period is associated far more prominently with the vocal trumpeting of domestic ideology for bourgeois women. Books, journals, and institutions peered closely at the maternal figure and judged her in need of counsel and reform. While the chorus of voices calling attention to women's domestic responsibilities probably reached a peak during the Second Empire, the years between 1830 and 1848 certainly marked a turning point in public discussion about mothers' responsibilities within the family. Moral motherhood became a dominant theme within the more general debate about family life and values.[34] As will become apparent, however, the valorization of motherhood focused not on women as individuals, but rather on their social role within the family. Calls then for improving women's education echoed many of the feminist appeals, but more carefully circumscribed women within a revitalized and moralized domestic sphere. Within this discourse about moral motherhood, two strands can be distinguished that correspond roughly with the respective positions of the authors of the texts under consideration. Catholic writers and the Catholic press emphasized the religious dimension of domesticity, while the women's press and more liberal authors presented their vision of domesticity in more administrative and economic terms. Naturally the two strands were rarely distinct, but by untangling the messages underlying each, it is possible to distinguish two visions of domestic womanhood, with very different implications.

Mothers and Mary: The Religious Dimension of Domesticity

As historians of religion have argued, the nineteenth century presents a contradictory face when considering religious practices and the weight of the Catholic Church in French society. Certainly long-term secular trends contributed to the phenomenon of de-Christianization as well as to more political expressions of anticlericalism. But this same century that paved the way for the separation of church and state in 1905 was also characterized by renewed Marian devotion, devotion to the Sacred Heart, and the great pilgrimages to Catholic holy places, such as Lourdes. Visions of the Immaculate Virgin proliferated in literature, art, and politics in both popular and more elite venues.[35] Recently historians have highlighted the gendered dimension of this religious revival. Ralph Gibson in particular has analyzed three areas that testify to the feminization of religion: devotional literature became more feminine and less austere, women increasingly formed the bulwark of practicing Catholics, and thousands of women became nuns.[36] Girls' education clearly played an essential role in this process of feminization, both in terms of the moral messages conveyed at home and in schools and through the growth of religious schools.

Between the 1830s and 1860, sermons, devotional handbooks, and manuals dealt constantly with the subject of women's responsibilities within the home. But as Hazel Mills has argued, the messages of this Catholic literature contained inconsistencies

that opened opportunities for women beyond the home: "Lurking within representations of woman's nature as essentially qualifying her for private responsibilities and
domestic duties was a powerful sub-text stressing her latent moral superiority. This
language of moral powers was available to legitimate some types of female activity
beyond the home."[37] Through the emphasis on the Virgin Mary as wife and especially
mother, devotional literature urged women (and girls) to imitate her spiritual virginity: "Motherhood became a means to female virtue that challenged the previous hege-
mony of virginity." Time and again women were reminded: "You are the living instruments, the visible leaders of a formidable spiritual power."[38] As mother-educators,
women contributed to the re-Christianization of society but also gained the moral authority to visit the poor or the imprisoned, to move beyond the confines of the home.

The clergy's contribution to the religious emphasis on motherhood was in part a
defensive reaction to the disturbing trends of modernizing French society, as well as
a rebuttal to feminist criticisms of the traditional family. The task of moral motherhood then was often presented as shoring up traditional values and traditional social
arrangements, but at the same time women were granted enormous authority within
the family, an authority that inevitably had broader social dimensions. As Father
Pierre Alexandre Mercier argued in his lectures for ladies and young girls: "Men
believe they do a great deal when they earn and administer their fortune, when they
govern their country; undeceive yourselves, fathers and administrators, it is your
wives, who, without your knowledge, are from the outset invested by Providence in
the growth and decay of the greatest treasures of the family and society."[39]

Re-Christianized motherhood gave women a critical educational role that Mercier
explicitly addressed: "The solidly virtuous women ... is on her own the education,
the school and the civilization of the family; she alone inspires sentiments of justice,
of generosity in wealth, of courage in work, of patience in distress, of resignation in
misfortune, the absolutely essential virtues for the restoration and maintenance of
the social order. Woman alone teaches her husband and children to turn their gaze
away from other's goods, even when the owner is egotistical and contemptible."[40] As
the source of critical moral and social values, mothers needed an appropriate education themselves, an issue that both lay and religious writers increasingly addressed.[41]

The success of Necker de Saussure's book L'éducation progressive, as well as that of
Louis Aimé-Martin's De l'éducation des mères de famille ou de la civilisation du genre humain
par les femmes, is emblematic of the audience that existed for writings about Christian motherhood. Aimé-Martin argued that women were the key to redressing contemporary French society's general malaise. Despite progress in the industry, the
arts, and letters, the spiritual or religious dimension of human experience was missing in France's modernizing impulse. Women needed to supply this essential spiritual dimension. His lengthy and at times erudite discussion of the need for stronger
moral and religious education deplored the frivolous and mechanistically intellectual

aspects of contemporary girls' education, but rather than propose a reform of existing schools, as feminist journalists did, he centered his discussion on the figure of the mother. Mothers, not schools, were given the responsibility for transmitting fundamental moral values to their young sons and daughters. As a result, he advocated a system of "mixed education" for both girls and boys where intellectual and physical capacities would be tuned within a day-school setting, so that students could return home for the ultimately more important messages of maternal education. Women's place was clearly within the home for biological, historical, and cultural reasons, according to Aimé-Martin. Throughout his text he emphasized the contours of women's power, or influence, as he frequently put it; based within the home, this influence nonetheless extended into society as a whole: "This is the central point, or rather, the synopsis of the education of mothers. The concern here is to get women to leave the narrow circle in which society confines them and to extend their thoughts to all those objects which make us better and happier. A religious, philosophical, moral world opens before them. Their mission is to introduce our childhood into this world, as into a holy temple, where the soul can study and recognize God's presence!"[42] Interestingly, he did not shy away from the long-term implications of his analysis as most maternal advocates did. Indeed he argued that once civilization had been achieved "men's rights will be recognized, woman will take her place in the state: she is housewife, companion and citizen; she is complete." But for the time being, in this "century of regeneration," "women must raise themselves to the highest magistracy through the simple accomplishment of their duties as wives and mothers."[43]

This text, which emphasized mothers' spiritual responsibilities in the modern world, was not, however, a practical handbook for young and inexperienced women. Other authors, both men and women, took up the challenge posed by clerics and Aimé-Martin, resulting in a proliferation of books and articles on the subject of maternal education.[44] Women's publications, in particular, popularized an increasingly widespread perception that mothers needed guidelines to perform their tasks with honor. While fashion concerns and leisure activities were not uncommon in this press, the dominant message it conveyed was the need to teach women how to assume their maternal tasks more efficiently. Religious messages played of course a role, but overall the press as well as conduct manuals increasingly established the home as the site where women exerted their newly codified role as domestic managers.

Managing the Home

David Lévi-Alvarès (1794–1870) is probably the pedagogue and writer most associated with developing a vision of the professional mother-educator. In 1820 he founded a day class in maternal education (the Cours d'éducation maternelle) where mothers accompanied their daughters to classes in order to guide their lessons better at home.

The courses, which took place only once a week for two hours, easily fit within a pedagogical paradigm that valued home education. Following Rousseau, he encouraged mothers to let "nature" serve as a pedagogical guide, but he also published a journal, *La mère institutrice* (1834–45), that helped mothers pursue the subjects raised in the classroom.[45] His journal printed pedagogical stories and information about cultural activities, and provided a format for the women poets and writers of this period, such as Victorine Collin, Marceline Desbordes-Valmore, and Fanny Richomme. Lévi-Alvarès firmly distinguished his efforts to promote women's roles from those presented in more radical journals such as the *Gazette des femmes*: "Women understand the dignity of their functions and the importance of their duties: the study of arts and sciences does not let them forget the modest occupations which are theirs alone; they do not seek to escape the limits that social propriety has traced; they know that in a woman pedantry, that inevitable scourge of the domestic hearth, would be a grievous anomaly in our morals."[46] His concern to circumscribe women's influence within the home, however, was accompanied by his desire to make women more efficient educators. The journal took on an increasingly educational tone, and in October 1841 it issued a guide titled *Bulletin créé spécialement pour les institutrices*, which provided detailed advice on how best to prepare for the Parisian teaching examinations required in order to work in a boarding school.

Pedagogic literature of the period similarly addressed this concern to educate women for their maternal responsibilities, echoing in this respect such British writers as Sarah Strickney Ellis or Harriet Martineau. The Protestant Nathalie de Lajolais wrote, for example, that "greater dignity, consistency, moral strength, and vigor in instruction, would allow women to become better teachers for their children, surer companions, and the universal instruments for happiness." At the same time, however, she also argued that girls' education should promote women's individual happiness: "One must raise girls for their happiness, *no matter what their future is in society*, rather than forming them exclusively for the habits and needs of men, rather than arguing in one hundred ingenious ways that man is the sole goal of their virtue."[47]

Although women's magazines presented a variety of messages, the concern to educate was omnipresent in their pages.[48] The *Journal des femmes*, for example, included information on literature, the sciences, the arts, fashion, music, drawing, and painting. More illuminating, however, is the attention this journal initially gave to such subjects as hygiene and domestic economy in an effort to define more clearly the "scientific" responsibilities of motherhood. As one writer argued in 1832: "Domestic economy is a science that women cannot escape."[49] Similarly, the *Conseiller des femmes* combined articles on fashion and theater with far more concrete advice on hygiene, education, psychology, and domestic economy.[50] The concern to codify motherhood appeared most openly in the pages of *La mère de famille* (1833–36). Founded by Madeleine Sirey, niece of the Revolutionary Honoré Gabriel Riqueti, comte de

Mirabeau, this influential Catholic journal developed a cult of the conjugal family where women played the starring role.[51] The journal's subtitle, *Journal mensuel, moral, religieux, littéraire, d'économie, de législation et d'hygiène domestique*, illustrates clearly how this press intertwined religious, moral, intellectual, and practical concerns in its effort to educate women to their role within the family. If women's religious role figured prominently in this journal's pages, it is perhaps more intriguing to note the weight attached to medical and hygienic issues that signaled the emergence of new responsibilities for the mother.[52]

The heightened attention given to women's responsibilities in the family during the July Monarchy can be explained in part as an effort to impose domestic order in reaction to the urban disorder that reigned without. But the association of women with the home involved infusing their role with new moral and public authority. As Sharon Marcus has argued, domestic manuals of this period described the home as "analogous to the sphere of political administration."[53] Women managed, administered, and ultimately controlled a domain whose significance was recognized as extending beyond the private sphere. This perception was widely shared in liberal and Catholic circles precisely because so many women authors assumed a public voice in this period in the burgeoning publishing market. As Paulin Limrayac, writing for the moderate *Revue des deux mondes*, noted: "The most appropriate role for women is in the family. The domestic hearth is their true fatherland [*patrie*]; public life for them is like a foreign land. Their advantages lie in private life. It is in this apparently narrow theater . . . that lofty intelligences and noble hearts develop."[54] He argued that women's authority appeared to be new in these decades, because the press gave them a far wider audience. From being "moralists who observe," women had become "moralists who teach," or act, in the public sphere. And while he rejected the words and actions of those women who sought emancipation, he approved of those who sought to regenerate society through their writings: "The talent that a woman can best exercise without usurping the role of a man . . . is that of the moral writer . . . to write in such an area, a woman does not have to don the halo which makes her an exceptional individual . . . what she writes in her books, she could say in her salon . . . she simply extends her conversation and enlarges her audience; she becomes an author, without ceasing to have been a woman of the world and a mother."[55] Thus Limayrac sought to reconcile women's public and private responsibilities, granting special authority to these now largely forgotten women moralists.

Bas-bleu, Education, and the Limits of Respectability

Contemporaries had a very different reaction, however, to those women writers who sought influence directly in the public sphere. The figure of the *bas-bleu*, in particular, generated a wide range of negative images, notably that of the world turned upside down.[56] The term *bas-bleu* came from the English term "bluestocking," which was first coined in the eighteenth century to describe circles of learned middle-class women; by the end of the century it had acquired overtones of pedantry. In the late 1830s Charles Philipon, the influential editor of the humorous journal, *Le Charivari* (1832–93) adopted the term *bas-bleu* in order to dissociate men and women of letters. Increasingly then, the term was used in a derogatory fashion to mock and ridicule women who had taken up the pen. Essays and plays appeared in the 1840s that took as their object the ridiculous, but nonetheless menacing, figure of the *bas-bleu*. Another literary genre also picked up the subject of the *bas-bleu*, the *Physiologies*, which focused on figures or constructs of everyday urban life. These cheap and slangy volumes dealt with such subjects as the poet, marriage, or the *bas-bleu*. In an age fascinated by and distrustful of appearances, this literary genre sought to catalog and describe social types and customs for the purpose of maintaining order. Within this genre, women writers were frequently the object of criticism.[57]

As Christine Planté has argued, the woman author was an invented figure of the nineteenth century, invested with a variety of ideological and cultural fantasies that speak more to representations of learned womanhood than to the realities of female writing. Balzac's little sister's eloquent criticism of the woman author in 1832 speaks tellingly to the anxieties associated with the woman author: "I find the reputation of the woman author scarcely desirable . . . it isolates us from our sphere, from our affections, from our gender; we become neither men nor women. What do you think of all this? Our mission is so inspiring elsewhere!"[58] More generally, contemporaries had difficulties naming the woman author. Should she be an *auteure*, an *autrice*, an *auteuse*, or an *autoresse*? As one critic put it: "How does one name a creature whose breast, destined to nourish children and harbor maternal joys, remains sterile and only beats with feelings of pride; whose mouth, intended to utter sweet nothings, opens to pronounce bold and noisy words?"[59] The education that allowed women to aspire to literary or artistic prominence could also unsex them, just as education could un-class workers if not carefully circumscribed. The frequent association made between the figure of the woman author and that of the *bas-bleu* highlights the problematic nature of women's increasingly visible presence in the publishing world. The criticism in this instance focused more on how women's cultural aspirations challenged the social order. At midcentury the *Grand Dictionnaire Universel du XIXe siècle* noted that a common synonym for *femme auteur* was *bas-bleu*.[60] Women authors violated established gender roles by claiming for women the world of production and creation while abandoning the feminine world of reproduction.

The relationship between the *femme-auteur*, the *femme de letters*, and the *bas-bleu* was not always clear, even in texts that sought to define the *bas-bleu*. Frédéric Soulié's *Physiologie du Bas-bleu* presented a whole range of figures from the aristocratic and imperial bluestocking to the married, virginal, or artistic variety. Although he stated that he was not speaking about the *femme de lettres*, his presentation did not offer a clear distinction except to the extent that the *bas-bleu* had less talent. The latter was depicted as a woman who sought a certain form of independence, challenged established gender roles, and conveyed unwomanly opinions. While he found the figure of the *bas-bleu* both within the family and in public, it seems clear that she presented a problem precisely because she failed to conform to the domestic ideal.[61]

The *bas-bleu* encapsulated the problems associated with women writing and the dangers involved in allowing women to pursue educations that gave them an unrealistic belief in their own talents.[62] Excessive devotion to the "literary-cultural" life led these women to undermine familial values and neglect their maternal responsibilities. This in turn represented a threat to a social order whose foundation rested on the family. Although not all women writers were single, of course, contemporary medical discourse reinforced the perception that women's development of their intellectual capacities inevitably was detrimental to their reproductive abilities. Honoré Daumier's caricatures are perhaps the most famous visual representation of this vision.

In no uncertain terms, Daumier condemned women's literary, artistic, and political aspirations through a series of caricatures in the 1830s and 1840s, most notably in *Les mœurs conjugales* (1839–42), *Les bas-bleus* (1844), *Les divorceuses* (1848), and *Les femmes socialistes* (1849).[63] The chronology of Daumier's themes reflects, of course, the increasingly vocal presence of women feminists and socialists in 1848, but it also suggests how contemporaries linked political and familial organization in their understanding of French society. In his examination of conjugal life, women authors, and socialists, Daumier consistently underlined women's capacity to undermine the social order when they stepped out of the private sphere.[64]

Daumier depicted the woman author or political figure in sharply unfeminine terms. Wild-eyed women with unkempt hair, barren or unattractive bodies, and unfashionable or masculine clothing proliferate in these series. Their activities invariably lead to a disastrous reversal of gender roles with husbands confined to the home and domestic duties while women aspire to roles for which they are clearly unqualified. Daumier makes clear that such behavior is learned and that education is at least in part responsible for the ensuing social or domestic turmoil. Thus he shows a young girl reciting a few poetic lines before an appreciative audience of her mother and three unattractive spinsters (Fig. 1): "Oh that they should curse me / Those barbarous parents who brought me life, / Oh Victor, oh my soul, to you goes all my love!" Daumier clearly pokes fun here at an education that encourages a young girl to reject her parents, to aspire to romantic love, and to produce mediocre poetry all in one. The counterpart to this image is one where a suitably domestic mother reads to her daughter who is dutifully embroidering while an imposing woman author exclaims (Fig. 2): "Ah! my dear, what a peculiar education you are giving your daughter?...

Fig. 1 Honoré Daumier, *Les bas-bleus*, no. 36 in *Le Charivari*, 26 July 1844. Daumier mocks the dumpy bourgeois women in this female salon who admire the mediocre poetic talents of a young girl.

Fig. 2 Honoré Daumier, *Les bas-bleus*, no. 35 in *Le Charivari*, 24 July 1844. The artist astutely captures the tension between two representations of womanhood: the ambitious and unappealing woman author and the traditional bourgeois woman teaching her daughter to sew.

why when I was twelve I had already written a novel in two volume and once finished, my mother prevented me from reading it as it was so precocious for my age."

Like many contemporary observers, Daumier repeatedly suggested that the quality of women's cultural productions were inferior. The prolific literary critic Jules Janin described the woman of letters as having suddenly grown in literature as a "mushroom grows on a dunghill"; he castigated her poor writing, her abandonment of filial, maternal, and spousal duties, and especially her lies, hypocrisy, and false declamations.[65] Women writers as well contributed to such critical portrayals of culturally ambitious women. Stéphanie de Longueville, for example, lampooned the "great lady of 1830" who "prates of physics and politics, of geology and of chemistry, of medicine and of astronomy, with the authority of a Franklin or a Montesquieu . . . and this in such a way as might half induce a belief in the reality of her erudition, were it not that one finds in the reviews and journals she has read in the morning, all the scientific trappings with which she bedizens herself at night."[66]

Satire directed against the figure of the cultured woman suggests the tensions inherent in expanding educational and professional offerings for women. When women aspired to literary fame, they tended to forget their place in the family. Similarly, when girls sought the benefits of a more serious education, they tended to forget their place in the social order. Contemporary fears about *déclassement* through education surrounded both boys and girls' education, but for girls, *déclassement* carried sexual overtones. It was commonly believed that an overly ambitious education either left girls ineligible in the marriage market or rendered them miserable in the home. Madame Bovary, most famously, found only disillusionment in her bourgeois marriage following her education at the hands of teaching sisters.[67] The journalist and literary figure Léon Gozlan more humorously depicted this situation when he showed the effects of a worldly education on a young girl whose parents marry her off to a druggist. As she settles into her new home, her romantic hopes and cultural aspirations are swiftly dashed as she answers commercial letters for her husband and sleeps beside a man clothed in wool stockings and a cotton bonnet. The young wife sadly concludes that the cultural polish of her education bears little relationship to the exigencies of running a household.[68]

Honoré de Balzac's novels offer undoubtedly the best-known examples of girls whose refined education led them to aspire beyond their social condition, thus leading them into lives as courtesans. In *Béatrix* for example, Mme Schontz is portrayed as a student from the Legion of Honor school at Saint-Denis. Upon leaving the school she becomes the mistress of a wealthy man, "led to this doubtful future through the fatal example of a number of her companions who like her had resources." Her brilliant education has exposed her to English, German, and Italian so that she can speak with authority about foreign literature: "She behaved with her talents like a well-bred person, she said nothing."[69] This vision was not solely the product of a literary imagination. Even the teachers at this prestigious school recognized the dangers of the education they offered, as the following letter indicates: "[Our students] who are unfortunately raised out of their class through an overly developed instruction, do not want to descend into practical life and are exposed as a result to seeking dishonorable modes of existence."[70] This stereotype of an education that led to prostitution echoed the criticisms of women's cultural productions that were frequently likened to forms of literary prostitution.

On another level, however, the theme of prostitution went far beyond discussions of education and women's access to culture. Saint-Simonian and feminist writings had developed a far-ranging critique of existing class and gender relationships that tended to posit certain experiences common to all women. The most powerful metaphoric link between working-class and bourgeois women was established around the figure of the prostitute, as all women were seen as being vulnerable to prostitution. As Claire Moses has argued, the *femmes nouvelles* of the 1830s and 1840s raised questions about good woman/bad woman stereotypes by denouncing marriage as a form of legal prostitution for the privileged classes. Young girls were essentially sold into marriage thanks to the financial arrangements that characterized middle-class familial strategies.[71] But this criticism of bourgeois marriages was not limited to the radical fringes of public discourse; on the contrary, politically moderate urban observers also criticized the economic calculations that guided marital strategies. In Emile de la Bédollière's poem "La jeune fille," a virginal young woman prays and communes with nature as she awaits the moment of her betrothal. Rather than a hymn to romantic love, however, the poem ends with the appearance of the attorney or the notary: "You will waste away, the sweet and pure victim, on the altars of financial interest."[72] This representation of daughters as the pawns in bourgeois economic dealings was far from unrealistic during the nineteenth century.

Discussions about the position of daughters in the impoverished middle classes raise a number of questions about the limits of respectability for bourgeois womanhood in this period and offer a way to understand more clearly the place teaching held for many. In 1832 Victorine Collin wrote a powerful article about the plight of the young wellborn Parisian woman whose family had no financial resources to dower her: "Most of you are destined to rot uselessly on this earth, to never wear the title of wife, to only caress the children of others." Rather than belabor this stark portrayal of failed domestic happiness, Collin highlighted the strategies young women could adopt in the face of economic difficulties. She proposed two honorable solutions, commerce and teaching, while acknowledging that some girls would "dishonor their family through their bad conduct," and a minority would brave class conventions and marry beneath them or be chosen on their intrinsic merits by a wealthy man. The vast majority, however, would turn to teaching: "Instruction is the great resource, the object of all parents, the gaping chasm that devours so many mediocrities, so many talents, so many beauties, so many individuals with repulsive traits, the countess without a title, the ruined heiress." Collin's pessimistic vision of the teacher's lifestyle reinforced her message that the plight of the impoverished educated woman was a sad one indeed in this age where economic calculations barred many women from the pleasures of domesticity.[73]

Collin's portrayal of the single woman, like that of the *bas-bleu*, contributed to the flourishing genre of physiologies and served to establish an enduring stereotype of the old maid. As Cécile Dauphin has shown, this figure became increasingly problematic in the nineteenth century, only acquiring positive characteristics at the turn of the century with the spread of professional opportunities for women.[74] Novelists and urban observers at midcentury had only negative comments to make about women who failed to conform to the domestic model. Both threatening and ridiculous, the old maid in many ways resembled the *bas-bleu*. Both were perceived as fundamentally unfeminine, and both disrupted a society founded on the principle of the family. Marie d'Espilly's particularly colorful depiction of the old maid described her as "a sort of wan vegetation that resembles moss and grows far from the rays of the sun." While she blamed the multiplication of these pathetic creatures on the age's cult of money, she also linked their presence to expanding educational opportunities for women. Like many of her contemporaries, d'Espilly reveals her unease at the workings of a liberal economy where women are commodities produced by an educational system gone awry. The old maid is in her words, the "product of a completely false, absurd, and withering education."[75]

These visions of single women were, however, more than cultural fantasies. Although the French never responded as strongly to the "redundant woman" problem as the English did, statistical studies have shown a similar "problem" at midcentury. In 1851 the population survey revealed that over the age of twenty, one in every four women was single; over sixty, one out of two women was single.[76] Single women undoubtedly were not all cold, dry, ugly, and without organs as Louis Couailhac claimed in 1841, but they were a social reality and one that posed particular problems in the middle classes.[77]

Discussions about women's place in the social order were very much a part of cultural life during the July Monarchy. Women petitioners, women journalists, and women authors all proposed models of French femininity that called into question gender relations through their focus on women's influence. The caricatures and moral portraits just examined testify to the unease such questioning generated. With the revolution of 1848, however, the woman question reemerged as a feminist press blossomed and feminist clubs pressed for women's inclusion in the emerging democratic polity.[78]

Women, Education, and the Revolution of 1848

The revolution of 1848 once again brought into the limelight debates about education and gender relations in the newly created Second Republic. As in the aftermath of 1830, the concerns of working women took precedence over those of bourgeois women, particularly given the Second Republic's commitment to the right to work. Schoolteachers organized to defend their vision in the Association fraternelle des instituteurs et institutrices et professeurs socialistes (founded by Pauline Roland), while others published the subversive journal, *L'émancipation de l'enseignement* (1848–49).[79] Jeanne Deroin, herself a schoolteacher, organized both the Club de l'émancipation des peuples and the Société mutuelle d'éducation des femmes, which defended the right of women to receive the sort of serious education that would give them access to the liberal professions.[80] She pursued her efforts in more explicitly political directions, as well, arguing that women be given the right to vote. Not surprisingly, however, women's social rather than political role received the most public attention in the new social republic.

Inevitably, consideration of women's social role involved discussions about education, particularly in 1848–49 as public education underwent hard scrutiny. The minister of education, former Saint-Simonian Hippolyte Carnot, proposed an ambitious law for public education in which both boys and girls would receive free, secular primary education. For women like Eugénie Niboyet and Joséphine Bachellery, the revolutionary context offered an unprecedented opportunity to challenge women's social and cultural inferiority and the more constraining elements of domesticity by advocating the creation of a state-supported system of secondary education for women.

Joséphine Bachellery, in particular, redoubled her efforts to link political and moral changes with educational issues by writing directly to Carnot to propose widespread reforms. In her "Considérations générales sur l'organisation de l'éducation publique des femmes," she called for the creation of a girls' *collège* and a superior normal school for women.[81] Quoting Rémusat's statement that "the moment of political reforms is that of educational plans," she urged the minister to seize the moment in order to allow the emergence of a model woman for the modern democratic world, an individual whom "all women will be happy and proud to resemble." Describing a situation of "absolute urgency," she insisted that women needed above all to learn that "the sacred dogma of universal rights is the grand duty of human solidarity." In Bachellery's eyes the moment had come to right a flagrant injustice, and her proposals clearly reflected her years of reflection on the subject. Writing as well in Niboyet's feminist journal *La voix des femmes*, she hammered home her point that women needed to participate actively in the new order, "[with 1848] women ... will gain their part in the splendid legislative banquet which should offer this great nation new nourishment for soul and body."[82] Calling on women to shake off their chains and to liberate their minds in order to participate, she presented a vision of women's activism that was part and parcel of a broader social movement.

Bachellery's efforts to create the educational institutions that would allow women to participate on an equal footing with men were echoed in the pages of *La voix des femmes* as Delphine Gay, Niboyet, and others argued that women should have the same access to public education and vocational schools. Niboyet urged the opening of a reading room for women at the Bibliothèque Nationale and opened public courses for women in April. Other writers called for women's access to the university in order to become lawyers and doctors.[83] These plans to improve women's status reflected a general concern that women participate in the administration of the *cité* just as they had been granted such authority within the family.[84]

What distinguished these appeals for developing girls' education from earlier calls, however, was the emergence of an explicitly anticlerical rhetoric.[85] Bachellery warned Carnot that the Republic could not afford to leave girls' education in the hands of nuns and private schools because otherwise "the social revolution will not take place either in substance or in form."[86] Interestingly, she articulated a vision of a community of "wisely emancipated" women who would lead the way and offer their example to both men and women: "Nothing should prevent them from teaching those around them and to communicate a love of the Republic." Nuns, of course, were women, but she urged these "misguided sisters . . . to refuse perpetual vows and the isolation of the cloisters."[87]

Although most of these suggestions were not put into action, an important exception was the emergence of vocational courses for women workers, thanks to the efforts of Elisa Lemonnier. These courses first emerged in 1848 and assumed a more concrete existence in 1856, becoming the Société de protection maternelle and then in 1862 the Société pour l'enseignement professionnel des femmes.[88] For Françoise Mayeur this represents one of the most important educational legacies of 1848.[89] By recognizing women workers' right to vocational training, Republicans opened the way to envisioning women as individual economic agents.

The revolutionary context provided an opportunity for a questioning of women's roles that was far more public than the earlier discussions analyzed so far. Most emblematic of the attention given to gender roles was the decision to ask the prolific writer Ernest Legouvé to offer a series of well-publicized courses on the history of women at the prestigious Collège de France. In April 1848 Legouvé, whose father was also known for his "feminist" opinions, began his lectures, which were then published under the title *Histoire morale des femmes* in 1849. Interest in this text was such that it appeared in ten separate editions before 1896 and was translated into Spanish, English, and Russian, while sections appeared in Italian. As Karen Offen has persuasively argued, Legouvé's *Histoire* deserves close attention for the ways he articulated an argument for women's "equality in difference" at midcentury.[90] Moreover, the rhetoric of his argument offers exceptional insight into the complicated ways in which women's public and private responsibilities were conceptualized.

Legouvé's widely attended lectures denounced the weight of women's social, economic, and legal inferiority in French society and proposed changes to allow women greater rights and autonomy. From the outset, however, he positioned himself as a moderate, situated between two extremes: on the one hand, he shied away from the "romantic" socialist position that advocated sexual emancipation, but on the other hand, he denounced the inequities of the conservative traditionalist position. Change was necessary in his opinion, but it was couched in terms that were intended to appeal to fathers and husbands. As a result, he advocated marriage reform as well as civil reforms that would give women greater autonomy within the family. Like earlier reformers as well, he championed educational reforms and particularly emphasized the need for the state to provide public education for girls. Speaking with the authority vested in the Collège de France, he denounced the current state of affairs: "The state pays for a university for men, a polytechnic for men, a school of arts and industry for men, normal schools for men — for women, what does it create? Primary schools! Why stop there?"[91] While Legouvé stopped short of advocating women's participation in politics, he did urge the development of professional opportunities for women, particularly for single women whose plight he highlighted in his lectures. Specifically, he argued for women's admittance to the "private" professions (as writers and teachers), as well as access to the "public and social professions" (as notaries or lawyers).[92] He insisted as well that certain professions be reserved for women, particularly those that involved contact with other women, such as in prisons, in medicine, or in teaching.[93]

Unfortunately, the hopes of 1848 were soon dashed; just as the Second Republic reneged on its commitment to work, so the more feminist challenges met with defeat. A notable exception to this tale of disappointed expectations was the birth of vocational education for women, thanks to the efforts of Elisa Lemonnier. But it is important to emphasize that the debates of the previous two decades as well as the outburst in 1848 did produce a number of new arguments concerning gender roles and especially the role of girls' education in an emerging democratic order. Unlike the first revolutionary moment, the emphasis on educating mothers of future citizens was not uppermost. Instead women such as Bachellery or Deroin sought to place women more actively in civil society. As Joan Scott has insightfully argued, Deroin claimed politics as the domain of women by equating household and state, thereby abolishing the spatial distinctions between public and private. Feminists did not abandon the maternal figure in their rhetoric; on the contrary, they emphasized it. "When the subject of rights was inserted into a network of duties, as it was in 1848, feminists had no trouble finding a woman who met the definition of citizen ... the mother. Here was an identity achieved through the performance of socially attributed duties, the very model for the meaning of reciprocity and obligation."[94] But Deroin's mother, like Bachellery's women and girls, understood their responsibilities to include both rights and duties that went beyond the domestic sphere. So too did Ernest Legouvé, whose writings inspired a generation of feminists in the early Third Republic. He offers perhaps the most useful perspective for understanding the contradictions of the revolutionary interlude.

Legouvé's concern to foster legal and educational reforms resonated widely with earlier feminist campaigns once the more radical calls for sexual emancipation had vanished, and in this respect his proposals resemble those of many 1848 feminists (with the notable exception of the vote). Similarly, his support of motherhood echoed the pronouncements of the moralizing domestic discourse that developed during the July Monarchy. His discussion of work opportunities, however, reveals a fundamental tension in the relationship between educational reforms and women's roles. While advocating *public* state education for girls, he oscillated in his discussion of the most obvious products of such an education — the *femmes de lettres* or the teacher. Arguing that women's destiny was to love, he then went to say, "but only at this price will women be able to become women of letters without ceasing to be women, and society will no longer reproach them for this occupation which broadens the domain of public thought without pulling them from their private duties."[95] Despite his efforts to challenge a hierarchical understanding of the relationship between the sexes, Legouvé's reformed sisters remained second-class citizens in comparison to their brothers. Education, in his view, was clearly the road for women's emancipation. Still his promotion of public professions remained tied to what Offen describes as a "functional utilitarian vision of women's social role in family life."[96]

By midcentury women's education had entered public discourse in an unprecedented way thanks to the mobilizing impact of both a feminist and a woman's press. As education was linked to other social and legal reforms, it became an issue of political concern even if the political implications only played themselves out in the period after 1850. As contemporary writers recognized, things were changing in the 1830s and 1840s, and part of these changes involved questioning the place of women in a shifting and uncertain world. No clear answers emerged from these discussions: biology might explain some aspects of the relations between the sexes, differences in education explained many others. Again opinions on what that education should involve were varied, and relatively few advocated aligning girls' education with boys', but the Catholic clergy joined both the feminine press and feminists in arguing that "good" mothers needed more "serious" education.

These debates about bourgeois women and their appropriate role in French society were part of far broader debates about the shifting contours of bourgeois society. Education in general received careful attention, given the regime's commitment to a form of limited meritocracy.[97] But meritocracy was not open to everyone; women in particular were excluded from this system that promoted a chosen few on the basis of their individual accomplishments. Instead, efforts to promote women's status in society were redirected into the family. What in the end were the implications of these debates for women of the middle classes? Did these minority voices make an impact on how the domestic was configured in the Second Empire, widely considered the heyday of domestic ideology? What influence if any did these voices have on the schools that increasingly framed girls' educational experiences? Ultimately, these debates about girls' education did produce some results, as the following chapters will show. As institutions proliferated, rulings were elaborated in an attempt to define more clearly the shape of girls' secondary education. But these debates also produced a series of enduring feminine stereotypes whose significance bears consideration in this exploration of the relationship between intellect, education, and the bourgeois woman. Saint-Simonian and feminist challenges to the status quo generated powerful counterimages of unfeminine bluestockings, often cast as prostitutes of the mind, debasing the quality of literature with their inferior products. While the bluestocking threatened to unsex women, the image of the educated woman courtesan raised a whole series of anxieties against which educational institutions both explicitly and implicitly sought to defend themselves.

4

Independent Women?
Teachers and the Teaching Profession at Midcentury

The socioeconomic changes associated with the process of urbanization in France opened opportunities for educated women that have frequently been ignored in the secondary literature. Indeed, the dominant account of the impact of industrialization on gender roles has emphasized how the separation of home and workplace served to drive women into the home. More nuanced readings of this process reveal, however, the limits of this domestication — if one looks more carefully at all levels of the middle class and not just its upper reaches. Moreover, if one shifts one's consideration from industrialization to urbanization, the impact of change appears considerably more complex than the model of domesticity suggests. As noted in Chapter 3, the growth of a cheap press as well as the development of the book industry offered educated women countless opportunities to voice their opinions and to gain readerships. Recent work on women authors in the mid-nineteenth century reveals the presence of many now-forgotten individuals who lived by the pen, often writing for other women. Their publishing success testifies to the sharp growth of female readership in the middle decades of the century.[1] Clearly, writing offered some women a degree of financial independence generally not associated with women of the middle classes.

More than writing, however, teaching provided opportunities for educated women. Through teaching, women carved out a public role in French society whose significance has not been thoroughly explored. The rising interest in girls' education provided cultural impetus to the growth in institutions for girls. For the middle classes, most female establishments were boarding schools, run by either lay or religious women. Although other possibilities existed for educating girls — day classes, correspondence classes, and private tutoring, these represented minority options in France in the nineteenth century.[2] As a result, institutional growth generated a demand for women teachers and administrators, who came for the most part from the educated middle classes. A young woman's entrance into the world did not automatically imply entrance into the marriage market. On the contrary, many young women delayed this moment, temporarily or permanently, by becoming assistant teachers in boarding schools or entering the novitiate of a religious order. Only recently has historical scholarship revealed the extent of this phenomenon, which suggests that prescriptive insistence on women's role as wives and mothers was not as widely followed as one might imagine. Claude Langlois's sweeping study of religious orders, in particular, has highlighted the considerable attraction of religious life for women in the nineteenth century. Less well known is the considerable growth of lay institutions for girls that depended on the presence of both single and married women to function.

This chapter focuses on women teachers both as a social group and as individuals positioning themselves with respect to families, the state, and the church. While historians have long noted how teaching constituted one of the rare respectable professions for a middle-class woman, they have not considered the implications for an understanding of middle-class womanhood. In part this inattention stems from how lay schoolmistresses and nuns couched their educational project in the language of moral motherhood. In doing so these independent women sought to distance themselves from other available models of learned womanhood — in particular, the figure of the bas-bleu. Around 1848 the debates about women's place in French society spawned the figure of the female intellectual, whose claim to a public voice generated both ridicule and anxiety. In this context, donning the robes of masculine professionalism posed particular problems. Religious women teachers sought refuge in their corporate identity while laywomen teachers had to tread a thin line indeed to ensure their cultural respectability within French civil society. As a result, the professional trajectories of these women have received virtually no attention.[3]

The Laywoman Teacher and the Move Toward Professionalization

Women teachers had to contend with a series of images about women, education, and schools that durably influenced how they presented themselves. As the previous chapter has shown, these images proliferated in moral, religious, and pedagogical texts destined for young girls and women, but also in the literature related to urban life. While these documents presented quite different messages, the underlying image they offered of the woman teacher was remarkably similar: she represented a poor substitute for the figure of the maternal educator. At best she was a second choice. This vision of lay teacher as substitute mother sits uncomfortably with the realities of the emerging corps of female secondary-school teachers. For despite the absence of a state-supported system of secondary education for girls, institutional growth created a situation where the values associated with an emerging professional ethos increasingly fashioned teachers' working lives.

Images of the Laywoman Teacher

As the discussion of the *bas-bleu* and single woman has suggested, public rhetoric had little use for the independent laywoman. Although teaching represented the obvious honorable solution for young women from the impoverished middle classes, it was rarely presented in the period from 1840 until the 1860s as a positive choice for intellectually or professionally ambitious bourgeois girls. Instead, countless contemporaries characterized teaching as a last resort for young women who could not find husbands. The absence of clearly defined professional qualifications contributed to making institutional girls' education the object of frequent criticism. Writings that addressed the issue of girls' education tended to focus on a series of interrelated problems that all underscored the limited cultural authority granted to women teachers, as opposed to mothers. To begin with, writers dissected the underlying motives that pulled women into teaching. Unlike taking religious vows, the desire to teach was somehow always tainted with less honorable concerns. Second, contemporaries criticized the ethos underlying existing girls' schools, in particular the excessive attention to the decorative arts and worldly talents. Third, critics often linked this frills-oriented education to the evils of institutional competition. In an unregulated educational market parental demands rather than pedagogical criteria dictated school programs. Finally, medical science bolstered critical visions of girls' schools in general by suggesting that girls' bodies and minds risked overstimulation within a public institution. Lay women teachers far more than teaching nuns bore the brunt of these negative representations.

Public discussions about women teachers and girls' education extended beyond pedagogical circles and the feminine press. Not surprisingly, the same urban observers who contributed to the negative stereotypes concerning unmarried women and bluestockings frequently included women teachers in their criticism. Marie d'Espilly argued in her essay that an overly sophisticated education produced a surplus of single women, who were then condemned to lives as governesses, schoolmistresses, and ladies' companions:

> In the past it was the absolute lack of intellectual culture, today it is an instruction and talents incongruent with certain social necessities that condemn women to being single. The old maid encumbers institutions, fills with her name articles about governesses, lady's companions, language lessons, music lessons, etc., etc., in the *Petites Affiches*. One finds her in our *athénées*, our public and private lectures, seeking no doubt to braid a wreath

with the few flowers she has picked in the field of science or of art, a wreath that will console her in place of the marriage garland which will never decorate her virginal brow.[4]

Similarly, the poet Louise Colet (who was also Flaubert's lover) painted a dismal picture of the life and qualities of the *institutrice*. For Colet, these young women from the middle or lower middle classes could be divided into three categories: those who had a teaching vocation, those who were ambitious, and those who taught out of self-sacrifice. Colet harshly criticized all three types, presenting teaching not as a freely chosen profession, but rather as a means to a less than honorable end. In her essay, the first type of teacher begins her career as a teacher's aide in the boarding school where she was raised. Her superficial education coupled with an absence of imagination and insight are scarcely the stuff of the true teacher. Her principal aim is to seduce an eligible bachelor uncle; and if this fails, "she purchases a boarding school the way one buys a notary's office with a clientele that already exists, and then she struts around for the rest of her life." The ambitious schoolteacher aspires as well to a match above her station, and not to excellence in teaching. If she fails in her goal, she becomes a canoness. Finally, Colet presents a more acceptable vision of the devoted schoolteacher, the sweet young girl whose family falls on hard times who goes into teaching as a *demoiselle de compagnie*. But once again, her path is not smooth, and she is made to suffer the humility of class snobbery in the grand family that employs her. Like other authors in this series, Colet thoroughly demystified the cult of the devoted teacher.[5]

Ecarnot's biting criticism of the country school for young ladies presents a similarly unflattering representation of schools and schoolteachers. The essay begins with a sweeping condemnation of present-day girls' education ridiculing those schools which teach everything regardless of student's rank, fortune, or natural intelligence: "The daughter of the pastry-cook is taught literary composition; the labourer's daughter, logical analysis; the shoemaker's daughter, astronomy, the tanner's daughter, the art of poetry." The failure of these schools to form "economical, sensible, and useful housewives" is blamed both on the spirit of the day and on the schoolteachers themselves. Not surprisingly their reasons for going into teaching resemble those presented in Colet's essay: as orphans with a smattering of accomplishments, they hope that teaching will be the way to find a husband.[6] These satirical portraits naturally emphasized the baser, more commercial reasons that led young women into teaching. As a result, they contributed to a public perception of teachers that was a far cry from the selfless, devoted substitute maternal figure of pedagogical literature. The currency of this perception is perhaps best reflected in Flaubert's *Dictionnaire des idées reçues*: "Women teachers. Always come from an excellent family that has experienced misfortune — Dangerous within homes: corrupt the husband."

Given these negative cultural associations, it is not surprising that the women's press wrote little about the lay teacher. Anne Hettler's exploration of six such journals in the Second Empire reveals that teachers were relatively absent from these magazines, which preferred to concentrate on the figure of the maternal educator. *La mode illustrée* criticized boarding-school teachers for offering girls solely a worldly rather than a moral education because of the pressure of their clientele.[7] The highly influential author of *Le journal de Marguerite* (1858), Victorine Monniot, presented a more nuanced vision of lay teachers in her substantial didactic oeuvre. While praising the maternal educator, she also depicted the governess as a second and indispensable mother.[8] The author's early experiences as a governess herself undoubtedly influenced her representation of such teachers, but she was careful to depict them within the home, and not in boarding schools, motivated by the same moral convictions as mothers: "I cannot believe, as some argue, that there are women teachers so ignorant of their holy function to consider it a business. Naturally we need some form of pecuniary compensation for our noble labors . . . but we give back far more than we receive; we dispense that which cannot be paid for and that is what confers dignity on our profession."[9] The image of the Christian teacher in Monniot's writing bore a striking resemblance to that of the teaching nun: "She must always be pious, humble, modest, and charitable. . . . She must make studies agreeable for her students and virtue enticing."[10] Teaching here was clearly not a career but a vocation.

In sum, the figure of the lay schoolmistress carried mixed cultural messages that made it difficult for these women to position themselves clearly in civil society. Whether as a governess within a family or a headmistress running a school, the woman teacher appeared increasingly out of place within a discourse that valorized the home and home education for its daughters. Suspicions about the reasons that led women to run schools for money also extended to the ethos of these schools.

Professionalization in a Feminine Key

> [Mme Bascans] loathed anything that seemed like business in the noble
> task of teaching.
>
> — Hippolyte Maze, Mme Bascans, 1801–1878

The proliferation of both primary and secondary girls' schools in the years from 1830 until 1880 created a complicated administrative problem for the Ministry of Education and for the municipal authorities in charge of regulating the local educational scene. The uncertain status of women teachers and their schools resulted in a host of local rulings and decisions at odds with the general centralizing ethos of the French University.[11] Despite the relative confusion during this period about what constituted secondary education for girls and what should be required to run a secondary school, certain guidelines emerged that increasingly defined what it meant to be a secondary-school teacher. These guidelines were part of a process of professionalization within the female teaching corps, which is not always easy to discern for several reasons. To begin with, contemporaries frequently portrayed women teachers and their schools in very different lights, emphasizing far more the commercial nature of existing boarding schools and the superficiality of girls' studies, rather than teachers' academic qualifications. Second, the sources concerning laywomen teachers are scattered and fragmentary, since they belonged to the private sector and fell under the responsibility of the prefect, not the rector who oversaw public education. Finally, as the quotation from Maze suggests, the pervasiveness of a domestic rhetoric for bourgeois women not only influenced how teachers presented themselves but also tended to obscure how women's teaching did acquire professional characteristics in the period before the education laws of the Third Republic. As a result, historians have not appreciated the extent to which the laywoman teacher emerged as a professional figure in the mid-nineteenth century.

Professionalization carries a variety of meanings in different national contexts. Anglo-American historians of education have increasingly used professionalization as a framework to understand changes over time. In general the term is used to describe the impact of the development of teacher training, increasing specialization, the creation of fixed criteria for promotion, a rise in teacher's social status, and the emergence of professional associations. Often associated with these changes is the emergence of a professional consciousness centered around a set of learned values and habitual responses, what Burton Bledstein has described as professionalism.[12] In France teacher professionalization was not associated with establishing independence from the state, but instead can be seen as part of a dynamic involving four players: the state, the church, lay teachers, and families. The negotiations and conflicts that underlay this process had, of course, a gendered dimension, since both men and women were teachers.[13]

For male primary lay teachers, the process of professionalization involved distancing themselves from the model of the lay cleric and hence allying with the state in its efforts to develop normal schools, examinations, and inspections.[14] For both elementary and secondary female schoolteachers the situation was more complicated, given the weight of cultural models of womanhood, the widespread presence of teaching nuns, and the absence of clear consensus on what constituted girls' secondary education. Moreover, the state was far less persistent in its efforts to establish training institutions, to raise teaching credentials, and to systematize inspections for girls, allowing nuns to set up schools with little administrative oversight. Still, as schools multiplied during the July Monarchy, educational authorities responded with two important educational measures. In 1836 an ordinance known as the Pelet law extended to girls most of the provisions of the 1833 Guizot law on primary education except the most significant: the obligation for towns to open girls' schools and for departments to create normal schools.[15] In the wake of this ordinance, the prefect of the Seine passed another rule in 1837 pertaining to the secondary level of girls' schools, the *maisons d'éducation de filles*.[16] Described by earlier educational historians as the first charter of girls' secondary education, in reality it differed little from the text of 1821 discussed in Chapter 2. What was different, however, was the attempt to generalize this ruling throughout France.[17] Both of these measures established guidelines for acquiring teaching diplomas and established, in principle, a distinction between the primary schoolteacher with her *brevet de capacité* and the secondary teacher with her more advanced diploma.

The 1837 rule concerning secondary education focused on women teachers and their qualifications in an effort to raise the general level of girls' education and to guarantee moral standards. To begin with, it simplified the three-tiered institutional hierarchy created in the 1821 ruling by eliminating the lowest level — the *école secondaire*. Henceforth, only *pensions* and *institutions* remained, but new requirements were added for those women seeking to open such schools. The head of a *pension* was expected to be able to teach a wide variety of courses: moral instruction, religion, reading, writing, French grammar, arithmetic, French history, modern geography, and aspects of physics and the natural sciences, in addition to drawing, music, needlework, and foreign languages. Women who wanted to run *institutions* also needed to know literature, style, ancient geography, ancient and modern history, and cosmography. The jury that granted diplomas was to be composed of seven members, five men and two women who were appointed by the prefect.[18] Finally, the rule created a special inspection committee composed of at least five members. The minister of education appointed committee members who were expected to meet once a month and hear reports from inspectresses. In cases where the ruling was not observed, this committee had the power to revoke schoolmistresses' authorizations. As in the 1821 ruling, inspectresses formed an essential aspect of the emerging secondary system; while their responsibilities remained largely unchanged, the entire apparatus of surveillance became more professional as inspectresss had official checklists to guide them in their work and were expected to attend the monthly inspection meetings.

Despite this attempt to establish a more codified and controlled institutional landscape, the ruling failed to correct long-standing shortcomings. The fact that this so-called charter did not extend beyond the department of the Seine and perpetuated a system where each departmental prefect decided whether or not to implement it presented obvious limits to its effectiveness. Moreover, the ruling exempted day classes from its consideration and preserved the nuns' exemption from teaching examinations. Finally, it officially equated secondary schools with boarding schools so that the men and women who ran schools without boarders (*externats*) did not fall under its provisions even if they offered advanced education.[19] Given the proliferation of schools since the early 1820s and a more prevalent social demand for girls' education, however, the Parisian administration showed greater zeal in enforcing the new ruling. Specifically, in 1839, the Ministry of Education appointed M. Legros to oversee the work of the inspection committee.[20] Legros's task was to act as mediator between the ministry and the municipal committee members who oversaw the accreditation and surveillance of lay schoolmistresses.

Legros found a powerful collaborator in the person of the prefect of the Seine, Barthelot de Rambuteau, who also took seriously the need to reform girls' secondary education. He persuaded the Conseil royal de l'instruction to establish more rigorous procedures for the transfer of boarding schools from one owner to another. This was an attempt to prevent headmistresses from making private arrangements between themselves that short-circuited official authorization procedures. Too often the prefect was presented with a *fait accompli*; once a school was up and running, it was difficult to intervene.[21] Legros also insisted on the need to make provincial teachers recertify when moving to Paris, because provincial teaching standards were generally lower than those established for the department of the Seine.[22] Then in 1844 the city of Paris bolstered its female inspection team through the creation of the first paid inspectorate for women, following the example provided in 1837 by the creation of the first inspectresses general of nursery schools. Three women were appointed to serve as *dames déléguées*, coordinating and overseeing the activities of the other volunteer inspectresss.[23]

These efforts to establish guidelines for girls' secondary education spread to the provinces as the Ministry of Education urged each department to write up its own *règlement*, preferably relying on the criteria already established for the department of the Seine. Provincial responses to this directive offer insight both into the practical difficulties of implementing administrative control and into the ideological resistance it encountered. The administrative personnel often had difficulties incorporating women teachers and their schools into the increasingly complicated institutional machine.[24]

The prefects of isolated departments as well as those in heavily clerical regions tended to oppose the generalization of the Parisian ruling. For some, the reasons given were that no higher schools for girls existed, while others argued that the sole presence of religious institutions rendered such a ruling unnecessary. In both cases it is striking to note the failure to imagine the development of girls' secondary education as well as the resistance to conceptualizing religious education as subject to control. On a practical level, many prefects responded that they simply could not organize separate inspection committees and separate examination juries from those already existing for primary education.[25] Their proposals to have female boarding schools under the administrative oversight of primary inspectors exemplified the difficulties in establishing a clear distinction between primary and secondary education. Many responses also insisted that the concept of inspectresses made little sense in the provinces. In the Ile-et-Vilaine, for example, the prefect noted that lady inspectors were both too modest and unqualified to offer advice to teachers.

The prefects of more populated urban departments welcomed the ruling with more enthusiasm, often stating their support for the principle of establishing an institutional hierarchy in girls' education.[26] Overwhelmingly, however, prefects in such departments responded that the fine distinctions established between *institutions* and *pensions* at the secondary level were not pertinent in their department, even though they defended the need to distinguish clearly between secondary and primary education.[27] Interestingly, the prefect of the Cher noted the need for this basic distinction in order to end "the charlatanism of advertisements that headmistresses publish"; in an unregulated institutional landscape, women like men sought to deceive potential clients about the "wares" they were peddling.[28] The overall reaction to the attempts to impose regulations throughout France suggests that by the 1840s administrative personnel recognized the limits of hearsay or local knowledge in an increasingly mobile society, and so they welcomed the opportunity to impose administrative clarity on a female educational landscape whose contours remained unclear. The more practical questions raised illustrate the difficulties involved in fixing the division between what constituted primary or secondary education for girls, and the resulting problem in determining the difference between a simple *institutrice* and a *directrice de pension*. In 1849 the rector of Lyons wrote to the prefect in some alarm that primary schoolmistresses were calling themselves "mistresses of ladies' boarding schools," thus avoiding the inspection of primary inspectors.[29] More positively, a local educational official in the department of the Vienne wrote that while no women teachers had secondary diplomas, their institutions were recognized as such: "They are granted public confidence. The teachers with higher diplomas are considered to be headmistresses of *institutions*, because they have given proof of their ability and because they have the right to run a boarding school."[30] Dossier after dossier reveals the tensions between an ostensibly meritocratic administrative ethos, intent on establishing professional guidelines, and social practices where class and gender considerations prevailed.

The extensive comments transmitted by the prefect's councillor in the Eure-et-Loir offers a good example of how contemporaries linked educational and social hierarchies and how concerns about female gender roles prevailed over establishing professional qualifications. This councillor perceived *institutions* as schools for the "superior classes," who in his department were educated at home. *Pensions*, then, were intended for the *classe moyenne*, which he defined as the class that "encompasses most of the bourgeoisie, commerce and agriculture; that class is the only one where children receive an education in a boarding school." He saw the distinction between *institutions* and *pensions* not in educational but in social terms, and he judged such a distinction inappropriate: "With respect to public spirit, a distinction such as that which is proposed would only tend to provoke precisely those sorts of social classifications which are rampant in the provinces despite the equality of fortunes and positions."[31] Similarly, his discussion of headmistresses and teaching aides reveals how moral concerns prevailed over professional issues. He emphasized that since the majority of headmistresses were married, one should also insist on proofs concerning the husband's morality. Inspections should focus, not on teaching methods or tools, but rather on the hygienic measures of each school in order to reduce the "number of weak, frail, nervous women that are so numerous in the middle class [*classe moyenne*] and who give birth to fragile, rachitic individuals thus preventing the emergence of a generation of strong and vigorous men."[32]

In other departments, however, more professional concerns did surface. In particular, several reports called for the state support of normal schools: "Wouldn't it be possible to organize normal schools for the training of both teachers and teachers' aides, as exists in primary education for men?"[33] It was more common, however, for reports to highlight the need to differentiate more clearly the content of the certifying examinations for primary and secondary education. Several prefects argued, relatively accurately, that the *diplôme de maîtresse de pension* was similar to the *brevet supérieur* created in the 1836 ordinance concerning primary education. They worried then about what distinguished the more qualified secondary teachers from elementary teachers. A final issue that emerged frequently in these reports concerned the qualifications and age of teachers' aides. Some worried that at age sixteen, *sous-maîtresses* were too young to assume their required responsibilities, while others highlighted the age gap between eligible *sous-maîtresses* and headmistresses, who could only take their position at age twenty-five. As a report from the Vosges noted, a nine-year "novitiate" was too long. This comment strongly suggests that teaching as a *sous-maîtresse* was considered a form of apprenticeship for the position of headmistress; teaching then had become a career for women with a recognized trajectory.[34] The use of the term "novitiate" certainly indicates, however, that contemporaries saw similarities between religious teaching orders and an emerging corps of lay female teachers.

Provincial responses to the 1837 ruling suggest that in most departments this discussion about girls' secondary education was premature. While some interest did exist to develop this sector, the relative dearth of lay female teachers rendered the ruling inoperative. Public interest in girls' education in the 1830s and 1840s failed to convince most prefects of the need for a more professional definition of laywomen teachers. Echoing a similar lack of interest in the development of female primary normal schools, the administration of the July Monarchy ultimately left individual headmistresses to determine the characteristics of girls' secondary education in the provinces.[35]

The Agents in the Push for Professionalization in the Middle Decades of the Century

Traditionally in France the state is seen as the primary agent of change despite ample evidence to the contrary. Application of the 1837 rulings clearly depended on agents of the state (as well as lay inspectresses). In addition, however, lay teachers, feminists, and the press all exerted themselves to establish a clear professional profile for the secondary schoolmistress, albeit with limited success. Feminists, in particular, focused on the need to establish training schools for secondary teachers. The most vocal critic of the contemporary institutional situation at midcentury was Joséphine Bachellery. As a Parisian boarding-school mistress herself, she adopted an insider's perspective that allowed her not only to criticize her fellow teachers but also to offer sweeping proposals for radical change. Beginning in 1838, she published letters in educational journals criticizing the superficial quality of most boarding-school education: "The most obvious indication of the complete moral and scientific nullity of women who run large boarding schools is their propensity to frequent 'le monde' . . . the piano has become the focus, while education is only accessory."[36] In Bachellery's opinion, public education needed to rethink its raison d'être and adjust to the presence of lower middle-class girls in institutions who needed a more "scientific" and vocationally oriented education. Her commitment to improving women's work opportunities crystallized around proposals to raise the status of women teachers. To begin with, she called for the eviction of male professors from girls' boarding schools, arguing that they monopolized the more challenging jobs and contributed to perceptions of female intellectual inferiority. Abolishing male teachers would enable women to pursue more interesting and challenging teaching careers.[37] Her commitment to the professionalization of female teaching emerged most clearly, however, in her call for the creation of a superior normal school run by the state. According to Bachellery, the existence of teaching examinations would accomplish nothing "as long as a normal school failed to give the numerous candidates moral and scientific inspiration."[38] The Second Republic's failure to create such a superior normal school left initiative for teacher training back in the hands of individual headmistresses.

Critics within the ministry echoed many of these arguments. In 1842, Étienne Kilian, a civil servant in the Ministry of Education, published a detailed analysis of the state of girls' secondary education in which he argued that girls' education suffered from its being left entirely to "private speculation." Despite the introduction of standards for teachers and institutional inspections, the market determined a school's success or failure; schoolmistresses inevitably catered to the market to the detriment

of serious education. He argued in particular for far more pervasive state intervention in the realm of girls' education: "Now is the time to consider whether it is not
opportune to organize girls' secondary education seriously through the creation of
schools, sponsored by towns, departments, or the state."[39]

The pedagogical press also contributed to these efforts to define and control girls'
secondary education. In particular, the *Revue de l'enseignement des femmes* (1845–48)
devoted considerable attention to the new rulings and made more widely available
information about teaching examinations and accrediting procedures. This moderate newspaper distanced itself from the more challenging anticlerical or feminist
positions of the period, but nonetheless contributed to establishing knowledge about
the emerging professional standards for girls' schools. Articles ranged in subject
from the opening of normal schools and normal classes to pedagogical suggestions
about prizes, while also covering the more political efforts of reformers to pressure
the government into pursuing reforms. While the *REF* was the only journal solely
devoted to girls' education, others also addressed issues concerning it.[40] The short-lived
Journal des maîtres de pension (1840–42) functioned as a placement bureau, publishing
advertisements from teachers peddling their services or from headmasters or mistresses selling their schools and equipment. Several years later the *Courrier des pensions* (October 1846–March 1848) appeared, which offered similar services. In a private market, such professional journals played a critical role in defining the profile of
the lay schoolmistress; their rapid disappearance reveals the precarious status of the
private sector.

The concern to improve the quality of girls' schools and to ensure the proper
qualifications of women teachers in the 1830s and 1840s was clearly part of a much
broader interest in determining women's place in a changing urban context, as the
previous chapter has shown. The ensuing rulings and regulations translated in many
ways the contradictory impulses of this cultural debate. Ostensibly, of course, the
new rules sought to ensure that schools and teachers contributed to the moralization of French society, but the effort to test and accredit women teachers increasingly defined the contours of a professional career where women could construct
independent lives and their own female spaces.[41]

Obstacles to Professionalization

The efforts to introduce order, hierarchies, and rules went furthest in the increasingly
complex Parisian educational landscape, where they also encountered inevitable resistance, primarily from women already running schools. Legros's reports as well as
those of inspectors allow one to identify the major obstacles to the emergence of
clear professional standards for laywomen. Legros's criticisms, in particular, reveal

how thoroughly intertwined the issues of intellectual, professional, and moral standards were.[42] Three main issues emerge in these documents that illustrate the limits of professionalizing efforts for women: individual teachers were reluctant to follow established certification and authorization procedures; the absence of training programs for teachers undermined efforts to improve teaching, and finally the presence of male teachers who held the more prestigious positions in boarding schools hindered efforts at specialization.[43]

Timid Women, Tough Examinations, and Confusing Procedures

Problems associated with teachers' failure to obtain the necessary diploma reemerged constantly from 1838 until 1853 when the secondary diplomas were legislated out of existence. At times the inspectresses noted deliberate violation of procedures as when a certified teacher requested authorization for a school that was actually run by a noncertified woman. More frequently teachers and especially teachers' aides failed to take the necessary examinations. In 1842, for example, only three out of sixteen teachers' aides had the required diploma in the fifth arrondissement in Paris.[44] Year after year inspection committees noted that certain teachers were not officially qualified, and yet their schools were not closed.

The failure to pass examinations appears to have been the result of two quite different causes that illustrate the cultural difficulties inherent in the professionalization process. To begin with, many teachers felt paralyzed at the prospect of speaking before a jury primarily composed of men. As a result, some teachers simply never showed up for the examinations. In 1846, 1,019 women signed up for the Parisian examinations but 25 percent failed to appear. Older, more established teachers also refused to submit to the certification process. Clarice Aublay, for example, stated:

> A downturn in my fortune forced me to return to teaching [she had taught at one of the schools of the Legion of Honor], for the past several years I have run a day school in the area of the Chaussée d'Antin. Today I would like to avoid, not the ordeal of the examination which I do not fear in any fashion, but a painful and embarrassing appearance in front of a public jury, from whom I fear I am not certain to obtain all the respect and good will which my age, my antecedents, my character, and my position would lead me to expect as a right. You understand, M. le Ministre, how disagreeable it would be for me to go sit on the same bench as numerous other candidates who are presenting themselves for an examination without any of the guarantees I offer.

Clothed in the mantle of feminine respectability, this teacher successfully petitioned the government to grant her outright the highest diploma, that of *maîtresse d'institution*.[45]

Second, the examination itself appears to have been rigorously administered in and around Paris. In 1841 the decision was made that if a candidate failed part of the examination, she failed it all.[46] Reports of the Conseil général du département de la Seine reveal that the examinations to receive a teaching diploma were relatively selective in the capital. In 1845 and 1846 approximately one-third of all candidates obtained diplomas in a given year. Between 1851 and 1856, the percentage of successful candidates ranged from a low of 28 percent to a high of 40.4 percent. These figures contrast nonetheless with Octave Gréard's assertion that prior to 1848 only 13.7 percent of the candidates for a *maîtresse de pension* diploma were successful.[47] Inspection reports do not confirm Gréard's bleak vision of teachers' qualifications at midcentury. True, many candidates failed, but given the number of candidates — 762 in 1846 alone in Paris — the juries could afford to be selective.

In the provinces fragmentary evidence indicate that examination juries were more tolerant and the number of candidates considerably smaller. Between 1842–47 two-thirds of the candidates in the Seine-et-Oise obtained their diplomas.[48] In Tarbes in southwestern France percentages varied widely: in February 1848 all five candidates obtained diplomas, but candidates in the summer session were less successful; only five of eleven passed. Comments on the successful candidates suggests, however, that standards were fairly low, since a woman who got a "nul" in French history passed, as well as several women whose levels in dictation, history, or geography were judged "feeble." Surviving examples of candidates' dictation certainly confirms the impression that provincial juries were quite tolerant. Three spelling or grammatical mistakes in this one short sentence still received the "mention bien": "The feminine boarding schools, situated in the department of the Hautes-Pyrénées, which are not primary schools, are divided into two distinct types of institution according to the level of instruction one receives." Still, a candidate who passed all subjects except for mathematics was required to repeat the examination at its next scheduled date.[49] It seems that some standards were in effect even there. Juries were apparently more demanding in Strasbourg, according to Amélie Weiler. In 1843 she noted: "The committee was very strict this year; out of sixty-five candidates, twenty-five only [38 percent] received their diplomas. My! what one demands of a woman! It is almost impossible not to lose one's confidence in front of five rigid professors who delight in intimidating and harassing the poor young women."[50]

Without access to the examinations themselves it is difficult to judge their significance or the legitimacy of Amélie Weiler's criticism; similarly, without comparable figures for other examinations it is hard to interpret these varied success rates. Ultimately the very existence of secondary diplomas marked an important step in the process of professionalization, even if they fell far short of putting girls' education on the same level as boys'. In the capital, annual inspection reports suggest, moreover, that the examinations contributed to raising the general level of teaching without necessarily weeding out unqualified teachers. In 1849 a written composition in French history was introduced into the examination to improve the quality of history teaching, and two years later inspectresss wrote that all aspects of girls' education were improving because of the examination, although they continued to think teachers needed more practice in reading.[51]

Knowledge about the existence of secondary qualifying examinations appears to have been well disseminated in Paris by the mid-1840s, but the same was not true for the provinces, where considerable confusion reigned about what constituted a secondary diploma. In 1843 the rector of the Academy of Clermont wrote to his colleague in Strasbourg expressing his uncertainty about how to distinguish primary boarding schools from secondary schools: "In your academy have these institutions [the *pensions* and the *institutions de demoiselles*] become confused with primary level boarding schools as elsewhere?"[52] The ministry itself worried that since inspections were carried out under the aegis of primary instruction, "[the delegation of inspectors] may contribute to confusing even more the distinctions between primary girls' schools . . . and the *institutions* and *pensions*."[53] This uncertainty had direct consequences on the procedures adopted in various departments to authorize schools. In Strasbourg, for example, headmistresses ceased to obtain secondary diplomas in the mid-1840s and instead passed examinations for the primary level.[54]

Administrative interest in promoting secondary-level teaching diplomas was a clear effort to establish the parameters of girls' secondary education. In practice, however, the distinction between women who ran secondary schools and those who ran primary ones was less obvious. Many women, particularly in the provinces, convinced local authorities to honor their primary diplomas, anticipating in effect the disappearance of secondary degrees, for in 1853 girls' secondary education fell victim to the conservative backlash of the early Second Empire. In the wake of the 1850 Falloux law, the government decreed on 31 December 1853 that all girls' schools were part of the primary system: "Henceforth all institutions devoted to women's education, no matter what level, are subject to the dispositions that control primary instruction." These schools continued to be divided into two "orders," with first-order schools being the higher level; the administrative expectations for first-order schoolmistresses were very similar to what had been expected of a woman running a *pension*, but far less than what had been expected of a headmistress of an *institution*.[55] For lay schoolmistresses the most significant change was probably the lowering of the age requirement for opening a school from twenty-five to eighteen. But the most controversial aspect of this decree involved making clear that inspections did indeed concern both lay *and* religious schools. The boarding schools run by cloistered nuns were subject, however, only to inspections by members of the clergy.[56]

This administrative step backward can be seen as the simple recognition that without the study of Greek and Latin, which constituted the heart of boys' secondary education, girls' education had no real claims to secondary status. The ministry's delegate himself admitted in 1845 that he saw little distinction between the curricula of the primary and secondary boarding schools.[57] Certainly, the elimination of secondary diplomas and inspection committees simplified and clarified the female educational landscape; moreover, the lowering of the age requirement was a much-needed response to the realities of women's teaching careers, which began well before twenty-five for many. Unquestionably, however, this measure represented a setback to the efforts of reformers. Relegating all women teachers and their institutions to the primary level dashed feminist hopes and was consistent with other conservative educational initiatives during this period. In particular, the ministry also circumscribed male normal school education in a direct response to schoolteacher militancy in 1848.[58] Press censorship prevented radical voices from protesting this measure, but it seems likely that both the promoters of this decree and its opponents recognized that it effectively squelched the more ambitious plans of educational reformers.

In reality, however, the decree did not have much impact on schooling practices or on contemporary perceptions of girls' schools. Indeed for the general public the distinction between primary and secondary girls' education had far more to do with social aspirations than with intellectual qualifications. Inspectresses, as well, continued to highlight qualitative differences between institutions, while Parisian examination juries continued to award the secondary-level diplomas at least until 1858. Clearly the concept of girls' secondary education did not disappear even if it vanished as a statistical category, rendering quantitative approaches to its study very difficult.[59]

The failure of the French state to pursue the initiatives of the 1830s and 1840s following the 1848 revolution represented a notable setback to the process of professionalization. Most important, however, no consistent efforts were made to provide professional training for secondary teachers, thus leaving this training up to individual initiatives and the hazards of individual experiences. In Paris the only subsidized effort to provide pedagogical training for schoolteachers began in 1828 when the prefect of the Seine, Gilbert de Chabrol de Volvic, appointed a Mme Stévens to train prospective candidates. She was paid a remarkable salary of twelve hundred francs per year in exchange for services once a week. From 10:00 a.m. until 4:00 p.m., she gave lessons to candidates at the Hôtel de Ville, corrected their notebooks, and decided when they were qualified to pass the examination although she herself did not have a teaching diploma. The Parisian prefect refused, however, in 1835 to grant her school the title of École spéciale pour les institutrices, arguing that the department had no real need for a normal school, given the presence of many qualified women teachers in the area.[60]

As the numbers of girls' schools grew, however, the absence of training schools for teachers became more problematic.[61] Joséphine Bachellery most vocally championed the need for a superior normal school for women at a time when the state was making a concerted effort to develop male normal schools. In 1848 numerous voices reinforced her call, without success. Interest in such a school or schools continued, however, in the aftermath of the revolution, as the *dames déléguées* frequently reiterated the need for such an institution, particularly with regard to the training of teachers' aides.[62] Indeed, *sous-maîtresses* were consistently represented as the weakest link in the emerging system of girls' secondary education. Inspections revealed that aides performed important pedagogical tasks in most schools, and were in effect the teachers in smaller institutions. As a result, their working conditions and training increasingly formed the object of the most telling criticisms concerning the status of women teachers.

Teachers' Aides and Male Professors

The position of *sous-maîtresse* was seen as a way to get hands-on professional experience.[63] Until the 1853 decree, aides were expected to work in schools from the age of sixteen until twenty-five, when they could take the examinations to become schoolmistresses. But ill-paid and overworked, these women tended to stay for only brief periods of time in any one institution. In 1847 statistics concerning 172 aides in one area of Paris showed that well over half (ninety-three) remained only a few months in an institution, and an additional thirty-two only spent a year before moving on.[64] This extreme mobility weakened, not only their own pedagogical training, but also that of their students as well. Another major shortcoming for this group of women was their reluctance to take the required examination to become a *maîtresse d'étude*. Inspectresses also cited low salaries and difficult working conditions as the reasons why the more qualified young teachers fled the boarding-school setting. The bottom line was that no one took their situation seriously enough; their meager salaries dissuaded cultured young women from envisioning a "career" that promised so little.[65] And yet many schools depended on them to teach the lower classes and to keep order.

Report after report criticized the absence of appreciable improvement in the quality of teachers' aides from the mid-1840s until 1862, often judging them inexperienced and frivolous. Inspectresses proposed a variety of measures to improve their teaching: the creation of pedagogical training sessions in good boarding schools, the formation of normal schools, and the distribution of teaching awards. In the end, the lowering of the age to earn a *brevet de premier ordre* probably helped many women move more quickly from aide to teacher. Without question, however, the mediocre working conditions for women at the bottom rungs of the educational hierarchy slowed the progress of professionalization.

At the upper rungs of this same hierarchy, the significant presence of male teachers in female boarding schools was a final issue that plagued efforts to establish a professional corps of women teachers. Male teachers were common in Old Regime schools, often offering courses in the more "serious" subjects, such as history, literature, geography, and the sciences. This tradition continued in the early decades of the nineteenth century, generating relatively little comment. The reform efforts of the late 1830s and 1840s changed this situation as a number of voices called for the replacement of male with female teachers. This initial effort to promote women professors within boarding schools was clearly part and parcel of the broader concern to establish a female professorial career. The failure to challenge the position of male teachers in girls' education represents yet another limit to the professionalization of women teachers in France.[66]

Once again Joséphine Bachellery entered the fray, leading efforts to rid boarding schools of male professors. Indeed she placed this issue at the top of her agenda, declaring that "the first [measure], which would allow further improvements which are at present impossible, would be to entrust the teaching of women only to women themselves."[67] This would allow women to pursue intellectually challenging careers in teaching, although she recognized that such a reform hinged on other factors as well, most notably the creation of a superior normal school to train qualified women for these positions.

The woman of letters Louise Dauriat, whose positions were examined in Chapter 3, made the biggest splash in her effort to eliminate men from girls' education. She adopted a rhetorical strategy that emphasized the potentially immoral situations that male professors introduced, insisting that "it is only too true that among the teaching masters in both the sciences and in the arts there are a number who do not hesitate to envelop their young pupils in vile seductions." Moreover, she decried the 1837 ruling that allowed men to teach without proving their moral and intellectual qualifications through diplomas and certificates, as women were required to do. Like Bachellery's, her campaign against male professors was also an effort to create legitimate and honorable professional opportunities for educated women.[68]

Reactions to Dauriat's campaign clearly reveal how cultural visions of femininity at midcentury hampered the reform movement. Not surprisingly, the male teaching corps opposed her proposals: "If you eliminate male professors in the teaching of *demoiselles*, the following day all lay institutions will close, since their livelihood depends on men. Parents who are aware of the weak level of knowledge in convents and who want their children to have some instruction, leave their daughters with those female teachers who employ distinguished male professors."[69] For Lévi-Alvarès, women were incapable of offering "solid and serious instruction": male professors strengthened girls' minds through their virile lessons. Women had a place in education but not as the purveyors of intellectual culture, as the French language itself revealed: "*Instituteur* has a feminine, *professeur* does not," a group of male professors noted in 1845.[70] This self-interested defense probably overstated these professors' own influence in the age of maternal educators, but they undoubtedly had a point;

contemporaries associated the trappings of "science" with men. Even the reformist *REF* judged Dauriat's position critically, insisting that girls needed both the brilliance of male teachers and the maternal solicitude of women teachers. Inspectresses more pragmatically considered that abolishing male teachers was impossible, given their importance in girls' education: "At the moment we ask nothing better than to encourage professorships for women; prohibiting men, however, would not be a wise measure."[71]

Inspection reports show how men monopolized the more prestigious teaching positions within girls' boarding schools, leaving women teachers mainly responsible for supervisory tasks, elementary and moral education, and more feminine subjects, such as needlework, modern languages, and the arts. The larger boarding schools relied heavily on male teachers to teach "classical subjects" (history, literature, and the sciences), since it was often the quality of these teachers that gave a school its reputation. The prestigious Institut Beaujon, run by Mme Emilie Saint-Aubin Deslignières, used six men and no women to teach the "classical subjects"; women were relegated to less virile subjects such as languages and the arts.[72] As inspectresses reluctantly noted in 1853, family pressures worked against the development of women professors: "The older students prefer [men], families insist upon them." Figures concerning the numbers of male and female teachers within Parisian boarding schools confirm the effects of this preference; if one excludes teaching aides, men represented between 51 and 65 percent of the teaching personnel between 1845 and 1860. The reports register, however, a growth in the number of women teachers that began well before the Third Republic reforms: in 1845 boarding schools hired 341 outside women teachers, by 1860 this figure had reached 637 (in the same period the number of male teachers declined from 898 to 705).[73] In part, inspectresses noted this was a product of economic conditions. As lay headmistresses confronted the competition of religious schools as well as rent increases in George Eugène Haussmann's Paris, they had to cut budgets.[74] Since male teachers cost more than female ones, their numbers decreased in relative terms. But it may also be the case that the spread of girls' schooling by the 1850s meant more women had the necessary qualifications to teach, which meant in turn headmistresses had a wider choice. The growth in the number of women passing teaching examinations also supports this hypothesis. And inspectresses did indeed note that some schools maintained an excellent level of instruction without any male teachers at all. Still, the figures certainly suggest that in the capital city educational excellence required the presence of male professors.

The situation in the provinces appears quite similar for larger schools, although the evidence is far more piecemeal. Published programs for some institutions touted the lessons of male professors. In Versailles, for example, Mlle Edne Savouré announced that her students had lessons from male professors in history and geography as well as in literature.[75] Similarly, in the southwestern city of Tarbes the prospectus for the Institution Sainte-Marie, run by Mme Bernigole-Forcade indicated in 1841 that her husband "devotes the insights of his experience to the prosperity of the institution, which I founded with his help." This same document emphasized his, rather than her teaching qualifications, noting his twenty years of experience preparing young men for the *baccalauréat* in Bordeaux.[76] Inspection reports from Poitiers reveal the presence of male professors in the city's three major boarding schools in 1861; the pensionnat d'Aubigny, for example, employed ten teachers' aides and three male professors but no women professors. By 1866, these same three boarding schools had women professors as well.[77] The Dubois-Goblot correspondence reveals the presence in the 1870s of at least four male teachers in the Gellerat pension in Angers, southwest of Paris.[78] This boarding school, which also functioned as a normal course, relied on men for the teaching of writing, literature, English, and mathematics. Finally in Strasbourg, when outside professors are mentioned, men represented 83 percent of all such teachers (110 out of 132 cases).[79] Smaller schools in towns without a *collège* or a *lycée* probably did not use men professors, but their presence throughout France in larger institutions is clear testimony to the enduring prestige of "male" science that worked to the detriment of aspiring young women teachers.

In 1867 Victor Duruy urged the creation of secondary courses for girls; the teachers for these courses were all to be men. In introducing his proposal he insisted that girls' secondary education in France did not exist. Given the logic of this proposal, he might have added that no women professors existed in France, hence the need to draw on the three thousand professors of the male public secondary system.[80] On a certain level, Duruy was right. The early Second Empire had indeed eliminated secondary education for girls, as well as the secondary diplomas that had previously sanctioned this level of studies. The first woman to receive a *baccalauréat* (the male secondary diploma) did not do so until 1861. In 1867 only a handful of women had received the *baccalauréat*.[81] As historians have shown, Duruy's choice of male professors was both pragmatic and ideological: the men were available, *and* they were more likely to respect the strictly a-religious orientation he desired to impart. In particular, he did not want teaching nuns to be a part of his courses. Unwittingly, no doubt, this initiative also contributed to the historical erasure of the efforts to create a corps of qualified lay women professors.

Profiles of Parisian Headmistresses

Despite the absence of a normal school and the presence of male professors in boarding schools, teaching middle-class girls offered a career for many educated laywomen. The following analysis of Parisian headmistresses underscores their presence in the educational landscape throughout the nineteenth century, including after 1850 when nuns were increasingly active. Individual portraits are few and far between for these relatively obscure women, but the composite picture that emerges from my analysis shows a group of increasingly qualified women who set up schools that lasted. More interesting, the social origins of these women reflect how teaching had become an avenue for social mobility, giving lower middle-class women a certain degree of independence.

The quality of their teaching undoubtedly varied, but increasingly it bore the marks of professionalization with a training period, qualifying examinations, and inspection procedures. Evidence for this process is far more abundant for Paris than for other French cities, thanks in large part to the presence of inspectresses. Their reports reveal a trend toward increasing qualifications so that by the 1860s most headmistresses and their teachers had the requisite teaching diplomas. Moreover, in 1861 one out of every five headmistresses had the more difficult *brevet du premier ordre*.[82] Competition to attract students increasingly pushed women teachers to acquire the necessary teaching diplomas. In 1855, 476 women in Paris presented themselves for the teaching examination; seven years later this figure had risen to 689.[83] This reflects, I would argue, a new demand for the degrees that would allow women to open schools, not simply a fashion in bourgeois circles.

Analysis from Parisian trade books confirms the explosive growth in girls' boarding schools. Although numbers of students reached an all-time high in the 1840s, inspection reports during the Second Empire reveal the presence of between two and three hundred boarding schools, requiring much work on the part of the paid women delegates, who visited some fifty to sixty schools per year.[84] From early 1800 until 1880, the archives contain piecemeal information concerning over sixteen hundred women who ran schools, individually or with partners.[85] The evidence from this material suggests that running a boarding school represented a new career opportunity for upwardly mobile women. Certainly many institutions opened and closed rapidly, but almost one-half (800) of the women ran schools in Paris or its outskirts for over ten years, and a little over one-fifth (371) ran schools for over twenty years; the average length of activity was 12.8 years.[86] A mere 7.6 percent of the women opened and closed their schools within a year, and this percentage diminished in the second half of the century: prior to 1850, 46.6 percent of the schools closed within five years; for the schools operating between 1850 and 1880 this went down to 31.4 percent. Certainly there is ample evidence that many women did not spend their entire adult lives running schools; more surprising, many did.

Some thirty women devoted over forty years of their lives to girls' education. One such woman was Marie Félicie Leduc-Housset. Born in 1796, she opened a school on the rue du Faubourg Poissonnière in 1815, an institution that continued to attract boarders until 1864. Although she was among those women who had neither teaching diploma nor official authorization, her school was not the product of an amateur. In 1861 she had seventy boarders, ten of whom came from abroad.[87] She also employed twenty-five men and women as teachers, including six *sous-maîtresses*. Inspectresses evaluated her school very favorably, judging it to be an "excellent and significant institution." Opening a school was not just a temporary expedient in hard times, it had become for many a career.

Fragmentary evidence from birth and marriage certificates offers some insight into who these women were. In the first half of the century native Parisians dominated: 232 out of the 413 women for whom we have this information (56 percent) were born in the city. This figure dropped after 1850 to 42 percent as the capital attracted women from all over France and even from abroad: 26 out of 1,080 women were born outside France, including in the United States, Germany, Italy, Belgium, and Switzerland. Naturally this reflected the economic pull exerted by the capital, including in the field of teaching.

In sociological terms, boarding-school mistresses were not from the impoverished bourgeoisie, as contemporary portraits tended to suggest. On the contrary, well over half of these women came from the indeterminate lower levels of the middle class and the educated working classes (see Appendix 2). For the entire period, 47.6 percent had fathers who were skilled workers, artisans, small shopkeepers, or employees; another 6 percent were lower-level civil servants. The percentage of women from this background increased in the second half of the century, moving from 53.6 percent prior to 1850 to 60.9 percent. Since running a boarding school was a clear marker of bourgeois status, it seems clear that many women rose in the social hierarchy thanks to this activity. Corroborating evidence comes from an investigation of husbands' professions. Unlike the fathers, husbands were far more likely to be teachers themselves or low-level employees in either the private or the public sector. In other words, the study of marriage certificates suggests that a certain number of women married up. Elisa Benoist, for example, was the daughter of a pastry-maker. At age thirty she married a piano teacher, and a year later she opened a boarding school that continued for the next twenty-five years. One can speculate that the ambition to run a boarding school was part of a broader effort to ascend the social hierarchy.[88] While a father's or a husband's profession offers relatively limited insight into the sociocultural parameters of a headmistress' existence, its analysis highlights the opportunities teaching offered for motivated women from the lower ranks of the social scale.

The age at which a woman opened a school obviously had an impact on the length of her working life. The average age was a little over thirty-two. Although until 1853 headmistresses were not officially allowed to open schools before turning twenty-five, the trade book reveals many exceptions: 17.1 percent of those women whose ages we know were under the age limit, and this figure remains stable. At the other end of the age scale, a similar percentage of women (17.5 percent) began at age forty or over; a little less than half of these more mature women (46 percent) left their schools after less than ten years, although some undoubtedly had begun their teaching careers earlier in other cities. This was the case for Charlotte Bette, who was already forty-three when she first appeared in the Parisian trade books and then apparently ran her school a mere seven years. The archives reveal, however, that from 1830 until 1847 she was headmistress of a boarding school in Fontainebleau just outside Paris. From 1847 until 1850 her status was clearly in decline, since she was reduced to giving private lessons. Then it rose again with the opening of her school on the rue du Faubourg Saint-Antoine.[89] While difficult to trace, such trajectories were not uncommon, testimony to the fact that many women devoted their lives to teaching.

Both married and single women invested in this profession, with the former out-numbering the latter 59 percent to 41 percent in a field that is often portrayed as being restricted to single women. The concept of the "single" woman, however, deserves attention, since schools were often family businesses. Operating a boarding school could be both expensive and difficult for a single woman, which explains no doubt the numbers of sisters who worked together. Forty-three groups of sisters are indicated in the Parisian trade books, and undoubtedly many more headmistresses employed their sisters without listing them officially on the books. Virginie Rey, for example, drew heavily on her immediate family to run her institution, which specialized in teaching foreign languages, specifically Russian, English, German, and Italian. She is indicated in the trade book as running this school alone from 1853 until 1859. Inspection reports reveal hers was a relatively small school with twelve boarders and thirty-two day students. Her teaching diploma came from St. Petersburg, Russia, where her mother had also run a school. Within the school her brother offered courses in "the classics," while her two sisters, both listed as *sous-maîtresses*, taught in the school as well; one of them teaching English and Italian, although neither had a teaching degree.[90]

Another frequently encountered situation was the mother/daughter, aunt/niece, or wife/sister-in-law teaching pair. Elisabeth Debierne, the daughter of a stagecoach driver, obtained a teaching degree from the department of the Seine in 1837 at the age of twenty-one. She does not appear in the trade books as a headmistress until 1848, having married a middle-class widower Jean Rey in 1839 (he is listed as a "pro-priétaire" in the marriage certificate and as a "rentier" in the inspection reports of the 1850s). Nothing explains why she opened a boarding school with a Mlle Rey in the fashionable area around the Trocadéro in 1848, but it was not a mere whim, since she stayed in that quarter until 1904 when at the ripe old age of eighty-six she vanishes from the records. Also a qualified teacher, her co-headmistress, Adèle Rey, had a *diplôme de maîtresse de pension* from 1846. Adèle was not, however, her daughter. More likely she was the sister of Jean Rey, since she was born in 1803. Did she turn to teaching to stave off an impecunious old age as a spinster? Perhaps. At any rate she taught until her death in 1859. The school accommodated over one hundred boarders, with many foreigners, notably British girls (thirty-five are listed in 1854).[91] Running a boarding school may have brought economic independence, although this is difficult to trace, but it was rarely the enterprise of a lone woman.

An unusual document from the Haussmannian period gives some insight into the economics of running a school. In 1859, Mlle Laure Bronville brought suit against the expropriation board of the City of Paris, since her institution was destined to disappear thanks to imperial reconstruction projects.[92] She argued that she would lose her clients if forced to move and requested an indemnity of 70,000 francs! The documents present the following information, which suggests that teaching could indeed be a profitable business, if only for the woman in charge.

Table 1 REVENUES AND EXPENSES IN A PARISIAN BOARDING SCHOOL (1865)

Revenues		General expenses	
Source	Annual	Item	Annual
117 day students @ 920 francs per month	11,040	Teaching aide	300
6 half-boarders/year	1,536	Teaching aide	360
6 boarders	4,690	Music mistress	300
Plus heating	300	Singing master	240
Benefits from selling books, etc.	300	Teaching masters	300
Subscriptions, for New Year's party	500	Drawing master	216
		Servant	240
		Taxes	38
		Sweeping	11
		Sand for the garden	15
		Laundering	250
		Heating	180
		Lighting	115
		Rent	1,600
		Food for students, aides, and servant	2,000
Total revenues	18,366	Total expenses	6,165
Net annual profit	12,201		

SOURCE: *Mémoire en défense et expertise pour Mlle Laure Bronville (Pensionnat, demi-pensionnat et externat de demoiselles) contre la Ville de Paris* (1865).

NOTE: All revenues and expenses are in francs.

A majority of boarding-school teachers were married.[93] For some of these women marriage represented an escape from teaching, some 32 percent disappear from the trade books within five years of their marriage, but most continued to run their schools, at times with their husbands' help. Indeed the presence of many husbands within the teaching profession confirms the familial character of these enterprises. Take, for example, the case of Alexandrine Cornette. Born in 1797, she married Célestin Méry, a language teacher in 1827. In 1830 she opened her first school on the rue de Surène and then moved four times, ending up on the rue de Luxembourg in 1852, the year of her death. While she catered mainly to day students at the end, inspection reports reveal her husband taught history, grammar, and arithmetic for twenty years in her boarding school.[94] Even husbands outside the teaching profession helped out. Mathurin Simon, a doctor, taught physics and natural history to the thirty-seven boarders in his wife's school in 1845. Like many of these women, Antoinette Cantaloube Simon began her career relatively late, opening a school on the rue de Sèvres when she was already thirty-nine. Interestingly, she passed her teaching diploma in 1828, waited eleven years to put it to use, but then continued in the business for at least sixteen years.[95] Husbands who could teach were of course a precious aid, but the presence of a man cut two ways within the boarding-school setting. On the one hand, he helped to establish the familial image of a school, but he could also represent moral danger.[96] The one report that specifies the marital status of headmistresses, also noted whether there were sons from the marriage and whether these sons lived in the school.

Lay schoolteachers specializing in the education of middle-class girls were not unusual in the nineteenth century, despite the historiographic focus on nuns. On the contrary, within the capital lay schoolmistresses remained far more common than their religious counterparts well into the Third Republic. As the preceding discussion has emphasized, these women were increasingly subject to rules and regulations that established the necessary professional qualifications to run a school; the emergence of an inspection system ensured, to some extent, that these qualifications were respected. Naturally, this did not prevent under- or unqualified women from running schools of mediocre quality, but it did encourage many to seek the appropriate credentials. In the absence of normal schools, women increasingly acquired experience through a training period as a teachers' aide. The sociological study of Parisian headmistresses offers interesting insights into why women turned to this career. Contrary to the literary representations that began this chapter, teaching did not condemn women to a life of celibacy nor was it the forced choice of distressed gentlewomen. On the contrary, a majority married either before or during their teaching "careers," which often extended over several decades. And for many this marriage served to confirm a newly achieved middle-class status. While this does not tell us much about how these women experienced their careers, nor how this forged their sense of professional identity, it does suggest the emergence of new social strategies among women seeking to acquire the trappings of bourgeois culture, which could include leading professional lives. In the process, they studied and passed examinations. They rented or bought houses in which to lodge their students. They wrote up guidelines and submitted administrative dossiers for municipal approval. They hired teachers and teachers' aides. And they ensured the daily running of schools that harbored from a handful to over a hundred students. Some were more successful than others, but undoubtedly the administrative and logistical requirements of running such an operation helped forge professional modes of behavior and a new culture of professionalism among women from the upwardly mobile lower and lower middle classes. All this challenges us to reconsider these women's marginal status within the middle classes; teaching was not always a second choice.

5

VOCATIONS AND PROFESSIONS:
THE CASE OF THE TEACHING NUN

Nuns rubbed elbows with laywomen teachers in the French urban landscape and increasingly exerted their influence on the educational scene for middle-class girls after 1850. This chapter addresses this influence, while also seeking to position religious teachers more centrally in a social and cultural history of bourgeois women. Historians have too often assumed that taking the veil represented an antimodern reaction placing nuns under the control of the male church hierarchy while relegating them to the fringes of French society. Contrary to this interpretive tradition, I argue here that the structure and organization of those orders which catered to an expanding middle-class public offered important opportunities for single women in the nineteenth century to define their own spiritual and intellectual goals.[1] The closed female world of the convent was an important alternative to family life. It represented the possibility for a degree of autonomy and independence as well as the latitude to engage in public life in ways few secular women found possible. Above all, through their actions in the classroom and within the convent, teaching nuns exerted considerable cultural influence on generations of French middle-class girls whose significance was more subtle than earlier interpretations have suggested.

As many historians have argued, the vision of the teaching nun durably influenced the emerging female professorial corps in late nineteenth-century France. What characterized contemporary representations of the teaching nun and why did these images hold such cultural appeal? More important for my analysis, what relationship does this vision bear to the social realities determining a woman's decision to enter religious life? As the title of this chapter suggests, I am interested in exploring why women entered teaching orders. Naturally, spiritual reasons played an important part in this decision, but my focus will be on what sociocultural factors help to explain why religious life held growing appeal to women. I then seek to understand the relationship between the act of professing religious vows and the ethos of professionalism. As the previous chapter has shown, the legislation concerning female teachers had relatively little impact on nuns; and yet the very structure of the religious order, with its novitiate and its autonomy from outside interference, gave it more professional characteristics than the average lay boarding school. Finally, through an exploration of the religious culture within schools, I seek to understand the relationship between the characteristics of feminine religious identity and an order's sense of mission. In the end, what distinguished the religious teacher from her lay colleague? Ultimately this analysis should help us in the final chapter of this section to understand the contradictory messages of boarding-school life.

Taking the Veil

Nineteenth-century religious life opened up a range of activities for women, particularly within active congregations:[2] in 1878 seven women out of one thousand were members of religious orders, for a total of 135,000; female religious outnumbered male three to two. Taking the veil allowed educated women, in particular, to pursue both spiritual and intellectual goals more easily than the laywomen considered so far. In 1861, 65 percent of all sisters were involved in teaching, many in rural primary schools, but also a fair number in boarding schools.[3] The widespread social acceptance of religious life for women appears to support the argument that taking the veil was an easy choice for young women with uncertain futures. But careful examination of the entrance requirements of teaching orders shows that the act of profession required qualifications and commitment that deserve closer attention.

Representations of Religious Life

As the number of religious orders expanded at midcentury, so too did the rhetoric surrounding them. Despite the increasingly polemical character of this rhetoric, it is important to recognize that, for the general public, nuns possessed a degree of cultural authority, respectability, and ideological purity that their lay feminine counterparts did not.[4] Through their activities as teachers, nurses, and social workers, nuns were seen as critical players in the re-Christianization of French society. Unlike lay teachers, who were frequently represented as spinsters, pedants, or money-minded careerists, teaching nuns largely escaped these negative stereotypes outside anticlerical circles. Indeed, representations of teaching nuns tended to emphasize their selfless commitment to a higher good. Their celibacy was seen as chosen; their ambition, as nonexistent; and the pecuniary advantages of running a school, as irrelevant, since most orders used their boarding-school fees to pay for free schools for the poor.

Clearly, the social acceptance, and indeed success, of religious teaching orders stemmed in part from this perception that teaching for them was not a career or a profession but a vocation.

This acceptance can be seen in how nuns were treated in the urban tableaux. Maria d'Anspach glowingly wrote that "the nun by vocation is more than a woman because her mission is divine." In her description of the organization of religious life in a convent, she emphasized how such institutions usefully protected poor girls from the dangers of the outside world by offering them a home and family. In contrast to eighteenth-century criticisms of convent life, the author argued that things had changed; convents were no longer dumping grounds for unwanted girls or palaces of luxury.[5]

The rise of Marian devotions undoubtedly contributed to the cultural acceptance of religious life for women. Thousands of women joined confraternities where devotion to the Virgin Mary found more practical applications through service to the poor and needy. Indeed, Marian piety acquired missionary overtones in the increasingly feminized Catholic religious culture of midcentury.[6] Doing good through Mary gave meaning and structure to the lives of lay and religious women alike. At the same time, missionary zeal gave women license to act in public in new ways. The spread of confraternities both within schools and in French society offered opportunities for laywomen to take an active role in the redemption of mankind. As Hazel Mills has argued, the power which women acquired in public life "derived most particularly from the legitimacy of the structure of the female confraternity and of female philanthropy. This in turn derived from both dominant models of female virtue and the close similarity in the activities involved with those of the uncloistered nun."[7] Entering a religious order represented, of course, a far more dramatic commitment to the values embodied in these devotions, but these values were on a continuum with those expressed by a multitude of women from the lower and middle classes.

Historians interested in the feminization of religion over the course of the century offer a way to understand how nuns acquired such cultural authority despite their failure to conform to the premises of domesticity. Ralph Gibson's study of the relationship between French Catholicism and women has argued in particular that the growth in female religious orders ultimately stemmed from how Catholic values and rhetoric reinforced feminine gender typing.[8] Taking the veil was not seen as an act of independence or autonomy, but rather as an acceptable solution for women who might not marry. Female orders were under the spiritual authority of male clerics, who emphasized women's fundamental docility, weakness, and subservience. These characteristics, however, could be put to good use in teaching or in socially useful activities. As a result, young women were attracted to these institutions, which offered opportunities to do good apparently without challenging the tenets of a domestic discourse that associated women with the home and selfless action on behalf of others.

Naturally more negative visions of nuns existed as well, but they do not appear to have had the same kind of cultural resonance.[9] In anticlerical circles, the suspicion surrounding cloistered orders generated rhetoric about the wealth and worldly practices of certain nuns. Julie-Victoire Daubié, the first woman *bachelière*, was in many ways typical when she contrasted the opulence of the teaching congregations with the material poverty of laywomen:

> We know what riches and what influence our religious communities have acquired in recent years.... In their palaces [the convent] has spacious parlors, vast gardens, courtyards, magnificent vestibules, which parents prefer since they desire above all air and space. If we then visit the attic of a lay boarding school, the sight of the exhausted headmistress with her twenty to thirty students crammed into a dark, narrow, and unhealthy room highlights the realities of competition that exist between lay and religious boarding schools... teaching becomes an industry under these conditions, a speculation.[10]

Interestingly, however, her criticism does not address the figure of the nun herself, who remains outside the scope of her investigation of poor women's lives.

Iconographic representations of teaching nuns presented them veiled in the mantle of religious respectability, infinitely more virtuous and domestic than intellectual. In Figure 3, teaching nuns distribute prizes for work and good behavior, guide young girls in their religious duties, and offer examples of feminine industriousness during recreations.[11] The classroom is noticeably absent in this boarding school. Not surprisingly, nuns reinforced these cultural messages through their own efforts at self-representation, which tended to assimilate the religious sister with the domestic mother.

Nuns made an effort to present their institutions as families, and they urged their fellow sisters to adopt maternal attitudes toward their students: according to the rule of the Sœurs de Saint-Augustin de Meaux in 1856, "the sisters will demonstrate a maternal affection for the children and will show the same interest to all of them."[12] Not surprisingly, superiors chastised nuns who failed to conform to the prescribed maternal manner, recognizing the importance of maintaining a certain public image. The Sœurs de la Doctrine Chrétienne made it explicit how nuns were *not* supposed to appear: "A raised and mobile head, haughty eyes, a lively or a frigid figure, a graceless bearing... pretentiousness, a pedantic manner, excessive verbosity... all this is inappropriate to the religious habit."[13] The constitutions and rules that guided sisters' behavior emphasized their obligation to offer a model of Christian virtue to their students and their companions: "Lessons on religion and politeness must be

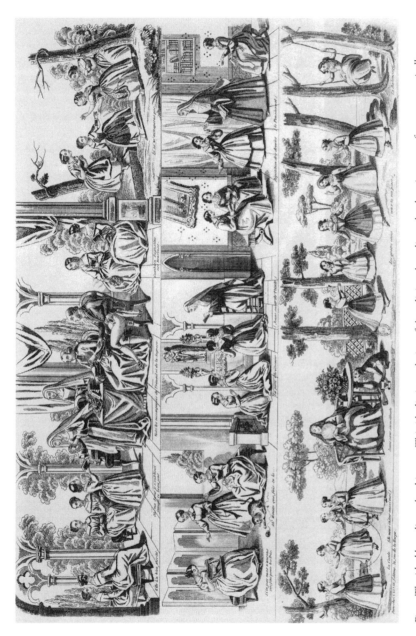

Fig. 3 The ideal boarding school in 1851. This idealistic rendering of the religious boarding school environment focuses on typically feminine activities, such as sewing and praying; the schoolroom itself is strikingly absent.

followed up by examples of piety and modesty; above all students must notice in their mistresses a significant aversion for worldly tastes, be it in the area of clothes, pleasures, walks. . . . Society, in all its perversion, condemns with its most malicious criticism traces of worldly education in a religious institution."[14]

Professional competence and qualifications played little role in the elaboration of a model of the teaching nun, and yet the structure and internal practices of teaching orders encouraged women interested in taking the veil to adopt modes of behavior and values that were not always in conformity with the images of self-effacement and self-sacrifice that so dominated representations of teaching nuns.

Entering a Teaching Order

Teaching orders established certain general entrance conditions based in large part on the particular profile of the order. Constitutions formalized some of these, but informal guidelines were more common. Specifically, admission into the novitiate as a more qualified choir sister required a legitimate birth, relative youth, good health, and basic literacy.[15] Aspiring nuns had to be sixteen years old, and in most cases, the prospective novice undertook a religious retreat before being admitted into the novitiate. During the novitiate, which could range from six months to three years, the novice took classes in spiritual and profane matters and generally experienced everyday convent life.[16] Throughout this period, the order tested candidates for their religious vocation and increasingly entrusted them with responsibilities according to their capabilities. The rigor of this training period depended a great deal on the size and stature of the order. Rural teaching orders often rushed their novices into teaching posts, whereas others took care to ensure their candidates were sufficiently trained. The Sœurs de Saint-Joseph established as of 1839 a three-year training period, one year as a postulant and two additional years as a novice, preferably within the novitiate in Lyons.[17] Then, depending on the opinion of the director of novices, the mother superior convoked her general council to vote on admission.

Since most teaching orders relied heavily on the financial resources of individual members, novices paid one fee to cover their training, lodging, and housing and another to cover the cost of their trousseaus. The sums required varied widely and depended in part on whether the order received public funds or not and on its own financial resources. While the Sœurs de Saint-Joseph could afford to admit many candidates for free because of such funding, the Congrégation de la Mère de Dieu asked for a hefty six hundred francs per year, and another twelve hundred francs for the trousseau and the cost of taking the veil. Claude Langlois's study shows that the fee for a year could be as low as two hundred francs, whereas six hundred francs appears to be the upper limit, fully equivalent to the cost of a better boarding-school education. Once past the training period, families were again asked to contribute to the upkeep of their daughters through the payment of dowries that also ranged widely in price, between one thousand and ten thousand francs, depending not only on the order's traditions and profile but also on the candidate's qualifications. Older candidates, who were considered bad bets, could be required to pay substantially more; Anaïs Cheval, aged thirty-six, paid eighteen thousand francs to enter the Mère de Dieu in the 1860s.[18] In many ways entering an order resembled getting married, except that the prospective teaching sister had far more occasions to have her commitment tested and found wanting. Entering an order was also far more codified than becoming a lay schoolmistress, and it included a training period. But these conditions do not shed much light on why young girls decided to take the veil, nor do they reveal much about what an order looked for in a prospective member.

The personal and intellectual requirements for taking the veil varied, of course, from order to order, but it should not be assumed that the process of selection was taken lightly. Indeed evidence suggests that future sisters had a relatively challenging experience overcoming the various hurdles required to take vows, since women who took vows rarely left religious life. Within the small and highly selective Congrégation de la Mère de Dieu only 10 percent of the women who took vows between 1806 and 1881 left, while only 3 of 132 Ursuline nuns in Périgueux left before their deaths and only 2 of 143 Visitation nuns.[19] Older and more established orders used the period of the novitiate to select relatively carefully those women who were considered to have the necessary moral and intellectual qualities to take vows.

What exactly did religious orders look for in a potential teaching nun? The guidelines for novice mistresses offer insights into how they sought nonintellectual and yet sensible young women. For the Sœurs de Saint-Charles, personality traits were emphasized; a candidate was expected to have "a good temperament, a solid spirit, a pleasing character, and a soul strongly bound to virtue." Somewhat more demanding, the Sœurs de Saint-Joseph de Lyon emphasized: "They do not need more than a modest talent to attend to the different ministries of our congregation. But they must have at least this humble measure of intelligence, . . . they must have more than heart and piety; they cannot do without a little sense and some knowledge."[20] The spiritual director of the Sœurs de la Doctrine Chrétienne de Nancy, the abbé Mougenot, warned more generally what novice mistresses should avoid: candidates from families "tainted by vices or with hereditary mental problems"; girls without judgment; girls with strange, somber, or capricious personalities; strong-minded individuals who refused to submit to a higher will; indolent or irresolute souls; and finally, impressionable women with strong inclinations.[21] This catalog of negative qualities confirms in many respects the primary importance attributed to character. As the century progressed, however, the more elite-oriented orders, like the Société du Sacré-Cœur, Sainte-Clotilde, or the Assomption, increasingly looked for intelligence in their novices in order to develop the quality of the studies they offered.

During the novitiate the candidate's moral and intellectual qualities were tested more or less thoroughly according to the order's personnel needs. The dropout rate during the novitiate varied greatly from order to order: in the Mère de Dieu more than half of the entering novices ultimately returned to civil life. Throughout France it seems that between 14 and 20 percent of prospective sisters abandoned the novitiate.[22] Piecemeal evidence suggests three main explanations for the failure to pursue religious life within a teaching order, and they all related to a novice's ability to adapt to the order's lifestyle and her obligations within an association of this sort. The most prevalent deterrent was the novice's health. Generally, the novice herself recognized her inability to function within an admittedly austere setting, but at times orders rejected women they deemed too fragile. Second, many novices left or were encouraged to leave because of their lack of aptitude for teaching. This could mean that the novice did not have the required energy or education, but it could also result from the perception that she did not have the moral stamina for her task, being either too affectionate or too violent for frequent contact with children. Finally, the order eliminated those novices who experienced difficulties following the daily rules, whether from "moral weakness," an "absence of straightforwardness," a "violent nature," or "too independent a spirit." The ideal novice needed to combine good health with pedagogical qualities and a relatively docile personality. In many ways it is not surprising that so many failed to meet this standard.

Those novices who persevered demonstrated, nonetheless, qualities and a degree of initiative that merit careful attention when considering the future lives of these women. Unlike bourgeois marriages where women themselves played relatively little role in choosing a spouse, or even in deciding whether to marry or not, taking vows with a specific order implied a far more active involvement of the female novice. Indeed, there are countless examples of young women who had to overcome parental opposition to become nuns. Given the relatively challenging admission procedure — be it finding the necessary sum of money, persuading parents of one's vocation, or rising to the challenge of a community's expectations — entering a religious order was not an easy solution for young women whose future seemed uncertain, no matter how positive the image of the teaching nun within French society. What then motivated women to join teaching orders, and how do these motivations shed light on the nature of the educational experience offered within religious schools? Using a collection of individual portraits, often culled from death notices, I highlight how sisters themselves framed the reasons for taking the veil.

Individual Portraits

The absence of detailed studies of individual orders makes it difficult to correlate taking vows with specific social and geographic backgrounds. Claude Langlois highlights the diversity of social origins and a process of relative democratization over the course of the century: the percentage of bourgeois sisters declined as that of women from rural origins rose. Those teaching orders which ran boarding schools tended, however, to recruit choir, as opposed to lay, sisters with urban roots and from lower middle-class to middle-class origins.[23] Not surprisingly, those orders which offered a semblance of a secondary education recruited women with some education themselves; this almost automatically eliminated women from the lower classes.

Death notices frequently mention the more contingent sociocultural explanations for a woman's having joined a specific order.[24] Male clergy often played a critical role, guiding young women toward institutions that they knew and could recommend. The friendships formed as a result of schooling experiences also explain many vocations; former students of religious boarding schools were particularly prone to enter religious life, based on their familiarity with the teachers whose ranks they sought to join. Fanny Kiesel attributed her vocation to the influence of an older student, like her from Brittany, who preceded her into the novitiate of the Mère de Dieu. For many, the decision to join an already familiar order was made relatively easily; the prestige of the Périgueux Ursulines' boarding school in the 1880s and 1890s inspired a great number of vocations.[25] Other women, and not just former students, opted more simply to join family members already present in an order. Théodore Humbert, for example, followed two of her sisters into the Sœurs de la Doctrine Chrétienne de Nancy.[26]

The taking of vows could also reflect an active ambition to lead a more fulfilling spiritual or professional life than the home life or the working world would permit. This was particularly true for women from working-class backgrounds, who undoubtedly led more comfortable and potentially stimulating lives within an order than they would have if they had remained at home or married within their social sphere. For Opportune Landivier, the orphaned daughter of an infantry sergeant, life as a teaching nun gave her opportunities that secular life could not. After graduation from the Legion of Honor school at the Loges in 1871, she spent seven years at home with her irascible widowed mother. The daughter, described as a woman with an "ardent temperament" and a "profound intelligence," fled her mother for her old associates, quickly rising through the hierarchy to become the mother superior of the order's house in Egypt.[27] Similarly, Jeanne Conte emerged from a modest background — her father was a carpenter and her mother a peasant. Thanks to her studies in a convent school, she decided to take the veil and devote herself to teaching, becoming headmistress of a school in the mid-1880s.[28]

Life in a teaching order gave women a form of cultural authority in French society and allowed them at times to thwart familial desires and to subvert norms of femininity in the name of a higher cause. For many women the decision to take vows cannot have been made lightly, given women's socialization to think of themselves primarily as family members. Isabelle Riembault joined the Mère de Dieu against her mother's will. The latter was chronically ill and wanted her daughter to remain at home.[29] Marguerite Bigot also opposed her Protestant family's expectations when she entered the novitiate in 1880, while Anne-Madeleine Magne, sister of Napoleon III's future minister of finance, became a novice at the Visitation of Périgueux in 1833 without her mother's permission.[30] There is widespread evidence that many families opposed their daughter's taking the veil. Victorine Lacour, for example, had to counter her father's desire to have her help out in his shop when she entered the Congrégation de la Doctrine Chrétienne.[31] The decision to pursue a religious life was, therefore, often a far more assertive gesture than has been acknowledged.

Biographies or death notices highlight, of course, the more spiritual reasons that influenced religious vocations. Clearly, a general climate of romantic asceticism often contributed to the decision to join an order. Marie Philippine Chappotin described her own adolescence, filled with extravagant self-punishments, in part as a product of the sense of despair she felt, surrounded by cousins and sisters who died early deaths. Entering a religious order seemed the only appropriate response: "All around me, more and more emptiness. What was worth loving? . . . What is earthly existence? A torment?"[32] More generally, internal documents emphasize the piety and virtue that characterized the early lives of future sisters.

Teaching Nuns and Pedagogical Training

Once a woman took religious vows, she entered a highly structured and disciplined environment whose contours only vaguely evoked that of the family.[33] Although the superior general was referred to as "mother" and the other members as "sisters," the family metaphor quickly broke down. Administrative and pedagogical responsibilities meant that these institutions were more like small businesses than families, and their evolution over the course of the century reveals a tendency toward increasing professionalization.[34] The concrete ways in which teaching orders sought to pursue their religious mission suggest the need to reevaluate the institutional legacy of religious education. Despite the fact that teaching sisters were not required to take teaching examinations, professional guidelines, training, and inspections were increasingly an aspect of religious life by the second half of the century.[35]

Constitutions and Rules

In order to receive official recognition, the state required religious orders to publish constitutions that established the basic guidelines determining congregational life. Most also wrote up rules where more specific organizational principles were detailed, including those concerning teaching. Examination of these rules reveals a widespread concern to establish clear-cut hierarchies and patterns of authority. In the discussion that follows the focus will be on those religious orders which offered boarding-school education. A superior general presided over these religious institutions. She was the "political" head, made strategic decisions, acted as the spokesperson with ecclesiastical and political authorities, and was in charge of appointments to positions within the order. The superior general was generally aided by a governing council composed of the assistant, the treasurer, the novitiate mistress, and a counselor. In centrally governed religious orders with multiple houses, each individual house had a local superior and usually a governing council, but they were ultimately under the authority of the central house.

Teaching responsibilities were similarly organized according to hierarchical considerations. The novitiate mistress occupied a special place, since she supervised the initial training of all incoming sisters. In houses that ran boarding schools, headmistresses of studies presided over the schools, while individual teachers were responsible for each class. Clearly some teachers developed strengths in specific subjects, but even the most prestigious boarding schools did not offer a secondary-style curriculum similar to that of boys where teachers specialized. This only occurred when orders hired outside, generally male, teachers to teach specific courses. The religious teacher was by definition a generalist. The Dames du Sacré-Cœur defended this principle along strictly gendered lines, arguing that specialization would render teaching sisters like male secondary-school teachers, thus robbing them of their maternal influence.[36]

The larger orders all made explicit the responsibilities incumbent on each level in the teaching pyramid, even if the general principle of equality among members was expected to prevail. Thus, the constitution of the Sœurs de Saint-Joseph reminded boarding-school mistresses that "the sisters employed in boarding schools . . . are neither of superior rank nor in a different category" from those "employed in day schools."[37] In practice, however, the headmistress played a crucial role in determining the success and good reputation of any given school, and so her appointment was a critical one. The Sœurs de Notre-Dame, also known as the Chanoinesses de Saint-Augustin, had a series of detailed guidelines for this position that emphasized the importance of organizing classes according to the academic level of students while also recognizing their social standing; in the placement of students in a classroom the rule recommended that girls from good families should be given the best places! The production of *femmes savantes* was explicitly not the goal of this elite-oriented institution: "The goal that teachers in a class must have is to form their students' hearts to the love of religion and all the virtues it inspires, rather than to embellish and cultivate their minds through human knowledge."[38] More important for the quality of the teaching offered, the rule insisted that the headmistress "be careful that the new teachers follow the ways of teaching and the customs of those who have preceded them . . . so that strangers do not criticize the frequent changing of teachers."[39] This concern for pedagogical practices was not isolated in the nineteenth century. Contrary to anticlerical propaganda, teaching orders were not peopled by ignorant, superstitious nuns.

Toward More Rigorous Academic Training

As the state began to intervene more actively in the development of a primary educational system in the 1830s, teaching orders also moved toward creating a more rigorous intellectual climate among their staff. This trend, however, was already evident in some places during the Restoration. The multifunctional Congrégation de Saint-Joseph in Bourg-en-Bresse in southeastern France had a dynamic novitiate headmistress, Mère St Claude, who expressed early concern for the training of future teachers. In 1826, she was appointed to establish a school within the novitiate. Young and inexperienced, she turned to the Frères des Écoles Chrétiennes, attending their classes and absorbing their pedagogical methods. This unofficial training then allowed her to set up classes for her novices, using a series of textbooks she coedited with the abbé Portalier, who was almoner of her congregation: *Méthode d'enseignement, Manuel grammatical,* and *Leçons de civilité.* By the early 1830s, this order was openly encouraging its nuns to take the state-sponsored primary teaching examinations despite their exempt status under the law.[40] In Normandy, the Tiers Ordre de Notre-Dame du Mont-Carmel offers an early example of concern to improve teaching in rural villages. As early as 1816, a member of this order, Mlle Cheruel, opened a boarding school for girls who intended to become teachers. Although she failed to obtain the title of normal school for her establishment, she nonetheless trained over three hundred teachers between 1809 and 1834.[41]

Teaching orders frequently used their clerical contacts to help them train both their novices and teachers. In the 1820s, the Congrégation de Sainte-Clotilde called on the male teaching staff of the reputable Collège Stanislas to give lessons to novices. Under the supervision of M. Dumont, the nuns gave lessons in literature, history, and science.[42] Jesuit fathers were often called on to impart both their knowledge and their pedagogical methods. This concern to train teachers more rigorously did not eliminate mediocre talents, and there is ample evidence that even within reputable orders teaching qualifications were weak, particularly in the first half of the century. In 1817, Ursuline Mother Sainte-Angèle Girodin reported on two of her nuns "who with much indulgence may become decent teachers. They are almost thirty, have no particular talent, and are in generally poor health, but the younger is courageous. I must confess, however, that they are not an encouraging beginning."[43] Similarly, death notices for the generation of women born around 1800 often reveal women with limited intellectual gifts. Witness the judgment rendered on Marguerite Sanciel, mother superior of a school of the Sœurs de la Doctrine Chrétienne in the Alsatian town of Cernay: "During her novitiate Sœur Marguerite gave us high hopes for the future, not because of any specific talent in the humanities, because in fact her skills were quite mediocre, but because of her excellent capacity for religious virtues."[44]

Teaching orders organized more actively to improve the quality of their teaching staffs beginning in the 1830s and 1840s through more rigorous novitiate training as well as through a form of continuing education. The Sœurs de l'Instruction Chrétienne de Saint-Gildas-des-Bois, for example, began to organize academic courses in their novitiate in 1833 with classes in reading, writing, spelling, mathematics, and handiwork.[45] The superior general of the Sœurs de Saint-Joseph de Cluny, Anne-Marie Javouhey, worked continuously to improve the quality of teaching in her missionary order. She explained in 1834 that she gathered all of the headmistresses in Paris so that they could get lessons from the best teachers of the capital and thus contribute to the reputations of their schools.[46]

The development of teaching diplomas and the spread of inspection procedures at both the primary and secondary level presented teaching nuns with a series of challenges. Until the Second Empire many orders, and particularly those which ran boarding schools, resisted inspections and refused to train their teachers for the official diplomas.[47] This hostility toward measures that threatened the independence of the teaching orders did not necessarily bespeak hostility to the principle of ensuring more rigorous training for teachers and novices alike. In large orders, the existence of boarding schools and the specialization of functions undoubtedly contributed to giving the novitiate a more academic cast for those novices who were destined to teach. The Congrégation de Saint-Joseph du Bon Pasteur in the central French city of Clermont-Ferrand had a common program for the novitiate and boarding school: in the morning novices joined boarders for lessons in mathematics, grammar, history, geography, and the decorative arts.[48] At the Congrégation de Saint-Joseph de Lyon, the length of the novitiate was extended to two years in 1839 and included an examination on secular subjects at the end. Novices had classes in grammar, arithmetic, history, geography, bookkeeping, and writing. In 1842, under the reforming impulse of Mère du Sacré-Cœur, a circular was sent to each community requiring that they maintain a library of classic and religious books; moreover, novices were to be sent back to the mother house for two months prior to taking their vows. Two years later, this same superior general created the position of *directrice des études* to coordinate the secular training of novices and the continuing education of teaching nuns. In 1858, the order insisted that all novices spend at least a year of centralized training in Lyons in order to maintain a common spirit and allow superiors to "make good placements later," as the rule specified.[49] The Sœurs de la Doctrine Chrétienne de Nancy offered a full range of academic courses in their novitiate in

1840 that included not only the basics but also cosmography, geography, secular history, elements of literature, and needlework. As a result, they prided themselves on offering an education equivalent to that of the better boarding schools for those novices who ended up not taking vows.[50]

While evidence of such training abounds in the archives of teaching orders, it is important to keep in mind that the focus of the novitiate was not instruction but spiritual development. Unquestionably those orders which mainly furnished teachers for primary schools did not spend much time on the academic training of their novices. What distinguished religious training from its lay counterpart, however, was the structure of the novitiate, which offered far wider possibilities for educational training for those novitiate headmistresses or superior generals who recognized that the academic qualifications of their teachers could contribute to the success of their schools.

As a result, the novitiates of major orders often became the site for the first normal schools in France; in 1844 the novitiate of Saint-Joseph de Lyon became a normal school for the southeastern departments of the Rhône and the Loire, a year later the Congrégation de Sainte-Chrétienne de Metz opened a normal school in Mézières in northern France.[51] In Lyons, the novices and apprentice teachers shared the same teachers, and student teaching was accomplished in the schools of the orders. The course of study in the normal school and novitiate was very similar from the mid-1840s until 1867, when the normal school program was extended a year and included topics not taught to the novices, in particular natural history, chemistry, and physics.[52]

The Sœurs de Saint-Joseph de Cluny had a project in the 1840s to open a normal school; although this project did not come to fruition, they did run a boarding school in Paris for those novices and young sisters who wanted to teach. The Sœurs de la Doctrine Chrétienne in Nancy ran their novitiate in Nancy as a normal school. Sister Saint-Claude at Bourg-en-Bresse moved from novitiate headmistress to superior general and published the *Manuel d'une religieuse institutrice*, which established guidelines for her community. Specifically, in 1847, she instituted annual examinations for all sisters who had less than six years of "professional" experience since taking their vows: "The honor, the progress, and the future of the order are all dependent on our sisters pursuing serious studies."[53] In Normandy, the Tiers Ordre de Notre-Dame du Mont-Carmel provided the principal impetus behind efforts to develop teacher training for rural teachers. Information about the normal course they ran in Avranches is more complete than elsewhere and reveals the very real concern to improve the quality of teacher training. In 1865, the three-year program devoted well over a third of its class hours to courses in arithmetic, history, geography, natural science, physics and chemistry, literature, and pedagogy. In the 1860s, the school accepted some seventy to eighty students, and between 1870 and 1877, 191 students received teaching diplomas. Many of the students in the school were in fact novices intending to devote their lives to teaching within the structure of a teaching order.[54] Indeed, until 1880 the female graduates of normal schools seldom actually went on to become primary teachers in the public sector, instead they turned to private education, as governesses, boarding-school teachers, or nuns.[55] Arguably then, the development of normal school training had more impact on religious teaching orders than on primary school education itself. The need to offer a teaching program, which often included courses in pedagogy, forced the teaching orders to establish standards for their teachers that had wide-ranging implications in the development of more professional standards. Their relative independence from state interference allowed individual orders to develop their own procedures of selection and training, albeit in a far less coordinated fashion than the emerging medical or legal professions.[56]

Contrary to both contemporary and historical perceptions, not all teaching sisters refused to sit for the state-instituted teaching examinations. By the second half of the century, some orders pushed their better teachers and future headmistresses to acquire teaching diplomas in order to give their institutions a better image. The religious boarding schools run by the Congrégation de la Mère de Dieu all had teachers who had earned their teaching degrees by the Second Empire; given the reputation of the schools of the Legion of Honor, which they ran, this is not very surprising.[57] In 1869 an astonishing 45.5 percent of the teachers in the Congrégation des Sœurs de la Sainte-Famille in Lyons had teaching diplomas, while the Sœurs de Saint-Joseph actively encouraged their members to pass the *brevet*. On the other hand, some orders consistently resisted obtaining these diplomas, such as the Sœurs de Saint-Charles and the Société du Sacré-Cœur who vehemently defended their right to declare their teachers qualified without requiring them to prove their skills before a male jury.[58] A nation-wide survey in 1864 revealed that many teaching orders established boarding schools where none of the teachers had teaching diplomas: of 2004 such schools, only 291 (14.5 percent) had headmistresses with *brevets*.[59] However, opposition to training teaching sisters for the state diplomas was not necessarily an anti-intellectual gesture, as the example of the Sacré-Cœur shows.

Founding mother Sophie Barat was concerned from the outset about the level of studies in her society's schools. By the 1840s, complaints about the quality of their teaching and the capacity of the sisters to teach led her to advocate more serious training.[60] To further this aim, she appointed a headmistress of studies in 1849, Mère d'Avenas, who did much to raise the level of studies, notably by publishing textbooks for the Society.[61] Under d'Avenas's direction the Sacré-Cœur created a "commission on studies and boarding schools" that emphasized the need to focus on teaching in the novitiate and urged the creation of a juniorate for pedagogical training. Revealingly, the commission argued that a juniorate was necessary to counter the competition from other teaching orders. Despite d'Avenas's concern, the Société du Sacré-Cœur implemented these suggestions slowly, not opening a juniorate until

1866. The course of study at the juniorate lasted two years and attracted those teachers who wanted to become head study mistresses. Pedagogical concerns dominated this institution: students were taught how to teach certain subjects and prepared teaching notebooks with lists of useful books as well as methods to transmit this knowledge. In 1884, the juniorate was divided into two levels: elementary and superior; the latter involved some 280 class hours in a wide range of subjects, including philosophy, history, literature, art history, and the sciences.[62] The Société du Sacré-Cœur was not isolated in this concern to bolster academic training, although the Sœurs de Saint-Joseph and de Saint-Charles did not open juniorates of their own until the final years of the century.

Another way to ensure quality teaching was through the establishment of inspection procedures within the order. In 1853, the appointment of ecclesiastical personnel to inspect boarding schools run by nuns put renewed pressure on the teaching orders to ensure that their teachers were qualified. Given the favorable religious climate, most accepted this outside scrutiny, which included examination of the school facilities as well as the teaching materials.[63] Many orders also established their own internal inspection systems both to enforce conformity to the ideals of the order and to maintain pedagogical quality within the classroom. When Sophie Barat noted criticisms about the quality of teachers in the Société du Sacré-Cœur in the 1840s, she created the position of *visitatrice*, who was responsible for inspection tours focusing on the studies within the Society's schools. She argued in particular that a "well-rounded mind, filled with science, was not harmful to inner life." A similar impulse led the Congrégation de la Doctrine Chrétienne to create *sœurs directrices* who investigated individual schools. Reports from such inspections reveal that they were taken seriously. At the schools of the Société du Sacré-Cœur, they contain countless references to teachers who were too focused on form rather than on content or on teachers who yielded too easily to parental pressure, allowing girls to advance despite weak performances. The frequent movement of teaching personnel within these schools was undoubtedly in part a product of such inspections.[64]

By the second half of the century, internal documents concerning the Ursulines reveal a similar concern to maintain a high quality of teaching. The mother house sent detailed questionnaires to the individual houses asking about their educational programs and the qualifications of their teachers. In the central French city of Blois in 1888, the headmistress was expected to keep a daily record of her classes that included the quality and quantity of homework required. The mother superior would then check this notebook every three months: "This experience has shown us that it is an excellent way to maintain the level of studies." This book allowed teachers to check what was done in previous years and harmonize teaching methods. In the summer, the Ursulines organized pedagogical conferences where the principles of the Jesuits, the Frères de l'Instruction Chrétienne, and the French University were all discussed and debated; teachers then had the opportunity to give mock lessons and receive criticism. As this same order noted: "We believe that religious communities have within them more such resources than any other sort of institution, because the experience of each individual becomes the patrimony of all."[65]

Unquestionably the major teaching orders responded to the expansion of girls' schooling through efforts to establish their pedagogical credentials. Annual letters, visits, inspections, and pedagogical conferences were all ways to communicate the characteristics of these credentials, particularly in the larger orders, whose schools developed throughout France and even abroad. Such efforts to ensure a certain level of instruction for girls should not, however, be overstated. First and foremost, religious teaching orders sought to communicate a particular worldview where religious and spiritual values predominated over intellectual concerns.

Religious Mission and Educational Strategies

Unlike most individual lay schools, teaching orders had a clear sense of mission that structured everyday life in religious schools. Although the characteristics of this mission evolved over time, particularly in reaction to mounting anticlericalism, the general features remained the same. Religious teachers sought to form good Christian women whose influence would then spread throughout society through their daily actions within the family and through their charitable actions in society as a whole. Generally, these teachers eschewed a proselytizing tone, since their cultural acceptance depended on avoiding overt efforts to recruit students as nuns. At the same time, most orders also steered away from advocating the training of intellectual women, given the bias against *femmes savantes* in nineteenth-century French society. Education rather than instruction formed the core of religious education. More important, perhaps, this education was endowed with missionary overtones; most orders saw girls' education as a means of uplifting and Christianizing specific social groups.

The spread of religious education for middle-class girls had broad cultural implications for French society. The religious goals of this education generated a series of educational strategies that introduced new practices and associations both within schools and without. Associations, such as the Enfants de Marie, clearly contributed to what historians of religion have described as a new and invigorated piety in the second half of the century. Without a doubt, religious teachers played an important role in instilling new modes of behavior and of action for middle-class women whose influence has too often been caricatured rather than analyzed.

Defining the Christian Woman

Annual letters, constitutions, general chapters, and rulebooks provide insight into the specific vision underlying teaching in religious schools. While all emphasize the importance of cultivating Christian virtues, one can discern significant nuances according to the stature of the order and the social milieu they targeted. Those orders which catered to a social elite clearly struggled to adopt an educational ethos that would attract students without betraying their religious vision. For them, family pressures often encouraged the development of a more worldly orientation, which some resisted better than others. The rules for the Sœurs de Notre-Dame specifically warned against this: "Inspire in them a disdain for society and a refusal of dangerous pleasures, as you must realize that your principal object and that of our institute is to form good Christians, not learned women."[66] This concern to avoid a superficial and flashy education is echoed in numerous sources, suggesting of course that many orders failed to comply. The Sœurs de la Doctrine Chrétienne de Nancy, for example, warned their teachers in the mid-1840s that far too many boarding schools were accused of providing a frivolous education where students were given a smattering of the sciences and art: "The Sisters who are in charge of our boarding schools must carefully avoid falling into this trap; on the contrary, they must inspire in their students the love of things solid, rather than brilliant; modest tastes and simple, but polite, manners; the love of piety, work and managing a household, in a word, ensure that their education is religious and exempt from all that favors vanity or that would enable students to leave their [social] condition."[67] Christian education was intended to contain troublesome social aspirations. In principle, religious schools sought to distinguish themselves from their lay competitors through their high moral tone; girls' education in this vision had a purpose, but this purpose was not to ensure upwardly mobile marriages.

The Dames de l'Assomption represent an unusual exception in their effort to promote more serious studies. Founded in 1839, this congregation was associated with the religious reform movement around such figures as Henri Lacordaire, Charles Forbes, comte de Montalembert, and Félicité Robert de Lamennais. Lamennais in particular emphasized the importance of girls' education in efforts to re-Christianize French society, an idea that founding mother Eugénie Milleret took particularly to heart.[68] As a member of the liberal aristocracy, she had the advantages of an excellent classical education but one that lacked religious depth. Her specific concern was to reach women, such as herself, members of the upper middle-class or the liberal aristocracy, and offer them a challenging intellectual and religious plan of study. Milleret argued that existing institutions were sadly inadequate and that Parisian elite convents were out of favor: "They suffer from one of three prejudices: political coloring, an absence of instruction, or the absence of good manners."[69] She proposed a plan of study for her students that noticeably surpassed the level of most girls' institutions at the time. Specifically, she urged the study of Latin and theology, which were traditionally off-limits for girls. Responding to criticisms, Milleret wrote: "Some say we are learned; nothing could serve us better in bringing us the children we seek."[70] She encouraged intellectual training for the way it shaped young women's characters:

> We push the level of instruction very far, but it is essentially the spirit in which we pursue it that distinguishes our education. I have no respect for a teaching of pure knowledge, I admire all that raises intelligence, that impresses on it a character of superiority in intellectual conceptualization and in Christian sentiments. Other schools, even religious ones, speak too much to the imagination and to sentimental faculties; we speak to [student's] intellect, in order to Christianize while developing it, we speak to the [student's] will to make it capable of abnegation and sacrifice.[71]

Her social Christian inclinations can be seen in the importance she placed on having her students help the poor.

More commonly, teaching orders had to guard against accusations of using their schools to recruit future novices. While such a practice was common, religious constitutions all insisted that this was not an explicit goal of religious teaching. The Congrégation de Notre-Dame wrote: "Nonetheless, despite the importance we attribute to all that concerns religion, we only develop in our school those pious practices that one finds daily in a Christian family."[72] The goal of religious education was to spread religious virtues throughout society, beginning within students' families. But this influence was expected to permeate all levels of society. The Sacré-Cœur, for example, expected to re-Christianize the elite; in 1876, Bishop Mermillod in Montpellier told them their mission was to "bring to life in the upper classes feelings of duty, sacrifice, and devotion to the church."[73] More generally, teaching orders expected their former students to work within charitable associations and to spread Christian values among the poor while setting an example through their own sacrifices.[74]

The characteristics of the Christian women that emerge from this variety of normative sources suggest that religious teachers constantly had to juggle between conflicting pressures. Teaching orders experienced internal pressures to recruit new members as well as external pressures from families to produce suitable marriage partners. These contradictory influences were not always resisted successfully. Nonetheless, a general consensus existed that religious education should prepare girls to be serious Christians in their families and in society, but the nuances attached to the term "serious" varied from order to order. For the Dames de l'Assomption, "serious" implied intellectual development, whereas more frequently it was associated with the development of moral virtues. In either case, however, teaching orders mobilized their considerable resources to encourage certain religious practices whose influence extended far beyond the convent walls. In this fashion nuns wielded a form of cultural authority that their lay counterparts simply did not have.

Instilling the New Piety

Numerous sources testify to the increasingly structured nature of religious life within convent schools. The diffuse piety that characterized school life in the initial decades of the century gradually assumed institutional form through the creation of sodalities that organized girls into religious groups. As a result, the daily religious rituals that framed boarding-school life were given a new setting and were endowed with explicitly missionary objectives. Young girls were encouraged to internalize certain values, but more important, they were urged to spread these values through specific actions and modes of behavior. Teaching orders contributed in particular to the vitality of Marian devotional practices that gained cultural influence after the pope's proclamation of Mary's Immaculate Conception in 1854.[75]

Within convent schools, a series of religious rituals structured daily life.[76] The First Communion, in particular, represented one of the transitional moments in a girl's life and was spoken about in terms that parallel descriptions of marriage. The traditional attire — long white gown and veil — reinforced the association between the two ceremonies. Private diaries as well as correspondence all confirm the impression that preadolescent girls took their First Communions very seriously. Sophie Simon at age twelve wrote long letters to her mother about her experiences under the guidance of the Mère de Dieu nuns. In these letters, religion is always present: "I await with great happiness the most beautiful day of my life — that of my First Communion."[77] But at the same time, the lavish ritualistic aspects undoubtedly contributed to the emotion this ceremony fostered. In 1878, Eugénie Servant, a student at a religious branch of the Legion of Honor schools scrupulously recorded her impressions of her own First Communion in her diary. Her emphasis throughout is on the ritual itself and not the inner transformations of this ceremony. Although she carefully describes her own attire and then the decorations at the chapel, at no moment does she address the personal implications First Communion held for her.[78] Above all, she suffered because her parents failed to attend this ceremony; she had wanted them to witness the ritual that granted her admission into a new group, that of the "premières Communiantes." Frequently religious rituals and activities were performed relatively automatically, although the underlying messages may indeed have been internalized. Writing about her religious education in the 1870s, Jeanne Crouzet-Benaben noted: "I accepted [religious truths] as they were, without any thought. They were dogma. As I was respectful of dogma, I gave myself up to the feelings and even the charming sensations that religion offers. I liked the atmosphere in the church, its silent coolness, the shadows that encouraged meditation, its smell of incense and melted wax."[79]

Religious associations for students, known as sodalities, first appeared in the 1820s and 1830s in the major teaching orders, but their numbers soared in the second half of the century, playing an increasingly important role in daily convent life.[80] Within these sodalities, young girls learned the value attached to Christian principles and were encouraged to put them into practice in order to gain recognition. A whole range of these associations catering to specific age groups gradually developed. At the Bénédictine school in Toulouse, young girls between the ages of seven and eleven could become members of "l'Enfant-Jesus," between eleven and thirteen they could join the "Saints-Anges," and finally, older girls had the privilege of becoming "Enfants de Marie."[81] These associations offered opportunities to participate actively in the religious life of the school through the creation of nativity scenes, for example. Teachers generally nominated students for admission, and members were then expected to follow the virtue of a saint throughout a month. In recognition of their piety, members earned the right to wear a special ribbon with the image of the Virgin Mary on it, and in religious ceremonies, Enfants de Marie tended to take center stage. In a school run by the Sœurs de Saint-Joseph in Cusset, Marguerite Rousset describes the Enfants de Marie reciting divine office with the teaching sisters on Christmas eve.[82]

Belonging to such a group played an important role in boarding-school sociability. For the individuals involved, becoming an Enfant de Marie meant not only official recognition but also more personal ties with other students in the school. When Eugénie Servant and her best friend were admitted, their first act was to exchange ribbons. Fellow Enfants de Marie stuck together within the boarding-school setting and were even perceived at times as being the policemen of the school.[83] The ribbon, the rituals associated with admission, and the weekly meetings all contributed to making this both a religious and a social association. Younger girls admired this organization, and teachers encouraged students to aspire to this particular model of adolescent girlhood.[84] Once admitted, students were encouraged to offer each other mutual supervision and guidance in attaining religious perfection. Those who failed to live up to the ideals of obedience and virtue in these organizations could be excluded. Mathilde Rousset, for example, was threatened with exclusion from the Enfants de Saint-Joseph because of her impertinence.[85] In schools run by the Ursulines, failure to live up to disciplinary standards also led to the temporary expulsion from such sodalities.[86] The sense of sisterhood that clearly marked members of a sodality may well have fostered the germs of vocation for certain students. At the Parisian school run by the Congrégation de Sainte-Clotilde, a register of forty-eight students who were Enfants de Marie after 1868 indicates that twelve (25 percent) became nuns themselves after leaving school; ten took the veil of their teachers.[87]

These religious associations served to incorporate young girls into groups that often enjoyed special privileges within the larger school setting. At the Assomption convent school, the Enfants de Marie had the "honor" of serving their classmates at meals, thus learning important lessons about religious humility.[88] The Ursulines of Blois in 1871 had a separate library of religious books for Enfants de Marie.[89] More important, these sodalities encouraged a missionary outlook that religious teachers clearly hoped would persist once students left the convent walls. The Ursulines in Clermont-Ferrand sought through their sodalities to excite the fervor of students by transforming them into "pontifical zouaves or Angels, pilgrims, or Harvesters."[90] Pilgrimages were also part of the rituals of some convent schools. Beginning in 1853, the Ursulines of Boulogne led their students throughout the main streets of the city in a pilgrimage to Notre-Dame de Boulogne. Citizens believed such practices explained why Boulogne was spared the ravages of the Prussian invasion in 1870.[91] Eugénie Servant describes in her diary how one of her religious teachers more informally created a feminine and pacific "crusade" that contributed to a selfless communitarian ethos. The crusade's goal was to use prayer as a weapon to convert infidels. In her words, this association was "for the most obedient girls. It involved contributing to our Mothers' good deeds as missionaries in Egypt through small sacrifices such as the renunciation of pride, victories over our own faults, and the patient enduring of small ordeals."[92] For Eugénie and her French schoolmates the infidels were an abstract concept, and clearly her appreciation of this crusade lay more in its social possibilities. Each crusader wore a red flannel cross on her left shoulder, and periodically the members got together and added up the total of their virtues. A similar eucharistic crusade existed at the Couvent des Oiseaux well into the twentieth century.[93]

Some orders worried, however, about the shallow character of these acts of piety fostered within convent sodalities. Within the Société de Sacré-Cœur, for example, a committee in 1869 warned that associations like the Enfants de Marie failed at times to produce the proper attitude: "We must be careful to avoid reproducing the actions of our students in our pious publications, this gives an ostentatious character to our good works which is inappropriate."[94] This revealing comment highlights how convent piety could become competitive, generating unfeminine feelings of self-satisfaction.

Thanks to its missionary zeal, convent-school piety was expected to have an impact well beyond the individuals involved. In particular, teachers fostered a moral worldview that encouraged young girls to assume responsibility for those less fortunate, notably through lessons on charity. Most teachers in both religious and lay girls' boarding schools encouraged their students to exercise charity actively from a young age. Mathilde Rousset noted in her diary that the Enfants de Saint-Joseph all contributed money to buy bread for the poor that they then distributed themselves.[95] In Lille, convent students often made a gift for an "adopted" child of the adjacent poor school.[96] Within the boarding schools of the Dames de l'Assomption, students belonged to associations that collected contributions for the poor.[97] Daily charitable endeavors included sewing for the poor or distributing food and clothes to the indigent.[98] At moments of national catastrophe, these charitable activities picked up in their intensity. Many schools had girls sew clothing for those stricken in the floods in 1877, and at the Legion of Honor students gave up their prizes so that the money could go to those in greater need. Similarly, when the nuns who ran the Notre-Dame boarding school in Toulouse urged their students to give up their prizes for the "Peter's pence" donation to the Vatican, this action was justified in these terms: "One only contributes to the serious education and the formation of useful women for society when one inspires in young children an awareness of the church's interest, the science of noble sentiments, and the energy of sacrifice."[99] Through daily activities and more unusual collective actions, girls in religious schools were taught to think about and succor those less fortunate. This training was expected to help middle-class girls learn their future role as ladies of charity.[100]

The camaraderie encouraged within sodalities and other religious associations was intended to continue once students left the school, and to form the basis for similar associations of adult women. In the Sacré-Cœur convent schools, inspection reports commonly refer to what were termed the "exterior congregations." Some of these sodalities included young girls who were not students, and others included adult women. In Quimper in Brittany, the exterior Enfants de Marie numbered some seventy girls, that of the sodality of Saint Anne one hundred adult women. In Amiens in 1875, the inspector noted: "The congrégation des Enfants de Marie is composed of 160 members, every year they have a retreat to which they invite society ladies. 400 to 500 people attend."[101] In a sense these sodalities prefigured associations of former students that did not emerge in France until the end of the century.

The social and missionary orientation of convent-school piety clearly extended beyond convent walls. Girls learned to identify with collective goals that involved both influencing their social peers through their example and succoring the poor through charitable actions. As *dames patronnesses*, Catholic women were expected to pursue activities learned in school, giving both time and money to those less fortunate. This piety was part of a broader movement that affected all social classes through the explosion of Marian piety and the tremendous growth in pilgrimages.[102] While this reinvigorated piety has been variously interpreted as a defensive reaction to the spread of secular values or as an antimodern reaction to modernity, these arguments do not address the social and cultural mechanisms that allowed this piety to spread. The organizational structure of religious life within female teaching orders encouraged the spread of Catholic values. Young girls were encouraged to see themselves as missionaries, an attitude that extended then into the organizations that structured the "leisure" activities of many adult bourgeois women. A religious sense of mission, however, did not necessarily imply the triumph of anti-intellectual attitudes.

In 1867 Dupanloup published his treatise *Femmes savantes et femmes studieuses* in which he argued that women needed more serious education: "Education, even religious [education] all too rarely gives young girls and women a taste for work.... I attribute this estrangement from work to their education [which is] limited, frivolous and superficial."[103] Shortly after the publication of this treatise, Dupanloup's name became associated in anticlerical circles with his opposition to Victor Duruy's attempt to create a system of public secondary courses for girls. The polemical and political nature of the debates surrounding these courses (analyzed in Chapter 7) has tended to obscure Dupanloup's initial position that girls needed mental instruction and not just religious education.[104] The bishop's concern to reconcile intellectual culture and piety was not a lone initiative in the conservative moral climate of the Second Empire. Instead there is ample evidence that his treatise developed ideas already under discussion in the more ambitious religious orders. By the 1860s, religious teachers were clearly aware that their educational offering had to adjust to broader changes within French society. As Mother Goetz, superior general of the Société du Sacré-Cœur argued in 1867, the Society needed "to preserve in its teaching the solidity and the ambition that places it at the level of contemporary needs, while offering to the young women raised in our schools, those precious lessons of faith, of duty, of solid virtue, of all the areas of knowledge which they should expect from us in order to receive a serious, complete and polished education."[105] In other words religious education required intellectual stuffing in order to serve its purpose.

The discussions within the Sacré-Cœur about the teaching of philosophy offer a revealing perspective on how religious education played into the gendered politics of the age. In 1866, Mother Goetz turned to the Jesuit Father Olivaint to ask him whether logic and philosophy, traditionally associated with boys' education, should enter their teaching program. His response was an unequivocal yes:

> Today men pride themselves on doing philosophy and all they produce are sophisms ... most are incapable of offering an education to their children; most frequently women are obliged to fill the role of men, they must, as a result, be able to correct certain words concerning the immortality of the soul, the existence of God, etc., which slip into conversations and attack the purity and the integrity of children's Faith. Hence it is appropriate that women know a bit of philosophy, and this should not provoke scandal.[106]

At the same time he cautioned the Society not to name these lessons "philosophy," as it would made them vulnerable to the accusation of wishing to form "grandes dames" or "savantes." By labeling their classes "logic," they would appear more modest. Indubitably, Father Olivaint advocated these studies to further conservative ends and yet this should not obscure the fact that in the interests of re-Christianization, he was encouraging women to engage in theological debates, a strictly male terrain.

The women who would form generations of Christian women were not, however, mere pawns of the Catholic hierarchy. Teaching orders were, of course, subject to the influence of male spiritual advisers as the preceding example demonstrates, but women superiors maintained a great deal of authority both within their orders and without. As I have argued, entering a teaching order and assuming teaching responsibilities within it required women of action and decision. It is not surprising then that at times they were perceived as masculine. Most famously, King Louis-Philippe is said to have exclaimed about Superior General Anne-Marie Javouhey, "Madame Javouhey, what a great man!"[107] While these women were teaching piety, obedience, and submission, their lives offered very different messages.

Boarding Schools:
Location, Ethos, and Female Identities

The middle decades of the nineteenth century witnessed steady growth in the number of girls' "secondary" schools, which pushed female teachers toward acquiring increasingly professional qualifications. Despite the absence of state support for the development of girls' secondary schools, a network of such schools materialized in the French urban landscape in the years from 1850 to 1880. This network and its relationship to primary schools must be acknowledged in order to understand the strategies individual headmistresses adopted in order to attract students during this period. By the middle decades of the nineteenth century, the lower middle and middle classes had a wide range of institutions from which to choose; not surprisingly, these schools offered a diversity of educational options that render simple conclusions about the characteristics of this education inaccurate. Despite the emphasis on domestic ideology within the bourgeoisie, girls' schools often emphasized skills and values that were not domestically oriented. In turn students received a variety of educational messages whose meaning they struggled with during their adolescent years. Finally, the school experience itself had an impact on emerging gendered identities.

Institutional Locations and Strategies

Efforts to quantify the number and availability of girls' secondary schools in France at midcentury are doomed to failure. Because the state had no official hand in the operation of these schools and indeed legislated the secondary level out of existence in 1853, official educational statistics are of little use in charting the growth of girls' secondary schools. Figures for girls' primary schools testify to a huge growth in schools, the majority of which were run by nuns: in 1837 some 14,100 girls' schools existed, this figure jumped to 27,300 by 1863.[1] Secondary schools similarly multiplied but concerned a mere fraction of the female school-age population. Nonetheless, these institutions marked the urban landscape and attracted the attention of educational authorities. In 1864 a nationwide survey of boys' secondary education included a few final questions concerning girls' boarding schools. Clearly, in the Ministry of Education's perspective, boarding schools constituted secondary education for girls. The results of this survey offer a general vision of the educational map at a specific moment and shed insight on the range of schools existing in the mid-1860s.

Putting Girls' Schools on the Map

Despite gaps, the survey revealed that boarding schools were scattered throughout the country.[2] The location of schools reflected traditional patterns in schooling, notably the educational advance of northern France and the relative dearth of schools in Brittany and the rural center.[3] Still the map reveals some surprises. Northeastern France appears underrepresented, given a historical tradition of female literacy, while one would not expect the heavy concentration of schools in the rural departments around Lyons, in the collar of departments in western France (notably the Loire-Atlantique and the Ile-et-Vilaine), or in the southwest. The presence of major, and even medium-sized, cities often explains these surprises: Nantes, Rennes, and Caen for the western departments, Toulouse, Bordeaux, and Montpellier for the southwest. Nonetheless, the pattern revealed by the survey is in part a reflection of how inspectors interpreted the questions. The minister asked rectors and inspectors to specify "How many boarding schools are run by lay women? How many by religious teachers? How many have the *brevet de capacité*? How many only have the letter of obedience?" Clearly, some inspectors included all schools that took in even a handful of boarders, while others focused their attention more on secondary institutions.[4] As a result, in the very rural Puy-de-Dome, the rector noted some 108 religious boarding schools — just behind the departments of northern France and that of the Rhône — scattered throughout the countryside, catering to students whose families lived in isolated hamlets. The report specified that only five women had the *brevet supérieur*, four of whom ran schools in Clermont-Ferrand and one in Thiers. Clearly, most of these schools were not secondary institutions, and not all inspectors included such schools in their reports. In Alsace, for example, a mere twenty-eight schools were noted for the two departments, despite a far stronger educational tradition than in the Massif Central. Here it appears that the inspector did not include village schools that took in a few boarders.[5]

A comparison of the survey results concerning lay and religious teachers further explains some of the initial surprises. Areas with dynamic teaching orders were well represented, notably around Lyons where the Sœurs de Saint-Charles and the Sœurs

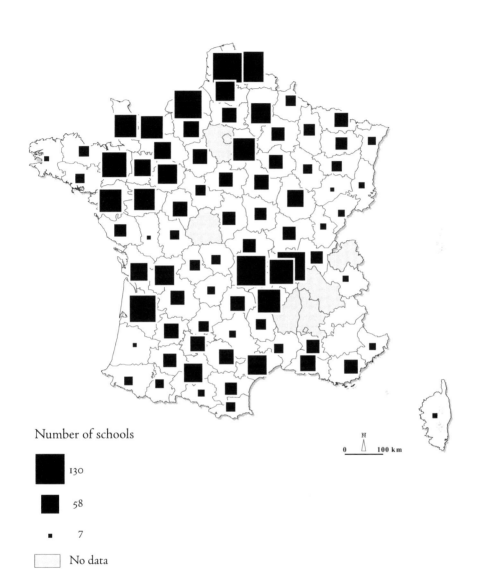

Number of schools

130

58

7

No data

Map 1 Girls' boarding schools in France in 1864.

de Saint-Joseph were based. Similarly, in Brittany (excluding the western tip) numerous religious orders ran boarding schools (83 percent of the 356 recorded schools in this academy were run by nuns). Overall, religious boarding schools predominated, representing two-thirds of the total number of schools: 2,338 out of 3,480. Given the large numbers of lay schools in the department of the Seine and in the Seine-et-Oise (neither of which were included in the survey), however, these results should be readjusted with that in mind. Religious schools were certainly in the majority, but lay schools were far from absent.

The survey showed that boarding schools were present virtually throughout France, most probably in cities. The judgments about the quality of the education offered suggests, however, a spottier picture, even if one needs to consider that respondents' answers often reflected their political orientations as they took sides in the religious conflicts of this period, notably to defend lay over religious institutions. Notwithstanding, a general picture of the perceived quality of girls' education does emerge from the question concerning "the general situation of girls' boarding schools in your area with respects to (1) morality, (2) education, and (3) instruction."

Overall, most inspectors considered that the morality and education offered in these schools ranged from excellent to satisfactory; less than 2 percent of the departments had schools that were considered mediocre or poor in this area.[6] The quality of the *instruction*, however, was judged far more severely: over 25 percent of the departments had "inadequate" schools, and another 15 percent were considered to have schools that varied considerably in quality. More specific comments shed light on what were considered problems. Frequently inspectors deplored the effects of a course of study that focused too exclusively on memory. In Lyons the rector blamed families for the absence of "solidity" in girls' education: in the course of four years of study "their memory is overloaded to the detriment of their judgment."[7] In the Vendée in western France where religious schools were dominant (twenty-five out of the thirty-one schools), the inspector similarly regretted the influence of parents that produced an education "which gives children narrow ways of reasoning; out of concern for their innocence, the world as it is today is not taught."[8]

The survey also inquired about the professional qualifications of women teachers and whether institutions underwent inspections. Contrary to the situation in Paris, the results showed that the vast majority of women teachers taught without having an official teaching degree beyond that of the nun's letter of obedience: out of 2,295 women teachers, only 291 had diplomas.[9] The question concerning inspections revealed a variety of practices, but in most departments inspectors reported that inspectresses no longer visited schools, if indeed they ever had. As a result, most schools were inspected either by ecclesiastical authorities or by the inspectors of the primary system. The inspectors frequently noted that headmistresses requested such inspections as a way of establishing the quality of their institutions, presumably to attract further clients.

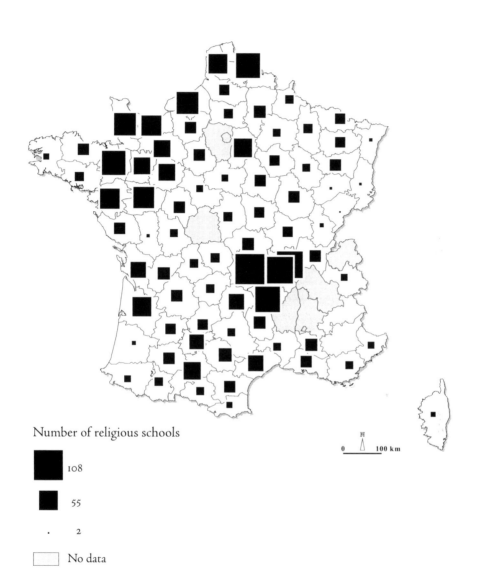

Number of religious schools

108

55

. 2

No data

Map 2 Religious boarding schools in France in 1864.

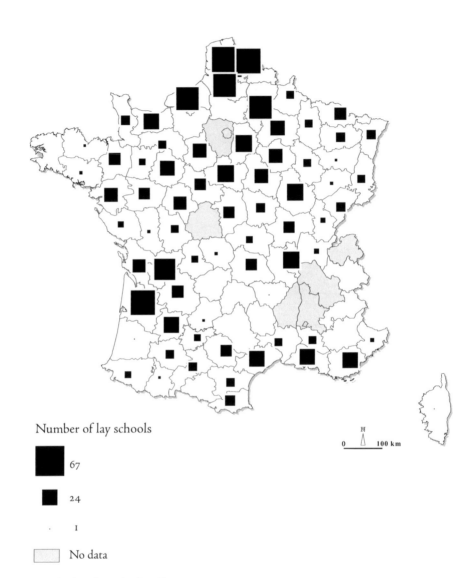

Number of lay schools

67

24

1

No data

Map 3 Lay boarding schools in France in 1864.

Finally, the survey inquired about the advisability of extending normal course education as well as creating a higher-level diploma in order to improve the training for teachers at secondary schools. Very few inspectors (six all told) thought that normal schools were needed to improve the level of the instruction offered. On the contrary, inspectors insisted that they needed teachers for rural schools so that there was no need to offer more secondary-level training. Consistently, the reports noted that only cities required more advanced schools. Nonetheless, in twenty-one departments (out of seventy-seven that responded to this question) inspectors did support the creation of a secondary diploma for women teachers.

The arguments for and against such a diploma reveal the absence of consensus about why girls should study in the first place. Those opposed to such a diploma argued in time-honored fashion that such a diploma would only nourish a girl's sense of vanity or inspire unsatisfied desires. In common with arguments concerning boys' education, other inspectors brandished the specter of *déclassement*: "Offering girls an opportunity to receive more developed instruction would pull them out of their social class and expose them to the dangers of an instruction and an education which is not in line with their fortune."[10] Occasionally inspectors urged the addition of certain subject matters to the existing *brevet complet.* In the Bouches-du-Rhône, the report argued that foreign languages and music should be added, since these subjects were "a necessity in the education of women who will live in society," but it saw no need for women to learn algebra or ancient languages.[11] Interestingly, in the Alpes-Maritimes, where Nice is located, the inspector saw no need for a new diploma but did urge the creation of a girls' *lycée*: "By pulling the monopoly of girls' education from the hands of private industry and religious corporations, [the state] would exert a long-lasting and useful influence on families. It would offer as well a secure position for many people, wives and daughters of civil servants, hence procuring precious advantages for the state." In the Gard, the inspector defended the creation of a higher diploma as a way to inspire emulation among candidates for the teaching profession: "In a few years individuals holding this diploma would found institutions, and the result would be an increasingly pronounced movement in favor of girls' instruction."[12] This argument, like that of the inspector for the Alpes-Maritimes, clearly envisioned a system of girls' schools similar to what existed for boys. More commonly, however, inspectors reasoned more in terms of what women needed to fill their role in society. In this respect opinions diverged; one inspector defended a very literary education for city schools where girls would study history, literature, the literary history of France, and the French language. In the Academy of Lyons, on the contrary, the rector argued for a far more practical orientation, adding courses in commercial law, domestic economy, and womanly duties (!) to the existing *brevet complet.*[13]

This diversity of opinions highlights the absence of consensus at this period about girls' educational needs above the primary level. The survey's national scope revealed major differences between regions and suggests widely varying educational strategies throughout France. Inspectors reasoned one way when discussing departments where the clientele of boarding schools was mainly the daughters of small landowners and wealthy agricultural families (the case of the central department of the Creuse) and another when discussing departments where a major city generated a wider range of social demand. In Bordeaux, for example, the inspector urged the creation of a secondary diploma as a way to attract the daughters of rich families. In the end, Victor Duruy used the results of this survey to conclude that secondary education did not exist for girls — a *political* interpretation which failed to do justice to the complexity of the situation. Ultimately, the attempt to garner a national snapshot foundered for lack of sufficient information concerning existing institutions. Analyses of individual cities, and particularly Paris, reveal more clearly the extent to which a hierarchical network of girls' schools had emerged at this period offering a range of educational opportunities to a broadly defined middle class.

Profiles of Urban and Institutional Diversity

The period between 1850 and 1880 saw a considerable growth in the numbers of girls' schools opened in Paris, with religious schools representing a clear minority.[14] In 1855 twenty-two religious boarding schools in Paris and four in the suburbs educated a total of 1721 students, compared with 320 lay boarding schools educating 13,529 students. In 1864 the number of boarding schools remained steady at 316 with 12,000 students; whereas there were 957 public and private primary schools, educating 79,521 girls.[15] The urban changes wrought by the baron Haussmann did not, however, drive boarding schools from the center of the city; instead, numbers grew with new institutions sprouting along the periphery, most prominently in the wealthier northwestern sections of Paris. Rents may have forced some schools from the heart of Paris, as inspectresses argued, but headmistresses also relocated to areas where they could attract wealthy clienteles. Inspection reports indicate that in these middle-class boarding schools tuition costs ranged between 800 and 1000 francs per year, during the Second Empire, at a period when primary schoolmasters only earned 700 francs per year after five years of experience. Therefore, as day schools opened for girls throughout the city, boarding schools settled in solidly bourgeois areas on the right bank, in the eighth, sixteenth, and seventeenth arrondissements. These areas in northwest Paris were also known for the quality of their air — an important selling point in the school brochures — and the schools there had far larger courtyards and gardens for their students than were available in the center of the city.[16]

The schools that peppered the Parisian landscape during this period ranged considerably in size, but many accommodated sizable student bodies. In this respect many girls' boarding schools came to resemble boys' institutions, rather than surrogate homes. Large schools with over a hundred boarders were relatively rare within Paris, instead they operated in the suburbs where space and gardens were more available. There were, however, exceptions. The select Institut Beaujon, situated in the aristocratic area around Saint-Germain, educated 120 boarders, including some 30 foreign students. The better religious boarding schools generally accommodated between 50 and 60 boarding students. In 1855 a survey indicated the following numbers: the Congrégation de la Mère de Dieu, rue de Picpus (64 boarders), the Couvent de l'Assomption (62 boarders), the Dames de l'Abbaye aux Bois (57 boarders).[17] Small boarding schools existed as well, often catering to specific clienteles. Rose Coulon, a Protestant headmistress, had a total of nineteen, mainly Protestant, young women in her school; twelve were considered boarders, and seven were "élèves en chambre," more casual students who generally attended the school for a year. Of the nineteen, eleven were foreign students (six British, three American, one Russian, and one Dutch). Virginie Rey's school taught thirty-five students, but only four were boarders. Her school was known for the quality of its lessons in Russian, English, German, and Italian.[18]

Lay and religious schools attracted students from families with a broad range of social, cultural, and professional aspirations. Moreover, their appeal extended far beyond the borders of France. Between 1852 and 1860, 3,070 foreign students attended classes in Parisian schools. Of this number English students far outnumbered other nationalities (49.6 percent of all foreign students), followed by Americans (14.7 percent), and then Poles (8.8 percent).[19] While some institutions offered a form of finishing education for aspiring socialites, others proposed a serious course of study organized rigorously by classes. Given the number of available institutions, families could afford to pick and choose; the successful headmistress was the one who established a specific identity for her school. Unquestionably, Paris offered an exceptionally wide range of girls' schools, dominated in no uncertain terms by lay rather than religious teachers. Within provincial cities this range was necessarily more restricted, but nonetheless what emerges from studies in various cities is a corresponding diversity that suggests that a secondary educational network for girls was in place by the 1860s.

Thousands of girls' schools opened and shut in provincial French towns and cities over the course of the century.[20] Clearly a demand existed for girls' institutions, which explains an often bewildering complexity of institutional offerings throughout the urban landscape. More important, however, the multiplication of schools contributed to generating a demand, as recent analyses have shown.[21] Lay boarding schools tended to far outnumber those of religious orders, as in Paris, but they were also more ephemeral. A few examples drawn from departmental almanacs highlight this general trend. In the Alsatian capital Strasbourg, sixty-nine lay schools and only three religious schools opened between 1800 and 1870, but unlike their lay competitors, the religious schools never closed their doors.[22] In the far smaller working-class city of Troyes (population of 25,000 in 1851), the departmental almanac reveals that forty different schools opened between 1834 and 1875; of these, only five were run by nuns. In Chartres (population of 17,028 in 1861) a mere eighteen lay schools opened between 1845 and 1890, in part no doubt because of the reputation of three major religious schools run by the Sacré-Cœur, the Providence, and the Sœurs de Saint-Paul. During the Second Empire the proportion of lay schools to religious schools in cities continued to favor the former despite what the national survey of 1864 had shown.[23] While the evidence from trade books should be used cautiously, it seems clear that even if the number of schools run by nuns increased during this period, lay schools continued to hold their own.

Headmistresses opened and shut their institutions with considerable regularity throughout the century, although often the buildings themselves continued to be girls' schools.[24] Despite a large percentage of ephemeral institutions, however, what is most striking is the consistent presence in most cities of a few long-lasting lay schools that benefited from local esteem and patronage. A surprising number of head-mistresses successfully competed with the financial resources of religious orders even after 1850 and the expansion of religious education. In Alsace between 1800 and 1870, headmistresses ran their schools for an average length of fifteen years, but Mlle Barbenes established a record of forty-five years of service and a generous handful of headmistresses functioned between twenty-two and twenty-eight years.[25] In Besançon between 1821 and 1881, headmistresses operated an average length of 10.13 years, with the longest-lasting staying open for thirty-seven years. Fourteen out of the seventy-nine schools (17.7 percent) operated more than twenty years; while thirty-one (39.2 percent) lasted less than five years, a pattern that resembles what I discovered in Paris. In Chartres, despite an overall average for lay schools between 1845 and 1890 that was only 7.7 years, three such schools were in operation for twenty-three to twenty-eight years. These schools were widely recognized as superior institutions where most future teachers received their early education and training.

Both lay and religious schools attracted a wide range of clients from the middle classes. As in Paris, the cost of provincial boarding schools largely determined the nature of the student body, and this cost varied widely depending on the city and the number of available institutions. In general boarding fees ranged from a low of 400 francs per year in religious institutions to a high of 1,000 francs per year. In Strasbourg, for example, families could choose from a wide range of differently priced institutions; the religious schools run by the Congrégation de Notre-Dame and the Benédictines du Saint-Sacrement cost a mere 400 francs per year, and this price remained stable throughout the century. Lay schools had an average cost of 650 francs per year but could be as expensive as 1,200 francs with ornamental arts included.[26] The most expensive institutions justified their high prices by the number of male teachers they employed. Mlle Knoderer, for example, charged 1,200 francs per year, but her students had access to seventeen outside teachers; Mlle Paulus who offered lessons herself and only used five outside teachers charged 600 francs per year. Consistently throughout France religious boarding schools seem to have charged lower fees than lay schools, in part simply because their infrastructure allowed them to cut costs.[27] But fees also varied depending on the desired clientele, and the more elitist religious institutions tended to align themselves with the more expensive lay schools in their city. In Toulouse, for example, the most expensive boarding school was run by the Sacré-Cœur; although the boarding fee for a year was only 650 francs, the cost of lessons in music or the arts could almost double this annual fee (in 1878–79 it was estimated at 1274 francs).[28]

Within this general price range, boarding schools effectively excluded the daughters of working-class families, but they nonetheless catered to a broad range of families from the lower middle classes to the aristocracy. In Laval the school of Mlle Mouliès and Mlle Sainte-Marie attracted students from both the bourgeoisie and the nobility.[29] In Toulouse the clientele of boarding schools has been more precisely described as coming from the world of magistrates, high-ranking civil servants, and military officers.[30] In Angers in the 1870s two sisters from a family of midlevel civil servants in Mlle Gellerat's well-respected school wrote in their correspondence that although the other students were nice, practically all were from commercial families: "They are not at all the same sort. They are all amazed that *maman* is educated."[31]

Religious schools frequently accommodated a relatively diverse clientele but they were often strictly segregated by class: at the Couvent du Saint-Nom de Jésus in Tarbes, boarders were daughters of landowners from the area while day students were the daughters of officers, lawyers, and shopkeepers.[32] In Ambert in the Massif central, the Ursulines maintained three schools, each for a particular clientele: the first, with some 80 to 100 boarders, had six classes and catered to an urban population. The second, more populous boarding school educated 140 to 150 daughters of rural families along the same educational lines as the first. Finally, the third category of students came from the lower classes; here some 80 students received a manual primary education free of charge.[33] In the boarding school run by the Congrégation de Notre-Dame in Molsheim, a small Alsatian village of 3,500 inhabitants, the student body's social mix was equally diverse: 25 percent came from agricultural families, another 32 percent from families who ran shops or businesses, 15 percent had fathers who taught or worked in the liberal professions, and a small handful even came from the working class.[34] This diversity, however, was undoubtedly greater in small towns where no other educational options existed, and there is no clear evidence from the archives that the students in Molsheim mingled freely.

Religion also played into the success of individual boarding schools. While lay schools all taught religion, they consciously courted those families who did not want their daughters to be taught by nuns or be tempted by the religious life. In cities, such as Strasbourg, where a middle-class Protestant or Jewish population existed, schools opened that catered specifically to these groups. In Montpellier, the trade book specified that Protestant headmistresses ran two of the nine lay schools. Finally, some headmistresses catered to a foreign clientele. In western France, in particular, a number of cities such as Caen, Rouen, or Honfleur boasted boarding schools for British girls who crossed the Channel in order to acquire the trappings of what was perceived as an elite French education.[35]

Information about the clientele of girls' schools is necessarily incomplete but the accumulated pieces suggest that headmistresses targeted not only specific social groups, religious groups, and nationalities, but some focused as well on certain age groups, establishing their schools more clearly within an emerging network of primary and secondary education. Examples from two cities highlight the strategies that underlay the success of certain schools. In Nantes in 1861, inspectors recognized that of the thirteen schools that took in boarders, four or five were of high quality. The better institutions ranged in size from a mere 30 students to 125 students, with eight to forty boarders. Prestige did not, however, depend on size, since small "familial" schools often had excellent reputations. Student numbers were important, however, in establishing class size, since by the 1860s most schools organized their student bodies into classes, more or less according to age — a trend that was visible in the Paris region twenty years earlier. As a result the age range within a school was also a factor when families decided to enroll their daughters.

Educational statistics during the Second Empire divided the student body into the following age categories: below seven years old, between seven and thirteen, over thirteen years old. Naturally the type of education varied widely depending on the age. Middle-class families generally hesitated to send their daughters to a school before the age of seven, although widowed fathers often did. Still, as the charts from Nantes and Poitiers reveal, many institutions did have a certain number of young girls, and some schools, such as that of Midoux or Saint-Grière in Poitiers, catered to this age group. In Nantes, Clémentine Duplessy briefly ran a sort of primary school, which the inspectors described as "nulle." The more successful small institutions focused their energies on attracting "older" students (girls over thirteen), who attended classes in order to acquire a more advanced education. In Elisabeth Priet's school, which was considered one of the best in Nantes, sixteen of her forty students were over thirteen, and none were under seven.[36] In Poitiers, Mme de Chateaurocher had almost 70 percent of her student body in the upper age range. Larger institutions could afford to accept a wide range of ages. Religious schools, in particular, often showed the least specialization in terms of age groups, although boarders tended to be over ten.[37] Certain well-established boarding schools, such as that of Mme Eulalie d'Aubigny in Poitiers, clearly established a reputation for training older students, who came to attend classes at a more advanced level as well as to take lessons in the

Table 2 AGE RANGE OF STUDENTS WITHIN INDIVIDUAL SCHOOLS IN NANTES (1861) AND POITIERS (1866)

	No. of students	< 7 (%)	7–13 (%)	> 13 (%)
Nantes 1861				
Mlle Anne NAN	80	25.0	40.0	35.0
Mlle Elisabeth PRIET	40	0.0	60.0	40.0
Mme Hermine GILLOT	109	9.2	63.3	27.5
Mlle Marie DOMINIQUE	66	15.2	54.5	30.3
Mlle Clémentine DUPLESSY	67	52.2	41.8	6.0
Mme Marie-Anne BESNARD	110	13.6	42.7	43.6
Mlle TAUTAIN	96	10.4	55.2	34.4
Widow Marie-Anne Thérèse TOUZE	46	19.6	69.6	10.9
Mme Louise LASNIER	25	0.0	56.0	44.0
Widow Julie MASSON de BELLEFONTAINE	58	20.7	53.4	25.9
Widow Marie BUCHMULLER	48	16.7	60.4	22.9
Mlle Jeanne BOUQUE	60	16.7	75.0	8.3
Mme Clément MATHON	18	22.2	66.7	11.1
Total number of students	823			
Poitiers 1866				
Mlle Eulalie D'AUBIGNY	101	4.0	39.6	56.4
Mlle Clara BOFFINET	87	17.2	41.4	41.4
Mlle de CHATEAUROCHER	44	9.1	22.7	68.2
Mme MIDOUX	70	28.6	50.0	21.4
Mme de SAINT-GRIÈRE	37	32.4	67.6	0.0
Mme PECHEL	21	19.0	81.0	0.0
Mlle Amandine NEIL	14	0.0	71.4	28.6
Total number of students	374			

arts.[38] Since schools made a profit from these lessons, the age range of a school's clientele also reflected the strategic decisions made by a headmistress.

While it is difficult to generalize from the example of these two cities, it seems that only headmistresses in larger cities consciously set about to attract specific age groups. In Carcasonne (a city of approximately 15,000 inhabitants) where some 702 girls received an education within a boarding school, either as boarders or day students, no school distinguished itself for its "higher" education in 1867: 10 percent of the students were under seven, fully 77 percent attended between the age of seven and thirteen, and a mere 12 percent pursued their studies over the age of thirteen (despite the availability of male teachers from the local *lycée*).[39] Statistics, however, fail to reveal the more subtle differences that distinguished one school from another. In 1848 Augustine Dubois wrote proudly to her brother: "Our boarding school is now considered the most prosperous in our town [Pont Audemer in Normandy];

we take in the oldest *demoiselles*."[40] This does confirm that "better" schools were those with older students. Headmistresses necessarily operated within specific sociocultural contexts, and their ability to generate a demand for a certain type of education depended on a number of factors, including the presence of boys' schools (with their accompanying masters), the characteristics of the local middle classes, and the number and nature of rival institutions. What emerges clearly when one moves from the level of the city to individual institutions, however, is that headmistresses increasingly positioned themselves explicitly with respect to specific clienteles and recognized that in order to attract students they needed to provide a certain type of education. When one examines more closely what this education entailed, however, it becomes apparent that by the Second Empire headmistresses believed that girls' education should more than destine them to become good wives and mothers.

Academic Culture *au féminin*

A variety of sources reveal the ethos underlying girls' schools: rules and timetables, school advertisements, and printed prize-giving speeches. While historians have often relied on rulebooks to characterize the education offered in schools, I argue that the other two sources — advertisements and speeches — provide an equally revealing perspective on what teachers sought to transmit and on what they thought their clients wanted. Contrary to my own expectations, these two sources reveal a surprising range of educational objectives that undoubtedly had repercussions on the students within these schools.

Headmistresses Present Their Schools

School advertisements sought to sell the merits of specific institutions.[41] Not surprisingly, then, they replicated the stereotypes associated with girls' education. Virtually all of them insisted on the place of religion and morality in their programs, frequently emphasizing that their goal was to produce "tender and obedient girls who will become virtuous wives and good mothers."[42] In addition, many headmistresses vaunted the quality of the (male) professors who gave lessons in their school, or highlighted the possibility of learning a wide array of decorative arts. The advertisements combined descriptions of the content and ethos of the educational program with statements about the school environment, especially the quality of air and a ready access to gardens. Clearly the prose of such advertisements was repetitive, as Henri Léon suggested in his humorous portrayal of 1855. Supposedly parodying some three to four hundred advertisements, he describes the institution of Mme Prude-Boniface as being placed in the healthiest quarter of Paris, with large, well-heated dormitories, and healthy meals in sufficient quantity. Family members contributed to the lessons in religion and morality while the overall morality of the teaching environment was guaranteed by the presence of married male teachers.[43] Léon's portrait, however, obscures the variety of messages conveyed in such documents, which in fact present a far less aseptic and normalized environment than he suggests.

Specifically, school advertisements reveal an awareness that girls' education in fact served a variety of ends. By emphasizing course content, future careers, or the overall environment, headmistresses conveyed very different orientations, presumably in order to attract specific clienteles. Small, relatively nonacademic institutions generally highlighted the maternal solicitude of the teachers and the familial ambiance they sought to cultivate. The prospectus for Mme Shanahan's school for English and French girls in Paris, for example, specified that she would not indicate what she taught but rather how she envisioned her maternal obligations: "The life style … completely resembles family life, it only differs through being more regular and precise in the work and by a greater degree of emulation in the accomplishment of duties."[44] Similarly, the advertisement for the Institution Ste-Marie in Tarbes represented the teaching staff as a family: Mme Estelle Bernigole-Forcade's husband aided in the classroom, while her mother, the widow Jouvel, offered the students the maternal touch.[45] Protestant institutions frequently played up the familial character of their schools; in the Alsatian village of Barr, for example, the small number of students attending the school there was intended to reproduce "family life and the influences of the paternal household."[46]

At midcentury most institutions devoted some space to the quality of the education offered and when possible insisted on their longevity as a way of signifying their professional success. By the 1870s many schools indicated that they prepared their students for the various teaching examinations. Mme Legrand in Paris mentioned that fact first on her advertisement. Religious boarding schools in particular sought to emphasize their awareness of changing opportunities for girls. The nuns running the school of the Congrégation de Notre-Dame in Paris specified that they were "not only aware of contemporary needs but also of the prejudices that exist against religious houses in this respect."[47] Certain boarding schools stated more explicitly their concern to train girls to earn a living in a clear departure from the domestic orientation of most advertisements. Consider, for example, Mme Michel de la Thulière in the Parisian suburb of Ivry: "Honest people note with sorrow the great number of intelligent young women who languish in idleness and ignorance in the midst of an enlightened and industrious nation. … The founder of this institution proposes … to prepare useful women for society, and to offer them the means to acquire the talents that will allow them to get by honorably in the world. … All of the students at Sainte-Thérèse receive instruction so that in the future they are able to shine either in commerce or in teaching."[48] As more vocationally oriented schools developed for girls, such as the École Guépin in Nantes, some headmistresses recognized a clientele existed and accordingly adjusted their educational claims. As a result, in Bordeaux and Nantes boarding schools competed with more explicitly vocational higher primary schools.[49]

Admittedly, most boarding school advertisements advocated a thoroughly domestic vision of their students' future while seeking to attract specific categories of students. Relatively laconically, the Institution du Sacré-Cœur de Jésus in Besançon specified their interest in the "middle classes" in 1861. Run by the notoriously aristocratic congregation founded by Sophie Barat, this statement presumably was an attempt to attract a more socially diverse student body.[50] Mme Kahn's brochure (Fig. 4) devoted three quarters of the front page to a drawing of her school. The relatively austere institutional facade opens outward onto groups of young girls playing within a carefully enclosed "natural" space. This Jewish school clearly sought to attract an international clientele, since the borders of the drawing advertise the school in both English and German, although the Jewish character of the school only appears in German. The stated course program included the typical assortment of classes in history, mythology, geography, and natural history, but also mathematics for commercial purposes.[51]

Speeches delivered at prize-giving ceremonies reveal more explicitly the diversity of objectives underlying girls' education at midcentury.[52] Headmistresses or their representatives — husbands and priests — delivered such speeches before mixed audiences of local notables, parents, and the students themselves. Surprisingly, given the public and very ritualized nature of such occasions, headmistresses at times seized the opportunity to present frankly feminist visions of girls' education. In sharp contrast, priests tended to reproduce the stereotypes concerning girls' maternal futures, presumably with the headmistresses' approval.

I have found no published speeches by nuns; instead, at religious schools priests commonly took the floor to make speeches that read very much like sermons. M. Bonin, for example, emphasized the church's need for Christian mothers and added, "Who better to prepare girls for their holy maternal duties than these good nuns, these quiet creatures, these angels more than women, who have given all else up to care for girls."[53] In a similar vein, the abbé Brière described female teachers as the necessary helpmates of priests, "who by associating themselves in a way with priestly vocation, comment on, repeat, and assiduously inculcate the priests' lessons."[54] Abbé Boulage vaunted in particular the advantages of moral education and sought to inspire a love for the boarding school in the students of Mlle Ernestine Pfeiffer's school in Troyes.[55] The spirit of sacrifice and the love of others were intended to shape the hearts and souls of these future mothers.

Clergymen at times took more progressive positions. The abbé Hébert-Duperron, for example, urged the students of Mlle Hirche's boarding school in Vesoul to study

Fig. 4 Advertisement for Mme Kahn's Jewish Boarding School in Paris (ca. 1880). This sort of advertisement proliferated during the nineteenth century as headmistresses sought to attract a clientele for their schools.

to pass the teaching examination, arguing that in this day and age girls needed such examinations in the event of catastrophe. While he stressed that he did not want girls to become *savantes*, he nonetheless repeatedly praised those girls who distinguished themselves in their studies.[56] As an inspector of the Ministry of Education for the Academy of Besançon and the author of guidebooks for teachers, Hébert Duperron clearly conveyed the message that girls should take pride in their education and set themselves goals.

Headmistresses more frequently presented an active and even heroic vision of French femininity to galvanize young women to develop their reasoning capacities in order to confront an uncertain future. The Saint-Simonian Joséphine Bachellery developed a distinctly feminist perspective in the speeches she delivered before her Parisian students in the 1840s, even if she often used religious imagery to convey her meaning. This combative headmistress believed that education should prepare girls for a profession and give them the confidence to believe in themselves and to take control of their own destinies. Drawing on the example of the mother of Christ, she argued that "thanks to Mary, women's existence has become freer and more intellectual." This vision of active, professional women did not survive her move to Saint-André in the Isère. In the 1850s, before a provincial audience, she spoke of the need to develop a girl's intelligence, which is "the sunbeam that brings us closer to God." Women remained active in her speeches, but their activity was more clearly confined to the domestic sphere. A similar orientation emerged in the speeches of Eugénie Dubois. Although she said girls needed solid knowledge, this was principally in order to allow them to fulfill "their saintly and noble mission with intelligence and devotion."[57]

Some headmistresses reflected more closely on the prize-giving ceremony itself and developed a gendered perspective on the concept of emulation. Like Mme Campan at the beginning of the century, several of these speeches explicitly argued that emulation should be a feminine practice. Mlle Lequien, for example, lauded the pedagogical aspect of prizes that taught young women "the only honorable path to success is through true merit." Harking back then to the influence of women in the past and particularly to women's contribution to the progress of civilization and language, she advocated offering girls a more serious education which she encouraged them to pursue once back at home.[58] Mme Alvarès in the small town of Caussade (Tarn-et-Garonne) sought to associate emulation with feminine virtues in an obvious effort to dissociate it from a masculine spirit of rivalry: "[Emulation] will make you a strong woman according to God; it is emulation that gives you that moral superiority." On a more challenging note, Mme de Loziéras in Senlis (Oise) argued that emulation was "the mother of civilization, the sciences, and the arts," as well as the reason behind the emergence of many remarkable women now writing for young people.[59]

Unlike the speeches addressed to boys, the speeches addressed to girls appear more openly gendered, concerned with developing specifically feminine characteristics and roles. The themes of virtue, maternity, family, piety, and religion appear over and over again. According to Viviane Isambert-Jamati, boys were encouraged to identify with the more "universal" concepts of "truth, beauty and good." Unlike girls, their position in the social hierarchy was more explicitly specified, and they were also urged more to think about how their actions influenced the nation. Common to both, however, was the emphasis on the need to work and to live disciplined lives.[60]

As the variety of themes suggest, headmistresses envisioned their task in very different perspectives despite the normative weight of a domestic ideology. What inspired the rhetorical flourishes that led one woman to describe the action of famous women in the past or the other to advocate education in order to "protect yourself against unplanned circumstances and the rude blows of fate"[61] are difficult to ascertain. Some women clearly spoke from their own experience while others sought to reassure families. In any event these documents suggest that pedagogical goals within schools for the middle classes were far from homogenous.

Classroom Programs and Practices

By the Second Empire middle-class boarding schools offered a relatively established range of courses that resembled in many respects the modern curriculum within boys' schools with its emphasis on history, geography, literature, and modern foreign languages.[62] School programs testify to a broad consensus that the well-educated young lady should be familiar with the humanities, have a smattering of knowledge about the natural sciences, be able to converse in foreign languages, be competent with needle and thread, and possess a certain number of talents. School programs and pedagogical objectives varied, however, according to the social characteristics of the clientele, but they also both responded to and helped to shape familial demand. The nature of this demand began to change during this period, however, as career opportunities for women expanded. As a result, a number of schools began to offer a more explicitly "useful" plan of study that paralleled the emergence of higher primary education within the educational system.[63] A few vocational schools for girls were founded in the 1850s and 1860s, but more commonly headmistresses subtly reoriented their program to address a growing demand for genuinely useful skills.

At the top of the social ladder the call for change was relatively muted, and evidence from the more socially exclusive institutions reveals a conception of girls' education that was both encyclopedic in its range while remaining narrowly focused on the marriage market in its objectives. The memoirs of the comtesse Puliga offer insight into one such a school — the Institut Beaujon in Paris, run by Emilie Saint-

Aubin Deslignières. This large boarding school (112 students in the 1850s, including some 105 boarders) rigorously organized the academic day, providing some eight hours of study or classes a day for the older students. As in most such schools, the morning was devoted to academic lessons, generally offered by teachers within the school, while in the afternoon male and female teachers came to teach individual courses on both academic subjects and the arts. Six male professors handled the academic subjects, while mainly women offered lessons in the arts and languages: six men came to teach the piano, music, drawing, and painting, compared to seventeen women who gave lessons in music, including the harp, English, and German.[64] The school hired well-known male figures: Alphonse Dantier taught history and literature, Eugène Cortambert geography, and Emmanuel Le Maout science. Despite the emphasis on repetition and memorization, the comtesse Puliga remembered an education that was challenging thanks to a rigorous examination system (every four months students had two weeks of oral examinations) and relatively open-minded. Her long descriptions of her male teachers make clear that she associated them more with her intellectual training than her women teachers.

The memoirs are revealing as well about the objectives of this education. Alongside book learning, students spent many hours learning to decipher music, draw, paint, and speak foreign languages, all skills that were directed toward making them more eligible on the marriage market. Unlike in less elite institutions where such skills were seen as potentially productive, the comtesse is explicit in her memoirs that "marriage was the openly stated goal toward which we were being led."[65] Indeed she wrote that students had no doubts about their futures — they knew they had to learn to converse agreeably and to dance. Not surprisingly, she never mentions needlework, supposedly a mainstay in girls' education. For the elite, at any rate, it was less essential than for other social groups.

This vision of the cultured woman harks back in many ways to an eighteenth-century model and was far less evident in less socially distinguished institutions. In 1865 an Ursuline manual for girls' boarding schools emphasized: "Nothing makes a young boarder more interesting than perfect docility; even if she lacks intelligence, talent, and natural grace, she merits praise and love if she is docile."[66] This anti-intellectualism was not, of course, universal in the 1860s and 1870s. Still, the Ursulines resisted forming "modern" women who took teaching examinations:

> In Clermont some students want to prepare for diplomas and we have presented some of our students with success. But this examination illness has not yet reached epidemic proportions, and we hope that this classical land of good judgment, as our Auvergne is called, will not urge mothers to have a diploma from the Academy.... We seek to turn our older students into women of taste rather than learned women; and although we teach mathe-

matics, mineralogy, and physics, etc., we reserve our strongest efforts to the
teaching of the purity of the language, the formation of style, and historical
studies.

The future woman of taste was nonetheless introduced to a broad range of academic
subjects and allowed to develop her intellectual skills through access to a natural history study, a botanical garden, and treatises on archeology and geometry, as well as
by keeping a literary journal.[67]

Within the Société du Sacré-Cœur the concern to develop the academic quality
of their program became particularly evident after midcentury when the order created a special Conseil des études and then periodically held meetings to discuss ways
to reform the curriculum. From the outset the committee members deplored the
frivolous and overly devout character of girls' studies in their elite-oriented schools.
The issue of appointing outside male teachers was nonetheless rejected for fear this
would reveal too openly their incompetence. Instead, the commission recommended
hiring professors to train the teaching nuns themselves. In opposition to common
practice in the better lay boarding schools, they advocated maintaining classes under
the pedagogical guidance of one teacher rather than the creation of courses by specialists. The fear expressed was that courses encouraged teachers to become like the
teachers of a *collège*: "Soon one will no longer find any sign of that special maternal
behavior."[68] This effort to propose a more serious and yet domestically oriented curriculum gradually won acceptance in the order's governing body. By 1864, the order's
general council declared that class programs needed to be modified in order to
respond to broader cultural changes. Specifically, the council recommended that the
final class become more challenging and that students have fewer but longer lessons.
The revised program in 1866 remained, nonetheless, encyclopedic in its scope in
keeping with prevailing attitudes about what the cultured woman should know. The
final class, in particular, had students study grammar, rhetoric, universal history,
cosmography, arithmetic, ancient and sacred literature, physics, chemistry, and archeology. Comments about pedagogical practices reveal, however, that for the most part
students learned their lesson by rote and were incapable of applying their knowledge
to unknown situations.[69] A mere three years later the Conseil des études proposed
more changes that reveal an important shift in the elitist orientation of this teaching
order. The final class took on a far more modern cast. Instead of universal history
and ancient literature, the Conseil advocated contemporary history and the literary
history of the nineteenth century. The physics and chemistry were to be those elements that could be applied to industry. The future homemaker was also instructed
in the basic elements of common law as well as in practical hygiene and domestic
economy. Foreign languages retained their place in the curriculum, but the Conseil
recommended that students should only study one at a time in a far more serious

fashion. Rather than thirty minutes a day, they advocated an hour three times a week. Finally, Christian philosophy was added to the program in order to develop students' logical powers.[70] Although the educational ethos remained profoundly conservative, the revised program was intellectually ambitious.[71]

More modest lay schools adapted their teaching more easily to the prevailing demands of their clientele. The Dubois sisters in Pont Audemer, for example, only offered three different classes for the approximately eighty students they taught at their peak. Catering to the daughters of shopkeepers, small-scale industrialists, as well as farmers, they appear to have remained modest in their educational objectives. Without having recourse to outside teachers, the course program remained limited to the teaching of history, geography, the natural sciences, literature, and arithmetic, as well as the obligatory courses in needlework. Unlike the Institut Beaujon, the decorative arts were not in high demand, reflecting no doubt the cultural realities of a small provincial town. The Dubois were not in the business to produce the Emma Bovarys of the provinces. Indeed their correspondence reveals that in 1874 they had only one student studying drawing, two studying the piano, and a handful studying English.[72]

While needlework was universally present in school advertisements and school programs, memoirs and student diaries speak relatively little about such practices. Based on her study of girls' private writings, Colette Cosnier has argued that when girls and women write about sewing they tend to highlight their commitment to behaving in an appropriately feminine fashion, while suggesting that it was not their activity of choice.[73] The literate girls who have left us diaries rarely wax eloquent about the pleasures of stitching and darning. Eugénie Servant wrote occasionally about sewing as a student in a Legion of Honor school, but she always emphasized her weakness in this matter, whereas she excelled in academic subjects.[74] The far more conventional Mathilde Savarin, also writing in the 1880s, peppers her diary with references such as the following: "Went to mass, did my embroidery all morning." Appropriately enough, she accepted without question a schedule divided between church and feminine activities. A few days later she recorded that in a charitable gesture to a friend, she had mended her stockings.[75] Girls in boarding school undoubtedly spent hours engaged in needlework while listening to pious texts; for those who chose to write about their schooling experiences, however, this rarely took central stage.

By the 1860s the relatively modest objectives of many boarding schools were increasingly challenged both by competition from other institutions and by familial demand to prepare their daughters for active futures. This period witnessed the emergence of the first professional schools for women, such as that founded by Elisa Lemonnier in Paris in 1862. In response to concerns about the plight of the single woman, Lemonnier designed a program offering a solid primary education in three years that included as well some physics, chemistry, hygiene, and linear drawing.

After three years students had access to special courses in commerce, bookkeeping, commercial law, and industrial drawing as well as in various branches of the textile trade.[76] Similar vocationally oriented schools for girls also appeared in Nancy, Nantes, and Bordeaux.[77] The schools of the Legion of Honor reorganized their curriculum as well to respond to the growth of working opportunities for women. In 1861 the school at the Loges had a decidedly lower middle-class student body with over 60 percent coming from families of noncommissioned officers. The teachers feared that their students would leave school with ideas too exalted for the realities of their social backgrounds and prospects for the future. Reform entailed eliminating physics, literature, cosmography, and the natural sciences from the curriculum so that students could concentrate on apprenticeship training at the end of their studies. After two years of elementary education, the last three years of study were spent learning such skills as silk embroidery, clothes-making, lace-work, painting on porcelain, and the making of artificial flowers. In this way "the students who leave this school will be ready to care for themselves without any outside aid, whether they end up getting married or remain celibate." The more solidly middle-class students at Ecouen also experienced curricular reform, as the teaching order in charge of this school geared their program to preparing students for the teaching examinations, including more training in geometry, cosmography, pedagogy, and rhetoric.[78]

The development of more vocationally oriented institutions reflects how girls' education was gradually emerging into a coherent system with increasingly diversified objectives for primary, higher primary, and secondary education. However, the institutional studies of these new schools reveal an overlapping between the clientele of these schools and the presumably nonvocational boarding schools in cities. While most boarding schools did not overtly advocate careers outside of teaching, more and more they did encourage their students to entertain aspirations that were not strictly domestic.

Examinations and Diplomas: New Feminine Educational Aspirations?

The growth in the number of young women who sat for teaching examinations provides an interesting way to explore the ethos of bourgeois girls' education between 1850 and 1880. Historians have tended to present this growth as a fashionable trend, following the analysis of Octave Gréard, inspector for the Academy of Paris in the 1880s.[79] The latter noted that between 1855 and 1880 far more women than men sat for and obtained their teaching certificates: out of a total of 33,616 *brevets de capacité*, 24,171 (72 percent) went to women; in 1881 alone 3,807 women obtained such *brevets*. These diplomas opened the door to both primary and secondary teaching, given the disappearance of secondary-level degrees in 1853. Gréard insisted, however, that for most young women "their concern is not to obtain a professional degree. The diploma certifies their studies, it's a modest diploma of intellectual nobility that one seeks to obtain in a public fashion."[80] This verdict, however, may have been more applicable to the capital than to other cities. Analysis of individual schools and teaching practices suggests, on the contrary, that professional ambitions may have joined forces with the typically French emphasis on *émulation* to produce a generation of schoolgirls who pursued their studies with a variety of objectives in mind.

Virtually all boarding schools devoted some space either in their study program or in their advertisements to the question of emulation. Through a system of good and bad points, teachers sought to foster a certain attitude toward studying that influenced girls as much as it did boys, for whom academic success translated more directly into professional opportunity. The debate over prize-giving ceremonies, particularly whether they should be public or private, continued throughout the century, which is testimony to the importance attached to prizes within French culture as a whole. As the study of school advertisements showed, however, by the 1860s and 1870s headmistresses increasingly presented teaching examinations as one of the major objectives of their plans of study, a shift in emphasis that undoubtedly had repercussions within the classroom.

On a general level, the esteem attached to examinations and prizes can be seen in the publicity around these events. In Toulouse the results of examinations at the École Fénelon were printed in the local press, whereas in Poitiers the Société du Sacré-Cœur published a brochure in the 1860s that presented lists of students, the nature of their prizes, and their geographic origins.[81] Marie Fortine's school in Arrau (Hautes-Pyrénées) advertised the existence of two public examination sessions for the parents.[82] While the French educational system traditionally valued prizes, teaching examinations represented an important shift in emphasis within schools. These examinations took place outside school walls, were administered by men, and played no role in the subtle rankings within the schools themselves. They brought girls into a more public realm and opened up opportunities for girls who succeeded.[83]

Undeniably the interest in passing such examinations increased in the second half of the century. In Toulouse, for example, Germaine Bourgade found that only 69 young women obtained a *brevet simple* or *complet* between 1833 and 1850, as compared to 400 young men. Between 1851 and 1867 the number of women to obtain such diplomas soared to 463, almost rivaling the 525 young men who succeeded during the same period.[84] While normal schools would have been the logical place to prepare such examinations, their numbers were few and far between before the state mandated their creation in every department in 1879.[85] Moreover, the decision to attend a normal school represented a clear vocational orientation that most bourgeois women and their families hesitated to take.[86] Consequently, as the demand for teaching examinations increased, certain boarding schools acquired a reputation for their preparation. In Angers, the community recognized that "the Picherat boarding school has a long tradition; studies there are strong. Every year several young women take and generally pass examinations. There are many students."[87] Nonetheless, when the Goblot sisters, Madeleine and Germaine, decided to pursue their quest for the *brevet* in Angers, they enrolled in the school run by Mme Gellerat, who hired outside teachers to provide lessons in literature, English, and mathematics. Their letters home reveal clearly that this decision represented a deliberate career strategy, as their mother intended them to take over their aunt's boarding school in Pont-Audemer. In Rennes the city council offered thirty half-scholarships for worthy young women to attend a school for young ladies founded in 1844; here students prepared for the *brevet*, and when they succeeded, a philanthropic committee placed them in suitable jobs.[88] Even Mathilde Savarin, whose academic training does not appear to have been first rate, writes that her classmates prepared for and took the examinations for the *brevet*.[89]

While there is clear evidence that more and more girls studied for and passed teaching examinations in the second half of the century, it is not clear why. Was it indeed a mere fashion in educated circles to present a daughter who had a *brevet*? Many bourgeois families seem to have seen the *brevet* as a useful certificate to ensure the transition from adolescence to womanhood. For lower middle-class women, however, this *brevet* was a ticket allowing them to open their own schools. Unquestionably, however, the quest for the *brevet* reveals the ambiguities evident within the emerging system of girls' education. These ambiguities surface even more clearly when one explores more carefully the characteristics of schoolgirl culture at this time.

Schoolgirl Culture and Feminine Identity

By the second half of the century girls' schools peppered the urban landscape addressing a clientele with varied motivations for sending their daughters to school. What sort of culture existed then within these schools and how did incipient professionalism mix with the messages of domesticity? This section explores the boarding-school environment both in its material organization and in its moral contours. By paying special attention to schoolgirl writings, I seek to understand how girls experienced their daily lives and what values they consciously or unconsciously adhered to. The logic of institutional life generated modes of behavior and ways of thinking that did not directly conform to the dictates of domestic ideology. Indeed, as primary school-teachers increasingly opened boarding schools for lower middle-class girls, this environment became characteristic of French institutional life with an influence far beyond that of the bourgeoisie.[90]

Configuring the Educational Space

The physical space of boarding schools heavily conditioned the patterns of everyday life. The process of opening an institution required headmistresses to undergo inspections that ensured the building was appropriately organized to accommodate boarding students. Inspectors investigated the layout of dormitories in relation to classroom space and the private rooms of the headmistress, and also noted the position of the school with respect to the surrounding urban space. The architectural plans that headmistresses were required to submit with their applications to open a school all tended to emphasize the hermetic quality of the school as a whole. Although many small institutions were simply converted houses, the plans carefully noted the walls that sealed girls off from outside influences as well as the garden that introduced girls to more natural pleasures.[91]

Walls and enclosure were a striking aspect of boarding-school life and one that students internalized. Henriette Berthoud described the courtyard of the normal school in Sainte-Foy in the following terms: "Narrow, dark, surrounded by high walls; for newcomers it appeared vaguely sinister, but one got used to it."[92] Surveillance often underlay the concern about spatial arrangements within boarding schools, as comments concerning architectural plans indicate. In 1843 Emma Tautain was given authorization to take in twenty-six or even twenty-seven boarders if she removed certain walls and opened up spaces in the dormitory to watch over students.[93] While inspectors worried about surveillance, headmistresses worried as well about public perceptions. The Dubois-Goblot correspondence shows how headmistresses negotiated their contacts with their potential clients. In 1878 the Dubois sisters invested heavily in the remodeling of their lobby, clearly imagining that the ensuing sense of luxury would attract parents. Apparently their decision was well founded, as they proudly quoted the mother of one of their boarders saying: "You are now in a little castle."[94]

For the students living within school walls, spatial configurations were the physical manifestation of underlying educational principles. As I have argued elsewhere, rules and regulations structured everyday life within French schools.[95] These rules dictated how each moment of the day was to be spent, and they established a clear sense of hierarchy between students and teachers and between students of different classes. Rules, both implicit and explicit, governed as well the use of space within boarding schools. Dining tables, for example, established internal hierarchies. In Mme Neymarck's Parisian school, special students were given the privilege of eating with the headmistress, while in Marguerite Rousset's religious boarding school one of her punishments was to eat alone with the teachers.[96] In the boarding school of Mme Saint-Aubin Deslignières, British girls ate separately from the French girls and enjoyed certain favors: their table had a table cloth, they were given potatoes, their desserts were more varied, and above all they were allowed to speak while the other boarders were condemned to silence.[97] The recreational space of the garden was another area where students experienced how internal hierarchies structured spatial practices. Eugénie Servant described how two alleys divided the garden into four quadrants where each class played, keeping carefully to its own quadrant. A fence surrounded this play area, ostensibly to protect the students from the "wolves" without.[98] Finally, in large boarding schools, such as those of the Legion of Honor, each class had its own dormitory.

The emphasis on rules and internal hierarchies introduced a sense of moral rigidity that permeated daily life. These rules reinforced Catholic messages and stimulated students to perform as expected. Adèle Riobe, for example, noted in her diary at the age of fifteen that she worked hard, since she knew the sacrifices her family had made for her education.[99] Girls were taught to know their place both within the school and within society according to a code imposed from above. Naturally some students accepted this constant discipline more easily than others, but all acknowledged that it affected their schooling experience. In her memoirs, the comtesse Puliga emphasized the school's separation from the outside world; students within were subject to regulations that bode no exceptions: "Bending to the rule became inevitable." In retrospect she acknowledged the need for such discipline, which in her mind fortified both body and spirit.[100] Élisabeth de Bonnefonds thought the rules of her religious boarding school provided necessary structure to her life.[101] The memoirs of Émilie Darnay are equally positive in their judgment of the effect of these rules in a lay provincial boarding school: "Fifty years later I think back with delight to this blessed house ... where authority was expressed equally and mildly, where surveillance was enacted with tact and discretion."[102]

Eugénie Servant's diary offers a more immediate perspective on these rules, uncolored by the passage of time. Her initial reaction was one of revolt. When the nuns cut her long blond hair upon arriving, Eugénie protested:

> The rulebook! ... Always the rulebook. ... How I detested the insufferable rulebook!

But little by little the rigidity of the rules ceased to be resented:

> The miracle [of being happy at Ecouen] had nonetheless occurred. How? ... I hadn't realized it myself; despite missing my parents terribly, I soon succumbed to the goodness of the Mothers who sought to replace my family. I ended up obeying the rulebook, not because I had no energy to resist it, which would not have been noteworthy, but because I no longer found it detestable. At this point I was content with my life.[103]

In a sense, the structure provided by the rulebook was a comfort to Eugénie, who missed her family's familiar codes and values. Pious students, in particular, internalized rules that they presumably believed came from God. In the memoirs of Eléonore de Gaulmyn, a young classmate describes her failed attempt to make her more virtuous friend break the rule of silence. Humbled by Eléonore's refusal, the young woman takes this as an additional sign of her perfection.[104] Not all students accepted the constraints of daily life, and it is particularly striking to note how young diarists expressed their sense of confinement in spatial metaphors, frequently referring to their school as a prison, whose walls represented a barrier separating them from their families.[105] In retrospect, Juliette Lambert humorously described her first day in school in the following terms: "The main door of the school, the prison! opened. It closed behind us with a thunder clap. We entered the courtyard where the younger and older students were assembled. Mme Dufey, the headmistress, appeared. She had a mustache, I found her ugly, and she terrified me."[106] Domestic rhetoric notwithstanding, girls clearly perceived their schools not as homes in any conventional sense but as institutions.

The Lessons of Community

Rules existed for a purpose that went beyond producing docile, obedient young women. Descriptions of boarding-school life suggest that the physical and moral organization of daily life operated on two levels. On the one hand, the emphasis on discipline and surveillance reinforced hierarchies and banished intimacy in order to ensure a respect for rules. On the other hand, the consequence of these rules was to generate a sense of belonging and a moral community that was a vital and recognized aspect of boarding-school life. Teachers and headmistresses consciously sought to fashion a collective ethos where individuals devoted their energies to promoting the group. In aspiring to belong, however, students discovered that the line between emulation and competition was very fine. Teachers used emulation to promote a sense of community while condemning the masculine spirit of individualism that competition generated.

On a most basic level, girls' institutions generated an initial sense of belonging through the uniforms that boarding schools required upon entrance. Uniforms visually marked students, indicating they were part of a larger whole. Henriette Berthoud blessed the fact she was given a uniform, arguing that personal clothes led to "sensations of vanity, luxury, pride"; writing in retrospect, she applauded how school life encouraged "salutary emulation."[107] Larger schools often imitated the practice of the schools of the Legion of Honor of assigning a belt color for each class. Belts marked out a hierarchy between the classes, and younger girls were expected to aspire to the colors of the more advanced classes. Eugénie Servant describes how these signs of belonging were also used to exclude the unruly. When Jeanne B. responded impolitely to one of her teachers, the headmistress placed Jeanne in the middle of a classroom and threw the green belt of the youngest class at her feet exclaiming: "Take off your white belt, mademoiselle, and put on this one. You have conducted yourself as a person without heart or reason, all of your classmates are indignant." This expulsion from the group of whites lasted for an entire day when Jeanne was also kept physically separate from them in the dining hall, in the chapel, in the classroom, and in the dormitory.[108] Similarly, when Marguerite Rousset misbehaved, the nuns in her boarding school excluded her from the sodality of Saint Joseph. And what is more unusual, when she received bad marks, she was also excluded from all lessons and all homework. As a punishment she was required to "copy the Christian doctrine rather than anything that might be useful."[109] Some teachers clearly set more stake on the moral lessons of community than on any sort of intellectual goal. Unlike in boys' schools, these lessons were rarely enforced through physical punishments.[110]

Teachers worked hard at inspiring the collective adherence of their students to certain ideals. Virtue, obedience, honesty, and piety were certainly among the openly proclaimed ideals of girls' education, but so too was hard work, including intellectual work. Girls were expected to internalize these ideals through a constant effort at self-evaluation. A sixteen-year-old normal school student in Le Mans poignantly described this effort in her diary: "I'm going to put everything around me in order so that I'll be able to do the same to my heart. Then I hope that my efforts to become a well-behaved, hard-working student will have results. Each evening I'll examine my conscience. I'll note the little victories which I've won over myself and I think that by noting them down I'll be able to make them grow in number day by day."[111] Given the encouragement girls were given to keep stock of their actions and thoughts, it is scarcely surprising that diary writers scrupulously noted down both their good and bad points. Unlike Catholic confession, self-evaluation was not always directed to finding faults.[112]

Universally, boarding schools used a system of merits and demerits as well as medals to reinforce the importance of certain ideals and establish rankings within groups. Medals were a means of both enacting hierarchy and creating a sense of belonging. Girls' private writings are replete with statements reflecting their desires to become members of this or that group or their pride at achieving admission. Eugénie Servant, for example, admires the students who are members of a literary society in her school and would deeply love to become a member. More commonly, as described in Chapter 5, girls expressed their joy at becoming a member of a religious association, such as when Sophie Simon wrote to her mother saying she had been admitted to the Association des Saints-Anges.[113] Members of religious sodalities all wore identifying ribbons, which were a constant reminder of the importance of conforming to certain rules of behavior.

The better, more academic schools actively encouraged a sense of competition among students, as the diary of Eugénie Servant reveals. In 1880 she was in her fifth year of school at the Legion of Honor preparing for the examinations of the *brevet* (although it should be noted at no time does she link this examination to a potential future as a teacher). Her teacher, Mère Saint Eugénie, took the preparation for this examination very seriously and encouraged the pursuit of academic excellence following a time-honored method developed by the Jesuits. She divided the classroom into two competing camps and placed the top two students as the military leaders of their "battalions."[114] The students then battled it out in the classroom. Thus the constitution of groups and hierarchies could have ambiguous effects, far removed from considerations of domestic and moral virtue. More generally, the public proclamation of "good" and "bad" students was expected to generate a desire to excel for those who were not among the chosen few and a sense of community for those who were. Mathilde Salomon, the directress of the famous Collège Sévigné (founded in 1880), frowned on this approach, characterizing it as "this accounting of merit which creates an inferior quality of emulation."[115]

Within such a system, self-pride had to be sublimated and jealousy squashed, which was not always easy. At age fifteen Mathilde Savarin had to struggle with conflicting emotions when her classmates received recognition that she did not: "Only another month and a half to spend in this blessed school where I have received notions and examples of virtue; shortly I will return forever into my family's bosom where I am destined to fill the role of 'angel of the home.' Confession this morning; also today a music competition where I had to stifle my jealousy at L. Rimard's two prizes."[116] This intriguing passage highlights the tensions young girls experienced as they both recognized and accepted the values of domesticity without being able to suppress their sense of self.

Within the boarding-school community the lessons of community involved as well a constant struggle to banish the intimate. Intimacy between students, intimacy between students and teachers, and the intimacy of self-discovery were all vigorously denounced both in rulebooks and in school practices, as women's writings confirm. At the schools of the Legion of Honor linguistic regulations served to highlight differences between students in each class as well as banning familiarity within individual classes: "The *tutoiement* was forbidden and we could only call by name the students in our own class. With all the others we were supposed to say 'Mademoiselle.'"[117] The comtesse Puliga describes a far more draconian system at the Institut Beaujon where students lost their names and became numbers — Mademoiselle 23 or Mademoiselle 71.[118] The general evolution within girls' schools during this period was toward greater formality, as institutions abandoned the pretense of being surrogate homes.

The constant focus on groups served as well to prevent the development of intimate relationships. Teachers separated pairs and discouraged signs of affection between students.[119] Religious schools, in particular, inveighed against "particular friendships" in their rulebooks, whether between nuns or between nuns and their students. In place of freely chosen friends, teachers in boarding schools consistently encouraged a system of "little mothers," where older students were put in charge of younger ones. Rather than view this as an anxiety about lesbianism, whose very conception did not exist at the time, I would argue these warnings about close friendships speak more powerfully to the value attached to community in such settings.[120] Pairs undermined the community.

Uniforms, medals, sodalities, and the class itself all functioned within boarding schools to create a set of common moral values, but the community thus forged differed in notable respects from the family. Student writings highlighted this in the descriptions they offered of their teachers and particularly the headmistress, who frequently failed to conform to traditional gender stereotypes. Schoolgirls described women who inspired respect and at times fear, figures who appear more masculine than feminine. The young Protestant Henriette Berthoud for example, described the headmistress of the École normale of Sainte-Foy in these terms: "I feared her considerably, I would never have thought of approaching her for a hug or kiss."[121] The comtesse Puliga similarly presented Mme Saint-Aubin Deslignières as a distant and universally feared women, even if she nuanced this by writing that all students nonetheless considered her to be fair. The mother of one of Mlle Gellerat's students in Angers, wrote in her correspondence that this women scolded her students frequently, using fear as a pedagogical tool.[122] Religious women did not escape such masculine stereotyping as Eugénie Servant's diary reveals as well. The teacher who pushes her class to pass the *brevet*, Mère de Gethsémani, is described as having "firm and well-defined features, a strong, masculine voice," and being very strict. This description is all the more striking in that she describes other teachers in characteristically feminine terms: Mère Sainte-Thérèse is "young and pretty, and wears her nun's habit with elegance."[123]

Naturally, students also described teachers who played maternal roles in their lives, but headmistresses frequently assumed more masculine traits. Young women intuitively perceived these increasingly "professional" women as relatively distant male figures. Whether this reflects an effort to recreate the boarding school in familial terms is another story.[124] What seems likely, however, is that these varying models of womanhood undermined the effect of a domestic discourse. Indeed the hierarchy and distance that community life imposed precluded the intimacy of familial relationships.

Bending Rules and Writing the Self

Schoolgirls did not accept the dictates of institutional life without question. Although private writings reveal little trace of outright revolt, adolescent girls learned to bend and adapt rules as they forged their own sense of self. Signs of this effort to develop a sense of self can be found both in the daily practices of boarding-school life and more directly in the personal writings that form the source material upon which much of this analysis is built. Although the diaries for this period remain quite conventional, they nonetheless reveal aspirations and practices that speak to an emerging adolescent culture from the 1850s on whose values were neither those of the moral community just described nor those of domestic womanhood.[125]

Diary writing testifies to how young girls aspired to intimacy, which group life effectively squashed. Eugénie Servant devoted many pages to her special friendship with Virginie, which began in her second year at school and lasted for the following four years. They marked their friendship by studying and playing together, teaching each other words of Italian and Spanish, and even tying their uniform belts together in class. Although their teachers clearly tolerated this friendship, they were regularly punished for actions that were perceived as threatening the unity of the larger peer group. Thus when the two of them wrote out a motto to describe their friendship—"Long live Pleasure [Virginie's nickname] and long live Gaiety [Eugénie's nickname]"—and then intertwined their names and initials, the headmistress of their section subjected them to public ridicule. Similarly, when Eugénie was caught waking Virginie up in the small hours of the morning, she was banished to the dormitory of the youngest students.[126] Pauline Weill, although less expansive about her friends in her Jewish boarding school, asked her cousin and classmates to write in her diary. Cousin Sophie then wrote, "I wish to respond to your sweet letter, dear Pauline, in which you expressed your sincere friendship toward me; rest assured I feel the same and I want to repeat in my Alsatian dialect the affectionate feelings I have for you." Indeed, Pauline writes that although her years in the school were filled with "bad moments" "and sad, boring days," her most positive memories are of moments in bed with four or five friends, "chattering away like magpies."[127]

In her memoirs Jeanne Crouzet-Benaben waxed eloquent about her adolescent friendships in the 1880s at the Collège Sévigné. She clearly perceived adolescence as a specific turning point in young girls' lives, when secrets replaced games and when "friendship" (amitié) replaced "camraderie." She describes then keeping a notebook that testified to these secrets and friendships and even writing up a questionnaire for a friend to fill out in a religious notebook. Writing at the age of seventy, she was at pains to emphasize the pure nature of these friendships while recognizing, nonetheless, their exclusive and jealous nature.[128] The diary of the anonymous young apprentice teacher at the Le Mans normal school reveals more passionate longings to establish intimacy, in this case with one of her teachers. Her diary is in fact addressed to "Miss," whose every look and action inspired strong reactions. Clearly Miss sought to distance the volatile sixteen-year-old, but when she allowed greater intimacy—a hug in the morning for example—the writer accepts her daily routine far better:

"So all my day went better, and I stuck to all the rules."[129] The writer also shares her hopes and despairs with another student, Marie Savare, who is the only person she appears to trust. Clearly, this young woman had problems internalizing the values of this feminine community, torn between a form of hero worship for Miss and a serious crush on an anonymous "him." She felt constantly on the margins at the normal school; not surprisingly, she ended up dropping out.

Boarding-school life also involved many minor transgressions, venturing into areas of the school or the garden that were off-limits or merely looking at objects or people that were forbidden. Pauline Weill argued in her diary that "one cannot find a slyer, craftier person than a boarder."[130] Indeed diaries and memoirs are replete with references to adolescent defiance of rules. At age fifteen Mathilde Savarin confided this amusing anecdote to her diary: "Ah, how curiosity and disobedience are the daughters of Eve! We were forbidden to go into the garden in front of the castle because of the statues; I wanted to go there with some friends, I looked at one or two, which were not at all indecent, but there was a practically naked Amphitrite [goddess of the sea] at the bottom of the garden, I didn't look at it and left."[131] While internalizing some aspects of the school rules, notably the rejection of physical nudity, she nonetheless broke other rules when venturing into the park. Thirteen-year-old Marguerite Rousset's diary also describes many minor escapades, which are generally the source of some remorse. Having only recently celebrated her First Communion, her high-spirited antics reveal more her concern to play and have fun than an inward quest to understand herself. The older Jeanne Crouzet-Benaben noted that some girls at the Collège Sévigné escaped from study hour to go smoke cigarettes, although she did not participate because her "petite mère" prevented her. More audaciously, Pauline Weill describes escaping from her Parisian school to have her fortune told.[132]

The primarily spatial transgressions described above were frequently coupled with more cultural transgressions, particularly the sort of reading that led to Emma Bovary's downfall. Ample evidence describes how girls smuggled illicit books into school and then shared them with friends or their diaries. Age-old prohibitions about female reading practices, which were constantly reinforced in school lessons, failed to prevent girls from peeking into forbidden texts. But even accepted texts could be read in inappropriate fashion. Valérie Feuillet describes her stay at the school of the Couvent de la Visitation in Caen as a period when she escaped family pressures by plunging into piety. Trundled home by her concerned parents, her books were then burnt and her harp hidden. Many years later she described this period of adolescent crisis as reflecting a desire to be loved for what she thought, not for what she did.[133]

The decision to write a diary reveals most clearly the conflicted manner in which girls internalized the messages of boarding-school life. Diaries were used in two distinct fashions within the boarding-school setting. On the one hand, they were proposed as a pedagogical tool primarily as a means of self-evaluation. They were intended to make girls reflect on their behavior in order to conform to a well-established norm of obedient and virtuous femininity. Such diaries were scarcely private writings, since teachers or mothers then corrected them, and they often involved younger girls, around the age of the First Communion. On the other hand, some girls adopted diary writing as a way of coming to terms with their emerging sense of self. Taking to the pen rather than to the needle, adolescent girls sought to make sense of their lives through their writing, while also testifying to their sense of individuality.

This exploration of teachers, academic studies, and student lives reveals many similarities with what we know about British girls' education in the nineteenth century and testifies to a common way of envisioning gender roles in middle-class Western European society. Within France this organization of schoolgirl life and the values it transmitted were not limited, however, to bourgeois education. Normal schools, which attracted students of humbler origins, operated along very similar lines, while textbooks reinforced precisely the same feminine values of docility, obedience, and hard work.[134] The changes noted in French girls' education with the rise of expectations concerning what girls should study and for what purpose echo well-documented evolutions in Great Britain as well as in Germany.[135] Commonly, historians of British women's history have linked the vitality and strength of the late nineteenth-century feminist movement to improving educational opportunities, the appearance of reformed high schools and access to university degrees and training. Ironically, concern to prepare women more thoroughly for their domestic responsibilities opened doors for lives within the public sphere, a situation that Martha Vicinus has eloquently described in her study of the reformed boarding schools.[136]

My analysis of girls' education in France between 1830 and 1880 has emphasized a trend toward professionalization among teachers and an increasing focus on examinations within schools, both features that have been highlighted in the British case as well where examinations and competitiveness were traditionally considered unwomanly.[137] Indeed the emphasis on examinations and training that emerge in the last quarter of the century in England may have been partly inspired by French examples. Mary Carpenter and Frances Goodman, both English reforming schoolmistresses, attributed their own effort to introduce standards and examinations to their formative experiences within French schools.[138] And yet, despite the French willingness to encourage girls to emulate, the introduction of higher standards for teachers, and the general effort to provide middle-class girls with educations that would allow them to pass teaching examinations, French women failed to develop a vibrant feminist culture comparable to that which emerged in Great Britain. Are there ways of reading French school culture to understand this?

Obviously the biggest difference between French and British girls' education lies in the presence in France of religious women teachers and schools whose dominant concern was to inculcate Catholic values. Within these schools, but also more generally within lay schools, the regimented quality of daily life pushed girls to seek identification with social and religious groups that gave meaning to their lives. Schoolgirls' writing testifies to the importance of the moral and religious communities that structured their boarding-school existences, where individual aspirations only emerged with difficulty. Alice Bizot, student at the Couvent des Oiseaux in Paris, for example, wrote eloquently about becoming a member of a religious sodality, but her individual successes generated more conflicting sentiments. In 1857, she described aspiring to a school prize "solely to please her beloved mother," and in her final year, she tried *not* to win prizes so that her friends might.[139] Obviously, counterexamples can also be found, but these represent far more the exception than the norm. Juliette Lambert, for example, learned from her father the importance of work, not just to attain independence but also to achieve a sense of self-identity:

> Work, work, become somebody. There's no other way for a woman to conquer her liberty and develop her personality. While feeding and raising my daughter, I worked, I completed my instruction, which was pushed to an extreme in some areas, notably insufficient in others. Then, having written some insignificant essays, one fine day, in disgust after reading the insults Proudhon directed against Daniel Stern and George Sand in his book: *La justice dans la Révolution*, I wrote *Idées anti-Proudhonniennes*. That's when I began my literary life.[140]

In general, however, the conflicting messages of French schoolgirl culture did not produce rebels, or even many feminists of note. It is striking, in comparison with either England or Germany where such women educators as Dorothea Beale, Frances Mary Buss, or Helene Lange people the feminist landscape, that one finds few French equivalents except tardily among the ranks of Protestant Republicans. French schoolgirls may have learned to take examinations and to take their studies seriously during this period, but this rarely translated into an awareness of gender inequalities that merited direct challenge in their adult lives.

PART III

National *and* Political Visions
of Girls' Education

The final section of this book leaves the terrain of individual schools and their teachers to consider representations of girls' schooling from a more political and national perspective. The classic political interpretation of the period from 1850 until 1900 emphasizes the advent of the Third Republic and the bitter struggle between the values of the Republic and those of the Catholic Church, which culminated in the enormously divisive Dreyfus affair. Republicans portrayed this struggle in starkly dichotomous terms: the forces of democracy and the modern world were pitted against those of reaction and the past. Education played a pivotal role in this increasingly polemical opposition between two worldviews. Fearing the influence of teaching nuns in girls' education, anticlerical reformers sought more and more energetically to tear women from the hands of the church by proposing a new public system of secondary education: *collèges* and *lycées* for girls. These new institutions did not embrace the more radical feminist propositions, such as coeducation or a rigorously equivalent curriculum between girls and boys, but they did introduce new twists in the domestic model that opened the way to alternative visions of bourgeois femininity. Chapter 7, which addresses the confrontation between Republicans and Catholics over women's minds, emphasizes the need to read the political struggles of the period through lenses that consider the centrality of gender roles within these debates. Cultural issues, and notably education, were at the heart of efforts to define democracy and an emerging civic society in the second half of the nineteenth century.

The vision of women as the unwitting agents of reaction is relatively familiar. Consider, for example, the Republican reformer Camille Sée deploring the characteristics of the young woman leaving her convent school "with practically nonexistent instruction and an education that has trained her heart to hate all of the principles, all of the ideas that underlie the France of 1789 and our institutions."[1] And yet, beginning in the early decades of the century, women, and particularly nuns, were very much a part of the French civilizing mission both in the colonies and elsewhere; when the French exported their educational models they accepted that "reactionary" women would spread the seeds of civilization. Orders, such as Saint-Joseph de Cluny, were in fact agents of the French state, paid to produce French Christian families in often hostile lands. Chapter 8 then considers the far less familiar story of the French educational mission overseas. Discourses about women's education and gender roles developed in France, as in Britain, within a broader imperial context that spanned the entire century.

The same groups of women participated in efforts to reform girls' education at home and provide models of femininity abroad. Inevitably, the institutional links between the home mission and the civilizing mission had repercussions on both.[2] The effort to spread Catholic values, to inculcate habits of work and discipline, and to domesticate family life was unmistakably an effort to transpose bourgeois values onto foreign populations. The civilizing process described by Norbert Elias had ramifications well beyond Western Europe. As in earlier chapters, I emphasize the paradoxes this process generated for the women involved. The women teachers who urged girls to be good wives and mothers lived themselves very different lives, venturing into unknown lands and climates, confronting little-known social systems and settings, making do without the familiar landmarks of French urban society. The decision to participate in this mission made them exceptional women, far removed from the model they sought to promulgate.

This analysis also addresses how national features defined an evolving system of girls' education. By considering the characteristics of French institutions both in Africa and the United States, I emphasize how women implicitly and explicitly promulgated French (middle-class) cultural values that transcended the political divisions noted previously. By bringing together the insights of educational, missionary, and gender historians, Chapter 8 de-centers our reading of French girls' education. What changes when it is considered from the imperial margins of the French state in Saint-Louis, Senegal, or the cultural margins of French influence in Saint Louis, Missouri? Together these final two chapters use debates about girls' education as well as the study of schools to offer historians a fresh angle from which to understand not only the cultural politics of the Second Empire and early Third Republic but more generally the gendered characteristics of national bourgeois identity that had emerged by the second half of the century.

7

Political Battles for Women's Minds
in the Second Half of the Nineteenth Century

The years following the revolution of 1848 were critical in determining the terms of the debate concerning girls' education for both the middle and the working classes. The Falloux law in 1850 gave girls' primary education a boost by requiring villages of eight hundred inhabitants or more to open girls' schools, but it also allowed nuns to acquire an increasing dominance. With the advent of a more liberal Empire in the 1860s public debate reemerged about the goals and objectives of education in general, and in this increasingly charged political climate discussions about girls' education took on a polemical tone, constituting one of the rallying cries of an emerging Republican opposition.[1] Echoing Jules Michelet's earlier pronouncements against the clerical influence over women, such major political figures as Jules Simon and Jules Ferry introduced girls' education into public debate.[2] In particular, these politicians made family life and the relations between husband and wife a political issue:

> There is going on today a silent but persistent struggle between the society of the past . . . with its edifice of regrets, beliefs, and institutions which does not accept modern democracy and the society that emerged from the French Revolution. Women cannot be neutral in this combat; optimists, who do not want to see the heart of the issue, can imagine that women's role is negligible . . . but they do not perceive the secret and insidious support she offers to this society of the past and that we wish to banish forever . . . he who holds the woman, holds everything, because she holds the child as well as the husband.

In this oft-quoted speech, Ferry concluded by arguing that girls' education was the key to democratic politics: "Democracy must choose on pain of death; citizens must choose; woman must belong to science or to the church."[3]

While such statements were not new in the 1860s, their impact spread and, most significantly, received close attention within the Ministry of Education. With the appointment of liberal minister Victor Duruy in 1863 anticlerical Republicans discovered a champion for their viewpoints, and for the first time since Napoleon I founded the schools of the Legion of Honor, bourgeois families discovered a political figure who astutely recognized the political significance of their daughter's education, albeit in somewhat different terms than the emperor some sixty years earlier.

Duruy's decision to create secondary classes for girls briefly placed gender and bourgeois culture at the center of political debates in the late 1860s. In the turmoil surrounding these courses clerics, feminists, and Republicans articulated a wide range of positions that reveal not only the strength of traditional Catholic visions of womanhood, but also the emergence of new professionalized identities for women. The polemical character of the debate hardened and radicalized both individual and collective positions about women's place in French society, producing strict oppositions between clerical and anticlerical attitudes.[4] What has been less noticed, however, is how the debate introduced sexual politics into the discussions about who should teach girl students.

This chapter begins by examining how the French state sought to establish girls' secondary education, initially through Duruy's secondary courses in 1867 and then through the creation of *lycées* and *collèges* in 1880. In particular, I am interested in the rhetoric employed to disqualify existing institutions and female teachers, both lay and religious. At the same time, the reemergence of a feminist press and the development of feminist organizations allowed a somewhat different perspective to emerge concerning girls' education. This perspective drew heavily on earlier discourses about professionalization but gained far broader attention in the context of a democratizing society. Moreover, the use of comparisons with other national settings gave both feminists and their anticlerical colleagues a political tool to criticize existing educational paradigms in French society. Finally, the chapter concludes with an analysis of the religious and clerical response to these debates. The church's concern to maintain its control over women's minds produced a variety of political responses, not all of which were conservative.

Challenging the Church's Empire: The State's Response

Victor Duruy was appointed minister of education in 1863. Although a liberal and a deist, the fifty-two-year-old historian had gained Napoleon III's favors and had been named inspector of the Academy of Paris in 1861. Still, his appointment as minister was a surprise, testimony to his integrity and to the emperor's esteem for his reform efforts. Duruy's first action on learning of his appointment was to send Napoleon

III a program of action, which included the organization of girls' education. He argued: "A portion of our contemporary difficulties stem from the fact we have left education in the hands of people who are neither of their time, nor of their country."[5] The results of the survey on secondary education that he initiated in 1864 (analyzed in the previous chapter) served to confirm his impression that nuns dominated girls' education. His solution then was to urge the creation of secondary courses, thus initiating the French state's intervention in girls' secondary education.[6] Building on what appeared to be a cultural consensus about the need to develop girls' schools, Duruy's initiative nonetheless represented a highly political response to the "problem" of girls' education.

The Duruy Courses

His call for reform began by stating: "One must found secondary education for girls, which in point of fact does not exist in France."[7] Duruy proposed the creation of secondary courses — not boarding schools — to improve bourgeois family life:

> Young girls receive the education of the heart and their first religious teachings in the domestic home, in the familial sanctuary.... To fortify [a woman's] judgment and to enrich her intelligence, to teach her to govern her mind and to place her in a condition to assume, with another person, the tasks and responsibilities of her life without departing from the role that nature has assigned to her, a woman needs strong and simple instruction. The latter adds the strength of straight thinking to religious feelings, as well as enlightened reasoning to the dangers of the imagination.[8]

The decision to leave religious education in the home or in the churches represented a dramatic departure from institutional girls' education even if the stated objectives of this education were far from revolutionary. By distinguishing instruction from education, the courses proposed "a combination of general literary instruction, the study of foreign languages, and drawing with practical demonstrations of scientific knowledge." In principle the three-to-four-year course of study resembled special secondary education for boys, minus Latin and Greek. In terms of content, the Duruy courses were indistinguishable from the better programs in existing boarding schools. Like most boarding-school headmistresses, Duruy emphasized that these courses were not intended to produce *bas-bleus*, but rather informed and rational private women. And yet professional concerns were not absent even if the minister's public rhetoric did not emphasize them initially. His private writings confirm that he saw the need to open "honorable careers" to women, and these courses were also expected to train qualified secondary-school teachers.[9]

The state was unwilling, however, to use public funds for these courses, so town governments were urged to take the initiative, provide locales, and pay the professors out of the fees collected from the students. The absence of qualified women teachers led Duruy to recommend using male professors from the secondary schools. Courses run by male teachers already existed in France, notably in Paris. What distinguished these courses, however, was the concern to organize the courses in a three-to-four-year cycle so that each individual course contributed to a coherent educational program. Girls were expected to attend from the age of fourteen to eighteen, accompanied by their mothers or governesses, as they did in Lévi-Alvarès's Cours d'éducation maternelle. Duruy's intent was to distinguish his creation from such worldly gatherings as the lectures at the Collège de France, even if he praised such gatherings in the provinces. In 1866 he wrote to the Empress Eugénie about the conferences offered in the Academy of Nancy: "These evening chats on literature, science or art are an agreeable diversion from the banalities of provincial life, and in a certain measure they fill the emptiness we leave in [women's] minds. But I don't want to make women into *bas-bleus*. A mother's influence on her son and on his thinking is too important for us not to be anxious when we see women remaining outside the intellectual life of the modern world."[10]

Between 1867 and 1870 approximately sixty courses opened throughout France, but many failed after less than a year, and in 1870 the Franco-Prussian War ended this experiment in liberal reform. In 1878 a mere ten still survived.[11] The actual course content varied widely from town to town, although in most cases no real cycle of studies was ever established, since they closed down so rapidly. Mayeur's analysis of twenty-nine of the course programs confirms nonetheless that in most cases towns offered a relatively broad program.[12] A system of subscriptions for the different classes meant, however, that students did not respect this breadth, picking and choosing the classes that interested them. Moreover, the general refusal to take examinations meant that the *cours secondaires* resembled worldly gatherings more than their creator had intended. In Nîmes, for example, the courses began with a dictation, and students then took notes. They handed in written work, which was corrected and annotated without any verbal explanations "so not to vex people," but they did not take examinations.[13]

The courses were most successful in cities with significant middle-class non-Catholic populations, such as in Bordeaux, Montpellier, Nîmes, Guebwiller, Wissembourg, and Mulhouse, as well as in cities with strong liberal or Republican traditions, such as Rouen, Orléans, Amiens, Périgueux, and Auxerre.[14] Local institutional offerings for girls also often determined the fate of these courses. In major cities, such as Toulouse or Strasbourg, where there existed well-respected boarding schools, both religious and lay, no courses were ever founded. The strength of clerical opposition condemned these courses in Nantes, Brest, Angers, Laval, and Le Mans.[15] The attitude of local lay teachers could make a difference, notably in Clamecy in the center of France, where Mme Germenot actively enrolled her students, but also in Vesoul in the east and Metz in the north, where Mlle Hirsch and Mme Mamer both did the same.[16] Elsewhere, however, lay mistresses either saw the courses as a form of competition (Périgueux) or feared clerical reaction if they sent their students. In Avignon for example, one headmistress declared to the principal of the *lycée*: "I am so appalled at the idea of these courses, that not only I do not want anyone to even imagine that I might take my students there, but I do not want anyone to know you even came to speak to me on this subject."[17]

Administrative reports reveal, moreover, that despite occasional local enthusiasm, most courses at their peak attracted very few students, most of whom were Protestants or Jews.[18] The cost of the courses — which ranged roughly from thirty to seventy francs a trimester — restricted their access to the middle classes. Analyses at the time reveal the courses mainly attracted the daughters of middle-ranking civil servants, particularly teachers, as well as those of employees, and shopkeepers. A few elite families also supported Duruy's creation, such as the marquis de Moustier, the empress, who sent nieces, and a few wealthy Protestant families, but bourgeois Catholic families shunned this liberal initiative.[19] Clerical opposition, which I will explore later in this chapter, condemned Duruy's initiative to failure, since in the end only some two thousand young women attended these courses between 1867 and 1880, a small handful compared to those who were educated in boarding schools. Still, these courses merit attention, since they heralded the state's involvement in girls' secondary education and its commitment to a nonreligious content. As a result, when Sée began his campaign to create girls' *collèges* and *lycées*, both political and public opinion was already familiar with the terms of the debate and its stakes.

The Camille Sée Law

On December 21, 1880, French Republicans passed the Camille Sée law, creating a national and public system of *collèges* and *lycées* for girls.[20] The law was passed at the same time as the Ferry laws, which concerned primary education. Because it concerned middle-class education, the flavor and tone of the new schools bore little relation to those of the primary system, where education became compulsory, free, and secular. The feminine *collèges* and *lycées* were neither obligatory nor free, and religion remained in the curriculum as an elective. Like Duruy before him, Sée was concerned to provide a serious education that would allow women to become the intellectual partners of their husbands. The report presenting the law described these schools as a means for women to exert their intellectual faculties in order to return to their families "adorned with all the graces of the mind and prepared to fulfill [their] maternal duties, that is to teach."[21] Despite the demands of feminists groups at the time, the Sée law created a secondary school system that was detached from any professional preoccupations, since the course of studies did not lead to the *baccalauréat*. By creating a separate curriculum, sanctioned by a uniquely feminine degree, the French Republicans who defended this bill proclaimed their adherence to a vision of bourgeois femininity whose cultural sway was already under attack at the time. As Françoise Mayeur has pithily argued, Sée's concern was to strip girls' instruction of all utilitarian concerns.[22] Paradoxically, this law, which Republican historians hailed enthusiastically, badly misjudged the changing aspirations of the French middle classes.

The debates surrounding this law, which lasted from 1878 when Sée first introduced his proposal until December 1880 when Republican solidarity won the day, clearly reveal how women's place in French society had acquired national and patriotic meaning. As Philip Nord has argued, Republicans predicated the triumph of democratic institutions and practices on the moral reform of the middle-class home.[23] But Republican discourse also linked secondary girls' education, democracy, and national values: "The absence of secondary education for women maintains intellectual anarchy in the nation. Most women remain unfamiliar with the ideas and the sentiments of modern and Republican France. Some say the German schoolteacher beat France [in 1870], but France had a shortage of soldiers and citizens. It's the French female teacher, the French mother, who will form future robust generations of citizens and soldiers."[24] Without a doubt, the state's decision finally to intervene in girls' secondary education represented a political decision, governed far more by national and Republican preoccupations than by a liberal concern to educate women as individuals. Republican pedagogues owed greater allegiance to Rousseau than to John Stuart Mill.

The issue of religion within the curriculum polarized opponents and supporters of the bill. The cultural association of women and religion made it inevitable that even the suggestion that religious instruction would not be present in the curriculum would raise Catholic hackles. The Catholic opposition attacked the bill as another step in a "series of attacks against God and religion."[25] In the name of freedom of conscience, they argued that the state could not refuse Catholic girls a religious education. The conservative senator Pierre Charles Chesnelong, in particular, denounced the state's intention to use public funds to banish religion from the curriculum: "The religious neutrality that you proclaim is but a chimera, and your godless education will become over time an education against God."[26] In the end the senators voted that religious education by ministers of the different religions would be available upon parental request in both day and boarding schools.

The debate over whether the new institutions would be boarding schools or day schools raised another set of issues whose implications speak to the Republican discomfort with the professionalization of girls' education in general. Sée wanted to open boarding schools in order to allow girls from rural areas to benefit from this education. The Republican Paul Bert led the opposition to this aspect of the law and eventually won, although municipal councils could vote to create boarding schools, if they were prepared to fund them.[27] Mayeur has argued that the defeat of the boarding school option reflected an important shift in French bourgeois attitudes toward the surveillance and discipline characterizing such institutions. At a time when boys' boarding schools were coming under attack, opponents argued it was unseemly to propose such organizations for girls: "This cloistral regime, similar to that of the barracks and the convent, does it really seem so desirable that we wish to spread it to girls' education?"[28] But in fact girls' boarding schools were already widespread. On an ideological level, the Republican opposition emphasized its refusal to undertake the moral education that went along with housing girls for twenty-four hours a day. Republican arguments speak more, however, to an undercurrent of anxiety about the professionalization of middle-class girls' education than to any real opposition to the principle of educating girls in boarding schools. Deputy and former minister of education Agénor Bardoux expressed this anxiety most clearly when he asked how the state would find administrative personnel.[29] Obviously such schools would require women administrators, and yet supposedly women were not destined for such tasks.

The law established a three-year cycle of studies with an additional two-year program for the more intellectually ambitious. Even so, the five years of girls' secondary education remained two years shorter than that of boys. The program diverged little from the standard fare of better boarding schools: modern languages and French literary classics, history, and an introduction to such scientific studies as geometry, chemistry, physics, and natural history. The most unusual aspect of the curriculum was the decision to replace religious instruction with moral instruction, although parents could request to have their daughters attend religious classes. Sée had championed the study of philosophy, but this lost out to moral instruction. The feminine cast of the educational program can be seen in the concern to develop gymnastics to ensure the "future of the race," as well as hygiene, domestic economy, and needlework. Three hours a week were devoted to the arts, especially drawing and music, given "the influence that women exert on art and taste."[30] All told, nonetheless, classes occupied less than twenty hours a week, compared to boys who had on average twenty-five hours of classes a week in 1880.[31] The Republican concern to form French mothers, revealed itself most clearly in the refusal to sanction these studies with a "practical" degree. The *diplôme d'études secondaires* opened no doors except those of the conjugal home.

This issue of professionalization reemerged when the state created the École normale supérieure de Sèvres in 1881 to train the future secondary-school teachers of the new girls' *lycées* and *collèges*. Normal school training implied professionalization, but as Jo Burr Margadant's study of this school has shown, the Sèvrienne tradition was from the beginning torn between the contradictory impulses of Republican meritocracy with its underlying liberal belief in individual merit and a conviction that the new profession would create "distinctly feminine traditions based on expectations for their sex within the home."[32] The decision to train women teachers to teach other women teachers and students was not, however, a neutral one. Although men taught girls in other countries, and the Duruy courses had used men as well, when the state finally decided to create a girls' secondary system, it assumed the need for women teachers. As one observer noted, "It would have been impossible, given public opinion in this country, to place men at the head of girls' schools."[33] Sée actively encouraged the feminization of the profession of secondary school teaching on two grounds. First, he argued, it was important to provide professional opportunities for impoverished middle-class women. Second, he insisted on women's special aptitude for teaching, echoing arguments elaborated in the revolutionary aftermath. By naturalizing women's pedagogical potential, Sée implicitly reaffirmed the socially conservative implications of his reform. Yes, Republicans wanted thinking and rational wives and mothers, but they were far from advocating a rethinking of gender roles that would have led women to assume more active lives in public.

Nonetheless, the state's creation of a public system of secondary schools for girls in 1880 reflected a major shift in French educational politics even if public opinion remained largely indifferent.[34] Bourgeois girls' education was no longer the privilege of solely private initiatives, be they religious or lay. In practical terms, however, the Republican concern to form the "future mothers of men" did not represent a radical departure from the Napoleonic vision almost eighty years earlier. While Catholics deplored the creation of what Senator Desbassayns de Richemont described as the "University's feminine wing," feminists quickly regretted how the new program failed to promote feminine professional concerns. Hubertine Auclert, in particular, denounced the law's shortcomings: "The law on secondary instruction for girls was approved by the Legislature, but the *status quo* remains. . . . As long as women are only able to acquire knowledge that they cannot use, this knowledge will bring them nothing for themselves, women will continue to be worth only the money they possess."[35] By turning now to this feminist discourse about secondary school education for girls, it is possible to see how another set of concerns fashioned the debate about women's place in French society in the last quarter of the century.

In a Different Key: The Feminist Position on Girls' Education

Although feminists per se played a negligible role in the state's decision to create *lycées* and *collèges* for girls, they nonetheless used the issue of girls' education to develop a political argument about the need to reconsider gender roles and attributes.[36] For feminists, like the Republican educational reformers, the issue of who controlled women's minds was an important one, but by turning their attention more closely to how women would then use their minds, they moved the debate from the family to civil society. The "feminist" voices of the French Revolution, the Saint-Simonian period, and the revolution of 1848 had all addressed the issue of girls' education, but in the 1860s and 1870s education became an explicitly political issue, as women like Julie-Victoire Daubié questioned the place of women in the French political economy. By arguing that women should be given the means to achieve economic independence, feminist voices linked educational reform to far broader reforms in the family, in civil society, and ultimately in politics. Feminists generally supported the positions of such men as Duruy and Sée, but the more radical voices envisioned a far different future for women than the home.

The reemergence of feminist themes occurred a decade after 1848, in response to the misogynist or antifeminist pronouncements of intellectual figures on the left, notably Jules Michelet and Pierre-Joseph Proudhon.[37] Well known for his famous statement in 1846 that women had only two possible roles, that of housewife (ménagère) or harlot (courtisane), Proudhon continued to develop his antifeminist perspectives in such writings as De la justice dans la Révolution et dans l'Eglise (1858) and La pornocratie, ou les femmes dans les temps modernes (1875). De la justice offered a supposedly scientific analysis to demonstrate women's "physical, intellectual, and moral inferiority." Michelet's writings in L'amour (1858) and La femme (1860) were more effusive in their praise of women's special attributes, but he too argued for women's difference from and hierarchical inferiority to men. Coming at a time when the biological sciences were increasingly establishing women's "natural" inferiority to men, these statements stimulated a number of responses. Although far less well known than the male writers, women like Juliette Lambert and Jenny d'Héricourt wrote detailed counterarguments that created a common store of concepts for latter battles. And among the recurring themes these new feminist voices articulated was the need to rethink the ethos and the objectives of girls' education.

Juliette Lambert (later Adam) was the first to challenge Proudhon's text, in her Idées anti-proudhonniennes sur l'amour, la femme et le mariage (1858). The daughter of a leading Republican figure in her home town in Picardy, Lambert achieved national recognition both though the salon she ran in Paris and through her influential literary magazine, La nouvelle revue. In 1858, however, she was only twenty-two, albeit well connected to leading intellectual figures, such as Charles Fauvety and Charles Renouvier.[38] In her Idées anti-proudhonniennes she refuted Proudhon's arguments, but also emphasized that for women to assume responsibilities in French society they needed to be educated for a professional future, since "work alone has emancipated man and work alone will emancipate woman." The sorry state of women's education produced mere dolls, she argued, hence the need for reform. Her autobiography highlights her own eclectic educational experiences; while she did attach some benefit to her formal education in a boarding school, she attributed her later notoriety more to the lessons and encouragement of her father. He urged her to seek real work and to acquire independence and freedom of thought.[39]

Her contemporary, the Protestant feminist Jenny d'Héricourt, also saw women's education as a key to their emancipation: "It is radically false that nature made men rational and women emotional; it is education and morals that made them thus: feelings and rationality are equally distributed. . . . The brain is the instrument of progress."[40] In her writings, she refuted Proudhon's biblical, historical, and natural evidence for women's inferiority and pleaded for expanding women's professional opportunities. This plea was clearly grounded in her own experiences; before becoming a midwife and acquiring a degree in homeopathic medicine, she was a teacher and the proprietor of a boarding school on the rue de Picpus in Paris and thus well situated to understand the importance of education.[41]

The feminist call to improve women's education frequently drew on the Republican and anticlerical arguments developed earlier: by reforming education, family life would be regenerated.[42] Maria Deraismes's opening speech at the Grand Orient in 1867 developed precisely this argument: "[We need] complete instruction for women; the true key to progress is there. The home must no longer be a setting for narrow thinking and mean calculations; we must stop having great ideas brush up against the doors of the home without being welcomed in."[43] An articulate orator, Deraismes devoted her adult life to promoting women's rights and emancipation. In particular, she collaborated with Léon Richer in the feminist newspaper *Le droit des femmes* (1869–91) and was a founding member of the Association pour le droit des femmes. Her lectures and her political commitment to the Republican anticlerical cause made her a public figure: in 1881 she served as vice president of the first national Anticlerical Congress, and in 1882 she became the first woman member of the Masonic lodge, Les Libres Penseurs du Pecq. Less radical than such contemporaries as Hubertine Auclert, who devoted her energies to winning the vote for women, Deraismes focused on the historical, moral, religious, and social factors that maintained women in a state of subservience to men. Her oft-repeated conviction was that women's inferiority was a human invention, and education, particularly religious education, was largely to blame. More interesting, she argued that the current state of women's false education was not only a catastrophe for the family but for the nation as a whole: "The elimination of women from the administration of general concerns causes considerable damage to nations and impedes their development."[44] She insisted that women were capable of administering, working, and creating on a par with men: "When called upon, [women] know very well how to administer, they run businesses well, and many have made fortunes. . . . In the arts, in the sciences, in politics, in literature women have risen to the level of genius. In a given situation, woman's inferiority to man, stems from not having received the same professional education."[45]

In a more prosaic tone, the feminist weekly *Le droit des femmes* reiterated the message that women needed to develop their reason in order to assume their responsibilities in civil society and to exercise power.[46] Frequent articles about girls' education reported on developments in vocational training, the Duruy courses, and higher education. Somewhat surprisingly, the arguments for such an education were rarely couched in liberal or individual terms, instead the authors repeated the classic Republican argument based on the need to improve family life. This was the viewpoint developed by Félix Hément in the first issue of the journal in April 1869: "It is high time that a solid and appropriate instruction cease to be the unique privilege of men: [women require education] not only to form them better for the society in which they live, but also to prepare mothers for their providential role. By sharing this privilege, men will still achieve the greater well-being."[47] The newspaper also publicized the existence of associations, such as André Léo's Société de revendication des droits de la femme. Justifying their creation of a lay primary school, Léo and her fellow feminist signatories wrote: "The key to our difficulties and the object of our struggles is new teaching for a new society. . . . The means that has been chosen is schooling and to begin with, naturally, a primary school. But a school created to prepare citizens and not subjects, to develop reason, not to lead it astray, to stimulate children's initiatives rather than to stifle them."[48]

The fiery socialist Hubertine Auclert also saw women's education as a critical issue. In an interesting inversion of the traditional argument, however, she insisted: "Women must vote in order to be educated. Young girls will never have serious instruction, a scientific and rational instruction, until women have the right to debate budgets, to introduce a pair of scales in the budget of public instruction, and to establish the principle of equality for all children in these scales, that is to say, the same number of schools, the same quantity of science for girls as well as for boys."[49] Consistently she insisted that education and citizenship were intimately interconnected, but she openly mocked those who argued that women needed instruction before acquiring the vote, noting in 1881 that illiterate and uneducated men were allowed to vote.

Feminists were aided in their efforts to promote girls' education at the primary level by Jean Macé's Ligue de l'enseignement, which was founded in 1866. Particularly strong in the north and east, the Ligue promoted primarily popular coeducation but was also attentive to the needs of middle-class girls; in Marseille, for example, the Association phocéenne pour l'instruction des deux sexes emphasized the emancipating possibilities of education and attracted 2,500 members.[50] Feminist alliances with Freemasons and Republicans gave a decided anticlerical tint to their calls for an improved education for girls, making this issue an overtly political struggle between liberal Republicans advocating reason and Catholics advocating faith.[51] Nonetheless, the objectives of this education often remained highly traditional. Richer himself argued: "The question is not to have both sexes always and ever follow an absolutely identical curriculum. No. Given the difference of occupations appropriate for men on the one hand and for women on the other, what we ask for women is an equivalent education to that which men receive. This instruction may be different if women themselves desire it but it cannot be inferior."[52] Ultimately, the feminist call for reform acquired the greatest bite when it turned to the issue of vocational education. Julie-Victoire Daubié, in particular, moved the discussion about education onto new ground as she argued for changes that would allow women to achieve greater independence in the economic sphere.

Education, Professionalization, and Women's Independence: Julie-Victoire Daubié's Contribution

The 1860s witnessed the emergence of a number of new institutions and associations that promoted the professionalization of girls' education. This period was also one of considerable questioning about the objectives of boys' education, with the emergence of special secondary education. Given these educational developments for boys and the intellectual climate that allowed figures such as Adam, d'Héricourt, and Deraismes to acquire some notoriety, it is less surprising that vocational schools multiplied after 1860, following the example of Elisa Lemonnier's Parisian Société pour l'enseignement professionnel des femmes in 1862. Most of these initiatives developed in ideological tandem with Republican and anticlerical goals. In the working-class city of St. Etienne, for example, the municipal council pressed for the creation of a superior school for girls in 1867: "In order to create the nursery from which capable subjects will emerge, able to enter into all careers, accounting, drawing, teaching, and so many others which would be far better filled by women than by men."[53] In the end the city opened a secondary course along the lines advocated by Duruy (hence far less vocationally oriented), but unlike the other courses it was free and lasted until 1889. The development of vocational courses for girls began in earnest in the late 1860s, spawning as well an accompanying pedagogical literature.[54] For the most part these initiatives to develop trade schools or higher primary schools, which also had a vocational orientation, were inspired by a concern to provide greater opportunities to lower middle-class girls, but they did not have explicit feminist objectives.[55] These were most apparent in a few isolated associations whose members explicitly linked education and women's emancipation. This was the case with

Elisa Lemonnier and Mme Adolphe Bertillon's Société pour l'enseignement professionnel des jeunes filles as well as with André Léo's society, Société de revendication
des droits de la femme, founded in 1869.[56]

Like Joséphine Bachellery during the July Monarchy, a few women teachers adopted
openly feminist stances, using their experiences as educators to argue for the need to
reconceive girls' education. Among the more dramatic of such teachers was Céleste
Hardouin, the head of a Parisian boarding school; she split with the more moderate
Léon Richer in 1875 in order to found the Ligue française pour l'amélioration du
sort des femmes.[57] Two other boarding-school teachers struck more moderate notes.
The most renowned, Marie-Joséphine Marchef-Girard, a teacher and the future
head of the Collège Sévigné, criticized lay education for "answer[ing]" neither to the
demands of the present nor to concerns for the future," while religious schools failed
to instill a sense of the "fatherland, society, the world, or the family."[58] Marchef-Girard
endorsed a domestic vision of women's role in society but this did not preclude, in
her opinion, the need to train a professional corps of women teachers.[59] Similarly,
headmistress Mme Caubet-Darius urged the government to create a superior normal school for women in 1869, echoing the ideas of Bachellery in 1848.[60] Increasingly,
educators were pushing the boundaries of women's sphere.

The most articulate defense of women's right to a vocational education came from
Julie-Victoire Daubié, whose experiences battling to have her educational qualifications recognized led her to privilege education in her analysis of the plight of the
"poor woman." Well known as the first woman in France to receive a *baccalauréat*
degree in 1861, she devoted her adult life to promoting women's causes, especially in
the pages of the feminist paper *Le droit des femmes*. In 1859 her prize-winning response
to a competition launched by the Imperial Academy of Lyons brought her ideas to
public attention. Her essay in response to the question about how to improve the
economic situation of women principally in moral terms was first published in
the *Journal des économistes. Revue de la science économique et de la statistique*, between
1862 and 1865, and then in an abbreviated version under the title *La femme pauvre au
dix-neuvième siècle* in 1866.[61] The latter was reissued in 1870 after receiving an honorable mention at the Universal Exhibition of 1867.[62] Now hailed as a feminist classic,
Daubié's text deserves special attention for how she intertwined economic and moral
issues to make girls' education a political issue.

Daubié devoted well over a third of the initial version of her essay to girls' education, paying particular attention to the situation of women teachers. Her primary
argument was that women teachers suffered from what she termed the "university
and convent monopoly." By this she meant that lay teachers suffered discrimination
both from the competition that religious orders offered and from men who received
unfair advantages thanks to the existence of normal schools and fellowships within

the French University. Specifically, she highlighted the difficulties of women laboring within the private sector when a powerful male public sector existed in education. Her essay drew on both anticlerical and feminist arguments to denounce the conditions under which laywomen teachers taught: "*Our boarding schools are free* [in the sense of private] *institutions!* Free! But of what, I beg you! Free to turn their backs in humility and receive legislative kicks and whiplashes as well as monastic blows."[63] She then offered numerous examples to show how laywomen suffered from the unfair competition of religious orders, given the high cost of acquiring a school and a clientele. More significant, she highlighted the gendered nature of anticlerical politics in France, arguing that the University paid little heed to the place of women professionals in contemporary struggles: "If the University with its science, its subsidies, and its privileges complains of the encroachment of the clergy . . . if the alarm of famous orators and eminent writers have divided France into two rival camps, I ask you once again what are the chances in this struggle for poor women . . . after having ground us with the university anvil and the clerical hammer you dare speak about our freedom!"[64] Drawing on commonly used rhetoric, she associated the plight of laywomen teachers with that of prostitutes, describing the "mercantile" policies of boarding schools in evocative terms: "They spread their wares like in shops, they set up stages like in theaters, they powder like actresses and flatter like parasites."[65] Like Jules Simon writing about women workers at the same time, Daubié emphasized the thin line that existed between honest working women and fallen women but offered concrete feminist solutions that her male colleagues eschewed in their defense of the family wage.[66]

Her impassioned plea to reconsider the status of women teachers was ultimately a political argument about the need to reconsider the relationship of women to the teaching state in order to offer women the same rights and privileges as men. By emphasizing how men enjoyed privileges in girls' education, she asked why women did not enjoy the same privileges in boys' education. And, above all, she advocated a common education for boys and for girls: "Whenever the object of science is to reveal truths, a mode of teaching that does not apply to both sexes is by definition bad." Like many before her, she drew on the argument about family life but she added a feminist political twist by emphasizing as well women's individual rights: "Next to the social advantages of this common education one should consider as well the personal rights of women, taxpayers like men, they should find the same security and the same possibilities as men do in professional careers."[67] For Daubié, women's emancipation went hand in hand with their access into higher education, which then opened professional doors.[68] While she ultimately concluded that the moment was not yet ripe to create a women's university in France, all of her other solutions emphasized offering women the same economic, professional, and personal opportunities that men enjoyed. By moving the argument about girls' education from the terrain of family politics to that of economics and the state, Daubié highlighted the political nature of contemporary thinking about gender roles, but she also showed how this thinking was rooted in national stereotypes whose underpinnings needed to be questioned.

On the Political Uses of Comparisons

The political battle for women's minds occurred in France at a time when educational matters acquired an increasingly international perspective. The Universal Exhibitions, in particular, offered occasions when nation-states could present their specific strengths, and educational innovations played a significant role in these events. In France interest in foreign educational systems developed in the second half of the century as politicians and reformers sought to structure the increasingly diversified educational offerings.[69] In the aftermath of the French defeat to Prussia in 1870, much ink was spilled debating the comparative merits of the Germanic and French primary educational systems, since the Prussian victory was frequently attributed to the superiority of the German schoolmaster. The curiosity about foreign systems included attention to girls' education, particularly girls' secondary and higher education, where many perceived the French to be lagging behind their neighbors.[70] Both Republicans and feminists drew on international comparisons to further their reform efforts; in some instances these comparisons were clearly intended to stimulate a national reflex, but in other instances the intent was more nuanced. In particular, feminists used examples from other national contexts to criticize French educational paradigms, notably its centralization. More interesting, feminist explorations of gender roles and attributes allowed them to reveal how national stereotypes determined these roles and locked women into situations of inferiority. The discussion about coeducation in particular offers a way to understand how reformers used comparisons to denounce the ideological underpinnings of the developing French educational system for girls.

Julie-Victoire Daubié offered the most systematic use of international comparisons in her effort to change the status of women in French society. In *La femme pauvre au dix-neuvième siècle* Daubié titled a section of her initial essay "Panascopic glance over women's primary, secondary and professional education in the two worlds." By highlighting the variety of opportunities available to girls in the Scandinavian countries, in northern Germany, and especially in the United States, she presented a stark contrast with her earlier analysis of France. She used a similar comparative approach when analyzing the professional condition of women in volume 3 of *La femme pauvre*; here, she cited John Stuart Mill to argue that access to higher education in other countries was paving the way for women's emancipation. Alas, the situation was far different in France. She argued in effect that her home country's level of civilization was inferior to that of the other countries she had discussed because of an absence of liberty:

> If we examine Europe, we see a society that develops women's intelligence in direct relation to the price they attach to general morality. In civilizations where responsibilities have given birth to liberty, moral forces reside in the power represented by secular instruction, justice, and administration. Harmony then exists in the education of boy and girl adolescents who do not need to be preserved from any corrupting contact, and schooling takes place in day schools where the sexes are united.[71]

Daubié insisted throughout this section that the ideal mode of education for both boys and girls was coeducation within day schools, rather than the strict separation of the sexes within boarding schools that characterized secondary education in particular. And yet she did not advocate such a system for France. Her reasons for not doing so are highly revealing of the connections she established between gender roles, education, and the reigning system of political economy. For Daubié, like Hubertine Auclert, political changes had to occur before real educational reform could take place: "Coeducational and day schools, as well as individual initiative in teaching may justly be considered elements of social harmony; but these liberties depend on the security and public order that proceed from justice in civil relations; it is for this reason such relations cannot exist in France or other European governments where the irresponsibility of all means that the necessary relations for social harmony depend on each individual."[72] The French political economy, which gave free rein to the individual without guaranteeing justice within civil society, condemned coeducation. Given the incivility of French society, educational reform for girls was inevitably tied up in political reform.

The political use of international comparisons developed in the debates surrounding the creation of the Duruy courses. The liberal and anticlerical press, in particular, drew on foreign examples to argue for the need to develop girls' education in order not to appear retrograde. The Bonapartist and anticlerical paper *L'opinion nationale* cited the United States, while the more official *Revue de l'instruction publique* used examples from northwest Europe.[73] In this highly politicized context, former University professor Célestin Hippeau published in the *Revue des deux mondes* his description of American girls' and former slaves' education in the United States. The juxtaposition of girls and slaves was intentionally polemical; Hippeau suggested throughout his essay that a liberal education freed both women and slaves from the chains of tradition and history. He concluded his article by writing: "Let us finish by proposing the example offered by the United States as a way to encourage those generous spirits who consider that the increasingly widespread diffusion of wisdom is an essential condition for political and social progress." His detailed presentation of girls' secondary and higher education showed that women were capable of the same studies as men: "The admirable results women's studies have achieved are the most triumphant answer to all those objections that emerge whenever the question of the intellectual emancipation of women has not moved beyond mere discussion."[74] At the same time he criticized European states and France in particular where "some go so far as to claim [women] do not have sufficient intelligence for higher scientific studies." Hippeau and his governmental sponsors clearly sought to influence public opinion to support the Duruy courses.

Feminists and their allies often went a step further in their use of the comparative method, developing analyses with the intent of providing a model for French reforms. The Freemason Eugéne Pelletan, for example, argued frequently in his conferences that the French should seek inspiration in the American model of higher education for women: "One must create the modern woman, the American woman, to wit, the woman."[75] The development of international feminist congresses encouraged such comparative methods, as delegates from each country presented synopses of the situation in their country. At the first International Congress for the Rights of Women in 1878, speakers defended coeducation as "a strong stimulus for the progress of studies and of morals."[76] Similarly, the Republican feminist Clarisse Coignet championed a reform of girls' education in 1871 that also established the principle of coeducation.[77] In the aftermath of such congresses, the feminist press frequently used examples from the United States or Switzerland to suggest alternative ways to conceive girls' education.

A similar intention underlay Sée's detailed study of girls' education in other countries that introduced his presentation of the proposed law. Beginning with the United States he offered sketches of twelve different countries, drawing on the reports that were presented at the 1878 Universal Exhibition. The American situation, in particular, was presented as a success story for girls' education, given the presence of institutions for higher education such as Vassar and Wellesley. Sée then examined school systems in decreasing order of perfection, placing Switzerland, Germany, and Italy immediately after the United States: "The Swiss Republic, like the American Republic, has proclaimed men and women equal in instruction ... giving in this way satisfaction to moral law as well as the interest of the family and the nation."[78] By positioning France at the end, Sée clearly suggested his country's backwardness in this domain. Indeed his description of the historical context in France paid little heed to the tangible progress stimulated by private initiatives; instead, he adopted the official vision that before the state took an interest in it, no secondary education existed for girls.[79] Despite his favorable analysis of the American system, however, Sée did not advocate adopting similar measures. Instead, his law created a public system of girls' secondary education, but did nothing to encourage women's access to higher education.

The use of national comparisons in the debate about girls' education served then both as an example of what one could seek to achieve and as a stark reminder of the limits of educational reform. The decision to marshal comparative figures appears to have been used more commonly on the left than on the right. For the latter, the politicization of debates about girls' education led to an increasing defense of tradition and the weight of history, although not always with reactionary results.

Culture and Politics: The Religious Response

Historians of education have long argued that the second half of the century ushered in a new era of acrimony in educational matters. In the realm of girls' secondary education, Catholics and anticlericals both used the battle over women's minds as their respective rallying cries. The Republican rhetoric cited at the beginning of this chapter presented the struggle within French families as a series of sharp oppositions between the past and the present, between reaction and democracy, between superstition and rationality. Obviously in practice these distinctions were not so clearly drawn, but the power of this rhetoric had enduring consequences both for the relations between anticlerical reformers and their opponents and for the vision of girls' education that emerged in the early Third Republic.

The debate about who should educate women, along what lines, and for what purpose was never as simple as the preceding series of oppositions would suggest. Françoise Mayeur has skillfully demonstrated the complexity of the religious response, notably when considering the position of liberal Catholics. In particular, she has shown how the debate over the Duruy courses led the major protagonist in the public controversy, the Bishop Dupanloup, to alter his original position, becoming increasingly dogmatic in his refusal to endorse the state's initiative.[80] Undeniably, the decision to exclude religious subjects from the Duruy courses was what rankled most, but the extended public controversy that followed the creation of the courses carried two other important themes that speak to how educational issues carried both political and sexual overtones. First, the Catholic opposition to what Dupanloup termed a "university of women" highlighted the fears about women's access to male spaces. Second, the use of male professors in these courses introduced a sexual dimension to the debate. By denouncing the immorality of placing young girls with male teachers, the Catholic opposition sought to undermine the entire project, but they also unwittingly joined hands with the feminists in promoting the idea of the woman professor. And it is precisely in this area that nuns achieved new momentum in the closing decade of the century. Mère Marie du Sacré-Cœur's publication of *Les religieuses enseignantes* in 1897 placed certain Catholic teachers at the vanguard of reform efforts in girls' education — an ironic twist whose significance bears closer examination.

Challenging the Duruy Courses

The clergy, and especially the bishop of Orléans Felix Dupanloup, led the opposition to Duruy's initiative. The latter, however, was no enemy to girls' education. On the contrary, he represented the liberal wing of the Catholic party and had already published on the need to provide girls with a more serious program of study: "The painful truth I want to state here, is that even religious education . . . too rarely gives young girls and young women a serious taste for work."[81] Like Victor Duruy himself, he argued for the need to improve the quality of intellectual interactions between husband and wife, and he thought women should have access to careers as writers and artists. He proposed an intellectual program for girls that included literature, mainly from the seventeenth century, some Latin (in order to read religious texts), history, the arts, and Christian philosophy, as well as some knowledge of law, aesthetics, sciences, applied sciences, social economy, and natural history.[82]

Despite Dupanloup's concern to fortify girls' education, he responded in vehemently negative terms to Duruy's proposal to create secondary courses.[83] His first pamphlet began rather moderately, protesting against the minister's argument that no secondary education for girls existed in France. But as he continued, he became progressively more polemical, insisting on the immodest nature of these courses that placed women in public spaces and in the public eye: "What I dislike is not the publicity of their actions [*œuvres*] but that of their persons."[84] He attacked in conclusion the creation of this "women's university run by men," arguing that it was unthinkable — indeed horrifying — to imagine young girls traipsing into public spaces to listen to men lecture on potentially scabrous topics. By focusing on issues of morality and propriety, Dupanloup initially downplayed the threat these courses supposedly posed to religious values. Instead, he hammered home the idea that women belonged in the home and that their education was "women's business": "Girls' secondary education is in the hands of women, I ask that it not go into the hands of men. Young girls are raised for private life, in private life; I ask that they not be led to the courses, the examinations, the diplomas, the ceremonies that prepare men for public life."[85] Repeatedly, Dupanloup emphasized the dangers of certain subject matters, noting some professors taught Rabelais and the private poetry of Voltaire.[86] More suggestively, clerical journalists published songs and broadsheets that evoked the amorous possibilities these courses offered. Parents should be warned: girls and their governesses would undoubtedly succumb to the charms of young bachelor professors.[87]

Dupanloup's writings in many ways encapsulate the range of cultural tensions concerning girls' education. Not only did he inveigh against the idea of women invading male spaces, but he also explicitly drew out the implications of such an education: "You want women freethinkers, unbelievers, more than that, women doctors of impiety, professors of atheism, a type of unknown woman who would be dreadful."[88] Here he went several steps further from the common discourse about an education that declassed individuals. Duruy's courses, in his opinion, both desexed and displaced its unfortunate victims by pulling women from the arms of the church and the family. The ultramontane newspaper *L'univers* pursued this line of reasoning, arguing that the courses were part of a general program to emancipate women: "The emancipation of women means pulling her from the obligations and the occupations of her state, from the virtues of her sex, to make her emulate and equal men in the functions of civil society."[89]

Dupanloup's deepest concern, however, was the threat these institutions posed to religious values, and his defense of these values reveals clearly how religion had become domesticated. As a result, he presented what he described as Duruy's anticlerical project as an effort to undermine the family and domestic values. Inscribed in his defense of religious values was a deep-seated belief in the fundamental difference between men and women. This led him to adopt relatively contradictory positions; although he stated that women were naturally purer than men, he also judged them to be weaker. As a result, women needed religion to protect themselves against their own weaker natures. Getting rid of religion meant eliminating the "surest bulwark for their virtue, the most important force against themselves." In the same vein, he argued: "Everywhere women's honor must seek refuge against their weakness and their modesty near the altar."[90] Like his feminist sparring partners, Dupanloup drew on French national stereotypes, but he used them to defend the clerical position. His essay *La femme chrétienne* concluded with an argument about why the courses were against French nature. Every nation, in his view, had an education that corresponded to its nature, and for French women this implied a focus on religion. Since all of Europe recognized the superiority of French women, courses that would lead women to lose their sense of virtue could only be catastrophic. As a result, he wrote, his defense of the church was not self-interested; on the contrary, he was defending humanity in general.[91]

It seems likely that this sort of argument made less of an impact than the virulent campaign waged against the courses in individual cities. In these campaigns questions of propriety and morality were given greater attention than the actual content of the courses. Sexual politics joined with religious politics to win the day. But the clerical success in this campaign can be seen in some respect as a swan song.[92] For the most part, Catholics failed to capitalize on their success with respect to the Duruy courses and did little to bolster girls' education along the lines that Dupanloup had initially suggested. Mayeur has noted a few exceptions to this inactivity, notably that of the abbé Dadolle, a professor at the university in Lyons, who in 1881 opened a philosophy course to women.[93] Once the Republicans came to power, the balance of power shifted considerably, and the church progressively lost its foothold in girls' education. In 1886 the Goblet law pushed women religious out of public primary schools, and in 1904 the teaching orders lost the right to teach in France at all. And yet despite these political defeats, the church continued to have an impact on girls' secondary education, most notably through the image of the woman teacher that emerged in the final decades of the century.

As I have argued elsewhere, in the polemics surrounding the Duruy courses, Dupanloup positioned himself as the defender of women teachers against Duruy who placed girls' education in the hands of men.[94] The representations of womanhood that emerged in this debate, juxtaposed nuns and home life with women freethinkers, male professors, and the abandonment of the domestic sphere. Ironically, when the state finally created a system of secondary education for girls, the image of the virtuous nun produced in the debates of the Second Empire became the model for the new women professors.[95] How then did nuns respond?

Reforming Nuns and the Fate of Catholic Education

Few studies consider how the teaching orders reacted to the state's new initiative in girls' secondary education.[96] We know that bourgeois families continued to send their daughters to religious boarding schools, but beyond that we know relatively little. Until the late 1890s, most teaching orders failed to react to the challenge posed by public secondary education for girls. Beginning in the mid-1890s, however, they began to initiate changes. In 1896 the Sacré-Cœur, for example, opened a normal school for nuns in their novitiate in Conflans.[97] But the concern to improve religious education only attracted public attention in 1897 when Mère Marie du Sacré-Cœur published *Les religieuses enseignantes*, which brought the issue of girls' education back into the political spotlight. Although Mère du Sacré-Cœur's reform initiative failed, it does illustrate my earlier argument that some nuns were fully aware of the need to bring their teaching practices and contents in line with a modernizing world.

Adrienne Laroche (1856–1901), the future Mère Marie du Sacré-Cœur, was born into a petit bourgeois family in the Auvergne.[98] She followed her religious vocation at an early age and entered the convent of Notre-Dame in Issoire near Clermont-Ferrand. Despite the fact that nuns did not need educational diplomas, she pursued her studies and obtained both the *brevet élémentaire* and the *brevet supérieur*. During her novitiate she was struck by the mediocrity of her pedagogical training and quickly acquired the conviction that religious women's training was inadequate. Initially, she sought to create a normal school within her order, but under the influence of the abbé Naudet, who became her spiritual director in 1895, she moved her campaign into the public sphere. Thanks to the influence of powerful supporters, and most notably the vicomtesse d'Adhémar, the abbé Frémont, and the Catholic writer Georges

Guyau, her project acquired a national dimension that brought it to the attention of the Catholic hierarchy. Specifically, she wanted to create a normal school for teaching nuns in order to offer them the same kind of intellectual training that secondary women teachers then enjoyed thanks to the École normale supérieure de jeunes filles. Not wishing to provoke the ire of the major elite orders, such as the Sacré-Cœur and the Assomption, she insisted that her school would be directed toward the more modest orders, who did not have the means to offer a serious program of study for their nuns. She sought to attract supporters then through the publication of *Les religieuses enseignantes*, a book that primarily justified the need for such a school.

Her general argument was that teaching orders had failed to respond to the state's challenge: "Religious teaching orders are destined to disappear if they do not do what is necessary to withstand competition." Her proposal was an effort to counteract state reforms by providing qualified teachers within religious schools. Following the line of Dupanloup in his more liberal phase, she argued that young women needed serious educations in order to hold their own in social and political debate: "One must know a bit about the world, know the works in literature and philosophy, which are destined to exert an influence, have knowledge of those important ideas that stir up the masses, know the church's thinking on these matters in order to enlighten others, rather than be limited to incomprehension."[99] Throughout *Les religieuses enseignantes* she emphasizes that faith and reason are not incompatible and that Christianity would only benefit from promoting more serious studies for girls.

Her book galvanized public opinion through its criticism of religious education and its praise of public secondary education. Not surprisingly, many on the Catholic right responded in harshly negative terms. The bishop of Annecy, Monsignor Turinaz, protested that there was no need for such a school, that Catholic education was under no threat from public education and that her normal school would result in the disappearance of "true housewives and true mothers, in order to create *déclassées* exposed to all perils."[100] Others reacted vehemently to her undoubtedly impolitic suggestion that French Catholics look to the United States as an example. Like Daubié before her, she traced a highly favorable portrait of American girls' education, noting in particular the rigor of academic studies at Wellesley, which formed, nonetheless "learned Christian women, Christian wives, and Christian mothers."[101] For writers, such as Émile Keller, vice president of the Société générale pour l'éducation et l'enseignement, this sounded like antipatriotism of the worst sort: "We view with sadness that peevish spirits announce the so-called inferiority of our boarding schools for girls . . . and that, in the name of democracy and modern thinking, they call for French women to adopt those foreign programs that in America have produced lawyers, doctors, accountants, civil servants, everything, except mothers. Soon we will be turning them into soldiers and the triumph of civilization in the twentieth century will be to produce a regiment of amazons."[102]

Adhémar, who wrote a book defending Mère du Sacré-Cœur, argued that nuns themselves responded favorably to her proposal, recognizing the justice of her criticisms. Those who refused to support the project openly feared its inevitable association with the feminist movement: "We run the risk of being towed along by the feminist movement, which tends to denature women's role in the family and society rather than claiming their legitimate rights."[103] Mère du Sacré-Cœur responded to the attacks on her position in "La Formation catholique de la femme contemporaine," which she published as a preface to the fifth edition of *Les religieuses enseignantes* (1899). In it she tried not only to correct misunderstandings but also to propose a pedagogical approach to the education of girls. While recognizing the similarity between her goals and those of feminism, she urged Catholics to respond positively to the existing situation. Feminism, in her opinion, represented the "increasingly clear affirmation of woman's character, her personality, her family rights, and her relatively undefined need to extend her influence. This is an extremely important movement and the church should be in the vanguard."[104] In essence she defended a form of Catholic feminism that would not destroy the family.

In the end, Mère du Sacré-Cœur's normal school never saw the light of day for reasons that speak to the political charge of educational reforms. She and her allies were branded as democrats. Conservative Catholics mobilized against her project, which they saw as promoting free thought as well as sapping the foundations of the family. In 1899 the Sacrée Congrégation des Evêques et Réguliers in Rome issued a condemnation of her book, thus ending all hope. Although she opened a boarding school in the final years of her short life, nuns' teacher training did not get the boost she had hoped for. Indeed the early years of the new century were inauspicious ones for teaching orders. In 1904 the prime minister Emile Combes pushed anticlerical legislation to a new extreme by forbidding all religious orders from engaging in teaching activities. Teaching nuns were forced either to leave France, to close their schools, or to secularize. In a very material sense the state appeared to have won both the battle and the war.

And yet, the story is not so simple, for girls' Catholic education certainly did not just disappear. Historians have amply demonstrated the very thin veneer of the secularization process.[105] In most instances women donned lay clothing and continued to teach as they always had. Adolescent girls continued to imbibe Catholic values and messages. Within Paris, private secondary education thrived, a refuge for those who opposed the supposedly atheist orientation of the state-supported system. Moreover, the calming of religious tensions after 1904 allowed new Catholic reform initiatives to succeed, although by then nuns were not the beneficiaries. In 1906 Mlle Desrez opened the École normale catholique to prepare teachers for secondary teaching within the private sector, and to allow girls to pursue secondary studies in an environment untroubled "by a neutral or atheistic teaching."[106] In Paris this sparked a number of new creations that catered specifically to adolescent girls who wanted a serious education. In 1908 Madeleine Daniélou opened the École normale libre, which prepared girls for university examinations; more rigorous studies could also be found at the Cours Montalembert (1907), the École la Bruyère (1908), and finally the Collège Hulst (1914), which was founded to prepare girls for the *baccalauréat*.[107] The educational programs of these institutions often went beyond what was being offered in the state-run *collèges* and *lycées,* most notably they provided courses in Latin and Greek. In a striking reversal of the position taken over the Duruy courses forty years earlier, the private Catholic sector had become more receptive than the state to the educational demands of girls from *les classes moyennes,* since these schools openly prepared girls for the *baccalauréat.*

Feminists were also present in these efforts to align girls' secondary education with that of boys'. Educators such as Jeanne Crouzet Benaben pushed to have the girls' secondary curriculum lead toward the *baccalauréat,* rather than the professionally useless *diplôme d'études secondaires.*[108] Finally in 1924 the Bérard law extended the public secondary program for girls from five to six years and introduced an optional curriculum that allowed girls to prepare for the *baccalauréat.* Léon Bérard presented this measure, however, in a politically moderate fashion: "On the one hand my concern is to open classical culture to a small elite of students and, on the other hand, to offer to the vast majority of young women in our *lycées,* whose sole ambition is domestic life, precisely the advanced education which the legislators in 1880 had envisioned."[109] Contrary to his expectations, girls flocked into the new option. Although couched in traditional language, Bérard's law radically altered the ethos of girls' secondary education as it had emerged in the early nineteenth century and been confirmed in the Camille Sée law. Without instituting coeducation, it nonetheless allowed girls to pursue the same studies as their brothers, opening up new educational and professional possibilities that many were quick to seize.[110] But it would take more to change solidly entrenched attitudes that bourgeois girls were principally destined for the home. True, the array of opportunities for educated women expanded in the interwar period, but educational equality did not erase gender differences. Despite the anxiety generated by the war years that France had become a "civilization without sexes," the historical development of girls' education left a heavy legacy of female difference.[111] Women increasingly had access to "male" knowledge and "male" programs, but education alone was not sufficient to change enduring cultural attitudes about gender specificities.

By the turn of the century few questioned middle-class women's right to have an education but its purpose was indeed disputed. Many, on both the right and the left, continued to argue that girls' education served essentially private ends, to bolster the intimacy between husband and wife and to ensure the proper education of young children.[112] But the political battles of the previous forty years had left their mark, so that most recognized that girls' education had implications that carried over into the public sphere. On a certain level, the struggle between the church and the Republic to control women's minds made women pawns in a political contest about the ideological characteristics of the future. But women teachers and activists were part of this contest and helped to frame both its content and its outcome. In the process, the opposition between lay and religious teachers or male and female teachers ceased to have the same significance. Instead the stakes were more clearly defined as being between Republican and Catholic education. In effect this reflects the success of the professionalization process; women had won the right for professional training and were increasingly taking advantage of opportunities to take the *baccalauréat* and gain access to the university and the professions. By 1900 there would be no turning back, even if the new Catholic schools continued to rely on male professors because of chronic shortages of qualified teachers.

The politicization of girls' education and its stakes and the ostensible success of the Republican state did not erase the fundamentally gendered ideology that had given rise to a secondary system for girls. As Jo Burr Margadant's study of the first *Sèvriennes* has shown, the new women professors continued to be torn between the meritocratic and universal values of the Republican university and a vision of the maternal educator that took shape in the 1830s. One might conjecture that the teachers within the Catholic sector were less torn, and yet both groups of women professors reached their positions through a professional process that undoubtedly left its imprint on their sense of who they were. Indeed the first Catholic women educators, unlike the *Sèvriennes*, had commonly competed with their male comrades to obtain *baccalauréats*.

The new opportunities in girls' secondary education at the turn of the century undoubtedly affected far more women than in earlier decades, but their significance lies less in their quantitative impact than in how French society as a whole understood the impact of this education. And here, I would argue, it was primarily the feminist movement that changed the terms of debate. By fighting to achieve equal opportunities in education and in employment, turn-of-the-century feminists like their predecessors had insisted on how these issues had political implications beyond the domestic sphere. But more and more they went one step further pushing for women's political rights as well. Although French women would only vote for the first time in 1945, women's suffrage was a public issue from 1900 on. And with suffrage, the issue of who controlled women's minds — the church, the Republican state, or individual women themselves — became a burning issue.[113]

8

Beyond the Hexagon:
French Schools on Foreign Soils

The French effort to establish standards in the education of bourgeois girls had an impact far beyond the hexagon. Frenchwomen set up s7chools for girls throughout the Western world, as well as in the colonies, spreading in this way a vision of French girls' education whose features have seldom been explored. The founding of girls' schools on foreign soils began well before the surge in French imperial activity under the Third Republic and contributed to the emergence of a specifically French model of girls' education that foreign observers recognized and at times admired. From the beginning of the nineteenth century then, French cultural reconstruction carried a gendered imperial dimension. The nuns and laywomen who sought to fashion serious Christian women in the postrevolutionary period also left France to set up girls' schools in Africa and the United States as part of a civilizing mission that had a distinctively French pedagogical twist.[1] Although the characteristics of this mission changed over time, the concern to spread French values consistently involved the schooling of both boys *and* girls. Teachers, like colonizers, saw women's status as one of the most telling signs of a country's degree of civilization. Improving women's status involved providing education.

This chapter seeks to highlight the characteristics of a French model of girls' education by exploring its interactions with other national and cultural traditions. My focus will be on French forays into northern and western Africa, as well as to Britain and the United States, roughly from the 1820s until the 1880s. The pedagogical thrust of the "civilizing" mission found voice in letters and bulletins that inspired French women both lay and religious to leave for foreign soils in the hopes of carrying on activities such as those they had initiated at home. The rhetoric surrounding efforts to achieve the "fusion of the races" in Algeria or acculturation in the United States reveals the strength of an imperial dimension in French educational goals that from the outset included women as both teachers and students. French teachers carried with them values and practices developed on the Continent and sought to implement them in a variety of contexts. The confrontation with ethnically and religiously diverse populations, however, forced women educators to adjust their goals and to modify pedagogical practices.[2] Still, their efforts left their mark on the societies they encountered. The comparison between the colonial situation and how schools evolved in the American setting highlights the interactions between culture and politics and emphasizes how the concern to educate girls contributed to establishing social, racial, and national boundaries within these different locations.[3] Ultimately, this chapter argues that concern for girls' education was part and parcel of a civilizing process that had an imperial dimension. Revealing this dimension illustrates why French girls' education makes a difference in our understanding of histories of cultural encounters.

The Imperial School: Women's Civilizing Mission in the Colonies

"Women will accomplish the civilizing action we have begun; they have the secret for calming tensions and troubles."[4] This statement by a government official highlights the recognition colonization required not just might and men, but also women with their gentler ways. More concretely, women as educators were seen as playing a critical role in the colonization project, as this woman journalist in 1883 argued: "We seek the means to publicize [the splendors of Algeria] and we have found an excellent one — it is to entrust women to spread these ideas to the entire nation. They can do it. They hold on their knees the generation who will replace us, the one that will undoubtedly accomplish the great work of colonization?"[5] But women served the colonizing mission not just at home; from the start, both lay and religious women accompanied male administrators in the French expansion into Africa, but also went on their own, notably to found schools or hospitals. In the French colonial context women often had a more visible cultural impact than the missionary wives who have received ample attention in the Protestant imperial context.[6] Particularly as members of religious orders, women staked their claim to status as cultural emissaries spreading the fruits of French civilization. In missionary news bulletins as well as letters, they communicated with women who stayed in France, allowing us to explore the motivations that led to their presence in Africa.[7] Moreover these same documents also shaped the vocations of future women missionaries, thus contributing to the reproduction of a specifically feminine civilizing mission.

This section will focus mainly on educational initiatives in Algeria and Senegal, highlighting how very different approaches came to resemble each other in these areas where contact with the French had very different histories. In 1830 the French began their military conquest of Algeria, and a large settler population soon followed to reap the benefits of Algerian colonization. This violent occupation of an ancient Muslim society established patterns of domination that strongly determined the sorts of schools the French founded upon their arrival.[8] By contrast, the French trading presence since 1630 in Senegal had produced a society that was relatively egalitarian in racial terms, in part because the white population remained numerically very small.[9] As an insignificant minority, the French colonial authorities were initially far more respectful of the local population. In the first half of the century both lay and religious women left their homeland to establish schools in both of these areas buoyed by faith in the virtues of assimilation or what contemporaries in Algeria described as the "fusion of the races."[10] While the meaning attached to the concept of assimilation changed over time and varied according to the speaker, it essentially represented a belief that Algerians or Africans could become like Frenchmen through a civilizing process that included education.[11] This belief immediately ran into difficulties for the Frenchwomen who sought to set up schools and confronted the realities of colonial politics and society. My analysis then considers how the initial vision evolved and, most notably, how the spread of girls' schooling in these locations led to policies of racial segregation with enduring consequences for the future.

Gendered Visions of the Missionary Ideal

As Alice Conklin's recent *A Mission to Civilize* has shown, the French civilizing mission has a long history that borrowed from many sources. The Third Republic's secular discourse about this mission was steeped in Enlightenment values, but intersected with a Catholic and missionary discourse that similarly emphasized what French values brought to non-Western areas.[12] Both men and women transmitted these values, although men have received far more attention than women, given their more public voices.[13] Women, and particularly nuns, wrote about the civilizing mission and positioned women as both agents and subjects within it. Their representations reveal how understandings of French femininity conditioned their approach to the civilizing ideal.

The impulse to go overseas depended on a variety of both sociocultural and spiritual factors. The familial religious environment undoubtedly had a strong impact as well as a young woman's educational experience and the books she had read. The autobiography of Rosalie Chapelain, founder of the African order the Filles du Saint-Cœur de Marie, inspired many young women to embrace the missionary cause. How they interpreted this cause was another matter. Other women had brothers or family members involved in missionary work and sought to imitate them.[14] The analysis that follows draws on documents and studies concerning a variety of orders; some were explicitly missionary in their orientation, while others were better known for their activities in France. Despite differences in the sorts of objectives pursued on foreign soil, the motivations women expressed when requesting to leave France bear many similarities.[15]

Before leaving France, women wrote of their motives in fairly abstract terms, reflecting a lack of clear knowledge about what awaited them in Africa. Instead their impulse to go abroad stemmed from the lessons of charity that pushed bourgeois women to help those less fortunate. Many women reproduced a discourse about self-sacrifice and even martyrdom that was common both in girls' education and in religious orders more generally. As one woman wrote: "Despite my reluctance and squeamishness, one day I must sacrifice all that is dear to me to follow our heavenly spouse to those foreign beaches."[16] Some women appear more simply to have been moved by curiosity or the spirit of adventure: "Will I dare to offer myself for this first voyage? I have a great desire to do so, while remaining completely respectful of the decision of my good superiors."[17] Naturally, many women referred either indirectly or directly to their desire to save souls: "No human motives explain my determination; God's will, his glory, and the desire to save souls have persuaded me to solicit this favor."[18] One candidate insisted that "even as a young girl, before my First Communion, my great desire was to grow older so that I could go to the savages [barbares]. By this I meant men deprived of faith."[19] Finally, some religious women saw their mission in both religious and patriotic terms: "Algeria has become a new France. [The Algerian mission] has the same claims on the religious devotion of our sisters as the motherland."[20] This combination of moral and religious arguments for participating in mission activities suggests that the civilizing mission for these women was primarily a spiritual or evangelical one, relatively distinct from the secular vision developed by Jules Ferry in the 1880s.

A common rhetoric informed much of the writing from the early decades of imperial expansion. Most frequently, nuns expressed their concern in the moralizing language that characterized the "home mission" as well. In other words, the attitude toward African populations mirrored in many ways attitudes toward the French rural or urban poor. Nuns saw their task as one of bringing spiritual uplift specifically to women who would then exert influence within their families. In Madagascar, for example, religious women sought to fashion "Christian women." Similarly, in South Africa, the Sœurs de la Sainte-Famille de Bordeaux opened schools in 1864 so that indigenous women would learn "the rules of Christian decency."[21] Once settled in Africa, however, religious women changed their tone and often their objectives, depending on the colonial context that prevailed. The abstract concern to save souls quickly translated into specific activities, since unlike Protestant missionary women, Catholic religious orders enjoyed an autonomy of action that enabled them to target female populations more easily. Upon arriving in Algiers, the Sœurs de Saint-Joseph de l'Apparition were quickly solicited by many women, both Muslim and Jewish, who sought their expertise for sick members of their family.[22] In this settler colony, however, the government specifically warned against seeking conversions, so the religious mission was enacted through example rather than through spreading the word. Indeed, in Algeria, the nuns' mission increasingly acquired the traits associated with the Republican *mission civilisatrice*; civilization for women in this version meant teaching concrete lessons in child-raising, hygiene, and basic literacy. Nuns, like European travelers, believed Arab women lived lives of indolence and sloth, contributing to the general decadence of Arab life.

In areas where Islam presented less of a political problem the religious mission remained uppermost. Anne-Marie Javouhey, the superior general of the Sœurs de Saint-Joseph de Cluny urged a more proselytizing approach, inspired in part by her direct contact with the African populations in Senegal and Gorée: "You wish to civilize Africa? Begin by establishing religion; reveal this religion as it should appear to a fanatical population that cannot yet understand but has eyes. Display it; pomp will attract people and respect will retain them, and soon you will change the face of the country. [Africans] are naturally attracted to religion, they like prayer; this is an important point and gives one great hope for success."[23] As a result, in Senegal this order did not hesitate to challenge traditional customs and beliefs, offering in their place what they unquestioningly considered the fruits of a superior civilization.

The nuns who traveled to Africa do not appear to have come with the same degree of ethnographic information as their male counterparts. Given the educational training and preparation they had in France this is scarcely surprising.[24] The intellectual preparation for these cultural encounters was often limited to a few sermons about the dangers and iniquities of Islam without attention to the prurient details of African women's sex lives that often informed male missionary reactions to indigenous societies.[25] As a result, it would appear that nuns had almost a Rousseauean vision of Africans as innocent and childlike, uncorrupted by the ways of the modern world. Anne-Marie Javouhey, in particular, reiterated this vision in her voluminous correspondence, which undoubtedly influenced the women who followed in her footsteps. Writing of "good," "pure," or "innocent" blacks, she defended a vision of African society that was eminently receptive to the values and virtues of civilization: "I like blacks much better [than whites]: they are good, simple, their only malice comes from us; it will not be difficult to convince them by example."[26] Civilization, in Javouhey's eyes, would offer religion, of course, but also a work ethic and knowledge to combat the laziness and ignorance that she identified as the main problem. From the outset she wanted to spread this civilization to both boys and girls.

Letters from Africa reveal subtle differences between the nuns and their male counterparts.[27] French nuns transposed their vision of French society onto foreign soil and assumed that families formed the cornerstone of other societies. Civilization meant spreading those values that ensured women would provide the moral lessons necessary to regenerate society from within. Educating girls and women constituted a religious and moral imperative whose repercussions were expected to have social implications, much like charity at home. Male missionaries, on the other hand, sought more directly to influence the political and socioeconomic structures they encountered overseas through the creation of a native elite.[28] No doubt male and female Catholic missionaries expected to interact mainly with persons of their own sex, which influenced of course their vision of what might be accomplished through their actions. For women, schooling constituted a civilizing imperative, but it encountered obstacles once in the field that often changed the nature of cultural interactions.[29]

Establishing Schools in a Foreign Setting

The nature of early colonial schools depended to a great extent on the local context and the type of financial, political, and religious support these women had from French authorities. Upon arriving laywomen and nuns adopted different strategies if they were in interaction with an existing settler population, with Muslims, or with families of mixed ethnic background. Similarly, women who received financial support from the French government had greater leeway than those who relied solely on their own resources. The diversity of clientele and institutional structures in colonial territories meant that the civilizing mission varied widely from place to place, even within the same religious order. Examples from different locations and types of schools illustrate how ideals fluctuated and evolved in response to local pressures, so that women teachers hesitated over whether to privilege moral, religious, educational, social, or national objectives. Despite variations, however, educators sought to introduce the French respect for order and hierarchy that underlay the schools they founded in France as well.

In areas where a settler population existed, most women teachers quickly shifted their initial interest from indigenous people to people of European origins. This was particularly true in Algeria where the colonial government vigorously forbade efforts to convert Muslims for fear of the political turmoil this might engender. In 1843 Bishop Dupuch in Algeria estimated there were some twenty-five to thirty thousand nominally Catholic Europeans whose daughters were in sore need of religious education. But even this population received very different treatment according to their social class, just as they did in France. The Sacré-Cœur, for example, focused its educational efforts on the European elite, opening a boarding school in Mustapha on the outskirts of Algiers, but it also offered more limited education to girls from the lower ranks of society. Bishop Dupuch described their enterprise in the following glowing terms: "An extremely handsome establishment; it includes a boarding school for young ladies that is on a par with the most respected institutions of this type in France; a day school directed toward officers' children who are stationed in great number in Mustapha and who cannot afford to pay for boarding their daughters; and a free work school for the poor girls of the area, which is as successful as it is perfectly managed."[30] Muslim girls were not present in any of these schools.

The dynamic provincial superior who supervised the expansion of the Sœurs de la Doctrine Chrétienne in Algeria specifically placed European conversions before those of the Arab populations: "Before considering direct efforts to convert Arabs, it is important to focus on regenerating as much as possible the European, and especially French, populations who come here seeking to make a fortune."[31] Between 1850 and 1866 the Sœurs de la Doctrine Chrétienne opened some fifty schools, catering to this poor, fortune-hunting European population.[32] Their institutional development was greatly facilitated by the financial support that the French government offered, but at the same time they respected the military and then the civil government's orders to practice religious tolerance. In reality, the absence of Muslim students meant that their civilizing efforts resembled those practiced among the rural poor in France. Religious instruction formed the backbone of a curriculum that focused on introducing orderly and domestic ways through lessons in needlework and basic hygiene. In many areas the sisters also ran local hospitals, which treated Muslims, orphanages, *salles d'asiles*, boarding schools, and workhouses, often using one building for several functions.[33]

A number of laywomen also opened schools in Algeria in the early years of colonial expansion. Although most of these institutions similarly catered to European girls, a few women proposed more venturesome cultural experiments that reveal the complexity of French attitudes toward the civilizing mission. As early as 1836 the colonial government gave their support for the creation of a school for young Jewish girls in Algiers run by a French Jewish headmistress Heloïse Hartoch.[34] According to the inspector of education in Algeria, "Israelites have no difficulty following the path of intellectual culture that we seek to clear for them." For girls, in particular, the inspector argued that the French could contribute mightily to the process of civilization, since "up until now women have never learned to read or write. . . . Through education and especially the education of women, we are preparing a salutary revolution in morals and in the spirit of families. . . . Popular instruction is one of the greatest benefits of modern society not only with respect to morality, but perhaps even more with respect to the domestic economy."[35] This enthusiastic endorsement of Hartoch's school underlines the extent to which French officials transposed the underlying tenets of a burgeoning domestic ideology to colonial societies. Jewish families in Algiers were less enthusiastic, however, and in 1843 the school boasted a mere sixteen students, despite Hartoch's ambition to educate one hundred.

A more unusual initiative, which prefigured later efforts on the part of the French colonial government, was that of Mme Allix-Luce, who founded a school for Muslim girls in Algiers in the mid-1840s. In her successful efforts to get official governmental support, she described her mission in high moral and patriotic tones: "I was intimately persuaded, particularly after our interminable wars, that civilization would be without effect as long as we did not reach the interior of families, and I felt I had sufficient courage to render a great service to my country even at the cost of some sacrifice." Specifically she sought to "change as rapidly and as quickly as possible the morals, habits, and native prejudices," and she argued the probable results of this education would be "the fusion of two civilizations which have been considered irreconcilable until now." She aimed to attract the daughters of indigenous elites: "These young girls will become, in the nature of things, the privileged wives of the most important men of their class, they will become our guarantee of the country's submission to our authority as well as the unimpeachable pledge of its future assimilation."[36] The government's financial support allowed her to institute an unusual procedure: she paid each girl two francs per day to receive lessons in reading and writing in both French and Arabic, while focusing most of her efforts on teaching them needlework.[37] Girls' schooling in Allix-Luce's eyes was the key to pacified colonial relations: "I keenly felt what important changes in domestic life can be produced by the direction given to the education of women, changes extending to society at large."[38] While pushing for governmental support of her school, she highlighted how Algerian women remained beyond the pale; in one letter she argued that the French state was prepared to pay for the food of four to five thousand prisoners but refused to pay for the education of one to two hundred girls. In her view women were the key to winning the Algerians over; if they were converted to the French cause they would then aid in the future assimilation of the races. Clearly, the conquest of Algeria was not solely a masculine enterprise. Nuns and laywomen were also present, opening schools for both European and Algerian Muslim girls in the hopes of forming a feminine population respectful of French values.

In Saint-Louis and Gorée in western Africa, the precociously international Sœurs de Saint-Joseph de Cluny operated a similar range of institutions while receiving financial support from the Ministry of the Marines and Colonies. Unlike the Algerian situation, however, the local European population was far smaller, and local colonial officials encouraged the idea of educating indigenous black girls, arguing "women exert a tremendous influence on the morals of this country, so one must act through them to give this population the love of work, as well as more industrious, more active and more French habits."[39] A "school for young negresses" opened in 1826, offering lessons in the rudiments, taught in French; the main object of this school was to teach cleanliness, how to run a house, and how to garden in order to form a "laboring class." The order offered an education similar to that provided to the rural poor in France with an important exception: the school was organized as a boarding school in order to plunge the young African girls into a structured French environment for a period of four years. This initial effort at assimilation ended in failure, however, as the school never attracted more than ten students, and in 1835 it disappeared. The local officials who had supported the school financially blamed the failure on the religious orientation of the school. Probably the decision to separate young girls from their families also contributed to its demise.[40]

A more radical project to transplant African boys and girls to the order's novitiate in Bailleul, France, envisioned the creation of a native class of nuns or teachers well versed in civilized ways thanks to their total immersion in French society. Javouhey defended her project in 1822, arguing that upon their return to Senegal these young men and women would help spread "the fundamental knowledge of civilization."[41] In 1825 eleven children between the ages of eight and ten were sent, including four girls. The students were chosen from mixed-race and poor black families, presumably under the assumption that they would part more easily with their children than the indigenous elite. Initial reports about the transplanted Africans were encouraging. The students were reported to be thriving, and the girls were praised, saying they would become excellent teachers in the decorative arts. Indeed, Javouhey announced her intention to send them back to the colonies with pianos and guitars. By the early 1830s, however, the project had begun to falter; between 1830 and 1834 ten African students died despite moving this "African seminary" from the north of France to the more temperate climate of Limoux near Toulouse. In the end the small numbers and the cost of this education contributed to failure as well; by the 1850s the nuns adopted other strategies to civilize the Africans. This experiment, however, reveals interesting contradictions in French attitudes toward education for colonized people. In particular, the decision to offer music lessons to lower-class African girls represented a radical break with traditional French conceptions of what constituted an appropriate education, and indeed the government questioned this, arguing "it would hinder this education's chance of success in its country."[42] Javouhey, on the other hand, defended the idea of an education that would develop the personality and offer an opportunity for social mobility. This unusually liberal vision was not particularly in evidence, however, on colonial soil.

In Saint-Louis and in Gorée the Sœurs de Saint-Joseph de Cluny taught a range of European, mixed-race, and black girls in their schools, but they maintained strict separation between black students and the small number of European girls as well as between Christians, Muslims, and animists.[43] The content of this education resembled French higher primary education with lessons in grammar, French history and geography, arithmetic for commercial purposes, and needlework, but these girls were also taught African history. The intent was to form good housewives who spoke fluent French. In the 1840s the French colonial administration advocated even greater assimilation in an abortive attempt to create a boarding school. Here they sought "to transform young Africans into true French people and to establish through affection the preponderance of France on the shores of Senegal."[44] This sort of idealistic project was predicated nonetheless on notions of cultural superiority; the fact that schools separated students by skin color and by religion only served to reinforce divisions within colonial society, divisions that would become more apparent in the period of consolidation after 1850.

This comparison of the situations in Algeria and Senegal highlights the very different approaches initially adopted with respect to the civilizing mission in these two colonial territories. Attitudes toward the education of orphans were similar, however, since they were considered in a sense to be outside their native cultures. Orphans were seen as an ideal population for educators seeking to promote a radical change in attitude through the creation of hard-working indigenous Christian families. In arguing for the need to open an orphanage in 1853 the Sœurs de la Doctrine Chrétienne wrote: "[We need to] teach them how to run a household, raise livestock, cultivate a garden, etc., because Algeria has sickened due to slothfulness, it will only gain strength through work."[45] In Senegal the Sœurs de Saint-Joseph de Cluny created orphanages in the hopes of marrying their pupils with those of male Christian missionaries, and they briefly operated an agricultural colony which Superior General Javouhey described as a "contributing to the grand project of civilizing Africa, creating a laborious agricultural people, composed above all of honest and good Christians."[46] Here the teaching orders directly acted on the indigenous populations, but as in France, they were careful to separate orphans from other categories of students, and the "civilization" that was proposed was a far cry from learning to play the piano and speak French.

With the exception of orphans, the nuns in Algeria focused on European populations, leaving most Algerian Arab women beyond the pale of civilization. This may in part explain why in post-1870 Algeria Julia Clancy-Smith notes that Arab women were used as a trope to demonstrate the native's inability to absorb French civilization.[47] In Senegal, on the contrary, the government considered the indigenous population ripe to receive the fruits of French civilization — no doubt in part because of the mixed-race population — and so various strategies were tested that ranged from total immersion in French society to the more limited and segregated schools in urban settings. The concern to make African girls more like French women was driven by an unquestioning belief in French cultural superiority and the conviction that "gallicized" women would effect moral reforms within their families. Over time, the emancipating ideals of some of these more radical experiments gave way to a vision that education served to prepare girls for their socially preordained place in society.

Revising the Mission: The Impact of Cultural Encounters in Algeria and Senegal

By the 1850s and 1860s a range of girls' schools existed in Algeria and Senegal; and as colonial authorities tightened their grip, the patriotic aspect of the civilizing mission took on greater significance. The local political context, as well as local recruitments, strongly determined how school offerings evolved over time. But in both contexts colonial officials and teachers increasingly interpreted civilization as a set of values that emphasized difference from native populations, rendering the ideal of assimilation illusory. In action the civilizing mission produced women who fit in neither their native society nor in French colonial society, thus highlighting the fundamental flaw in the initial project to make indigenous women more like Frenchwomen.

Two examples — one from Algeria and one from Senegal — serve to illustrate the decline of the assimilationist vision as both the French colonial administration and women teachers recognized the difficulties inherent in transposing cultural values onto foreign populations. By focusing on these difficulties we can see how understandings of French femininity informed the civilizing mission and ultimately contributed to reinforcing national, racial, and social differences between French and indigenous women.[48] The creation of Arab-French schools for both boys and girls in Algeria in the 1850s and their ultimate failure constitutes my first example; my second explores how the Sœurs de Saint-Joseph de Cluny sought to consolidate their presence in Senegal through their recruitment policies. Specifically, their decision to create an all-black, indigenous order, the Filles du Saint-Cœur de Marie, allowed them to reorient their educational mission toward mainly European populations.

In 1850 French colonial administrators created male and female Arab-French schools for the children of the indigenous elites in a variety of Algerian cities.[49] Through training in both the French and Arab language, the French sought to effect the "fusion of races," a concept that dominated French colonial educational policy in Algeria until the 1860s. These schools were primarily intended for indigenous students, although some European students were present in the boys' schools. The appellation "Arab-French" signaled the concern to provide native students with an educational environment that respected Arab culture while teaching French and providing the necessary tools for future assimilation. They were expected to gradually supplant Arab schools, through a process of cultural assimilation. By targeting the children of Muslim elites, colonial authorities expressed their belief that the values of French civilization would then trickle down to the popular classes, encouraging widespread assimilation with "naturally" superior French values.[50] The decision to create girls' schools alongside the boys' schools was undoubtedly motivated by the existence of Mme Allix-Luce's school in Algiers, which served as a model for the three other schools that appeared in Oran, Constantine, and Bone.

From the beginning Allix-Luce adopted the dominant colonial rhetoric and gave it a gendered twist to justify her initiative. She presented her school as an integral part of the civilizing mission: "It's the fusion of the two races, a previously insolvable problem which is now settled affirmatively."[51] The educational curriculum in these schools was initially fashioned on that of higher primary education in France; it included French grammar, history, and geography, in addition to a wide variety of needlework. From the outset, however, these schools attracted almost exclusively young and impoverished Arab women rather than the daughters of indigenous elites. In 1853 Rector Delacroix blamed the curriculum for attracting only the lowest classes: "Clearly the study of French is considered a very great danger for these young girls, thus pushing away from our schools all except those who are pressured by misery."[52] Inspectresses similarly emphasized that French grammar and geography bore little interest for these Arab students, but their arguments were more rooted in considerations having to do with the students' future lives: "What does it matter to these women who are destined to spend their whole lives inside their homes to know that the world is divided into several continents, to be able to say what is an ocean, a lake, a gulf. Alas! Won't this poor science render even more bitter their obligation to live only for the family. In a desire to make them happy, I fear we have gone beyond our goal and that we have awakened in them desires and sentiments that lead them away from honest and resigned lives."[53] As a result, both the colonial authorities and the teachers themselves quickly reoriented the civilizing mission for women to emphasize domestic "sciences" and the virtues of hard work in order to achieve "the moralization . . . of Muslim families."[54] In essence, the schools limited their action to promoting the same sort of domestic values that primary schools in France proposed for the lower classes.[55]

Within a decade, however, the Arab-French schools for girls had lost the support of the colonial government, and Allix-Luce's school, in particular, had been demoted to a mere workshop (*ouvroir*). The failure of this initiative was in part attributed to the odor of immorality that surrounded both Allix-Luce herself and her schools. Reports on this entrepreneurial schoolteacher revealed that she had lied about her husband upon first arriving in Algiers. The man who lived with her, was not in fact M. Allix, but rather M. Luce, who became her second husband in 1847. Colonial officials were, however, even more critical of the reputation of her school. Citing an Algerian member of the general council, one administrator wrote that "no self-respecting Muslim would ever send his daughter or choose a wife from this school."[56] In a final report on this experiment, Adolphe Michel emphasized the folly of seeking to include women in French efforts to assimilate the Algerian population: "This education that we seek to give to native girls will remain for a long time irreconcilable with the religious beliefs, the morals, and the domestic habits that the Arab world assigns to women. It's sheer illusion to believe that we are preparing social reform by teaching young Muslim women of the cities to read, write, and calculate using our methods. By raising them as Europeans in this way we render them unfit for Arab life; we are preparing concubines for Europeans, rather than wives for natives."[57] Both colonial authorities and indigenous elites interpreted the effects of French civilization on Arab women in sexual terms. In an unusual inversion of traditional accounts of colonization, white women in this setting, rather than reinforcing the boundaries between the colonizers and the colonized, encouraged an all-too-corporeal fusion between the races that proved in the long run to be all too problematic as well.[58]

By the late 1860s French administrators concluded that these efforts on behalf of both Arab girls and boys were misplaced; instead the French colonial administration encouraged the development of local "mixed" schools for the masses, and not the elites. Rather than separating Europeans and Algerians, the governor general of Algeria Marshal Patrice de MacMahon, decreed in 1867 that primary schools should accept "all children in a town, regardless of their race or religion" in order to effect "the fusion of the diverse populations that inhabit this country."[59] For Arab girls, however, educational efforts waned considerably after 1860. Religious orders in particular focused their efforts almost exclusively on European students. This turning away from Arab women created new separations in the civilian colonial society that emerged after 1871, separations both between Europeans and Algerians and even more notably between European and Algerian women.

In Senegal, the Sœurs de Saint-Joseph de Cluny dominated the educational scene to the exclusion of any other lay or religious teachers. As mentioned previously, their strategy differed from that in Algeria, since Senegalese girls were targeted from the outset. Here the existence of a relatively large mulatto population probably facilitated the decision to educate both European and African girls, although Nemo's research reveals that European and "assimilée" families largely dominated within the schools.[60] Black and Muslim girls were concentrated in the lower classes and kept separate from girls of European origin, both in day schools and boarding schools. The sisters justified this segregation with reference to the native culture. Given the recent abolition of slavery (in 1848), local elites refused to have their daughters on the same benches with the daughters of recently emancipated slaves. As a result, the order's educational efforts contributed to cementing differences between different categories of the population in Senegal.

Notwithstanding the diversity of the students in their schools, the sisters devoted a surprising amount of time to the decorative arts, even though, as in France, this training was associated with the trappings of elite culture. The teachers justified this education with the argument that the students themselves had insisted on becoming "civilized and learned."[61] Through this education the sisters demonstrated their belief in assimilation for *certain* categories of girls living in Senegal, notably the daughters of a native elite. But this assimilation had its limits, as is particularly evident when one considers the growth of the order and the recruitment choices that were made.

By midcentury the order's relative success in attracting students pushed the leaders to envision the local recruitment of Senegalese teachers. Until then the *Maison Mère* had been responsible for sending out women to the oldest urban centers, the coastal towns known as the Four Communes (Gorée, Saint-Louis, Dakar, and Rufisque).

Given the rigors of life in this area for Europeans, however, the advantages of local recruitment were obvious. The first Senegalese novice took her vows in 1856. Born in Gorée, she came from an elite mulatto family and had spent many years in France. Once a member of the order, she was placed in charge of the lower classes of African students. Others, however, did not follow her example, given local resistance to the very concept of celibacy. Those who sought to enter the missionary order were all products of the sisters' education and came from an elite mulatto population; in total a mere seven women joined the Sœurs de Saint-Joseph de Cluny.[62]

This lack of success encouraged Monsignor Kobès, a member of the Congrégation des pères du Saint-Spirit, or Spiritains, to create the Filles du Saint-Cœur de Marie. His primary concern was to encourage conversions, and he believed this would occur more easily if African nuns set the example. In 1858 he placed Rosalie Chapelain, a Sœur de Saint-Joseph de Cluny, in charge of this new order, which recruited from students of the sisters. While the Filles du Saint-Cœur de Marie offered some primary education, their focus was far more on religion, and they operated more in the countryside than in the cities. The creation of a separate order, however, definitively reoriented Saint-Joseph de Cluny's objectives so that by the second half of the century the sisters themselves opposed the recruitment of black nuns.[63]

By the last quarter of the nineteenth century French women were clearly part of the civilizing process in both Algeria and Senegal even if they targeted different populations; women then were far from absent from the imperial project. Their presence contributed in multiple ways to reinforcing the hierarchies that imperial expansion both explicitly and implicitly established. By separating girls into groups by ethnic origin, religious preference, and social class, lay and religious women teachers contributed to the establishment of boundaries that clearly proclaimed the superiority of French civilization. In Algeria, after 1870 the civilian government's suspicion of religious proselytizing meant that Arab women largely "escaped" the civilizing process, thereby contributing to gender differences in Algerian society.[64] The cultural and ethnic hybridization in Senegal produced a more complicated relationship between men, women, and the civilizing mission. Assimilation in this context, however, generated curious cultural phenomena whose implications deserve further exploration. While the daughters of *assimilées* learned to sing and play the piano, under the guidance of mainly French nuns, the Filles du Saint-Cœur de Marie dispensed primarily spiritual lessons to Senegalese girls. This hardening of racial boundaries prefigured twentieth-century developments in West Africa, particularly the principle of adapted education that in 1903 emphasized "evolution within their own classes" in order to avoid the production of *déclassés*.[65] French education for girls in both Algeria and Senegal, then, certainly contributed to asserting the superiority of French civilization over that of indigenous cultures, but the reorientation of their efforts away from native girls limited the impact of both religious and lay initiatives. Civilization understood as difference was partly a product of institutional development in Africa, and it was, of course, intimately tied to attitudes about race. Unlike French administrators, who remained ideologically committed for many decades to the principle of assimilation, the realities of everyday life led nuns in Algeria and Senegal to create schools that isolated European and white students from black, mulatto, and Arab students.[66] In the end, the French model of education in these two areas may have had more impact on other Europeans than on an indigenous African population. But as an ideal it remained influential even after the French left Africa in the early 1960s.[67]

The Catholic Mission in Protestant Countries

Both religious and laywomen contributed to the civilizing mission in Africa, serving, at times unconsciously, the imperial ambitions of the French state. But these same women also served to spread a French model of girls' education far more widely throughout the "civilized" world. Thanks to the action of nuns, lay teachers, and governesses, French women left their cultural imprint on much of Europe and North America. Contrary to the situation in Africa, French values and culture represented an alternative rather than a superior civilization in these noncolonial settings even if similar motivations impelled women to cross the seas. The spread of French girls' schools and the demand for French governesses even within Protestant countries testifies to the prestige attached to French education for middle-class women on both sides of the Atlantic. This section explores this success and seeks to define what constituted "Frenchness" by focusing more specifically on the initiatives that developed in the United States.

Recent work has begun to explore the impact of French nuns within Protestant countries, notably in England and in North America. Susan O'Brien, in particular, has investigated the expansion of Catholic religious orders in England and has argued for the persistence of "Frenchness" in the lives of the orders, despite adaptation to English ways and the recruitment of English nuns.[68] For the United States, Patricia Byrne has developed an opposing argument in her analysis of the Sœurs de Saint-Joseph; she notes their "Americanization" through the increase of spoken English, and the democratization of religious ways; at times adaptation went so far as an official split with the home French community.[69] Both historians, however, are more interested in the impact of French Catholicism on Protestant soils and its adaptations than in the educational model these teaching nuns brought with them. My concern here is to examine the motivations that pushed French women to settle in England and the United States and then look more closely at the schools themselves and their evolution. Contrary to Byrne, I argue that despite clear evidence of cultural adaptation, French women teachers nonetheless contributed to forging a specifically French vision of girls' education in "civilized" lands that persisted well into the twentieth century.

"Savages" and Protestants: Le Même Combat?

The archives of French religious orders present the expansion of their institutions into Protestant countries and into colonial areas in very similar terms. In both cases, a primarily spiritual mission inspired religious women to invest money and personnel in opening schools in often inhospitable lands. The founding mother of the Société du Sacré-Cœur, Sophie Barat, responded in these terms in 1841 to Mère d'Avenas, who wanted to found a house in Tunis: "I am pushed to consider England . . . my heart bleeds to continue pushing back this beautiful and important mission. . . . Why not look in that direction? Arabs tempt me less than the English; I believe we would be far more useful among the latter than on the sterile Tunisian beaches; I may, however, be mistaken."[70] In this case the challenge of converting Protestants won out over that of educating Muslim infidels, as the Sacré-Cœur established a series of houses in England: first in 1842 in Berrymead, then in 1843 in Cannington, and finally in Roehampton in London in 1851. For Sophie Barat, England was both a challenge and a mission, and she used foundations in Ireland as a way of moving into England: "Because if one considers the two locations proposed, this one [England] is more promising than Ireland because of the students. For prospective novices we would have many more in Ireland!"[71]

Unlike Senegal or Algeria, England scarcely represented the lure of the unknown, but it represented a challenge to Catholic religious women, and particularly French nuns: in 1887, thirty-two out of sixty-two apostolic congregations were French in origin, and French or French-speaking nuns from Belgium ran some ninety-five boarding schools.[72] Some of these foundations were a product of anticlerical policies in France, but prior to the 1880s, most religious orders opened schools in England with the same spiritual objectives that motivated the spread to Africa, Oceania, or the Far East. On English soil, the Fidèles Compagnes de Jésus were the most wholehearted in their efforts to convert Protestants through their schools. Founded in Amiens in 1820 by the vicomtesse Bonnault d'Houet, this small but wealthy order quickly expanded into both England and Ireland, opening their first English school in 1830 and then an Irish school in 1844. Claude Langlois characterizes them as the first to become a foreign order, and they quickly established an excellent reputation for their "French" curriculum.[73]

Undoubtedly, however, the United States represented a far more alluring destination for nuns seeking to spread the fruits of the French civilizing mission in the first half of the century.[74] Travellers to the American Midwest, in particular, imagined their task as heroically converting the "infidels," be they Native Americans or Protestants. The comtesse de la Rochejacquelin, who financed the trip of the Sœurs de Saint-Joseph de Lyon in 1836, explained her objectives in these terms: "I promised God, insofar as he would deign to bless their design, to send six Sœurs de Saint-Joseph de Lyon to North America to convert the savages, to teach their children and those of Protestant families, and to convert those to whom the missionaries, too busy and too few, are able to make but passing visits."[75] Almost twenty years earlier in 1818 Philippine Duchesne had led a first group of Sacré-Cœur nuns across the Atlantic hoping to bring civilization and religion to the "savages."[76]

The United States remained mission territory according to canon law until 1908, and many French nuns responded to the call. Elisabeth Dufourcq estimates that twenty different French religious orders contributed at least 5,950 sisters to the civilizing mission in the United States between 1840 and 1900.[77] The Ursuline foundation in New Orleans in 1721 was the earliest in the New World, but the real expansion of French orders in the United States came between 1830 and 1859, through the activities most notably of the Sacred Heart, the Sisters of Saint Joseph from Lyons, the Sisters of Providence, who settled in St. Mary of the Woods in 1840, and the Sisters of the Holy Cross, who settled in Notre Dame in 1843.[78] This presence of French nuns was far more evident in the Midwest, particularly in the annexed territories of the Louisiana Purchase, where schools in general were less developed and where missionary ideals remained strongest.[79]

Although knowledge about what awaited them in the New World increased over the course of the century, early recruits to the American houses came with the same sort of illusions that inspired women religious to participate in colonial expansion. But they were not the cultural emissaries of an expanding imperial state, even if the same conviction of their cultural and religious superiority carried them into North America. Nor were their main efforts directed toward the Native American population, despite their initial vocation: "They wanted above all, as this was the spirit of their vocation, to give themselves to the education of young savages . . . but this great work cannot begin and continue with any chance of success until religion's empire has established a sufficiently solid base among the civilized populations so that they offer the sort of example one might expect to the unhappy Indians."[80] As a result, the Sacred Heart, for example, waited some twenty years before attempting a Native American mission.[81] In practice, teaching creoles, Protestants, or "savages" turned out to be a very different task requiring different skills and forms of adaptation than the initial missionaries imagined.[82] As a result, schools often assumed very different characteristics both from what was imagined and from what existed in France.

French Schools on American Soil

In the United States, French orders did not have the financial support of the French government, and so the initial schools operated with limited budgets depending on local generosity, dowry payments, and educational income, as in France. Most commonly, nuns founded boarding schools, which generated income allowing them then to diversify their educational offerings. For the French, boarding schools were seen as the most efficient way to educate young girls far from the temptations of the outside world.[83] By targeting the local elite they sought to foster the emergence of Christian families who would then serve as examples of the virtues of French civilization. Local bishops in America defended this orientation, arguing, "For it is from the education of the upper levels of society that reform must come, and they are just as ignorant as the lower classes."[84] As in Africa, nuns imagined they would regenerate families thanks to women's influence within the family.

The early religious schools, however, very quickly took on some of the characteristics of their American setting. The example of the Sacred Heart institutions is particularly illuminating in this respect. The order rapidly opened five houses in the Mississippi River valley between 1818 and 1827. In 1841 a house was founded on the East Coast in New York; at this point, the Society had some 120 nuns in America, a majority of whom were of American origin.[85] Although the Sacred Heart established a reputation for offering a French model of education, this model had a distinct American flavor. As historian Nikola Baumgarten has persuasively argued, in Saint Louis, Missouri, the Sacred Heart contributed to the republican ideal of universal schooling through the variety of schools it opened.[86] Boarders and day students had access to a relatively rigorous plan of study based on the French plan of 1833. The Society also opened free schools that offered elementary education, and on Sundays the nuns opened their free school to black girls until 1847, when a Missouri law outlawed the education of blacks.[87] The early schools accepted many Protestants; in 1846 two-thirds of all boarders in Saint Louis were Protestants. As a result, Mother Duchesne openly worried about the absence of Catholicism in the Louisiana boarding schools.[88]

In the 1830s, the different American schools of the Sacred Heart had surprisingly contrasting images, dependent to a great extent on the personality of the mother superior. Philippine Duchesne, in particular, devoted her considerable energy in Saint Louis to the poor and, eventually, Native Americans. As a result, around Saint Louis day students and free students comprised the vast majority, whereas from the beginning the establishments around New Orleans attracted wealthy boarders. This variety both in clientele and type of school offered a sharp contrast with the schools in France. In the early 1830s Bishop Rosati described the Saint Louis schools of the Sacred Heart in the following terms: "The house is not elegant as your European convents, but it is suitable for this country."[89] The sisters of Saint Joseph from Lyons showed similar flexibility when they arrived in the Midwest in the 1840s, opening a middle-class academy but also running a day school, an orphanage, and a school for deaf children.[90] Despite this variety, French schools from the beginning cultivated a reputation for providing culture and refinement. In an advertisement for their academy in Cincinnati, the Sisters of Notre-Dame de Namur wrote: "The heart must be educated as well as the mind and adorned with those qualities which beautify manners and render virtue more attractive and amiable."[91]

Initial adaptation to conditions in the Midwest led to an unusual mixture of American and French ways. Students followed the French academic plan of study, but Catholicism was far less central to the educational experience. In order to accommodate and to attract a religiously and ethnically diverse student body, nuns downplayed cultural and religious proselytizing. Moreover, the physical proximity of boarders, day students, and poor students introduced more democratic practices within the schools in striking opposition to what happened in Africa or in France. The inspection that Mother Elizabeth Galitzine conducted of the Midwestern Sacred Heart schools in the early 1840s testifies to how American ideals had influenced how the institution operated. In the course of her inspections, she found many things to criticize: authority was lax, students were given inappropriate books, students danced too frequently, thanks to the presence of a violin-playing Negro, too many recruits were insufficiently pious.[92] In sum, it would appear that after some fifteen years in the Mississippi River valley, the Society's efforts to civilize the American population had gone woefully astray. And yet in institutional terms the Sacred Heart's civilizing mission in the United States was a clear success. After the initially lean years of the early 1820s, the Society boasted six highly respected academies, which catered to a mixed denominational elite. Newspapers and public opinion paid homage to the French nuns and to their institutions, whose prestige attracted an ever-growing number of students as well as American or creole religious recruits. Despite Galitzine's criticisms, clearly the Society exerted an influence, but what was the nature of this influence?

Beginning in the early decades of the century, frequent references to a French model or to French institutions testify to the cultural prestige attached to all things French. The Irish nuns of the Visitation, who ran a well-respected academy in Georgetown, Maryland, advertised in 1827 that their institution offered courses in "domestic economy, comprising the various exercises in Pastry and the culinary art, laundry, pantry and dairy inspection etc as conducted at the Academy of Saint Denis Banlieue de Paris."[93] Apparently these women considered the comparison with the school of the Legion of Honor at Saint Denis to be a selling point for prospective American families. Similarly, the Dames de la Retraite in Philadelphia advertised their school in 1833 as a "Young Ladies French and English Academy." Emphasizing an educational plan "as nearly possible similar to that which has inspired so much confidence in France," their brochure focused on the polish and refinement their schools offered in order to qualify young ladies for "refined and polite society."[94] As the number of French schools for girls increased in the United States, they created a French model of education that attracted attention and forged cultural ties between France and the New World.[95]

Adaptation and Change: The Emergence of a French Model for the Middle Classes

The missionary zeal that underlay the early midwestern foundations diminished as schools multiplied and the ethnic composition of the teaching orders evolved. Increasingly, French teaching orders shifted their focus from regenerating society to spreading Catholicism, with different strategies depending on the social class they targeted. As they settled in the New World, they experienced a variety of tensions that played themselves out in contrasting ways. Some did indeed "Americanize," through a general loosening of the social hierarchies that played such a prominent role in France: boundaries between categories of students were not as rigid, more contact was allowed between nuns and the outside community, and the distinction between lay nuns who did mainly domestic work and choir sisters was abolished.[96] Other orders, and most notably the Sacred Heart, clung to certain French traditions and evolved in a direction that increasingly distinguished their institutions from other American academies, Protestant or Catholic. Despite inevitable adaptation to the social and cultural mores of American society, French women religious introduced a way of ordering daily life and a vision of education that was perceived as specifically French, not just Catholic.

The astuteness with which individual orders adapted to American conditions explains in part the relative success of French convent school education.[97] After visiting the houses of the Sacred Heart, Elizabeth Galitzine emphasized in her report back to France in 1840 that success required respect for and adaptation to American customs rather than rigid adherence to a French model. She cautioned her superiors on the importance of recognizing other forms of belief and modes of behavior: "All that we can do and say for the success of our works and the good of the Society must vary according to circumstances, the time, the location, the people; what may be appropriate at one moment, is not at another; only flexibility and tact in the choice of methods will produce good results."[98] In practice this meant such things as accepting a less rigid organization of daily life, permitting the widespread use of English both in the classroom and among nuns, respecting Protestant prejudices against frivolous behavior on Sundays, and allowing day students to mingle with boarders. Throughout the world, the Sacred Heart insisted, however, that its boarding schools follow the French plan of study, which was *not* translated into English.

Nonetheless, the sorts of adjustments just described, as well as the recruitment of American nuns, produced an interesting melding of more open and democratic modes of functioning with a continued emphasis on what was seen as characteristically French, particularly the insistence on speaking in French, and certain forms of polite behavior.[99]

French nuns adapted their curriculum to American needs while retaining what was perceived as a French flavor.[100] The most notable change to the traditional French curriculum was the early addition of science classes. The Sacred Heart schools in frontier St. Louis, for example, studied natural philosophy, astronomy, chemistry, and geography in the advanced classes, while in 1842 the Maryland Carmelite Sister's Academy also advertised courses in natural philosophy, botany, and astronomy.[101] Carol Coburn and Martha Smith have similarly documented the weight of science lessons in the program offered by the Sisters of Saint Joseph of Carondelet. Their academy in Saint Louis, while advertising the quality of the "proper French education" they offered, nonetheless modified the content to suit the expectations of upwardly mobile American parents. In the 1840s their curriculum included French, Latin, German, sacred and profane history, geography, mathematics, rhetoric, botany, physics, chemistry, and astronomy. More tellingly, this order increasingly pushed course work in "ornamentals" to the sidelines of their academies at a time when such subjects continued to play a central role for French elites. By the 1860s their catalogs distinguished between the classical or ornamental curriculum and the "English scientific courses."[102]

"French" education for girls was increasingly associated with the education of elites. Contemporaries perceived the Sacred Heart, in particular, as offering an education "in the most elegant and fashionable manner."[103] Interestingly, it seems that as the Society's membership became increasingly international, its schools became more "French," with a more traditional commitment to educating the daughters of the "best families," as they had from the outset in France. As Susan O'Brien has noted in studying French nuns in England, this can be explained in part through the intensity of the order's founding narratives; moreover, the regular circulation of printed letters and annual reports and visiting inspectresses all contributed to enforcing respect for unity and for the Society's initial charisma.[104] As a result, the early diversity among the American schools of the Sacred Heart gradually disappeared.

A few examples illustrate this process. The school in New York, which moved to Manhattanville in 1847, catered to an elite. Its prospectus in 1864 stated that "the education of young ladies of the higher class was the special object of this institute" and the sizable board and tuition fee ($250) ensured this exclusivity.[105] Similarly, the school that opened in Chicago in 1858 quickly gained a reputation among the first families even if the Society also opened a free school that attracted far more students.[106] The prospectus for their Young Ladies' Seminary noted: "The Education course of instruction embraces the various elementary as well as the higher branches of a higher education. Propriety of deportment, politeness, personal neatness, and the principles of morality are objects of unceasing assiduity. An excellent Chemical and Philosophical Apparatus forms a valuable addition to the means of instruction. The French language is fluently and constantly spoken in this institution." In addition to intellectual subjects the nuns offered boarders courses in domestic economy for a basic fee of $140, while for an extra fee girls could have lessons in the German language, piano or guitar, drawing, and painting.[107] The educational program within Sacred Heart academies retained many elements of a French education, beyond the use of the language and the insistence on discipline, politeness, and good manners. For example, the focus on grammar, "orthography," and "epistolary style" in the last two years of study were hallmarks of a refined French education; epistolary style in particular was not commonly taught in Protestant academies.[108]

The appeal of this sort of education can be measured in part by the continuing presence of Protestants within the Society's schools, as Table 3 testifies. The presence of Protestant girls did not mean that Catholic rituals and lessons were any less important in daily life.[109] In Chicago, prospective students were explicitly warned: "All young ladies, for the sake of regularity are required to conform to the public worship of the house."[110]

"Frenchness" in girls' education in the United States was more than just a question of social elitism in the student body. It was also associated with an educational emphasis on ornamental accomplishments that American Catholics increasingly deplored, particularly as more serious college education for women developed. The newspaper *Catholic World* criticized convent academies in 1869 for their excessive attention to exterior graces, sentiments, and accomplishments, qualities that the journalist considered more appropriate to the social arrangements of Europe.[111] Music, however, was well appreciated. Writing about the curriculum of the Sisters of Charity in Frederick, Virginia, Theodora Guérin, mother superior of the Sisters of Providence of St. Mary of the Woods, exclaimed: "They teach the various sciences scarcely known in our French schools, but they excel in music, which is an indispensable thing in this country, even for the poor. No piano, no pupils! Such is the spirit of this country — Music and Steam."[112]

More broadly, French convent schools introduced an administration of daily life, which, despite adaptation, carried a distinctive French flavor. Indeed the perception that French nuns produced courteous, refined, and well-mannered young ladies was largely a by-product of the disciplinary project described in Chapter 6. Pedagogical methods, particularly those inspired by the Jesuits, crossed the Atlantic virtually intact. Most notably, convent academies adopted a weekly awarding of points as well as a solemn distribution of prizes that reproduced the emulation French pedagogues so valued. Also borrowed from French traditions were the elaborate prize-giving ceremonies, known as Exhibition Days on American soil.[113] Similarly, the focus on mem-

Table 3 STUDENTS OF THE ACADEMY OF THE SACRED HEART, CHICAGO AND LAKE FOREST, 1858–1910

	Total	Protestants	Protestants (%)	Jews
1858–1870	373	131	35.1	
1871–1880	360	62	17.2	3
1881–1890	414	85	20.5	
1891–1900	234	79	33.8	
1910–1910	538	109	20.3	

SOURCE: Brewer, *Nuns*, 89. She indicates as well that between 1841 and 1851 the Academy in Saint Louis educated 255 Protestants out of a total of 531 students (48%), and at the Clifton Academy in Cincinnati in the 1870s, 91 Protestant girls out of 192 total (47%).

orization was also very present, at least at Sacred Heart schools, if the well-known essayist Agnes Repplier's amusing portrayal is to be believed: "A competition in anything was an unqualified calamity. It meant hours of additional study, a frantic memorizing of facts, fit only to be forgotten, and the bewildering ordeal of being interrogated before the whole school."[114]

What distinguished French institutions from their American counterparts most clearly was this insistence on rules, regulations, and discipline even when these rules were modified to accommodate American mores. Agnes Repplier astutely noted in her memoirs describing her experience at the Sacred Heart in Philadelphia: "I am inclined to think that the habit of self-restraint induced by this gentle inflexibility of discipline, this exquisite sense of method and proportion, was the most valuable by-product of our education."[115] As a student she chafed at the constant control, the ringing of bells, and the speaking of French, but she appears nonetheless to have internalized the lessons in restraint that her teachers sought to instill. This is all the more striking in that her memoirs are testimony to how she and her fellow students rebelled against the rules of everyday life, to the point that she was in the end expelled from the Academy. A far tamer portrayal of French convent school life was published in the 1870s, but here as well the author emphasized the omnipresence of rules: "A Lady and a lay sister sleep in each dormitory, and neither by night nor day, from entering within, to departure from, the convent, are the scholars ever left alone. No communication with the day-pupils is permitted, no books or periodicals are read without examination." At the same time the rules were clearly not as strict as in France, since in this school teachers caught girls several times playing cards before the superior decided to put an end to this pastime.[116]

Mary McCarthy's memoirs, written decades after Repplier's, are an eloquent testimony to the continuing "Frenchness" of a Sacred Heart education. Placed at the age of eleven in the Forest Ridge convent in Seattle in 1923, she emphasizes the impact of a "highly centralized order, versed in clockwork obedience to authority. Their institutions follow a pattern laid down for them in France in the early nineteenth-century — clipped and pollarded as a garden and stately as a minuet."[117] Awed by the French words and the austerity of daily life, she describes an environment governed by rules she constantly circumvented, and where the rituals of form prevailed over content. This critical vision of French education in the twentieth century may not do justice to how the Sacred Heart adapted their education to American customs, but it certainly conveys how foreign and French this order still appeared to a young American, one hundred years after its arrival in the United States. True, Mary Elliott argued that although "the whole atmosphere we breathed had a strong unworldly, supernatural element . . . it did not seem foreign to us," nonetheless her memoirs emphasize throughout the nuns who spoke only French, the librarian who exuded "a real French, gentle, sentimental piety," and this order which distinguished between Ladies and lay sisters. Presumably families chose to place their daughters in such a school in part because of these differences.[118]

The focus on discipline, silence, and the rituals of Marian piety distinguished convent education from its Protestant variety.[119] But was there something specifically French about this form of Catholic education? Certainly the similarities among Catholic schools whose nuns came from Ireland, Germany, France, or America were far greater than their differences. Margaret Thompson presents a convincing argument for the relative flexibility of religious life in the American setting.[120] Should one then conclude that by the final quarter of the century the French civilizing mission in the United States had spent its force and that French nuns had been absorbed into the melting pot?

I think not. The recentering of educational goals on Catholicism rather than on civilizing had a tremendous impact on American society as a whole; French nuns and their schools are an important part of the story that transformed the fabric of American religious life. But there is more to their impact than that. Although the French teaching orders adapted and adjusted to American life, many maintained a carefully cultivated reputation for offering a "French" education to the daughters of wealthy or middle-class families. By the 1870s and 1880s this meant forming an articulate and polished young woman who could converse in French and play her role as hostess in a livingroom. Within school walls, a French education meant single-sex education (whereas American high schools were coeducational), relatively little social mixing, strict surveillance, and a demanding course load where memorization played an important role. That schools continued to advertise themselves as offering a French model of education strongly suggests that this represented something specific to an increasingly diverse American society.

Evidence of a French model for girls' education appears in scattered sources throughout Western Europe and North America. Irish historian Anne O'Connor has noted the tremendous weight in middle-class families on having girls learn French and acquire the trappings of a French education. French convent schools encountered swift success because they offered "an advantage for which [parents] would otherwise have had to go abroad." For the Irish, French education meant lessons in "politeness, deportment, good conduct, order, regularity, and application," but it also included an elaborate prize system and an education in good taste.[121] For Sissy O'Brien, who attended the boarding schools of the Faithful Companions of Jesus at Bruff, County Limerick, in Ireland, French education was a language, a discipline, and a way of organizing daily life. In her memoirs, *The Farm by Lough Gur*, she describes her nanny telling her, "That's the French way of making a bed: all the rules are French."[122] For upwardly mobile families throughout the Western world, French education transmitted the virtues of *politesse* and *goût*. At the same time the French model of education that had existed for boys in the early modern period had begun to lose its influence. By the 1850s on, the prestige attached to French education and the French language was gendered, at least within the Anglo-American world; for girls it produced polished women of the world, while for boys it smacked of effeminacy and superficiality.[123]

Positive perceptions of French education in certain circles did not preclude the emergence of visceral anti-Catholicism with its accompanying literature in both the United States and England. Most shocking perhaps was the burning of the Ursuline convent in Charlestown, Massachusetts, in 1834, when the nuns and their student boarders barely escaped with their lives. Anti-Catholic books and pamphlets presented the surveillance of French convent school education as an infringement of individual rights while separation from the family was seen as severing natural ties. In general this form of education was seen as despotic and prudish, more concerned with exterior forms than inner worth. As in France, criticisms of convent schools accused nuns of being disconnected from the modern world, incapable of forming good domestic wives and mothers. In 1870 a biting condemnation in the British journal *Fraser's Magazine* accused nuns of providing an education that "unclassed" young women: "The superficial accomplishments which form the ordinary convent curriculum are found totally useless in their homes."[124] More luridly, some of this literature borrowed from a time-honored anticlerical tradition in the condemnation of the immorality of convent life. By emphasizing the seclusion and separation of convent education, as well as the "abnormal" character of nuns, anti-Catholic propaganda implicitly, and at times explicitly, denounced the relationship between families and schools that underwrote the French civilizing mission.

Writing women into this mission offers a way to understand the strength of cultural and pedagogical imperatives in the imperial project. Particularly, it highlights how women carried an imperial vision to foreign shores and sought to influence societies from within through the creation of schools that would spread French values and ways of being. Educators envisioned their schools, however, through the lenses of their own experiences, and these experiences were fashioned in France for the early missionaries to both Africa and North America. The nuns and laywomen who set off to regenerate other societies saw girls' education as a way to reform indigenous families, but understandings of class inevitably bounded the reform project as it did within France. In Africa, the pedagogical enactment of class encountered the realities of race, producing schooling situations where class and race intersected to establish new hierarchies. In both Algeria and Senegal, nuns and laywomen initially sought to reform indigenous families, but by pulling girls away from their families they made them ineligible as marriage partners. As a result, French teachers were forced to redirect their efforts toward European populations or mulatto families, leaving an educational and racial legacy for the future. In Algeria, in particular, Muslim women were written out of the civilizing mission. The failure to enact the assimilation of Algerian women and, to a lesser extent, Senegalese women with French populations highlights the fundamental ambivalence of colonial discourse. Making these women into Frenchwomen was an impossible task that encountered the resistance not only of class and race, but also that of gender. Instead, the education nuns and laywomen provided contributed to a "learning of place and race," as Ann Stoler puts it, that was clearly inferior to that offered to bourgeois girls in France.[125]

In the Western world, French women educators' ambitions were different and reveal a national dimension to the civilizing process. Nuns and laywomen, including governesses, actively fashioned a vision of French girls' education that spread throughout much of the Western world and whose influence persists, unacknowledged, in many locations to this day. Carried in part by the ideals that spawned reforms within France, the "French" education that acquired a reputation in the United States and England had clear class overtones.[126] The women who established schools in these countries were in part disseminating the values of a consolidating bourgeoisie, and yet these values often acquired an aristocratic flavor, particularly within the context of a more democratic American society. The emphasis on acquiring the exterior signs of culture, through language, manners, and general deportment distinguished French education from that of other Catholic immigrant groups. French education offered American women poise and elegance, not just literacy. Ironically, given the efforts of such reformers as Joséphine Bachellery or Julie-Victoire Daubié, French girls' education acquired a reputation for precisely those characteristics they had struggled to eradicate in order to introduce a more serious and vocational orientation. This does not mean, of course, that French education abroad offered mere polish, but it does suggest that attention to exterior manners and accomplishments remained fundamental to the French bourgeois vision.

CONCLUSION

In 1900 Catherine Pozzi, the eighteen-year-old daughter of a well-established bourgeois Parisian family, wrote: "I'm eighteen. Since the 13th. Geez! I hate this age. Now I'm officially the marriageable young girl. Brrrrrrr! Thank goodness I trust my parents otherwise I'd kill myself! because I can't bear the mere idea of marriage." She went on then to protest against wasted opportunities: "I could have been somebody. I have capabilities within me which have never been developed. I've often felt within myself the seeds of great things, a vague impression of unexplored depths, the sensation that my whole being was being projected toward something. . . . My destiny! a destiny I imagined grand, terrible, splendid and that I called out to." This *cri du cœur* went on mingling self-reproach as well as criticisms of her father who failed to nourish her intellectually and spiritually: "Oh Papa, who might have created a mind, but who didn't, how I sense your guilt." Although she did not state it explicitly, she clearly linked her sense of failure to her womanhood, the "chair-de-fille" (girl's flesh), that made her a "coquette" and led her to fear for the future: "I'm afraid of what I'll do in the future. There are so many more demons than saints in this life!"[1] Catherine Pozzi wanted to be "someone"; as an eighteen-year-old bourgeois young woman she feared she would only be a wife.

Pozzi's sense of her own limited horizons is a useful reminder that despite the growth of opportunities for women over the course of the century, many bourgeois women continued to follow the dictates of a Napoleon or a Rousseau, marrying and devoting their lives to their husbands and families.[2] The fin-de-siècle New Woman attracted attention and provoked comment precisely because she was a symbol of rebellion against bourgeois domestic ideology.[3] In many ways the discourse surrounding her activities resembled that of early nineteenth-century commentators; doctors and psychologists marshaled scientific arguments to show that women belonged in the home and, particularly during puberty, should be careful not to exert themselves intellectually. The virulence of this discussion was undoubtedly greater in 1900 in response to evidence that women were not fulfilling their natural role—birthrates were falling—and yet the continuity with early debates is probably more striking than the discontinuities.[4] In 1900 as in 1800, many French men and women were uncomfortable with the idea that women had creative genius or simply intellectual and professional ambitions; many were threatened by women's efforts to venture into male spaces, such as the university, the liberal professions, and especially the world of politics.

Something had indeed changed, however, by 1900, and girls' education and women teachers had contributed to this change. To begin with, adolescents and women increasingly saw themselves as individuals with unique characteristics. As a result, more and more girls, like Catherine Pozzi, aspired to a life beyond the family and consigned their dreams and longings to paper in their diaries and correspondences.[5] Even those women who outwardly conformed to middle-class norms used writing more openly as a means to express themselves creatively.[6] In social terms, women had begun to enter the university and the professions, thanks to expanding possibilities to prepare for and pass the *baccalauréat*. These new students and women professionals were the proof that women could indeed follow university studies, practice law and medicine, and compete in civil service examinations.[7] And unlike Mme de Staël or Mme de Genlis, these women were not from the privileged aristocracy, but from the middle classes. Finally, politicians increasingly realized that women were a force to reckon with. Writing in the first all-woman newspaper, *La fronde*, high-profile journalists, such as Marguerite Durand and Séverine, kept women's issues and women's rights in the public eye. Unlike the Saint-Simonian and feminist press of the 1830s, which only reached a limited audience, *La fronde* made gender politics and gender identities the subject of public debate. As Mary Louise Roberts has argued, the newspaper presented "an image of women that was internally contradictory," thus rejecting notions of the eternal feminine and producing a female self that resisted fixed meanings.[8] Like it or not, women's nature no longer restricted them to the private sphere; women had become a factor to contend with in public. How had this occurred?

An obvious place to turn for an answer is to the history of French feminism, which is by now fairly familiar. Clearly, feminist campaigns and organizations contributed to changing laws and attitudes, particularly in the second half of the century. But this is only part of the story. I have argued in this book that education and schools were among the critical sites proposing new ways of positioning women in the family and in society. Pedagogues, teachers, the school environment itself, and the impetus of the civilizing mission contributed in multiple ways to redefining gender relations, although not always in feminist directions. The educational imperative led women to write, to publish, to found schools, to teach, to travel abroad, and to pester government officials throughout the century.

The postrevolutionary period left a complicated legacy for gender relations, particularly given the weight attached to the family as the bulwark of the new civic order. Women pedagogues helped then to construct a vision of the public and private divide, but their focus on an all-powerful familial metaphor meant that the tentacles of the private reached out into the public and indeed largely shaped its contours. The public was to be infused with the qualities that emanated from the family, such as honor and morality. In this fashion the more articulate teachers and pedagogues extended women's empire to society as a whole.

The qualities invested in the feminine and the messages conveyed through literature and schooling practices similarly muddy the binary oppositions so often used. Pedagogues might argue for women's natural religiosity but they also emphasized the need for rational study. This rational study could take the form of examinations and emulation that point to the importance of work and the work ethic in evolving female identities. Work, effort, and rationality were not the sole prerogatives of men. As Robert Nye has argued, the work ethic was central to bourgeois male honor, but the honorable woman also worked in nonremunerative but equally significant ways.[9] Indeed, the peculiar tension between forming girls who looked good in public and girls who worked well in private highlights how honor and appearances were central to the socializing messages of the early nineteenth century. Appearances were time and again the focus of reformist criticism, and yet the whole educational project revolved on the importance of appearances and concealment. Women should conceal their talents and their knowledge at the risk of appearing immodest; women should look beyond appearances to discern the true value of potential suitors and friends. Schooling practices, however, did not necessarily conform to this view — as my analysis has shown. Girls were indeed encouraged to perform, to appear in public, and to strive for public recognition in ways that directly contradicted the emphasis on concealment that feminine modesty entailed. The overt religiosity of certain educational institutions also turned girls away from the more serious pedagogical lessons on the importance of rationality and work. What sort of gendered cultural identity was likely to emerge from the constellation of conflicting messages and practices that the educational experience conveyed?

The second section of this book offers some provisional answers. The growth of schools in the years between 1830 and 1880 altered the socializing process for many bourgeois girls. Increasingly they spent some years within an institutional setting and received lessons conveyed by women who had studied in schools themselves, undergone some form of training, and taken examinations. The rise of the professional woman teacher — along with that of the woman writer — changed the tenor of debates about women's place in French society, raising the specter of the *bas-bleu* and the fear that gender roles would be reversed. While schools were rarely the site for open criticism of existing gender relations, they effectively opened new opportunities for women. As the social range of students in these schools expanded, teachers diversified their educational offerings and spoke more openly about the need to prepare girls for active futures. Within boarding-school settings, girls received very mixed messages about what femininity entailed and how being female affected their life choices. In these years when domestic values acquired widespread social and cultural acceptance, more and more girls studied to pass the educational examinations that headmistresses increasingly highlighted as the goal of their educational program. The education necessary to produce learned, serious, and domestic women opened door outside the home as well. Indeed religious messages and religious associations within schools undoubtedly contributed to the numbers of women who knocked on convent doors and consequently devoted their lives to teaching or nursing. Education also offered some women, such as Joséphine Bachellery and Julie-Victoire Daubié, the means to critique women's "natural" position within the home and to engage in public debate. For adolescent girls, however, the schooling experience provided above all lessons in community that challenged them to consider their individual positions within the group. Schools could not and did not replicate the family; instead they provided a disciplined environment where girls forged their sense of self in response to well-defined boundaries whose limits they spent their school years testing. It is these experiences that help to explain in part the sense of frustration expressed by Catherine Pozzi. Family and domesticity were the overt goals of girls' education, but not the concrete experience of many.

The apparently seamless fabric of the domestic woman began ostensibly to unravel in the second half of the century thanks to increasing professional opportunities and the impact of feminist voices. In this respect the state's tardy intervention in the field of girls' secondary education appears particularly out of touch with social and cultural realities. While the new *collèges* and *lycées* undoubtedly offered bourgeois girls a more rigorous education than existed in many boarding schools, they failed to adjust their objectives to the ambitions of these young women, who came increasingly from the lower middle class. As a result, the private Catholic sector took the initiative, preparing girls for the *baccalauréat* so they could join their brothers on the benches of university classrooms. It would be inaccurate, however, to understand the development of girls' education solely within this framework of Republican and Catholic political opposition. On the contrary, the weight of my analysis has been on showing how similar tensions traversed both lay and religious education for girls and that by exploring school settings in other lands what emerges most clearly is a French model of girls' education that appears relatively distinct from other national models.

Writing in 1910, Janet Erskine Stuart, superior general of the Société du Sacré-Cœur, wrote a book about Catholic girls' education that offers an illuminating vision of this model. Although she was herself English, and while her book addressed Catholic education in general and not French education, her arguments clearly reveal distinctly French pedagogical models and a conception of gender relations that appears specifically French. Her book first appeared in the United States under the title, *Education: How Old the New?* In 1914 it was translated into French under the less provocative title: *L'éducation des jeunes filles catholiques.* Stuart's concern was to promote a model of Catholic girls' education in the wake of widespread questioning about women's place in society. The years just preceding World War I were, of course, tumultuous ones for those concerned with gender relations, given the suffrage movements in England, the United States, and France, the three countries with which Stuart was the most familiar. In defending certain traditional, and specifically Catholic values, Stuart nonetheless proposed a relatively rigorous plan of study. Still, she was not promoting equality between the education of boys and girls; rather, she took pains to emphasize the limits of what was appropriate for girls — girls, unlike boys, did not need much math or Latin.

Stuart's defense of serious education recalls the position of many of her predecessors, most notably Albertine Necker de Saussure. Like the latter, whom she quoted directly, she argued for the need to reconcile religion and reason, thus justifying the development of philosophical studies for girls. Indeed, in terms of content, most of what she advocated, with the exception of philosophy, echoed the more enlightened position of early nineteenth-century educators: girls should study a little math; physical and natural sciences (the latter mostly via gardening); their country's language ("since a nation's spirit emerges in language and language gives the tone and spirit to the following generation"); conversational styles; modern languages; history; and subjects relating to practical life — needlework, hygiene, and cooking. More interesting, like Campan, she defended the study of dance, the arts, and manners, all subjects that had been repeatedly criticized over the course of the century as having more to do with old aristocratic values than those of the new middle classes. Her arguments clearly showed, however, that these subjects were not taught with the intent of forming salon hostesses. She presented dance as a natural way for the girl to express herself; art and music lessons instilled in girls "feelings of responsibility that find their source in the conviction that art exerts a great influence on character." She defended good manners as "the external expression of the intimate motives that guide our conduct."[10] Concern for the individual character was far more evident than a century earlier. Still what is most striking in her book is the relationship she implicitly established between her educational principles and women's place in society.

Stuart thought girls needed to learn work habits and the ability to be self-governing.

To achieve this she advocated a simple well-regulated life, where work was encouraged through a very familiar arsenal of prizes and rewards. She specifically defended boarding schools, where she believed teachers established greater moral influence and where the quality of professors was greater than at home. Within these schools, girls learned they were part of a broader world than the family, a point that was brought home through public prize-giving ceremonies and the associations and congregations within the school. History, through the communication of patriotic values, also contributed to making girls understand the country to which they belonged, while philosophy would allow girls to express their opinions and take initiatives beyond the confines of the home. Stuart, like Genlis, saw the education of girls as a complicated machine that required subtle adjustments according both to the student's and to society's needs. It was not easy to achieve the proper balance between serious studies and women's appropriate place; and indeed, she deplored the production of a large number of *"déclassées* whom this surfeit of education without any moral or religious counterweight has thrust onto the pavements of our great cities." Stuart was no revolutionary nor did her program appear to favor the emergence of the new woman: "Women's role is neither to initiate nor to create."[11] And yet her vision resembled those of many of her more radical predecessors. The public orientation of this education was a connecting thread with French girls' education from the beginning of the century. By forming girls' minds, taste, and bodies, Stuart sought like many pedagogues before her to extend woman's empire, even if she was unwilling to face up to what that might imply. Ironically, the very concept of woman's empire and its spatial location had considerably changed by 1900, thanks in large part to women like Stuart, who eschewed women's "traditional" role as wife and mother, opting instead to found schools, govern religious orders, or spread the messages of French civilization throughout the world. Stuart herself directed a society of several thousand nuns throughout the world, women whose schools defined a French model of girls' education for colonial subjects as well as for American, English, and Irish women.[12] While many French bourgeois women continued to aspire to lives of contained domesticity, others had learned that their empire no longer was the home; it had acquired an imperial dimension that allowed them to live on foreign soils, explore the characteristics of other cultures, and impart their vision of woman's proper place, a vision that bore little relation to the lives they actually lived.

APPENDIX I

The Women Pedagogues

Name	Estate	Nationality	Religion	Major work
Jeanne Louise Henriette Campan, born Genest (1752–1822)	bourgeois	French	Catholic	*De l'éducation* (1824)
Comtesse Françoise Thérèse Antoinette Le Groing la Maisonneuve (1764–1837)	aristocrat	French	Catholic	*Essai sur le genre d'instruction qui paraît le plus analogue à la destination des femmes* (1799)
Albertine-Adrienne Necker de Saussure (1766–1841)	aristocrat	Swiss	Protestant	*L'éducation progressive* (1828–38)
Elisabeth Charlotte Pauline Guizot, born De Meulan (1773–1827)	bourgeois	French	Protestant, converted to Catholicism	*L'éducation domestique ou Lettres de famille sur l'éducation* (1826)
Claire de Rémusat, born Claire-Elise Jeanne Gravier de Vergennes (1780–1821)	aristocrat	French	Catholic	*Essai sur l'éducation des femmes* (1824)
Fanny Mongellas, born Burnier (1798–1829)	bourgeois	French	Catholic	*De l'influence des femmes sur les moeurs et les destinées des nations, sur leurs familles et la société, et de l'influence des moeurs sur le bonheur de la vie* (1828)

APPENDIX 2

THE PROFESSIONS OF FATHERS AND HUSBANDS OF PARISIAN HEADMISTRESSES (1810–1880)

FATHER'S PROFESSION

	Total	%	Before 1850	%	1850–1880	%
Farmer/agricultural worker	9	1.1	1	0.7	5	1.1
Dayworker	15	1.9	2	1.3	12	2.6
Servant	3	0.4	8	5.3	14	3.0
Skilled worker	192	24.2	29	19.2	116	25.0
Artisan/shopkeeper	127	16.0	23	15.2	73	15.7
Employee	127	16.0	20	13.2	74	15.9
Merchant	39	4.9	12	7.9	15	3.2
Lower-level civil servant	40	5.0	9	6.0	20	4.3
Midlevel civil servant	10	1.3	2	1.3	6	1.3
High-level civil servant	3	0.4	2	1.3	0	0
Teacher	65	8.2	12	7.9	40	8.6
Artist/scientist	38	4.8	5	3.3	23	5.0
Soldier	45	5.7	12	7.9	21	4.5
Member of a liberal profession	42	5.3	10	6.6	22	4.7
Landlord / property owner	40	5.0	4	2.6	23	5.0
Total	795		151		464	

SOURCE: Information concerning social background is compiled from birth, marriage, and death certificates using the names of headmistresses registered in the *Almanacs de Commerce* for Paris.

Husband's profession

	Total	%	Before 1850	%	1850–1880	%
Farmer/agricultural worker	0	0.0	0	0.0	0	0.0
Dayworker	2	0.3	1	0.6	1	0.2
Servant	3	0.4	1	0.6	1	0.2
Skilled worker	91	12.1	15	8.6	47	11.7
Artisan/shopkeeper	37	4.9	11	6.3	19	4.7
Employee	216	28.6	35	20.1	129	32.2
Merchant	24	3.2	7	4.0	12	3.0
Lower-level civil servant	79	10.5	12	6.9	47	11.7
Midlevel civil servant	17	2.3	7	4.0	6	1.5
High-level civil servant	2	0.3	2	1.1	0	0.0
Teacher	140	18.5	36	20.7	75	18.7
Artist/scientist	51	6.8	16	9.2	25	6.2
Soldier	25	3.3	7	4.0	11	2.7
Member of a liberal profession	38	5.0	15	8.6	15	3.7
Landlord / property owner	30	4.0	9	5.2	13	3.2
Total	755		174		401	

source: Information concerning social background is compiled from birth, marriage, and death certificates using the names of headmistresses registered in the *Almanacs de Commerce* for Paris.

NOTES

INTRODUCTION

1. See George Sand, *Histoire de ma vie* (Paris: Flammarion, 2001).

2. Charlotte Brontë, *Jane Eyre* (London: Longmans, Green, 1959), 143.

3. See Bonnie Smith, *Ladies of the Leisure Class: The Bourgeoises of Northern France in the Nineteenth Century* (Princeton: Princeton University Press, 1981).

4. Private collection of Viviane Isambert-Jamati, prize-giving speech in 1866.

5. Mme de Genlis, "Zumélide ou la jeune vieille," in *Le Comte de Corke surnommé le Grand ou la séduction sans artifice suivi de six nouvelles* (1805), quoted in Jeanne Goldin, "De Félicité de Genlis à George Sand," in *L'Éducation des filles au temps de George Sand*, ed. Michèle Hecquet (Arras: Artois Presses Université, 1998), 176.

6. For the classic study of the Parisian bourgeoisie, see Adeline Daumard, *La bourgeoisie parisienne de 1815 à 1963* (Paris: SEVPEN, 1963). Her social and economic perspective highlights hierarchies within the bourgeoisie and justifies my frequent use of the plural "middle classes" to encompass social groups positioned from the lower middle class to the upper middle class.

7. For an overview of all levels of education in France, see Louis-Henri Parias, ed., *Histoire générale de l'enseignement et de l'éducation en France*, vol. 3, Françoise Mayeur, *De la Révolution à l'École Républicaine, 1789–1930* (Paris: Librairie Nouvelle de France, 1981). For a focus on boys' education after 1848, see Robert Anderson, *Education in France, 1848–1870* (London: Oxford University Press, 1975). For a useful document collection, see Marie-Madeleine Compère, *Du collège au lycée (1500–1850). Généalogie de l'enseignement secondaire français* (Paris: Gallimard, 1985).

8. For a controversial interpretation of educated women's influence within the family, see Mona Ozouf, *Women's Words: Essay on French Singularity*, trans. Jane Marie Todd (Chicago: University of Chicago Press, 1997). For the debates this book generated, see "Femmes: Une singularité française?" *Le Débat* 87 (November-December 1995), and Eric Fassin, "American Feminism in a French Mirror," *French Historical Studies* 22 (winter 1999): 113–38. See, as well, Michelle Perrot, "Pouvoir des hommes, puissance des femmes? l'exemple du XIXe siècle," in her collection *Les femmes ou les silences de l'histoire* (Paris: Flammarion, 1998), 213–26.

9. See, in particular, Suzanne Desan, *The Family on Trial in Revolutionary France* (Berkeley and Los Angeles: University of California Press, 2004), and Jennifer Heuer, "Foreigners, Families and Citizens: Contradictions of National Citizenship in France, 1789–1830" (Ph.D. diss., University of Chicago, 1998).

10. Sylvain Maréchal, *Il ne faut pas que les femmes sachent lire ou Projet d'une loi portant défense d'apprendre à lire aux femmes* (Paris, 1801).

11. Joseph de Maistre, *Lettres et opuscules inédits*, vol. 1 (Paris: A. Vaton, 1851), letter 41.

12. For an analysis of this discourse in the postrevolutionary period, see Geneviève Fraisse, *Reason's Muse: Sexual Difference and the Birth of Democracy*, trans. Jane Marie Todd (Chicago: University of Chicago Press, 1994).

13. Félix Dupanloup, *Femmes savantes et femmes studieuses*, 6th ed. (Paris: Charles Douniol, 1868).

14. See Dominique Julia, "Entre universel et local: Le collège jésuite à l'époque moderne," *Paedagogica Historica* 40 (April 2004): 15–31.

15. In addition to Sand, *Histoire de ma vie*, see Daniel Stern [the comtesse d'Agoult], *Mes souvenirs* (Paris: Calmann Lévy, 1877).

16. See Rebecca Rogers, "Retrograde or Modern? Unveiling the Teaching Nun in Nineteenth-Century France," *Social History* 23 (May 1998): 160–64.

17. See *Mère Marie-Eugénie Milleret. Fondatrice des Religieuses de l'Assomption. Actes du Colloque du Centenaire, Cannes, 24–25 avril 1998* (Paris: Éditions Don Bosco, 1999).

18. Archives de Paris, VD⁶ 159, inspection des maisons d'éducation de demoiselles, 1851–62.

19. Joséphine Bachellery, "Comment nous comprenons l'émancipation des femmes sous la République," *La voix des femmes*, 24–25 April 1848.

20. Lynn Hunt, ed., *The New Cultural History* (Berkeley and Los Angeles: University of California Press, 1989).

21. Françoise Mayeur, *L'enseignement secondaire des jeunes filles sous la IIIe République* (Paris: Presses de la Fondation Nationale des Sciences Politiques, 1977), and *L'éducation des filles en France au XIXe siècle* (Paris: Hachette, 1979).

22. In particular, see Rebecca Rogers, *Les demoiselles de la Légion d'honneur: Les maisons d'éducation de la Légion d'honneur au XIXe siècle* (Paris: Plon, 1992); Claude Langlois, *Le catholicisme au feminine: Les congrégations françaises à supérieure générale au XIXe siècle* (Paris: Cerf, 1984); and Philippe Lejeune, *Le moi des demoiselles: Enquête sur le journal de jeune fille* (Paris: Seuil, 1993).

23. Jo Burr Margadant, *Madame le Professeur: Women Educators in the Third Republic* (Princeton: Princeton University Press, 1990). Sarah Curtis's recent book, *Educating the Faithful: Religion, Schooling, and Society in Nineteenth-Century France* (De Kalb: Northern Illinois University Press, 2000), offers an important perspective from which to understand teaching nuns, but her focus is not on those women who formed the daughters of the middle class.

24. Two books chronologically frame my book: Desan, *The Family on Trial*, and Marie Louise Roberts, *Disruptive Acts: The New Woman in Fin-de-siècle France* (Chicago: University of Chicago Press, 2002).

25. See, in particular, Suzanne Desan and Carla Hesse, *The Other Enlightenment: How French Women Became Modern* (Princeton: Princeton University Press, 2001).

26. See, as well, Sharif Gemie, *Women and Schooling in France, 1815–1914: Gender, Authority, and Identity in the Female Schooling Sector* (Keele: Keele University Press, 1995). The focus here is on primary education and normal schooling and how this brought women into the public sphere. My focus is on the making of the middle classes.

27. See my overview of the historiographical debate on this issue, "Le sexe de l'espace: Réflexions sur l'histoire des femmes aux XVIIIe–XXe siècles dans quelques travaux américains, anglais et français," in *L'espace dans la pratique des historiens*, ed. Jean-Claude Waquet, Odile Goerg, and Rebecca Rogers (Strasbourg: Presses Universitaires de Strasbourg, 2000), 81–202.

28. The undermining of the concept of class itself is less developed among historians of France than among historians of England. See, in particular, the work of Patrick Joyce, "The End of Social History?" *Social History* 20, no. 1 (1995): 73–91.

29. Smith, *Ladies of the Leisure Class*, 7, 16.

30. Leora Auslander, *Taste and Power: Furnishing Modern France* (Berkeley and Los Angeles: University of California Press, 1996).

31. For specific studies that take a more cultural approach, see Douglas Peter Mackaman, *Bourgeois Culture, Medicine, and the Spa in Modern France* (Chicago: University of Chicago Press, 1998); Kathleen Kete, *The Beast in the Boudoir: Petkeeping in Nineteenth-Century Paris* (Berkeley and Los Angeles: University of California Press, 1994); Catherine Pellissier, *Loisirs et sociabilité des notables lyonnais au XIXe siècle* (Lyon: Presses Universitaires de Lyon, 1996); Philippe Perrot, *Les dessus et les dessous de la bourgeoisie* (Bruxelles: Editions Complexe, 1981); Peter Gay, *The Bourgeois Experience: Victoria to Freud*, 4 vols. (Oxford: Oxford University Press, 1984–1995); and Nicholas Green, *The Spectacle of Nature: Landscape and Bourgeois Culture in 19th-Century France* (Manchester: Manchester University Press, 1990). For an analysis that challenges the existence of the French bourgeoisie, see Sarah Maza, *The Myth of the French Bourgeoisie: An Essay on the Social Imaginary, 1750–1850* (Cambridge: Harvard University Press, 2003). Literary historians, in particular, have been influenced by the work of Norbert Elias, see *La dynamique de l'Occident* (Paris: Calmann-Lévy, 1975). His study of the civilizing process offers a stimulating perspective from which to approach the shaping of middle-class values. For a comparative analysis of the lower middle classes, see Geoffrey Crossick, "Formation ou invention des classes moyennes? Une analyse comparée: Belgique-France-GB 1880–1914," *Revue Belge d'Histoire Contemporaine* 26, no. 3/4 (1996): 105–38.

32. Carol Harrison, *The Bourgeois Citizen in Nineteenth-Century France: Gender, Sociability, and the Uses of Emulation* (Oxford and New York: Oxford University Press, 1999). Her introduction offers a very useful overview of the scholarship on gender and class.

33. Alain Plessis, "Une France bourgeoise," in *Histoire de France, Les formes de la culture*, ed. André Burguière and Jacques Revel (Paris: Seuil, 1993), 272.

34. See such classic studies as Leonore Davidoff and Catherine Hall, *Family Fortunes: Men and Women of the English Middle Class, 1780–1850* (Chicago: University of Chicago Press, 1987), and Mary Ryan, *The Cradle of the Middle Class: The Family in Oneida County, New York, 1790–1865* (New York: Cambridge University Press, 1981).

35. William M. Reddy, *The Invisible Code: Honor and Sentiment in Postrevolutionary France, 1814–1848* (Berkeley and Los Angeles: University of California Press, 1997).

36. See André Rauch, *Le premier sexe: Mutations et crise de l'identité masculine* (Paris: Hachette, 2000), and Gabrielle Houbre, *La discipline de l'amour: L'éducation sentimentale des filles et des garçons à l'âge du romantisme* (Paris: Plon, 1997).

37. Paulin Limayrac, "Les femmes moralistes," *Revue des Deux Mondes* 13, no. 4 (1843): 52.

38. See the stimulating analyses in Sharon Marcus, *Apartment Stories: City and Home in Nineteenth-Century Paris and London* (Berkeley and Los Angeles: University of California Press, 1999); Michael B. Miller, *The Bon Marché: Bourgeois Culture and the Department Store, 1869–1920* (Princeton: Princeton University Press, 1981); Lisa Tiersten, *Marianne in the Market: Envisioning Consumer Society in Fin-de-Siècle France* (Berkeley and Los Angeles: University of California Press, 2001); Vanessa R. Schwartz, *Spectacular Realities: Early Mass Culture in Fin-de-siècle Paris* (Berkeley and Los Angeles: University of California Press, 1998); and Edward Berlanstein, *Daughters of Eve: A Cultural History of French Theater Women from the Old Regime to the Fin de Siècle* (Cambridge: Harvard University Press, 2001).

39. See Rogers Chartier, *On the Edge of the Cliff: History, Language, and Practices*, trans. Lydia Cochrane (Baltimore: Johns Hopkins University Press, 1997).

40. In particular: Michel Foucault, *Discipline and Punish: The Birth of the Prison*, trans. Alan Sheridan (New York: Vintage Books, 1995); Michel de Certeau, *The Practice of Everyday Life*, trans. Steven Rendall (Berkeley and Los Angeles: University of California Press, 1984); Pierre Bourdieu and Jean-Claude Passeron, *The Inheritors: French Students and Their Relation to Culture*, trans. Richard Nice (Chicago: University of Chicago Press, 1979); Bourdieu and Passeron, *Reproduction in Education, Society and Culture*, trans. R. Nice (London: Sagewell Publications, 1977); and Bourdieu, *Distinction: A Social Critique of the Judgment of Taste*, trans. R. Nice (Cambridge: Harvard University Press, 1984).

41. Here I am thinking in particular of the following: Natalie Zemon Davis, *Women on the Margins: Three Seventeenth-Century Lives* (Cambridge: Harvard University Press, 1995); Joan Wallach Scott, *Gender and the Politics of History* (New York: Columbia University Press, 1988); Catherine Hall, *White, Male and Middle-Class: Explorations in Feminism and History* (New York: Routledge, 1992); Leonore Davidoff, *Worlds Between: Historical Perspectives on Gender and Class* (New York: Routledge, 1995); Martha Vicinus, *Independent Women: Work and Community for Single Women, 1850–1920* (Chicago: University of Chicago Press, 1985); and M. Perrot, *Les femmes*.

42. Pierre Bourdieu, *Masculine Domination*, trans. Richard Nice (Stanford: Stanford University Press, 2001).

43. See, in particular, Patrice Bourdelais and Bernard Lepetit, "Histoire et espace," in *Espaces, jeux et enjeux*, ed. Franck Auriac and Roger Brunet (Paris: Fayard, 1986), 15–26, and Daniel Nordman, "De quelques catégories de la science géographique. Frontière, région et hinterland en Afrique du Nord (19e et 20e siècles)," *Annales H.S.S.* 52 (September-October 1997): 969–86.

44. Chambre des Députés, *Débats parlementaires*, 30 May 1835.

45. Karen Offen, "The Second Sex and the Baccalauréat in Republican France, 1880–1924," *French Historical Studies* 13 (spring 1982): 252–86.

PART I

1. The most influential of these studies are Joan Landes, *Women and the Public Sphere in the Age of the French Revolution* (Ithaca: Cornell University Press, 1988), and Joan Wallach Scott, *Only Paradoxes to Offer: French Feminists and the Rights of Man* (Cambridge: Harvard University Press, 1996). For a theoretical interpretation of democracy that develops similar arguments, see Carole Pateman, *The Disorder of Women: Democracy, Feminism and Political Theory* (Cambridge: Polity Press, 1989). For a historiographic overview of this literature, see Dena Goodman, "Public Sphere and Private Life: Toward a Synthesis of Current Historiographical Approaches to the Old Regime," *History and Theory* 31, no. 1 (1992): 1–20, and Karen Offen, "The New Sexual Politics of French Revolutionary Historiography," *French Historical Studies* 16 (fall 1990): 909–22.

2. On the civil code, see Irène Théry and Christian Biet, eds., *La famille, la loi, l'État: De la Révolution au Code civil* (Paris: Éditions du Centre Georges Pompidou, 1989). On the debate about women's place in the new order, see Fraisse, *Reason's Muse*. For work that considers the historical significance of notable women authors of the period, see Madelyn Gutwirth, *The Twilight of the Goddesses: Women and Representation in the French Revolutionary Era* (New Brunswick: Rutgers University Press, 1992).

3. Hesse, *The Other Enlightenment*.

4. Desan, *The Family on Trial*, and her articles "War Between Brothers and Sisters: Inheritance Law and Gender Politics in Revolutionary France," *French Historical Studies* 20 (fall 1997): 597–634, and "Reconstituting the Social after the Terror: Family Property and the Law in Popular Politics," *Past and Present* 164 (August 1999): 81–12. Historians writing along similar lines include William Reddy, "Marriage, Honor, and the Public Sphere in Post-Revolutionary France: Séparation de corps, 1815–1848," *Journal of Modern History* 65 (September 1993): 437–72; Margaret Darrow, *Revolution in the House: Family, Class, and Inheritance in Southern France, 1775–1825* (Princeton: Princeton University Press, 1989); and Denise Davidson, "Constructing Order in Post-Revolutionary France: Women's Identities and Cultural Practices" (Ph.D. diss., University of Pennsylvania, 1997).

5. See Barbara Corrado Pope, "Mothers and Daughters in Early Nineteenth-Century Paris" (Ph.D. diss., Columbia University, 1981), and her article "Revolution and Retreat: Upper-Class French Women after 1789," in *Women, War, and Revolution*, ed. Carol R. Berkin and Clara Lovett (New York: Holmes and Meier, 1980). For the period of the Empire, see Elizabeth Colwill, "Women's Empire and the Sovereignty of Man in *La Décade Philosophique*, 1794–1807," *Eighteenth-Century Studies* 29, no. 3 (1996): 265–89.

CHAPTER 1

1. See Lynn Hunt, *The Family Romance of the French Revolution* (Berkeley and Los Angeles: University of California Press, 1992); Sarah Maza, "The Diamond Necklace Affair Revisited (1785–1786)," in *Eroticism and the Body Politic*, ed. Lynn Hunt (Baltimore: Johns Hopkins University Press, 1991), 63–89; Jacques Revel, "Marie-Antoinette in Her Fictions," in *The Staging of Hatred in Fictions of the French Revolution*, ed. Bernadette Fort (Evanston: Northwestern University Press, 1991), 111–29; Elizabeth Colwill, "Just Another Citoyenne? Marie-Antoinette on Trial, 1790–1793," *History Workshop Journal* 28 (1989): 63–68; and Dena Goodman, ed., *Marie Antoinette: Writing on the Body of a Queen* (London: Routledge, 2003).

2. Barbara Pope, "The Influence of Rousseau's Ideology of Domesticity," in *Connecting Spheres: Women in the Western World, 1500 to the Present*, ed. Marilyn J. Boxer and Jean H. Quataert (New York: Oxford University Press, 1987), 137–45.

3. For a recent overview of scholarship on Rousseau's sexual politics, see Helena Rosenblatt, "On the 'Misogyny' of Jean-Jacques Rousseau: The Letter to d'Alembert in Historical Context," *French Historical Studies* 25 (winter 2002): 91–114. For a sensitive portrayal of Rousseau's pedagogical vision with respect to girls and its influence, see Gilbert Py, *Rousseau et les éducateurs: Étude sur la fortune des idées pédagogiques de Jean-Jacques Rousseau en France et en Europe au XVIIIe siècle* (Oxford: Voltaire Foundation, 1997), 338–405.

4. Jean-Jacques Rousseau, *Émile, ou de l'éducation* (Paris: Flammarion, 1966), 475.

5. Ibid., 535.

6. Riballier, *De l'éducation physique et morale des femmes avec une notice alphabétique de celles qui se sont distinguées dans les différentes carrières des sciences et des beaux-arts et des actions mémorables* (Brussels and Paris: Chez les frères Estienne, 1790); see Py, *Rousseau et les éducateurs*, 377–80.

7. Cited in Dominique Julia, *Les trois couleurs du tableau noir, la Révolution* (Paris: Belin, 1981), 313.

8. Marquis de Condorcet, *Premier mémoire sur l'instruction publique* (1790; Paris: Éditions Klincksieck, 1989), 65–70.

9. Elke Harten and Hans-Christian Harten, *Femmes, culture et Révolution* (Paris: Éditions des femmes, 1989); this work includes a collection of revolutionary documents. For the classic argument about Republican motherhood in the early American republic, see Linda Kerber, *Women of the Republic: Intellect and Ideology in Revolutionary America* (Chapel Hill: University of North Carolina Press, 1986). For education during the Revolution, see Marie-Françoise Lévy, ed., *L'enfant, la famille et la Révolution française* (Paris: O. Orban, 1990).

10. For a summary of the impact of the Revolution on women's status, see Elisabeth Sledziewski, "The French Revolution as the Turning Point," in *A History of Women in the West*, vol. 4, *Emerging Feminism from Revolution to*

World War, ed. Geneviève Fraisse and Michelle Perrot, trans. Arthur Goldhammer (Cambridge: Belknap Press, 1993), 33–47.

11. His hostility to the author Germaine de Staël's public influence led him to exile her from the empire.

12. Napoleon I, "Notes sur l'établissement d'Ecouen" (15 May 1807), in Rogers, *Les demoiselles*, 332–35.

13. Colwill, "Women's Empire." Like me, she argues that problems of defining women's empire continued well after the execution of Marie Antoinette.

14. Cited in Octave Gréard, *Éducation et instruction. Enseignement secondaire* (Paris: Hachette, 1889), 1:214. For a nuanced portrait of de Staël that challenges American interpretations, see Ozouf, *Women's Words*, chap. 4.

15. See Elizabeth Colwill, "Laws of Nature / Rights of Genius: The *Drame* of Constance de Salm," in *Going Public: Women and Publishing in Early Modern France*, ed. Elizabeth Goldsmith and Dena Goodman (Ithaca: Cornell University Press, 1995), 224–42.

16. Hesse, *The Other Enlightenment*, 53. Between 1789 and 1800 she found 626 women's texts, 251 are on political topics and 39 on education. See *The Other Enlightenment*, 37, for figures on the number of women who published during this period.

17. See Carolyn Lougee, *Le Paradis des femmes: Women, Salons, and Social Stratification in Seventeenth-Century France* (Princeton: Princeton University Press, 1976). For early modern debates about the relationship of women and culture, see Linda Timmermans, *L'accès des femmes à la culture (1598–1715)* (Paris: Honoré Champion, 1993). For women's education, see Samia Spencer, "Women and Education," in *French Women and the Age of Enlightenment*, ed. Spencer (Bloomington: Indiana University Press, 1984).

18. For analyses of Fénelon, Maintenon, Lambert, Rousseau, Epinay, Necker, and Roland, see Octave Gréard, *L'éducation des femmes par les femmes: Études et portraits* (Paris: Hachette, 1889). Excerpts from the more prominent treatises are included in Paul Rousselot, *La pédagogie feminine: Extraits des principaux écrivains qui ont traité de l'éducation des femmes depuis le XVIe siècle* (Paris: Delagrave, 1881).

19. Martine Sonnet, *L'éducation des filles au temps des Lumières* (Paris: Cerf, 1987).

20. For an analysis of the effect of "trauma" on women's historical writing, see Bonnie Smith, *The Gender of History: Men, Women, and Historical Practice* (Cambridge: Harvard University Press, 1998).

21. The 1844 edition of this essay includes a biographical notice on the author. Information on her boarding school is contained in Bonneville de Marsagny, *Madame Campan à Ecouen. Étude historique et biographique* (Paris: Honoré Champion, 1879), 223. Information on her professional trajectory during the Restoration, when she edited the *Mercure* and the *Etoile*, can be found in Louis-Gabriel Michaud and Joseph-François Michaud, eds., *Biographie universelle, ancienne et moderne* (Paris: Desplaces, 1843).

22. See Ozouf, *Women's Words*, chap. 5. While she did not teach herself, she did help to establish schools in Lille in northern France.

23. She made an unhappy marriage to Pierre Dominique François Berthollet-Campan in 1774, who served in the household of the comtesse d'Artois. For more information on Campan, see Rebecca Rogers, "Competing Visions of Girls' Secondary Education in Post-Revolutionary France," *History of Education Quarterly* 34 (summer 1994): 156–63.

24. Biographical information on Pauline Guizot and Necker de Saussure can be found in Corrado Pope, "Mothers and Daughters," 118–41.

25. See Étienne Causse, *Madame Necker de Saussure et l'éducation progressive*, 2 vols. (Paris: Édition "je sers," 1930).

26. For an analysis of her educational writings, see Clarissa Campell Orr, "A Republican Answers Back: Jean-Jacques Rousseau, Albertine Necker de Saussure, and forcing little girls to be free," in *Wollstonecraft's Daughters: Womanhood in England and France, 1780–1920*, ed. Clarissa Campbell Orr (Manchester: Manchester University Press, 1996), 61–78.

27. The second edition of this work (1831) includes a biographical sketch.

28. Corrado Pope "Revolution and Retreat." She notes, in particular, how the prerevolutionary experiences of these women educators help to explain how they bridged in their writing the feminine ideals of sociability and domesticity.

29. I take issue with characterizing these women as representing a conservative reaction to the Revolution. See Marie-Claire Grassi on Rémusat, Campan, and Necker de Saussure, in "Le discours des 'éducatrices' en France entre 1760 et 1830," *Igitur. Gender, Letteratura, cultura* 1 (1993): 85–96. I concede that they accepted women's inferiority with respect to men, but their "domestic" project should not be judged retrograde for the period.

30. Claire de Rémusat, *Essai sur l'éducation des femmes* (Paris: Ladvocat, 1824), 24, 87.

31. Albertine Necker de Saussure, *L'éducation progressive ou étude du cours de la vie* (Bruxelles: Meline, Cans, 1840), 1:xviii–xix. Unlike the other texts, her book addresses both boys' and girls' education; she ends her study of boys' education at age fourteen but discusses the position of women from youth to old age.

32. Jeanne Campan, *De l'éducation, suivi des conseils aux jeunes filles*, 2d ed. (Paris: Baudouin Frères, 1824), 1:4.

33. Françoise Thérèse Antoinette Le Groing la Maisonneuve, *Essai sur l'instruction des femmes*, 3d ed. (Tours: Pornin, 1844), 7 and 90–91.

34. Rémusat, *Essai*, 27.

35. Necker de Saussure, *L'éducation progressive*, 3:17–18.

36. Fanny de Mongellas, *De l'influence des femmes sur les mœurs et les destinées des nations, sur leurs familles et la société, et de l'influence des mœurs sur le bonheur de la vie*, 2d ed., 2 vols. (Paris: L.-G. Michaud, 1831), xvii and 2:145.

37. Le Groing, *Essai*, 12.

38. See Rémusat, *Essai*, chap. 4, and Mongellas, *De l'influence*, 2:143–61.

39. Rémusat, *Essai*, 63.

40. Campan, *De l'éducation*, 1:5.

41. Guizot, *Éducation domestique*, letter 42.

42. Ibid., letter 30.

43. For an analysis of women and religion during the Revolution, see Olwen Hufton, *Women and the Limits of Citizenship in the French Revolution* (Toronto: University of Toronto Press, 1992), and Suzanne Desan, *Reclaiming the Sacred: Lay Religion and Lay Popular Politics in Revolutionary France* (Ithaca: Cornell University Press, 1990), 165–230. For the postrevolutionary period, see the articles by Jean-Pierre Chaline, Catherine Duprat, and Claude Langlois in *Femmes dans la Cité, 1815–1871*, ed. Alain Corbin, Jacqueline Lalouette, and Michèle Riot-Sarcey (Granat: Éditions Créaphis, 1997).

44. Le Groing, *Essai*, 113–15.

45. Necker de Saussure, *L'éducation progressive*, vol. 3, bk. 1, chap. 1; Mongellas, *De l'influence*, xi.

46. Rémusat, *Essai*, 9.

47. Guizot, *Éducation domestique*, letter 50.

48. Mme Bernier, *Discours qui a remporté le prix à la Société des sciences et des arts du département du Lot* (Paris, 1803), 19.

49. Necker de Saussure, *L'éducation progressive*, 3:137.

50. Guizot, *Éducation domestique*, letter 33.

51. Rémusat, *Essai*, 81, 200.

52. Mongellas, *De l'influence*, 2:150.

53. Le Groing, *Essai*, 27.

54. Campan, *De l'éducation*, 1:204–5.

55. Ibid., 259–64.

56. Ibid., 234.

57. The separation of students into classes by educational level was not widely prevalent in either boys' or girls' institutions. See Philippe Ariès, *Centuries of Childhood: A Social History of Family Life*, trans. Robert Baldick (London: Jonathan Cape, 1962), 176–88.

58. Campan, *De l'éducation*, 1:363.

59. Her proposition for a "cours d'études" for girls from the ages of seven until twelve suggests that intellectual studies were largely completed after the First Communion.

60. Harrison, *Bourgeois Citizen*, 1–9. She argues that emulation was a specifically male value in early nineteenth-century France; my research shows that some women pedagogues appropriated it for girls as well.

61. Campan, *De l'éducation*, 1:333–34. Campan's use of the term "public education" was common at the time to refer to education outside the home in an institution. Only later did the term "public" come to be associated with state-sponsored institutions. Her defense of emulation was not universally accepted in girls' schools; Mongellas, for example, criticizes it for developing envy. See Mongellas, *De l'influence*, 2:217.

62. See John W. Padberg, *Colleges in Controversy: The Jesuit Schools in France from Revival to Suppression, 1815–1880* (Cambridge: Harvard University Press, 1969), 233–35.

63. Joan Scott in her analysis of Olympe de Gouges argues that emulation "was the enactment of the continuing process of self-construction then reserved for men." The *Encyclopédie* defined "emulation" in heroic terms as that

"noble generous passion which admires the merit, the beauty, and the actions of others; which tries to imitate or even surpass them." Scott, *Only Paradoxes to Offer*, 188.

64. Campan, *De l'éducation*, 1:239.

65. Ibid., 236–44.

66. See Steven D. Kale, "Women, the Public Sphere, and the Persistence of Salon," *French Historical Studies* 25 (winter 2002): 115–48; Anne Martin-Fugier, *La vie élégante ou la formation du Tout-Paris, 1815–1848* (Paris: Fayard, 1990); and Elias, *La dynamique de l'Occident*, especially 181–318.

67. For an analysis of the intellectual and cultural influences in Necker de Saussure's writing, see Orr, "A Republican Answers Back," and Causse, *Madame Necker de Saussure*.

68. Necker de Saussure, *L'éducation progressive*, 3:142–57.

69. For a brief overview of Napoleonic boys' schools, see R. R. Palmer, *The Improvement of Humanity: Education and the French Revolution* (Princeton: Princeton University Press, 1985), 279–328. For a presentation of changes in the prescribed content of boys' schooling, see Compère, *Du collège au lycée*, 193–215.

70. Necker de Saussure, *L'éducation progressive*, 3:173–87; 389–407.

71. Ibid., 256.

72. Campan, *De L'éducation*, 1:283.

73. See Margaret Darrow, "French Noblewomen and the New Domesticity, 1750–1850," *Feminist Studies* 5 (spring 1979): 41–65.

74. Rémusat, *Essai*, 16.

75. Necker de Saussure, *L'éducation progressive*, 3:48–50; italics in the original.

76. Ibid., 3:50.

77. Ibid., 3:353.

78. See Renonciat's introduction in *Livres d'enfance, Livres de France*, ed. Annie Renonciat, Viviane Erzaty, and Geneviève Patte (Paris: Hachette, 1998), as well as Françoise Huguet, *Les livres pour l'enfance et la jeunesse de Gutenberg à Guizot* (Paris: INRP, Éditions Klincksieck, 1997); Isabelle Havelange, "1650–1830, des livres pour les demoiselles?" in *Les discours institutionnels sur la lecture des jeunes*, ed. Anne-Marie Chartier and Suzanne Pouliot, *Cahiers de la recherche en éducation* (Sherbrooke) 3 (1997): 363–76.

79. Jean-Noël Luc also notes European influences in the production of books for young children, in *L'invention du jeune enfant au XIXe siècle. De la salle d'asile à l'école maternelle* (Paris: Belin, 1997), 134.

80. See Isabelle Havelange, "La littérature à l'usage des demoiselles, 1750–1830" (Thèse de 3e cycle, École des Hautes Études en Sciences Sociales, 1984), 238; Isabelle Havelange, Ségolène Le Men, and Michel Manson, *Le Magasin des enfans. La littérature pour la jeunesse, 1750–1830* (catalogue de l'exposition) (Alençon: Imprimerie alençonnaise, 1988); and Michel Manson, *Les livres pour l'enfance et la jeunesse publiés en français de 1789–1799* (Paris: INRP, 1989).

81. Havelange's dissertation includes biographies of these authors; some are also analyzed in Hesse, *The Other Enlightenment*.

82. Smith, *Gender of History*; Denise Davidson, "Bonnes lectures: Improving Women and Society through Literature in Post-Revolutionary France," in *The French Experience from Republic to Monarchy, 1792–1824. New Dawns in Politics, Knowledge and Culture*, ed. M. Cross and D. Williams (New York: Palgrave, 2000), 155–71.

83. Quotation from Penny Brown: "'La Femme Enseignante': Mme de Genlis and the Moral and Didactic Tale in France," *Bulletin of the John Rylands University* 76 (autumn 1994): 22; italics in the original.

84. While including the "classics" of this literature, I have selected more systematically those authors who wrote at least in part for girls in schools.

85. This literature seems to confirm William Reddy's argument about the way honor played into feminine pedagogy: "The confusion of honor and religious virtue . . . had been for long, and continued for the nineteenth century to be, a central principle of feminine pedagogy in France. Manners, modesty and moral principles were instilled as elements of a seamless whole, so that regard for appearances and regard for right behavior were learned as aspects one of the other." It is interesting to note, however, how work also played into this pedagogy. See Reddy, *Invisible Code*, 73.

86. See, for example, Jean Nicolas Bouilly, *Conseils à ma fille*, 6th ed. (Paris: Louis Janet, n.d.); Mme Celnart [Elisabeth Félicie Bayle Mouillard], *Les institutrices réunies ou dialogues sur les arts et métiers* (Paris: Locard et Davi, 1825); Mlle Carreau [Mlle Vanhove], *Pension de jeunes demoiselles ou nouvelles propres à éclairer les jeunes personnes dans toutes les positions où elles peuvent se trouver dans le monde à la sortie de leur pensionnat*, 2d ed. (Paris, Caillot, ca.

1830); and Jeanne Campan, *Conseils aux jeunes filles; théâtre pour les jeunes personnes, quelques essais de morale* (Paris: Barrière, 1824).

87. The daughter of a mathematics professor, this woman married a magistrate employed as a counselor at the *Cour de Cassation* who went on to become a councillor of state. A precocious learner, she wrote over thirty-eight different books in twelve to thirteen years, in addition to writing for such periodicals as the *Journal des connaissances usuelles* and the *Journal des jeunes personnes*. She is particularly well known for her books on manners, notably her *Manuel de la bonne compagnie* (1832). See Marie-Claire Grassi, "Le savoir-vivre au féminin, 1820–1920," in *Du goût, de la conversation et des femmes*, ed. Alain Montandon (Clermont Ferrrand: Association des Publications de la Faculté des Lettres et Sciences Humaines de Clermont Ferrand, 1994), 213–32.

88. Mme Celnart [Elisabeth Félice Bayle-Mouillard], *La sortie de pension ou la bonne tante; ouvrage destiné aux jeunes demoiselles de 15 à 16 ans*, 2 vols. (Paris: Boiste fils ainé, 1825), 1:33.

89. Celnart, *Les institutrices réunies*, 6.

90. Julie Carroy, *Étude et récréation ou l'intérieur d'un pensionnat. Ouvrage divisé en 30 journées contenant plusieurs histoires morales et instructives* (Paris: Parmentier, 1825), 87–88.

91. Bouilly, *Conseils à ma fille*, 6th ed., 274.

92. Campan, *De l'éducation*, vol. 3.

93. In her focus on more serious children's literature, Havelange also notes that the authors advocated a new sober religion, directed toward civil life. Havelange, "La littérature à l'usage des demoiselles," 116–36.

94. Bouilly, *Conseils à ma fille*, 6th ed., 12–14. In Julie Carroy's *Zélie ou le modèle des jeunes filles* (Paris: Caillot, ca. 1830) the heroine is also warned about appearances and hypocrisy in others; see especially chapter 9.

95. Examples of this sort of lesson can be found in Carreau, *Pension de jeunes demoiselles*, notably the chapters "Bel esprit" and "La manie des sciences."

96. Quotation from Mme Laya, *Les trois sœurs, ou de l'éducation des filles* (1827) in Havelange, "La littérature à l'usage des demoiselles," 107.

97. See Adelaide Victoire Antoinette de Lussault Manceau, *L'ange de paix. Ouvrage dédié aux jeunes personnes*, 2 vols. (Paris: Marcilly, ca 1830). In this story the mother encourages the practice of ornamental accomplishments, while the grandmother seeks to instill simpler, less self-centered values.

98. Amélie Castel de Courval, *Les jeunes orphelines ou les contes d'une grandmère* (Paris: Vernaret et Tenon, 1825). This nonutilitarian presentation of acquiring an ornamental talent is all the more surprising in that she is most probably the widowed mother of three daughters, whom she placed in the schools for the Legion of Honor during the Empire.

99. See Carreau, *Pension de jeunes demoiselles*, chap.1.

100. This period is a transitional one for advice literature; it hesitated between offering lessons in civility and lessons in morality. For an analysis of this literature in England, see Elizabeth Langland, *Nobody's Angels: Middle-Class Women and Domestic Ideology in Victorian Culture* (Ithaca: Cornell University Press, 1995). She emphasizes the distinction between older courtesy manuals that valorized individual values such as honesty and fortitude and the new etiquette manuals that targeted the construction and consolidation of a social group.

101. Celnart, *Les institutrices réunies*, "Les etiquettes," 78, and "Les coiffures," 130.

102. Leora Auslander argues that after the Revolution class was defined by the means of production but also through knowledge and taste. Auslander, *Taste and Power*, 141. The prominence of discussions of fashion in this literature that sought to reconfigure class, social, and gender relations certainly confirms this argument. See, as well, Jennifer Jones, "Repackaging Rousseau: Femininity and Fashion in Old Regime France," *French Historical Studies* 18 (fall 1994): 939–96, and Montandon, *Du goût*.

103. Bouilly, *Conseils à ma fille*, 6th ed., 43–66.

104. Ibid., "Le petit dîner, ou les amies de pension," 173.

105. Ibid., "Les nuances de l'âge," 86. For a story with a similar theme, see Campan, "La famille Dawenport," in *Conseils aux jeunes filles*.

106. Bouilly, *Conseils à ma fille*, 6th ed., "Le premier pas dans le monde," 219.

107. See Goodman, *Marie Antoinette*. I am indebted in this discussion to the comments of Céline Grasser.

108. For fathers' influence in their children's education in the Old Regime, see Martine Sonnet, "Les leçons paternelles," in *Histoire des pères et de la paternité*, ed. Jean Delumeau and Daniel Roche (Paris: Larousse, 1990), 259–78.

109. Hunt, *Family Romance*, 175.

110. An estimated 1.3 million Frenchmen died in battle between 1790 and 1815. See Jacques Dupacquier, ed., *Histoire de la population française*, vol. 3, *De 1789 à 1914* (Paris: Presses Universitaires de France, 1988), 69.

111. See Michelle Perrot, "L'invisible frontière," in Corbin, Lalouette, and Riot-Sarcey, *Femmes dans la Cité*, 9–16.

112. See Rogers, "Le sexe de l'espace."

Chapter 2

1. See Claude Langlois and Serge Bonin, eds., *Atlas graphique de la Revolution française*, vol. 2, *L'enseignement 1760–1815*, ed. Dominique Julia (Paris: Éditions de l'EHESS, 1987). For girls' education, see my essay "L'éducation des filles à l'époque napoléonienne," in *Napoléon et les lycées: Enseignement et société en Europe au début du XIXe siècle, actes du colloque des 15 et 16 novembre 2002, organisé par l'Institut Napoléon et la Bibliothèque Marmottan à l'occasion du bicentenaire des lycées*, ed. Jacques-Olivier Boudon (Paris: Nouveau Monde Éditions, 2004), 275–90.

2. For a discussion of such interactions, see Martin-Fugier, *La vie élégante*; Pellissier, *Loisirs et sociabilités* (see introduction, n. 31); and Guy Chaussinand-Nogaret, ed., *Histoire des élites en France du XVIe au XXe siècle* (Paris: Tallandier, 1991).

3. See Sonnet, *L'éducation des filles*, 287.

4. Jeanne Campan, *Correspondance inédite avec la Reine Hortense* (Paris: Levasseur, 1835), 2:25–30, and *De l'éducation*, 1:336.

5. The *Moniteur* in 1801 published a list of the best and most fashionable boarding schools; there were thirteen for boys and six for girls out of a total of some seventy schools. Palmer, *Improvement of Humanity*, 283. For information about some of these girls' schools, see Louis Grimaud, *Histoire de la liberté d'enseignement en France* (Paris: Apostolat de la Presse, 1954), 3:278ff., 4:194–96.

6. See Catherine R. Montfort and J. Terrie Quintana, "Madame Campan's Institution d'Éducation: A Revolution in the Education of Women," *Australian Journal of French Studies* 33 (January-April 1996): 30–44.

7. Campan, *De l'éducation*, 1:315–16.

8. Goblet, *Dictionnaire administratif et topographique de Paris: Du commerce, des arts, et des produits en tous genres de l'industrie qui s'y trouve* (Paris, 1808). For information on the 1808 survey, see Claude Langlois, "Les effectifs des congrégations féminines au XIXe siècle. De l'enquête statistique à l'histoire quantitative," *Revue d'histoire de l'Eglise de France* 60 (1974): 39–64.

9. These figures come from trade books, as well as Grimaud, *Histoire de la liberté*, 5:535–36. For Paris, see Isabelle Bricard, *Saintes ou pouliches. L'éducation des jeunes filles au XIXe siècle* (Paris: Albin Michel, 1985), 64, and the trade book for the department of the Seine.

10. Langlois, "Les effectifs."

11. See Grimaud, *Histoire de la liberté*, 3:65–74.

12. See Claude Langlois, "Pesanteurs sociales et arbitrage politique. L'autorisation des congrégations féminines au XIXe siècle," in *Les contacts religieux franco-polonais* (Paris: CNRS, 1984), 415–24. By 1830 approximately 31,000 women lived in religious orders, although many of these women were not involved in teaching. Between 1796 and 1880 almost four hundred new congregations were created, and 48 percent of these creations occurred before 1830. Langlois, *Le catholicisme*, 203–5, and "Les effectifs," 56.

13. See Rogers, "L'éducation des filles." For the projects and discussions of the projects, see Archives Nationales (hereafter "AN"), AFIV 1047, 10 July 1810, AFIV 909, dossier 6. Léon Lecestre, *Lettres inédites de Napoléon Ier (an VII-1817)* (Paris: Plon, 1897), letter of 13 July 1810.

14. For the history of these schools, see Rogers, *Les demoiselles*.

15. Archives de Paris, VD[6] 367, no. 7, letter of the prefect to the mayor, 6 frimaire an 9.

16. Ibid., règlement pour les écoles de filles, 20 August 1810. The noted pedagogue Mme de Genlis was among these first women inspectors. For more information on these early schools, see Rebecca Rogers, "Boarding Schools, Women Teachers and Domesticity: Reforming Girls' Education in the First Half of the Nineteenth Century," *French Historical Studies* 19 (spring 1995): 153–81, and "La sous-maîtresse au XIXe siècle: Domestique ou enseignante stagiaire?" *Histoire de l'éducation* 98 (May 2003): 37–60.

17. See Raymond Deniel, *Une image de la famille et de la société sous la Restauration (1815–1830). Étude de la presse catholique* (Paris: Éditions Ouvrières, 1965).

18. Archives de Paris, VD⁶ 159, no. 2.

19. A. Verdet Lievyns and P. Bégat, *Les fastes de la Légion d'honneur (1803–1804)* (Paris: Au bureau, et chez B. Saint Edme, 1847), 1:27.

20. Archives of the schools of the Legion of Honor in Saint-Denis; personal dossier of Mme Séron.

21. Archives de Paris, VD⁶ 367, no. 9. No attempt was made, however, to distinguish between primary and secondary teaching qualifications. This period also saw the first laws on primary education for both girls and boys. See Antoine Prost, *L'enseignement en France, 1800–1967* (Paris: Armand Colin, 1968), 89–92, 162–66.

22. Copies of this ruling are in AN, F¹⁷ 12431.

23. This issue of inspection quickly became a thorny one as religious schools began to close their doors to outside inspections as early as 1830. Locally, inspectors and prefects were confused about their prerogatives with regard to convent schools. See AN, F¹⁷ 12431, and Mayeur, *L'éducation*, 94–97. In practice, inspection reports rarely included information on religious schools.

24. During the Restoration, the state paid fellowships for a few boarders with the Chanoinesses de Saint-Augustin (also known as the Sœurs de Notre-Dame); in 1821 the duchesse de Berry offered five such fellowships, and five came directly from the state. AN, F¹⁹ 6343.

25. Jeanne Étienne Marie Portalis, "Rapport sur les associations religieuses de femmes à sa Majesté Impériale et Royale" (24 March 1807), in *Discours, rapports et travaux inédits sur le Concordat de 1801* (Paris: Joubert, 1845), 503.

26. Campan, *De l'éducation*, 1:305.

27. For examples of fees in Paris, see Archives de Paris, VD⁶ 367, no. 7. In Strasbourg, boarding-school costs were similarly high, ranging from 700 to 1000 francs. Muriel Schvind, "L'éducation des demoiselles de la bourgeoisie: L'exemple du Bas-Rhin (1800–1870)" (maîtrise en Sciences Historiques, Université de Strasbourg II, 1995–96), 13.

28. "Cours d'éducation pour les jeunes demoiselles" (advertisement), *Journal de l'Yonne*, 25 nivose an X.

29. "Institution dirigée par les dames Ursulines de la congrégation de Paris" (ca. 1823), in Marie-Andrée Jégou and Marie-Odile Mesnil, "Les Ursulines françaises au XIXe siècle. Documents pour une histoire" (Amiens, 1985), typescript, 182.

30. For more information about changing attitudes toward hygiene, see Georges Vigarello, *Concepts of Cleanliness: Changing Attitudes in France since the Middle Ages*, trans. Jean Birrell (Cambridge: Cambridge University Press, 1988).

31. "Cours d'éducation pour les jeunes demoiselles" (advertisement), *Journal de l'Yonne*, 25 nivose an X.

32. Cited in Grimaud, *Histoire de la liberté*, 3:278–79.

33. For a general overview of this education, see Paule Constant, *Un monde à l'usage des demoiselles* (Paris: Gallimard, 1987), especially part 3, "Le point des connaissances."

34. *Affiches, Annonces et Avis divers de la Ville de Dijon*, 13 September 1813, 347.

35. Cited in Grimaud, *Histoire de la liberté*, 3:278.

36. Jégou and Mesnil, "Les Ursulines françaises," 182–83.

37. I have found little evidence for the existence of such inspectresses elsewhere in France prior to the 1830s.

38. Archives de Paris, VD⁶ 158, no. 3, inspection report for 12 May 1813.

39. Ibid., inspectresses' report to the mayor in 1812.

40. Ibid.

41. Ibid. Curiously, this same Mlle Sauvan was appointed head of a normal course in 1831. For a hagiographic presentation of this woman, see Emile Gossot, *Mlle Sauvan, première inspectrice des écoles de Paris. Sa vie et son œuvre* (Paris: Hachette, 1877).

42. Jégou and Mesnil, "Les Ursulines françaises," 185.

43. Archives of the Société du Sacré-Cœur (hereafter "ASSC") (Rome), series C-I c3 box 1, decision of the Fourth General Council in 1826. In 1820 the decision was made to allow the students to receive visits only one day a week. This move to isolate students from their families was echoed within religious orders, which increasingly limited the movement of their members. See Rogers, "Retrograde or Modern?" 150.

44. See Bricard, *Saintes ou pouliches*, 43–47.

45. Hortense de Beauharnais, *Mémoires de la Reine Hortense* (Paris: Plon, 1927), 2:21–122.

46. For more information on this institution and its origins, see Rogers, *Les demoiselles*, 17–70.

47. See Rogers, "Competing Visions."

48. Campan, "Mémoire pour la Reine de Hollande," 20 October 1809, in *Correspondance inédite*, 2:26–27.

49. Campan, "Sur une nouvelle organisation à donner à l'éducation des jeunes françaises," in *Correspondance inédite*, 2:54–55.

50. Archives of the Grand Chancellory of the Legion of Honor, *Règlement général de l'institut des maisons impériales Napoléon*. A more permanent rulebook was published in 1821 that differs only in minor ways; some subject matters were developed, and the list of appropriate books was expanded. For more detail, see Rogers, *Les demoiselles*, 181–94.

51. See André Chervel, *Les auteurs français, latins et grecs au programme de l'enseignement secondaire de 1800 à nos jours* (Paris: INRP, 1986). William Reddy argues that the study of Cicero and public rhetoric contributed to the importance of honor in schoolboys' education. See Reddy, *Invisible Code*, especially 24–38.

52. Archives of the schools of the Legion of Honor in Saint-Denis, *procès verbaux de concours*, 1828–40.

53. See Jeanne de Charry, "La Société du Sacré-Cœur: Institut contemplatif et apostolique," in *Les Religieuses enseignantes (XVI–XXe siècles), Actes de la 4ᵉ rencontre d'histoire religieuse à Fontevrault, 4 octobre 1980* (Angers: Presses Universitaires d'Angers, 1981), and Phil Kilroy, *Madeleine Sophie Barat (1779–1865): A Biography* (Sterling: Cork University Press, 2000).

54. Dominique Sadoux and Pierre Gervais, *La vie religieuse. Premières constitutions des religieuses de la Société du Sacré-Cœur* (Paris: Beauchesne, 1985), 66. This quotation and those that follow come from the 1815 Rule.

55. See Marie-Dominique Nobécourt, "Un exemple de l'éducation des filles au 19e siècle par les congrégations religieuses: Le Sacré-Cœur de Paris (1816–1874)" (Thèse de l'École des Chartes, 1981), and Marie-France Carreel, *Sophie Barat. Un projet éducatif pour aujourd'hui* (Paris: Éditions Don Bosco, 2003).

56. Darrow, "French Noblewomen and the New Domesticity." Havelange argues that the leitmotif of bourgeois — not aristocratic — girls' literature during this period was domestic economy. It is all the more striking that the aristocratic Société du Sacré-Cœur embraced this branch of study.

57. ASSC. The archives in Rome and Poitiers have these school plans, from which the preceding quotations come.

58. See Monsignor Baunard, *Histoire de la Vénérable Mère Madeleine Sophie Barat*, 2 vols. (Paris: Pousseliegue, 1892); Jeanne de Charry, *Histoire des constitutions de la société du Sacré-Cœur*, 3 vols. (Rome: General Archives of the Société du Sacré-Cœur, 1977); and Adèle Cahier, *Vie de la Vénérable Mère Barat. Fondatrice et première supérieure générale de la Société du Sacré-Cœur de Jésus*, 2 vols. (Paris: E. de Soye et fils, 1884). In 1830 the Parisian school had 160 boarders.

59. Under the Empire 19 percent of the students present were daughters of general officers and 43.5 percent of superior officers. Under the Restoration the percentage of daughters whose fathers came from the highest ranks had fallen to 11.4 percent, and those of superior officers had risen to 59.9 percent. Pierre Codechèvre, "Des maisons impériales à la maison royale de Saint-Denis," *La Cohorte, Bulletin de la société d'entreaide des membres de Légion d'honneur* 62 (1979): 17.

60. Nobécourt has argued that approximately 29 percent of the student body in Paris came from the aristocratic classes. "Un exemple," 397.

61. Campan, letter of 2 November 1811, in *Correspondance inédite*, 2:86.

62. Sophie Durand, *Mes souvenirs sur Napoléon, sa famille et sa cour* (Paris: Beraud, 1820), 164–65.

63. Rogers, *Les demoiselles*, 51. The correspondence of Nancy Macdonald can be found in AN, 279 AP 14; that of Annette de Mackau in AN, 156 AP II.

64. AD Ardennes, 21 I II.

65. Campan's correspondence testifies to how she negotiated marriages and places at court for her students.

66. Comtess de Bassanville, *Les salons d'autrefois, souvenirs intimes* (Paris: Brunet, 1863), 2:292.

67. See Nobécourt, "Un exemple," 362.

68. Sophie Barat indicates in her letters in 1825 that families in Niort, Bordeaux, and Poitiers were sending their daughters to a rival institution, the Couvent des Oiseaux, because of the steep fees at the Sacré-Cœur. Kilroy, *Madeleine Sophie Barat*, 177–78. For the tuition fees, see ASSC (Rome), series C-IV, history of individual institutions.

69. ASSC (Rome), series C-I c3 box 1, *Arrêté des trois conseils en une seule rédaction*.

70. Stern, *Mes souvenirs*, 157.

71. Cited in Kilroy, *Madeleine Sophie Barat*, 40, letter to Thérèse Maillucheau, 17 February 1818.

72. The Society purchased the Hotel Biron on the Rue de Varennes in 1820; this is now the Rodin Museum.

73. Cited in Kilroy, *Madeleine Sophie Barat*, 173.

74. This suspicion of the outside world is marked in the Society's emphasis on *not* taking in day students.

75. Kilroy, *Madeleine Sophie Barat*, 169. See as well in ASSC (Poitiers), Sophie Barat, *Lettres choisies de notre Bienheureuse Mère aux mères en charge* (Rome, Maison Mère, 1924), *Lettres aux maîtresses générales*, 57. Here she told Gramont that within the school charades should be infrequent and that students needed greater discipline.

76. ASSC (Poitiers), Beauvais, Affaire d'Olivier B05/117-2. The following quotations all come from this file.

77. ASSC (Rome), series D-I 1d box 1, Druilhet, *Conférences sur les devoirs*, 1827.

78. *Cours d'études à l'usage des élèves de la Légion d'honneur (classe violet unie et liseré)* (Paris, 1823–32).

79. Nobécourt, "Un exemple," 42–44.

80. See Rogers, "The Socialization of Girls in France under the Influence of Religion and the Church," in *Erziehung der Menschen-Geschlechter. Studien zur Religion, Sozialisation und Bildung in Europa seit der Aufklärung*, ed. Margret Kraul and Christoph Luth (Weinheim: Deutscher Studien Verlag, 1996), 139–58.

81. Stern, *Mes souvenirs*, 96. For more information, see Phyllis Stock-Morton, *The Life of Marie d'Agoult: Alias Daniel Stern* (Baltimore: Johns Hopkins University Press, 2000); and Whitney Walton, *Eve's Proud Descendants: Four Women Writers and Republican Politics in Nineteenth-Century France* (Stanford: Stanford University Press, 2000). I will be referring to Aurore Dupin and Marie de Flavigny by their far more familiar pen names: Sand and Stern.

82. Stern, *Mes souvenirs*, 142. See, as well, *Mémoires, souvenirs et journaux de la comtesse d'Agoult* (Paris: Mercure de France, 1990).

83. Stern, *Mes souvenirs*, 154.

84. Campan, *De l'éducation*, 1:387.

85. Marie Cappelle, *Mémoires de Madame Lafarge*, revised ed. (Paris: M. Lévy frères, 1867), 1:37.

86. Thérèse-Mélanie Martin, *Souvenirs d'une ancienne élève de la Maison de la Légion d'honneur d'Ecouen: Thérèse Mélanie Martin, 1807–1815*, ed. E. Joppé (Saint Dizier: Imprimerie de A. Brulliard, 1924).

87. Durand, *Mes souvenirs sur Napoléon*.

88. Ernestine Reboul, *Nouvelle réponse de Mlle Reboul, provoquée par la pétition de M. Loveday* (Paris: Chez Lamy, 1822), 28.

89. For a more detailed analysis of this case and its implications for familial politics, see Carolyn Ford, "Private Lives and Public Order in Restoration France: The Seduction of Emily Loveday," *American Historical Review* 99 (February 1994): 21–43.

90. Amélie Bosquet, "Une écolière sous la Restauration," *Revue Bleue*, 21 August 1897, 226. See as well the memoirs of Adèle Boury, who writes that she received basically a good education with perhaps too many religious exercises. *Memoires de Mlle Adèle Boury* (Paris: Vimont, 1833), 20.

91. Frances Ann Kemble, *Record of a Schoolgirl* (London: Bentley, 1878), 1:80–81.

92. Racine wrote these plays specifically for the students at Saint-Cyr. For the ethos of Saint-Cyr at its origins, see Carolyn Lougee, "Noblesse, Domesticity and Social Reform: The Education of Girls by Fénelon and Saint-Cyr," *History of Education Quarterly* 14 (spring 1974): 87–113. For information on these theatrical productions, see Sonnet, *L'éducation des filles*, 260.

93. This school hired as outside teachers some of the most preeminent artists of the day, including musicians from the Conservatory as well as Isabey, the painter and miniaturist. See Montfort and Quintana, "Madame Campan's Institution d'Éducation."

94. *The Journals and Letters of Fanny Burney (Madame d'Arblay)*, vol. 5, *West Humble and Paris, 1801–1803*, ed. Joyce Hemlow et al. (Oxford: Clarendon Press, 1975), 368.

95. Ibid., 369.

96. AN, 279 AP 14; letter of 8 germinal an 7.

97. Ibid., letter from Nancy Macdonald to her father, 25 vendémiaire an 9 (1800).

98. Ibid., letter of 25 August 1803; On 11 messidor she announced three first-place and three second-place prizes; in 1803 her sister received prizes in math and English, while Nancy triumphed in song and piano.

99. Ibid., letter of 7 June 1806.

100. Ibid., letter of 1 November 1807.

101. Private collection of Baron Pinoteau, letter of 13 February 1825.

102. For information on George Sand's educational experiences prior to the convent, see Goldin, "De Félicité de Genlis à George Sand," 163–77.

103. Stern, *Mes souvenirs*, 179–80.

104. For a biting criticism of anti-intellectualism in a school, see Bosquet, "Une écolière sous la Restauration," 230.

105. Stern, *Mes souvenirs*, 105. For more information on the abbé Gaultier's classes, see Mayeur, *L'éducation*, 67.

106. Sand, *Histoire de ma vie*, 921–26; Stern, *Mes souvenirs*, 176–78.

107. AN, 156 AP II 9, letter from Armand de Mackau to Annette de Mackau on 24 October 1808. See, as well, Annette de Mackau, *Correspondance d'Annette de Mackau, comtesse de Saint-Alphonse. Dame du palais de l'Impératrice Joséphine (1790–1879)*, ed. Chantal de Tourtier-Bonnazi (Paris: SEVPEN, 1967).

108. AD Ardennes, 21 J 11, letter from Henriod to Pascal-Diacre, 9 November 1813.

109. AN, 279 AP 14, letter from N. Macdonald to her father, 7 March 1808. For a study of friendships, see Anne Vincent-Buffault, *L'Exercice de l'amitié. Pour une histoire des pratiques amicales aux XVIIIe et XIXe siècles* (Paris: Seuil, 1995).

110. AN, 279 AP 14. The first letter cited is from 1807 when her father was probably sick. She continually defended her ability to assume a domestic role beside her father, insisting on her ability to sew; she wrote explicitly that she was not as ignorant in these matters as he believed. This sort of amorous expression of familial love also existed among brothers and sisters in the early nineteenth century. See Houbre, *La discipline de l'amour*, 138–46.

111. Mary Browne, *The Diary of a Girl in France in 1821* (London: John Murray, 1905), 87–101.

112. My reconsideration of these private institutions is not isolated; recently similar revisions have appeared among historians of girls' education in other countries. See Susan Skedd, "Women Teachers and the Expansion of Girls' Schooling in England c.1760–1820," in *Gender in Eighteenth-Century England: Roles, Representations, and Responsibilities*, ed. Hannah Barker and Elaine Chalus (London: Longman, 1997), 101–25, as well as the recent symposium in the *History of Education Quarterly* 41 (summer 2001): "Reappraisals of the Academy Movement," 216–70.

113. Bourg, *Mémoires de Mlle Adèle Bourg.*

PART II

1. For the complexity of the Parisian middle class, see Daumard, *La bourgeoisie parisienne;* for the relationship between the diverse middle classes and the male educational system, see Detlef K. Müller, Fritz Ringer, and Brian Simon, eds., *The Rise of the Modern Educational System: Structural Change and Social Reproduction, 1870–1920* (Cambridge: Cambridge University Press, 1987).

2. In addition to her historical studies, see Françoise Mayeur, "L'éducation des filles en France au XIXe siècle: Historiographie récente et problématiques," in *Problèmes d'histoire de l'éducation. Actes des seminaires organisés par l'École francaise de Rome et l'Università di Roma La Sapienza (janvier-mai 1985)* (Rome: École française de Rome, 1988), 79–90. For a recent overview of the field, see Patrick Harrigan, "Women Teachers and the Schooling of Girls in France: Recent Historiographical Trends," *French Historical Studies* 21 (fall 1998): 593–610, and Sharif Gemie, "Institutional History, Social History, Women's History: A Comment on Patrick Harrigan's 'Women Teachers and the Schooling of Girls in France,'" *French Historical Studies* 22 (fall 1999): 613–23. A useful comparative overview of new orientations as well as of the difficulties involved in conceptualizing this topic can be found in Marie-Madeleine Compère, *L'histoire de l'éducation en Europe: Essai comparatif sur la façon dont elle s'écrit* (Paris: INRP, 1995), especially 260–76.

3. Most notably the work of Isabelle Bricard, but even the far more nuanced study of Gabrielle Houbre tends to confirm this portrayal of an educational system that veiled girls in virginal innocence. See Bricard, *Saintes ou pouliches,* and Houbre, *La discipline de l'amour.*

4. Smith, *Ladies of the Leisure Class,* 172.

5. Exceptions include Maurice Crubellier, *L'enfance et la jeunesse dans la société française, 1800–1950* (Paris: Armand Colin, 1979), and Françoise Mayeur, *Histoire générale de l'enseignement et de l'éducation en France,* vol. 3, *De la Révolution à l'école Républicaine (1789–1930)* (Paris: Nouvelle librairie de France, 1981).

CHAPTER 3

1. See, in particular, Michèle Riot-Sarcey, *La démocratie à l'épreuve des femmes: Trois figures critiques du pouvoir, 1830–48* (Paris: Albin Michel, 1994); Marcus, *Apartment Stories;* Jo Burr Margadant, "Gender, Vice, and the Political Imaginary in Nineteenth-Century France: Reinterpreting the Failure of the July Monarchy, 1830–1848," *American Historical Review* 104 (December 1999): 1461–96; Walton, *Eve's Proud Descendants;* and Victoria Thompson, *The Virtuous Marketplace: Women and Men, Money and Politics in Paris, 1830–1870* (Baltimore: Johns Hopkins University Press, 2000).

2. I will be using the anachronistic term "feminist" to refer to people or to arguments that openly questioned gender roles during this period. See Karen Offen, "On the French Origin of the Words Feminism and Feminist," *Feminist Issues* 8 (autumn 1988): 45–51.

3. For a general overview of the Saint-Simonian movement, see Claire Goldberg Moses, *French Feminism in*

the Nineteenth Century (Albany: SUNY Press, 1984), especially chaps. 3–6. More detailed studies of the movement include Claire Goldberg Moses and Leslie Wahl Rabine, *Feminism, Socialism, and French Romanticism* (Bloomington: Indiana University Press, 1993); Riot-Sarcey, *La démocratie*; Evelyne Lejeune-Resnick, *Femmes et associations, 1830–1880* (Paris: Publisud, 1991); and Kari Weil, "A Woman's Place in the Utopian Home: The 'New Paris' and the Saint Simoniennes," in *Home and Its Dislocations in Nineteenth-Century France*, ed. Suzanne Nash (Albany: SUNY Press, 1993), 231–46.

4. Moses and Rabine, *Feminism*, 34.

5. See Riot-Sarcey, *La démocratie*, 37, and Claire Goldberg Moses, "'Difference' in Historical Perspective: Saint-Simonian Feminism," 17–84, in Moses and Rabine, *Feminism*.

6. Jeanne Deroin, *Profession de foi*, quoted in *De la liberté des femmes: Lettres de dames au "Globe," 1831–1832*, ed. Michèle Riot-Sarcey (Paris: Côté-femmes, 1992), 135–36.

7. Léon Abensour, *Le féminisme sous le règne de Louis Philippe et en 1848* (Paris: Plon, 1913), 89–107. See as well Marguerite Thibert, *Le féminisme dans le socialisme français de 1830 à 1850* (Paris: Giard, 1926), 261–62.

8. The expression "la femme nouvelle" was first used as the subtitle of the Saint-Simonian journal, *La tribune des femmes*.

9. Moses and Rabine, *Feminism*, 63. Guindorf organized the *Société d'Instruction Populaire*, to which she devoted her energy from 1832 until 1834. See, as well, Riot-Sarcey, *La démocratie*, especially 94–99. She committed suicide, like Claire Démar.

10. Cited in Evelyne Sullerot, *Histoire de la presse féminine en France, des origines à 1848* (Paris: Armand Colin, 1966), 170. Other studies of women journalists in the first half of the nineteenth century include Laure Adler, *A l'aube du féminisme: Les premières journalistes (1830–1850)* (Paris: Payot, 1979), and Walton, *Eve's Proud Descendants*.

11. Clémence Robert, in *Journal des femmes*, October 1833, cited in Riot-Sarcey, *La démocratie*, 95–96.

12. For more information on this learned society, see Riot-Sarcey, *La démocratie*, 305–6.

13. Historians frequently spell her name "Masure"; her father was, however, François Mazure, an inspector general of the educational system. Biographical information on her can be found in *De la liberté des femmes*, 142–43, and in Agnès Kettler, "De Francis Dazur à Sœur Marie des Anges: Les illusions perdues de Sophie Mazure," *Année Balzacienne*, 1988/1989, 45–71.

14. For more information, see Michèle Riot-Sarcey, "De la liberté de savoir au gouvernement des esprits. France première moitié du XIXe siècle," in *Lieux de femmes dans l'espace public, 1800–1930. Actes du colloque à l'Université de Lausanne, 11–12 nov. 1991*, ed. Monique Pavillon and François Valloton (Lausanne: Université de Lausanne, 1992), 107–22.

15. Abensour, *Le féminisme*, 135; Adler, *A l'aube du féminisme*. For a more detailed reading of Niboyet's intellectual evolution, see Riot-Sarcey, *La démocratie*, 130–40, 158–66.

16. See Michèle Riot-Sarcey, "Des femmes pétitionnent sous la monarchie de Juillet," in *Femmes dans la Cité*, 389–400, and Geneviève Fraisse, *Les femmes et leur histoire* (Paris: Gallimard, 1998), 281–88.

17. Sullerot, *Histoire de la presse*, 191–209.

18. Louise D'Ormoy, "De la nécessité de l'instruction des femmes," *Gazette des femmes*, 1 July 1836.

19. The subtitle of the *Gazette* is revealing: *Journal de législation et de jurisprudence. Littéraire, théâtral, artistique, commercial, judiciaire, de musique et des modes*. This article on women's instruction coincided with the Pelet law of 23 June 1836, which encouraged towns to open schools for girls. For another example of this concern for girls' education, see J. Dubreuilh's article "Instruction des femmes," in *Gazette des femmes*, 1 February 1837.

20. Reprinted in *La Mère de famille*, November 1834; emphasis in the original.

21. Chambre des Députés, *Débats parlementaires*, 30 May 1835. The quotation is reprinted in *Journal des femmes*, 15 June 1835.

22. For the history of women's normal schools in France, see Anne T. Quartararo, *Women Teachers and Popular Education in Nineteenth-Century France: Social Values and Corporate Identity at the Normal School Institution* (Newark: University of Delaware Press, 1995). The first superior normal school for women was the École normale supérieure de jeunes filles, which was founded in 1882 at Sèvres.

23. For more information on Jacotot, see Jacques Rancière, *Le maître ignorant* (Paris: Fayard, 1987), and Mayeur, *Histoire générale de l'enseignement*, 3:114–16.

24. For more information and an inventory on the pedagogical press during this period, see Pierre Caspard, ed., *La presse d'éducation et d'enseignement, XVIIIe siècle-1940. Répertoire analytique*, 4 vols. (Paris: INRP-CNRS, 1981–91).

25. *La tribune de l'enseignement*, 1 October 1838.

26. Analyses of medical discourse in particular have shown how gender differences became naturalized during this period. See Londa Schiebinger, *The Mind Has No Sex? Women in the Origins of Modern Science* (Cambridge: Harvard University Press, 1989); Jann Matlock, *Scenes of Seduction: Prostitution, Hysteria, and Reading Difference in Nineteenth-Century France* (New York: Columbia University Press, 1994); and Erna Olafson Hellerstein, "Women, Social Order, and the City: Rules for French Ladies, 1830–1870" (Ph.D. diss., University of California, Berkeley, 1980).

27. Joséphine Bachellery, *Lettres sur l'éducation des femmes* (Paris, 1848), 55. This collection contains all the letters she wrote to the *Tribune* as well as later letters addressed to Carnot in 1848.

28. For an analysis of the link between liberal political ideology and the emerging educational system during the July Monarchy, see Christian Nique, *Comment l'école devint une affaire d'État* (Paris: Nathan, 1990), and Pierre Rosanvallon, *Le moment Guizot* (Paris: Gallimard, 1985).

29. Bachellery, *Lettres sur l'éducation*, 48, 34.

30. The editor of this journal was Charles Richomme.

31. For information on Dauriat, see AN, F[17] 12432; her petition was printed as *Mémoire adressé à Messieurs les membres du Conseil Général du département de la Seine* (1846). In the end her petition was rejected, as the following chapter will show.

32. H.L.D. Rivail, *Projet de réforme concernant les examens et les maisons d'éducation des jeunes personnes* (Paris, 1847). Nicole Edelman has studied the gender politics of spiritism in France, which developed during the Second Empire. See Edleman, *Voyantes, guérisseuses et visionnaires en France, 1785–1914* (Paris: Albin Michel, 1995), 109–58.

33. Sandra Horvath-Peterson, *Victor Duruy and French Education: Liberal Reform in the Second Empire* (Baton Rouge: Louisiana University Press, 1984), 153. She notes that the Second Republic failed to pursue the project.

34. Deniel's study of the family in the Restoration provides a useful counterpoint for my discussion of the following two decades. The Catholic press he studies granted women importance within the family, but presented them as clearly dependent and inferior. See his *Une image de la famille*, chaps. 4 and 6. The religious revival of the 1830s and 1840s elaborated a very different vision.

35. See Stéphane Michaud, *Muse et Madone: Visages de la femme de la Révolution aux apparitions de Lourdes* (Paris: Seuil, 1985); Barbara Corrado Pope, "Immaculate and Powerful: The Marian Revival in the Nineteenth Century," in *Immaculate and Powerful: The Female Image and Social Reality*, ed. Clarissa W. Atkinson, Constance H. Buchanan, and Margaret R. Miles (Boston: Beacon Press, 1985), 173–200; Ruth Harris, *Lourdes: Body and Spirit in the Secular Age* (New York: Viking Penguin, 1999); and Raymond Jonas, *France and the Cult of the Sacred Heart: An Epic Tale for Modern Times* (Berkeley and Los Angeles: University of California Press, 2000). For an excellent synthesis of the century, see Jacques Le Goff and René Rémond, eds., *Histoire de la France religieuse*, vol. 3, *Du roi Très Chrétien à la laïcité républicaine (XVIIIe–XIXe siècle)*, ed. Philippe Joutard (Paris: Seuil, 1991).

36. Ralph Gibson, "Le catholicisme et les femmes en France au XIXe siècle," *Revue d'histoire de l'Eglise de France* 79 (1993): 63–93; idem, *A Social History of French Catholicism, 1789–1914* (London: Routledge, 1989).

37. Hazel Mills, "Negotiating the Divide: Women, Philanthropy and the 'Public Sphere' in Nineteenth-Century France," in *Religion, Society and Politics in France since 1789*, ed. Frank Tallett and Nicholas Atkin (London: The Hambledon Press, 1991), 29–54.

38. Donnet (archbishop of Bordeaux), "Instruction pastorale sur l'éducation de famille, Carême 1845," cited in Mills, "Negotiating the Divide," 40.

39. Father Pierre Alexandre Mercier, *Collection intégrale et universelle des orateurs chrétiens* (1863), cited in Marcel Bernos, "De l'influence salutaire ou pernicieuse de la femme dans la famille et la société," *Revue d'histoire moderne et contemporaine* 29 (July-September 1982): 457.

40. Ibid.

41. For an analysis of pedagogues' and moralists' interest in the early religious education of children by their mothers, see Luc, *L'invention*, 95–101.

42. Louis Aimé-Martin, *De l'éducation des mères de famille ou de la civilisation du genre humain par les femmes* (Brussels: Meline, Cans, 1837), 1:110.

43. Ibid., 91–92.

44. The most frequently cited texts include Amable Tastu, *Éducation maternelle: Simples leçons d'une mère à ses enfants* (Paris: Renduel, 1836); Augustin-François Théry, *Premiers conseils aux mères sur les moyens de diriger et d'instruire leurs filles* (Paris: Hachette, 1840); and Henri Louis Nicolas Duval (also known as Cardelli), *Conseils aux mères de famille ou manière de soigner et d'élever ses enfants jusqu'à l'âge de 7 ans, petit cours d'éducation physique et morale* (Paris: Johanneau,

1840). For a list of the most important nineteenth-century moral, pedagogical, and psychological texts, divided by the sex of the author, see Luc, *L'invention*, 485–89.

45. The subtitle of this journal was *Lectures religieuses, morales et littéraires pour les jeunes personnes et les jeunes gens*. For information on Lévi-Alvarès, see Mayeur, *Histoire générale de l'enseignement et l'éducation*, 69–72.

46. *La mère institutrice*, June 1836. Interestingly, Lévi-Alvarès confines the danger — the female pedant — to the domestic sphere, thus obscuring the greater threat posed by the public figure of the bluestocking.

47. Nathalie de Lajolais, *Le livre des mères de famille et des institutrices sur l'éducation pratique des femmes*, 2d ed. (Paris: Didier, 1843), 15–16. For a comparison with English rhetoric, see Davidoff and Hall, *Family Fortunes*, 80–192.

48. Patrick Bidelman offers these figures on the women's press: seventy-one journals appeared between 1800 and 1845 (compared to thirty-four by 1800). Of the seventy-one, forty-nine folded within two years, and only sixteen survived five years or more. Bidelman, *Pariahs Stand Up! The Founding of the Liberal Feminist Movement in France, 1858–1889* (Westport, Conn.: Greenwood Press, 1982), 21.

49. Article of 12 May 1832, cited in Adler, *A l'aube du féminisme*, 85. The tone of the *Journal des femmes* became more frivolous after 1834; in 1835 it adopts the subtitle *Revue fashionable*. Adler, 89–90.

50. The erstwhile Saint-Simonian Eugénie Niboyet founded the short-lived *Conseiller des femme*; her long-term interest in the social role of motherhood is evident in its pages.

51. Sirey also published a variety of handbooks and domestic texts that Adler has described as representing a form of maternal feminism in their conviction of women's moral superiority within the home. Adler, *A l'aube du féminisme*, 97.

52. For consideration of how women's bodies became the focus of medical attention in these years, see Yvonne Knibiehler, "Les médecins et la 'nature feminine' au temps du code civil," *Annales, E.S.C.* 31, no. 4 (1976): 824–45.

53. Marcus, *Apartment Stories*, 149–52.

54. Limayrac, "Les femmes moralistes," 52–53.

55. Ibid., 53.

56. See Janis Bergman-Carton, *The Woman of Ideas in French Art, 1830–1848* (New Haven: Yale University Press, 1995); Christine Planté, *La petite sœur de Balzac: Essai sur la femme auteur* (Paris: Seuil, 1989); and Florence Rochefort, "A la découverte des intellectuelles," *Clio. Histoire, Femmes et sociétés* 13 (2001): 5–16.

57. Women writers were venomously criticized in the *Physiologie de la presse* (1841) for getting undeserved publishing opportunities that they used to cheapen and sentimentalize literature. Bergman-Carton, *Woman of Ideas*, 77.

58. Laure Surville de Balzac, 23 May 1832, in *Lettres à une amie de province (1831–1837)* (Paris: Plon, 1932), cited in Planté, *La petite sœur*, 10.

59. Paul Gaschon de Molènes, "Les femmes poètes," *Revue des deux mondes* (1842), cited in Planté, *La petite sœur*, 23–24.

60. Planté, *La petite sœur*, 28.

61. Interestingly, he describes the conservative Société du Sacré-Cœur as an institution of *bas-bleu*. Frédéric Soulié, *Physiologie du bas-bleu* (Paris: Aubert, 1841), 37.

62. More sympathetic portrayals of women of letters existed, however; see the work of the popular caricaturist Paul Gavarni. Most commentators distinguished women writers from women artists; the latter were considered more respectable.

63. For more information on caricature and artistic renderings of women of ideas, see Kirsten Powell and Elizabeth C. Childs, eds., *Femmes d'esprit: Women in Daumier's Caricature* (Hanover: University Press of New England, 1990).

64. See Janis Bergman-Carton, "Conduct Unbecoming: Daumier and 'les Bas-bleus,'" in ibid., 65–86.

65. Jules Janin, "Le bas-bleu," in *Les Français peints par eux-mêmes*, vol. 1 (Paris: Philipart, 1861).

66. Madeleine Stéphanie de Longueville, "The Great Lady of 1830," in *Pictures of the French: A Series of Literary and Graphic Delineations of French Character* (London: Orr, 1840), 172.

67. The term *déclassement* has no English equivalent; it referred in this period to an education that left individuals with the cultural trappings of a higher class than their socioeconomic standing warranted.

68. Léon Gozlan, "Ce que c'est qu'une Parisienne," in *Le Diable à Paris: Paris et les Parisiens* (Paris: J. Hetzel, 1845), 1:61–63.

69. Honoré de Balzac, *Béatrix* (Paris: Gallimard, 1979), 400, 402.

70. Archives of the Congrégation de la Mère de Dieu (hereafter "AMD"), series 1F3, letter from the Superior General to Grand Chancelor Vinoy, 19 November 1871.

71. For the link between the new woman and the prostitute, see Moses, "'Difference' in Historical Perspective," 73–74. For an analysis of these familial strategies, see Adeline Daumard, *Les bourgeois de Paris au XIXe siècle* (Paris: Flammarion, 1970), 169–72.

72. E. de la Bédollière, "La jeune fille," in *Les Français peints par eux-même. Encyclopédie morale du XIXe siècle*, ed. Léon Curmer (Paris: Omnibus, 2003), 1:367.

73. Victorine Collin, "Les jeunes personnes sans fortune à Paris," in *Paris ou le Livre des Cent-et-Un*, 15 vols. (Paris: Ladvocat, 1832), 5:30, 43. Collin began her working life as a teaching aide and later earned a living as a journalist; interestingly, she does not present journalism as a viable option for the wellborn impoverished woman.

74. Cécile Dauphin, "Histoire d'un stéréotype: La vieille fille," in *Madame ou Mademoiselle: Itinéraires de la solitude féminine, XVIIIe–XXe siècle*, ed. Arlette Farge and Christiane Klapisch-Zuber (Paris: Montalba, 1984), 207–31.

75. Marie d'Espilly, "La vieille fille," in *Les Français peints par eux-mêmes*, ed. Léon Curmer (Paris: Omnibus, 2003), 999–1011.

76. Michelle Perrot, "De la vieille fille à la garçonne: La femme célibataire au XIXe siècle," *Autrement* 32 (June 1981): 227; Patrick Bourdelais, "Le poids démographique des femmes seules en France," *Annales de démographie historique*, 1981: 215–27; Cécile Dauphin, "Single Women," in Fraisse and Perrot, *A History of Women*, vol. 4, *Emerging Feminisms*. Perrot notes that there is no feminine in French for the words *auteur* and *célibataire*. For the English anxiety about redundant women, see Mary Poovey, *Uneven Developments: The Ideological Work of Gender in Mid-Victorian England* (Chicago: University of Chicago Press, 1988), and Vicinus, *Independent Women*.

77. See Louis Couailhac, *Physiologie du célibataire et de la vieille fille* (Paris: J. Laisné, 1841).

78. For an overview of feminist activities during the revolutionary period, see Moses, *French Feminism*, chap. 6.

79. See Maurice Gontard, *Les écoles primaires de la France bourgeoise (1833–75)* (Toulouse: CRDP, n.d.).

80. See Edith Thomas, *Les femmes de 1848* (Paris: Presses Universitaires de France, 1948), chap. 6; Jules Tixerant, *Le féminisme à l'époque de 1848 dans l'ordre politique et dans l'ordre économique* (Paris: Giard and Brière, 1908); and Moses, *French Feminism*, 28.

81. Her proposals are included in *Lettres sur l'éducation*. Gréard has reproduced her plan for a superior normal school in *Éducation et instruction*, vol. 1, annex 28.

82. Joséphine Bachellery, "Comment nous comprenons l'émancipation des femmes sous la République — 1," *La voix des femmes*, 19 April 1848.

83. Thibert, *Le féminisme*, 327–28.

84. Riot-Sarcey, *La démocratie*, 194–98.

85. For the general context, see René Rémond, *L'anticléricalisme en France: De 1815 à nos jours*, new and revised ed. (Paris: Fayard, 1999).

86. Bachellery, *Lettres sur l'éducation*, 228.

87. Bachellery, "Comment nous comprenons l'émancipation — 2," *La voix des femmes*, 24–25 April 1848. In Chapter 7 I will return to this issue of anticlericalism and the politics of girls' education.

88. See Thibert, *Le féminisme*, 331, and Charles Lemonnier, *Elisa Lemonnier: Fondatrice de la Société pour l'enseignement professionnel des femmes* (St. Germain: Imprimerie de L. Toinon, 1866).

89. Mayeur, *L'éducation*, 103.

90. See Karen Offen, "Ernest Legouvé and the Doctrine of 'Equality in Difference' for Women: A Case Study of Male Feminism in Nineteenth-Century French Thought," *Journal of Modern History* 58 (June 1996): 452–84.

91. Ernest Legouvé, *Histoire morale des femmes*, 5th ed. (Paris: Didier, 1859), 59.

92. Offen, "Ernest Legouvé," 469; Legouvé, *Histoire morale des femmes*, 366–90.

93. Legouvé's arguments echo those of Bachellery in her discussion of vocational education for women in 1839; see Bachellery, *Lettres sur l'éducation*, 48. For a recent discussion of the professional woman, see Linda L. Clark, *The Rise of Professional Women in France: Gender and Public Administration since 1830* (Cambridge: Cambridge University Press, 2000).

94. Scott, *Only Paradoxes to Offer*, 70. Claire Moses offers insights into how Saint-Simonian discourse influenced this evolution: for the Saint-Simonians the family was reconceptualized to include all of humanity — the family made social — while "the mother" "was the 'tie' that binds." Moses, "'Difference' in Historical Perspective," 58.

95. Legouvé, *Histoire morale des femmes*, 383.

96. Offen, "Ernest Legouvé," 474.

97. See the work of Christophe Charle for more information on the ethos and workings of French republican meritocracy. Most of his scholarship focuses, however, on the Third Republic.

CHAPTER 4

1. On female literacy rates, see James Smith Allen, *In the Public Eye: A History of Reading in Modern France, 1800–1940* (Princeton: Princeton University Press, 1991), 58–59, and Martyn Lyon, "Les nouveaux lecteurs au XIXe siècle: Femmes, enfants, ouvriers," in *Histoire de la lecture dans le monde occidental*, ed. G. Cavallo and Roger Chartier (Paris: Seuil, 1997), 365–400. On women writers during the July Monarchy, see Cheryl A. Morgan, "Unfashionable Feminism? Designing Women Writers in the *Journal des Femmes* (1832–1836)," in *Making the News: Modernity and the Mass Press in Nineteenth-Century France*, ed. Dean de la Motte and Jannene M. Prsyblyski (Amherst: University of Massachusetts Press, 1999), 207–32.

2. This is in contrast with England, where governesses were far more common. Alice Renton, *Tyrant or Victim? A History of the British Governess* (London: Weidenfeld and Nicolson, 1991).

3. Studies of women's professional trajectories in France tend to focus on the period of the Third Republic. See Mathilde Dubesset and Michelle Zancarini-Fournel, *Parcours de femmes, réalités et représentations. Saint-Etienne, 1880–1950* (Lyon: Presses Universitaires de Lyon, 1993). For the earlier period, see Rogers, "Boarding Schools" and "La sous-maîtresse."

4. D'Espilly, "La vieille fille," in *Les Français peints par eux-mêmes*, 1:1000.

5. Louise Colet, "L'institutrice," in *Les Français peints par eux-mêmes*, 1:651–60.

6. Ecarnot, "The Country School for Young Ladies," in *Pictures of the French*, 217–24.

7. Anne Hettler, "L'éducation des jeunes bourgeoises à travers la presse pour demoiselles sous le Second Empire" (mémoire de maîtrise en sciences historiques, Université de Strasbourg II, 1996–97), 23. The author uses *Le journal des demoiselles*, *Le magasin des demoiselles* (1844–96), *Le moniteur des dames et demoiselles* (1854–1902), *Le conseiller des dames et demoiselles* (1847–82), *Le messager des dames et demoiselles* (1854–56), and *La mode illustrée* (which began in 1860). Interestingly none of these journals publicized the creation of Duruy's cours secondaires in 1867, testimony to their disavowal of public education.

8. See Madeleine Lassère, *Victorine Monniot ou l'éducation des jeunes filles au XIXe siècle: Entre exotisme et catholicisme de combat* (Paris: L'Harmattan, 1999), 108.

9. Victorine Monniot, *Marguerite à vingt ans (suite et fin du Journal de Marguerite)* (1861), quoted in Lassère, *Victorine Monniot*, 110.

10. Quoted in Lassère, *Victorine Monniot*, 118.

11. The expression "French University" refers not just to higher education but also to the administrative system established under Napoleon that organized secondary education and incorporated schoolteachers into the civil service.

12. Burton J. Bledstein, *The Culture of Professionalism: The Middle Class and the Development of Higher Education in America* (New York: W. W. Norton, 1976).

13. Professionalization as a process has been studied far more systematically for men than for women. A few recent exceptions that focus on France and the teaching professions include Clark, *Rise of Professional Women*; Luc, *L'invention*; and Margadant, *Madame le Professeur*.

14. I have found the following useful in thinking about the process of professionalization: Peter V. Meyers, "Primary Schoolteachers in 19th-Century France: A Study of Professionalization Through Conflict," *History of Education Quarterly* (spring-summer 1985): 21–40; Harold Perkins, *The Rise of Professional Society. England since 1880* (London: Routledge, 1989); and Christine Ruane, *Gender, Class, and the Professionalization of Russian City Teachers, 1860–1914* (Pittsburgh: University of Pittsburgh Press, 1994). Marie-Madeleine Compère has noted that the process of professionalization is more often the object of study among Anglo-Saxon historians, while the French have traditionally focused more on questions of inherited traditions and meritocracy. Compère, *L'histoire de l'éducation en Europe*, 101–3. I would argue that the focus on traditions and meritocracy has contributed to erasing the presence of women from the history of French professions. See, for example, Christophe Charle, *Les élites de la République, 1880–1900* (Paris: Fayard, 1987).

15. No sanctions existed for towns that failed to open a girls' school. For figures on girls' schools, see Raymond Grew and Patrick J. Harrigan, *Schools, State, and Society: The Growth of Elementary Schooling in Nineteenth-Century France, A Quantitative Analysis* (Ann Arbor: University of Michigan Press, 1991), 121–46. For the Pelet law and on normal schools for girls under the July Monarchy, see Quartararo, *Women Teachers*, 36–53.

16. Rules or rulings (*règlements*) did not carry the same status as ordinances or laws. The government or administration passed such rules on matters of "secondary" importance in cases where a more general law was inappropriate.

17. In April 1838 the minister of education Salvandy sent the Parisian *règlement* to the prefect of the Seine-et-Oise saying, "It would be desirable that similar measures be adopted as regards *maisons d'éducation* in all of the departments." AD Seine-et-Oise, 30 T 1, letter of 24 April 1838. The prefects' responses to the Parisian *règlement* are in AN, F[17] 12432. For a general analysis of their reactions, see Mayeur, *L'éducation*, 59.

18. In Paris these diplomas were known as the "brevets de l'Hôtel de Ville" to distinguish them from the elementary-level diplomas that were delivered at the Sorbonne.

19. See Etienne Kilian's analysis of the ruling, in *De l'instruction des filles à ses divers degrés, institutions et pensions, écoles primaires supérieures et élémentaires* (Paris: Paul Dupont, 1842), 20–22.

20. A former lawyer at the royal court, Legros was appointed in February 1839 and served until 1848. Several of his reports can be found in AN, F[17] 12431. For more information on his activities, see AN, F[17] 12448 and Archives de Paris, VD[6] series. His position was eliminated when it was decided in June 1847 that the Parisian inspector of the academy could fill his role. He continued to comment on girls' education to the minister in early 1848.

21. The prefect was supposed to approve a transfer prior to the school's changing hands. Failure to conform could result in closure, although the archival record suggests these measures were rarely strictly applied. The need for such legislation indicates the extent to which schools did have lengthy existences.

22. AN, F[17] 12433, letters to the ministry dated 7 February 1838 and April 1842. The *conseil royal* issued a ruling concerning the ceding of *pensions* on 15 April 1842.

23. Archives de Paris, VD[6] 158, no. 3, règlement of 27 February 1844. See Mayeur, *L'éducation*, 92, for information on the first women delegates. The minister of education pressured the prefect of the Seine to create these paid positions, arguing that volunteer workers were inevitably less effective than salaried ones. AN, F[17] 12448. For information on nursery school inspectresses, see Clark, *Rise of Professional Women*, 19–25, and Luc, *L'invention*, 327–37. Female prison inspectresses were created in 1842.

24. See Félix Ponteil, *Les institutions de la France de 1814 à 1870* (Paris: Presses universitaires de France, 1966), and Nique, *Comment l'école*.

25. The departments concerned include the Charente, the Eure, the Gard, the Indre, the Isère, the Loiret, the Manche, the Haute-Marne, the Marne, the Orne, the Bas-Rhin, the Saône-et-Loire, and the Somme. Some argued they could not find female volunteers for the inspections; others argued that the scarcity of candidates rendered separate examination procedures unnecessary. AN, F[17] 12432.

26. Ibid. See reports from the Rhône, the Seine-et-Oise, and the Haute-Marne. The prefects from rural departments at times showed similar enthusiasm, for example, in the Gers. In Metz and Strasbourg, however, where there were many boarding schools as well, the prefect saw no need to establish a division between *institutions* and *pensions*.

27. Ibid. See the responses for the Bouches-du-Rhône, the Moselle, the Marne, and the Meuse.

28. Ibid. In the Moselle the prefect argued that the charlatanism of headmistresses existed only in Paris, not in the provinces.

29. AD Rhône, T 209, letter of 11 January 1849, quoted in Gemie, *Women and Schooling*, 44.

30. AD Vienne, 3 T 36, "Écoles de filles, 1836–1875," manuscript note added to the undated document "Considérations à l'appui du règlement sur les Pensions et Institutions de filles." This was written in the 1840s.

31. AN, F[17] 12432, report written by A. de Sauteul, the councillor of the prefect, on 5 October 1838.

32. Ibid.

33. AN, F[17] 12432, Prefect Baudoin of the Nièvre to the ministry, letter of 27 July 1838; the first normal school for girls was founded that same year but to train primary not secondary teachers.

34. Rogers, "La sous-maîtresse."

35. Given future attitudes toward clerical education there is a certain irony in the fact that departments often gave fellowships to girls to attend training courses in religious boarding schools prior to the creation of state-supported women's normal schools in 1879. See Françoise Mayeur, "La formation des institutrices femmes avant la loi Paul Bert: Les cours normaux," *Revue d'histoire de l'Église de France* 81 (January-June 1995): 121–30.

36. *La tribune de l'enseignement*, 1 March 1839. This article was reprinted for a larger audience in *La mère institutrice* in 1841 and again in Bachellery, *Lettres sur l'éducation*.

37. *La tribune de l'enseignement*, 1 April 1839, 222–25, reprinted as letter 5 in *Lettres sur l'éducation*. See Rogers, "Le professeur a-t-il un sexe? Les débats autour de la présence d'hommes dans l'enseignement secondaire féminin, 1840–1880," *Clio. Histoire, Femmes et Société* 4 (1996): 221–39.

38. Joséphine Bachellery, "Lettre à M. Lévi-Alvarès, professeur d'histoire, etc., sur les Inspectrices de la Ville de Paris" (Paris, 1844); portions of this letter appeared in *La mère institutrice* in December 1845.

39. Kilian, *De l'instruction des filles*, 23.

40. The *REF* was not a state-supported professional journal like the *Manuel général de l'instruction primaire*, which Guizot founded in 1832. See Nique, *Comment l'école*, 153–54.

41. For a similar analysis of the professionalization of nursery school teachers, see Luc, *L'invention*, 301–7.

42. This was not unique to female teachers. Similar concerns underlay the deliverance of the *agrégation* in male higher education, see Dominique Julia, "Le choix des professeurs en France: Vocation ou concours? 1700–1850," *Paedagogica Historica* 30 (1994): 173–205.

43. Legros attributed some of the blame to the women inspectors themselves who rarely attended the meetings of the surveillance committees, only sending in written reports. These bourgeois women, who spent the summer months in the provinces, took their responsibilities in a more amateurish sense than he would have liked. Luc notes resistance on the part of local notables to state efforts to require diplomas. Luc, *L'invention*, 306.

44. For inspection reports, see Archives de Paris, the VD⁶ series, especially VD⁶ 347, no. 15.

45. AN, F¹⁷ 12432. In 1838 when Salvandy acceded to her request, Clarice Aublay, née Hortode, was forty-three-years old. In 1839 she opened a boarding school that lasted some ten years. Foreign headmistresses similarly obtained diplomas without passing examinations.

46. Archives de Paris, VD⁶ 159, no. 2, decision of 27 March 1841.

47. See Gréard, *Éducation et instruction*, 125. Gréard's informant was probably basing her information on the number of candidates who signed up for the examination, not the number actually present. I too used the number who signed up for the examination to determine that 33 percent of the candidates in 1845–46 passed.

48. AN, F¹⁷ 12433, for the period 1842–44; for the entire period, see AD Seine-et-Oise, 30 T 1, Résultat numérique des examens pour l'obtention des diplômes.

49. AD Hautes-Pyrénées, T 39. This is the only department where I have found examples of the dictation given for the examination to be a *maîtresse de pension*. One candidate who failed made ten mistakes in that sentence. Strikingly, for an aspiring teacher, her dictation begins "les maison des ductions"!

50. Amélie Weiler, *Journal d'une jeune fille mal dans son siècle, 1840–1859*, ed. Nicolas Stoskopf (Strasbourg: La Nuée Bleue, 1994), 125–26.

51. In 1846 inspectors reported progress in the teaching of physics, chemistry, and natural history as a result of these subjects being part of the examination to become a *maîtresse de pension*.

52. AD Bas-Rhin, T, 1TP/PRI 256, letter of 4 October 1843, cited in Schvind, "L'éducation des demoiselles," 9.

53. AD Hautes-Pyrénées, T 39, letter from the ministry of 28 June 1847.

54. Whether this had any effect on the actual level of teaching is doubtful but it is curious to note the disappearance of the secondary diploma just at the moment of its overall generalization. Schvind found that of ninety-six teachers between 1820 and 1870 in Strasbourg, forty-six held the *brevet de capacité*, and only thirty-eight had a *maîtresse de pension* diploma; eight teachers had both diplomas. Schvind, "L'éducation des demoiselles," 41.

55. The *brevet de capacité du premier ordre* tested future teachers on moral and religious instruction, reading and writing, aspects of the French language, math and the legal system of weights and measures, French history, aspects of physical sciences and natural history, notions of literature, line drawing, music, and needlework. Hippolyte Fortoul, *Circulaire adressée à MM. les Recteurs, relativement à l'inspection des écoles de filles*. For the legislative texts, see Octave Gréard, *La législation de l'enseignement primaire en France de 1789 à nos jours* (Paris: Delalain Frères, 1891–1902), 3:562–73.

56. This issue of inspections in religious schools plagued the administration in the middle decades. Many nuns refused to allow inspectors access to their schools, and authorities were far from clear about their own prerogatives.

57. This was the official position taken by the ministry; see Henri Boiraud, "La condition féminine et la scolarisation des filles en France au XIXème siècle de Guizot à Jules Ferry" (Thèse d'État, Université de Caen, 1978), 346.

58. For an analysis of the 1851 male normal school curriculum, see Quartararo, *Women Teachers*, 54–59. For an analysis of the political implications of these changes, see Maurice Gontard, *La question des écoles normales de 1789 à nos jours* (Toulouse: CRDP, 1976).

59. For a reminder of the pitfalls involved in using educational statistics, see Jean-Noël Luc, "L'illusion statistique. À-propos de l'article de R. Grew, P. J. Harrigan, J. P. Whitney, 'La scolarisation en France, 1829–1906,'" *Annales E.S.C.* 41 (July-August 1986): 887–911.

60. Mme Stévens was born Marie Dupleix in 1795; she ran a boarding school from 1830 until 1842 on the Quai d'Anjou in the ninth arrondissement. The prefect in 1835 objected to the fact that her school was not a public institution open free of charge to all students but rather a private institution. See AN, F¹⁷ 12432. There is no indication

when the department ceased to pay her a salary. The first teachers in Parisian *salles d'asile* were also paid 1,200 francs per year, but their services were required on a daily basis. See Luc, *L'invention*, 23.

61. Normal schools and courses for female primary schoolteachers first appeared in 1838, but they were few and far between.

62. In 1852 they suggested the creation of a normal school where future teachers would receive lessons in pedagogy. Conseil général du département de la Seine, *Résultats de l'inspection des pensionnats*, 1852.

63. See Rogers, "La sous maîtresse."

64. Conseil général, *Résultats*, 1846.

65. For a particularly negative vision of the situation of teachers' aides, see Marie Sincère [Marie Dubreuil de Saint-Germain Romieu], *Les pensionnats de jeunes filles* (Paris: Deslosges, 1854), 27–36.

66. For a general discussion of male professors in girls' education from the 1830s until the 1880s, see Rogers, "Le professeur a-t-il un sexe?" Comparative perspectives are offered in James Albisetti, "The Feminization of Teaching in the Nineteenth Century: A Comparative Perspective," *History of Education* 22, no. 3 (1993): 252–63. In Denmark girls' academies also relied heavily on part-time male teachers who, like in France, frequently taught courses in several academies; see Carol Gold, *Educating Middle-Class Daughters: Private Girls' Schools in Copenhagen, 1790–1820* (Copenhagen: The Royal Library Museum Tusculanum Press, 1996), 125–27.

67. *La tribune de l'enseignement*, 1 April 1839.

68. Louise Dauriat, *Mémoire adressé à Messieurs les membres du conseil général du département de la Seine* (Paris, 1846); see as well the documents surrounding her campaign in AN, F^{17} 12432.

69. AN, F^{17} 12432, letter signed "professeurs" of 11 November 1845 to the members of the royal council.

70. Ibid.

71. Conseil general, *Résultats*, 10 November 1846.

72. Archives de Paris, VD^6 159, inspections de maisons d'éducation de demoiselles (1851–62), inspection of October 1851. Her school had 112 students, 105 of whom were boarders.

73. A table summarizing the presence of male and female teachers in Parisian boarding schools (1846–60) can be found in my article "Le professeur a-t-il un sexe," 227. Figures are compiled from Conseil général, *Résultats*, 1846–1860.

74. Haussmann, who was prefect of the Seine from 1853 to 1870, is best known for the urban planning he developed in Paris, notably the building and broadening of streets, the development of a sewage system, the creation of urban parks, and the construction of prestigious buildings.

75. AD Seine-et-Oise, 38 T 5.

76. AD Hautes-Pyrénées, T39, dossier Bernigole-Forcade; her school opened in 1842 and was still functioning in 1870; in 1858 she earned approximately 1,800 francs per year with her fifty-one paying students, see 1T 47.

77. The emergence of these women professors poses the questions of how inspectresses filled out their questionnaires. These "new" professors may simply represent the women who ran the school. AD Vienne, 10T 181, 1860–70. Mlles d'Aubigny's school was indicated in the departmental trade book from 1843 until 1873; in 1843 they had a declared revenue of 4,080 francs per year, see 10T 179.

78. Private collection of Viviane Isambert-Jamati; letter from Germaine to Eugénie Dubois, 23 December 1875.

79. Schvind, "L'éducation des demoiselles," 43.

80. For more information on Duruy's efforts, see Chapter 7.

81. The first women to obtain a *baccalauréat ès sciences* received it in 1863; between 1866 and 1882 a total of eighty-one women received the scientific or the literary baccalauréat. For a list of the first women *bachelières*, see Mayeur, *Histoire générale de l'enseignement*, 3:123.

82. Conseil général, *Résultats*, 1861.

83. Ibid., 1863, 347.

84. In 1848 a fourth woman delegate, the daughter of the poet Marceline Desbordes-Valmore, Ondine, was appointed to help out both in visiting schools and in attending the exams of the Hôtel de Ville. Francis Ambrière, *Le siècle des Valmore: Marceline Desbordes-Valmore et les siens*, vol. 2, *1840–1892* (Paris: Seuil, 1987), 199, 256, 448.

85. I have used the Parisian *Annuaire de commerce* to establish a list of institutions with their addresses over the century. Information concerning the boarding-school mistresses comes from the VD^6 series at the Archives de Paris, as well as from civil status registers.

86. This figure is based on headmistresses' presence in the yearbook even when their schools changed location. Since many women ran schools before coming to Paris or moved out of Paris after a number of years, this average is undoubtedly low. My study does not address the economics of running a boarding school, although if longevity is

some indicator of success, it would tend to support my argument that these institutions offered sizeable numbers of women a form of independence.

87. Archives de Paris, VD⁶ 347, no. 16.

88. Of the 140 women whose husbands were teachers, I know the profession of 77 of their fathers: 30 had fathers who were clearly lower class, working in agriculture, day labor, skilled labor, or as artisans or small shop-keepers; a mere 15 had fathers in the teaching, intellectual, or artistic professions.

89. Archives de Paris, Vbis R¹ 5, registre (1850–70).

90. Archives de Paris, VD⁶ 159, no. 1.

91. Ibid.

92. I do not know whether she won her suit.

93. Some of these women may in fact have been widowed, but this information is rarely indicated. An inspection in 1858 for the old sixth arrondissement lists twenty-three headmistresses and specifies that nine were single, two were widowed, and the remaining twelve women had sons. Archives de Paris, VD⁶ 367, no. 10.

94. Archives de Paris, VD⁶ 158, no. 3, inspection of 1848.

95. Archives de Paris, VD⁶ 575, no. 7, inspection of 1845.

96. See Rogers, "Boarding Schools," 173–77.

CHAPTER 5

1. The work of Claude Langlois has significantly reoriented the perspective historians now have of the feminization of religion. His quantitative and qualitative analysis of women religious congregations fits them squarely within the social history of the nineteenth century. See Le catholicisme. More recently he has offered a series of useful suggestions for further work in "Le catholicisme au féminin revisité," in Corbin, Lalouette, and Riot-Sarcey, Femmes dans la Cité, 139–49.

2. In the nineteenth century there was a distinction between active congregations composed of sisters and cloistered orders composed of nuns. For a summary of these distinctions, see Langlois, Le catholicisme, 13–17. In this chapter as in the rest of the book, I prefer the term "order," which is more familiar to English readers. I use "nun," "sister," and "woman religious" interchangeably; Anglo-American specialists of the subject prefer the last.

3. Ibid., 307–12, 323–30.

4. Several historians have highlighted the degree to which religious teachers, both male and female, benefited from popular approval even when accused of sex crimes. See Jean-Claude Caron's A l'école de la violence: Châtiments et sévices dans l'institution scolaire au XIXe siècle (Paris: Aubier, 1999), 263–69, and Caroline Ford, "Religion and the Politics of Cultural Change in Provincial France: The Resistance of 1902 in Lower Brittany," Journal of Modern History 62 (March 1990): 1–33. For an analysis of nuns' cultural authority within the Irish context, see Mary Peckham Magray, The Transforming Power of the Nun: Women, Religion, and Cultural Change in Ireland, 1750–1900 (New York: Oxford University Press, 1998), especially 74–86.

5. Maria d'Anspach, "La religieuse," in Les Français peints par eux-mêmes, 2 vols., ed. Léon Curmer (Paris: Philipart, 1861; new ed., Paris: Omnibus, 2004), 2:745–73.

6. See Claude Langlois, "Féminisation du catholicisme," in Le Goff and Rémond, Histoire de la France religieuse, 3:292–309, and Michaud, Muse et Madone, 23–55.

7. Mills, "Negotiating the Divide," 51. Her article explores the different types of confraternities. See Corbin, Lalouette, and Riot-Sarcey, Femmes dans la Cité, for a number of perspectives on how religious activities brought women into the public, notably the articles by Jean-Pierre Chaline and Catherine Duprat. For another vision of female confraternities and their meaning, see Smith, Ladies of the Leisure Class, chap. 5.

8. To add to this analysis, I would argue that Catholic rhetoric contributed to a specific vision of feminine qualities and characteristics at a time when significant numbers of women were demonstrating very different characteristics. See Gibson, "Le catholicisme." He argues that "the growth of teaching orders was not the cause of the feminisation of Catholicism, but the consequence; they responded to a preexisting demand" (84).

9. I have found little evidence for the nineteenth century of the kind of cultural fantasies about nuns that existed in the eighteenth century. René Rémond's L'anticléricalisme en France focuses almost solely on the actions and activities of the male church. I address the issue of anticlericalism in Chapter 7.

10. Julie-Victoire Daubié, La femme pauvre au dix-neuvième siècle, 3 vols. (Paris: Côté-femmes, 1992), 1:115.

11. "Le pensionnat de rêve en 1851," in Le Goff and Rémond, *Histoire de la France religieuse*, 3:306.

12. For examples of such recommendations, see Odile Arnold, *Le corps et l'âme: La vie des religieuses au XIXe siècle* (Paris: Seuil, 1984), 177.

13. Archives of the Sœurs de la Doctrine Chrétienne (Nancy) (hereafter "ADC"), *Annales religieuses des sœurs de la Doctrine Chrétienne, 1852–67*, Décision du chapitre général de 1849, 39.

14. Ibid., recommandations lors du 6e chapitre general, 12 July 1862, 344.

15. In what follows, I will be considering the training, qualifications, and motivations of choir, not lay, sisters. Lay sisters were second-class citizens in all orders, performing the basic domestic chores, while choir sisters taught in and ran the orders. For an analysis of entrance conditions in the Lyons region, see Curtis, *Educating the Faithful*, 43–49. For a more detailed analysis of one teaching order, the Congrégation de la Mère de Dieu, see Rogers, "Retrograde or Modern?"

16. Church law insisted that novices under twenty-one obtain parental consent before taking vows. For a description of this life, see Arnold, *Le corps et l'âme*, 39–161.

17. Curtis, *Educating the Faithful*, 51.

18. For the Congrégation de la Mère de Dieu, see AMD, series 1E2, "Schedule of vows, 1858–1902." For information on what individual women paid to enter congregations, see Langlois, *Le catholicisme*, 365–71. The amount to become a choir sister in the Congrégation de la Mère de Dieu appears to represent a high, with its suggested dowry fee of twelve thousand francs in 1851. Families could opt to pay a yearly pension.

19. See Rogers, "Retrograde or Modern," 156. Ralph Gibson, "Female Religious Orders in 19th-Century France," in *Catholicism in Britain and France since 1789*, ed. Frank Tallett and Nicholas Atkin (London: The Hambledon Press, 1996). Comparative data can be found in Langlois, *Le catholicisme*, 545–62.

20. Quoted from constitutions in 1854 and 1841, in Curtis, *Educating the Faithful*, 48–49.

21. ADC, *Entretiens familiers des sœurs de la Doctrine Chrétienne* (Nancy, 1850), partie historique, "Lettre circulaire de M. Mougenot, supérieur de la congregation, au sujet de sa nomination," 12 March 1851, 339–40.

22. These percentages come from Langlois, who nonetheless emphasizes that his results are based on a limited number of studies. See Langlois, *Le catholicisme*, 551–55.

23. See ibid., 601–25, as well as Rogers, "Retrograde or Modern?" 152–56. Langlois confirms the urban orientation of such congregations as the Sacré-Cœur, the Fidèles Compagnes de Jésus, and the Ursulines de Chavagne.

24. Death notices are a particular rhetorical genre. I have used the death notices of the Congrégation de la Mère de Dieu (AMD, series 3E,), as well as those published in the *Annales de la Doctrine Chrétienne* between 1852 and 1867. For another study of religious vocation using similar sources, see Elizabeth Rapley, "Women and the Religious Vocation in Seventeenth-Century France," *French Historical Studies* 18 (spring 1994): 613–31.

25. Gibson, "Female Religious Orders."

26. For a detailed analysis of the familial cultural climate that inspired religious vocations, see Yves Pourcher, "Les vocations sacerdotales et religieuses en Lozère aux XIXe et XXe siècles," *Le monde alpin et rhodanien* 2/3 (1985): 55–82. Within the Congrégation de la Mère de Dieu, I found at least fifteen groups of sisters who entered as novices as well as two nieces and aunts.

27. Landivier's obituary notice indicates Desjardin, a future superior general, "was able to sow and develop in her soul the seeds of a religious vocation." AMD, series E, cahier D.

28. Gibson, "Female Religious Orders."

29. AMD, series 1F7, letter of superior general Halley to the mother, 2 February 1867. In her letter Halley sought to convince the mother her daughter's vocation was not forced: "God alone is the master, he alone gives a vocation to everyone of his creatures . . . we never speak about such things."

30. Gibson, "Female Religious Orders."

31. See ADC, *Annales religieuses des sœurs de la Doctrine Chrétienne, 1852–67*, 191. For more examples of such reluctance on the part of parents, see Arnold, *Le corps et l'âme*, 30–35.

32. Yvonne Turin, *Femmes et religieuses au XIXe siècle. Le féminisme "en religion"* (Paris: Nouvelle Cité, 1989), 206–8. Chappotin ultimately founded the Institut des Franciscaines Missionnaires de Marie.

33. Recent feminist scholarship on missionary organizations has emphasized the bureaucratic nature of the latter, arguing for the ways in which bureaucracy has been traditionally gendered masculine. See Rita Smith Kipp, "Why Can't a Woman Be More Like a Man? Bureaucratic Contradictions in the Dutch Missionary Society," in *Gendered Missions: Women and Men in Missionary Discourse and Practice*, ed. Mary Taylor Huber and Nancy Lutkehaus (Ann Arbor: University of Michigan Press, 1999), 145–78. Similarly, one might argue that the bureaucratic structure of teaching congregations forced women leaders to assume masculine tasks.

34. The argument about religious congregations as businesses offering professional training and providing women with a sense of professional identity can be found in the work of religious historians Claude Langlois, Ralph Gibson, and Sarah Curtis. Historians of women have also made similar arguments; there is less scholarship on the subject for France than for other countries. See Dauphin, "Single Women," in Fraisse and Perrot, *Histoire des femmes*, 4:437–38; Martha Vicinus, "Church Communities: Sisterhoods and Deaconesses' Houses," in *Independent Women*; and Catherine Prelinger, "The Female Diaconate in the Anglican Church: What Kind of Ministry for Women?" in *Religion in the Lives of English Women*, ed. G. Malmgreen (London: Croom Helm, 1986).

35. Male religious orders were dispensed from obtaining the teaching *brevet* in February 1819; this privilege was extended to female orders on 2 April 1820. Exemption from certification was briefly revoked in 1830 and then reinstituted in 1836 for female teachers until the Ferry laws in the 1880s. Polemical debate about this measure really only developed after the 1850 Falloux law. Arguably a necessary measure given the absence of qualified teachers in the first half of the century, its practical justification was less convincing afterward. See Grimaud, *Histoire de la liberté*, 5:230–44, 254–55, and Mayeur, *Histoire générale de l'enseignement*, 3:306–13.

36. ASSC (Rome), series C-I c3 box 8, see the *Commission pour les études et le pensionnat* in 1851.

37. Cited in Curtis, *Educating the Faithful*, 69, from the constitutions of 1858.

38. "Avis pour les maîtresses du pensionnat," in Archives de la Congrégation de Notre Dame, *Règles et Méthodes dédiées aux Religieuses de Notre Dame* (Clermont-Ferrand: Imprimerie de la librairie Catholique, 1844).

39. "Règles de la préfète des classes" and "Avis pour les maîtresses du pensionnat," in Archives de la Congrégation de Notre Dame, *Règles et Méthodes*. Frequent shifting of teachers characterized teaching congregations in contrast to lay institutions. They were imposed from above as a way of ensuring humility; religious teachers learned through experience that they were not irreplaceable.

40. Turin, *Femmes et religieuses*, 119–20.

41. See Thérèse Perrée, *Le tiers-ordre de Notre-Dame du Mont-Carmel d'Avranches* (Coutances: Éditions Notre-Dame, 1965), 64.

42. Louis Foucher, *Mme Desfontaines et la congrégation de Sainte-Clotilde de 1757 à nos jours* (Paris: Institut Sainte-Clotilde, 1965), 83–84.

43. Jégou and Mesnil, "Les Ursulines françaises," 55.

44. ADC, *Entretiens familiers*, partie historique, 98.

45. Marius Faugeras, "Les Sœurs de l'Instruction Chrétienne de St-Gildas-des-Bois au XIXe siècle (1870–1869)," in *Les Religieuses enseignantes (XVIe–XXe siècles)* (Angers: Presses de l'Université d'Angers, 1981), 105.

46. See her correspondence in *Anne-Marie Javouhey: Fondatrice de la congrégation des Sœurs de Saint-Joseph de Cluny. Lettres*, 4 vols. (Paris: Cerf, 1994), especially 2:63, letter 296, to a mother superior in Saint-Denis (Bourbon Island), 29 August 1834.

47. The issue of inspections within religious schools posed problems throughout the century and generated a wealth of administrative correspondence, as education inspectors queried their superiors about the extent of their prerogatives in the face of congregational hostility to such inspections. See AN, F[19] 6354 and 6247. In 1819, the mother superior of the Présentation de Marie in Bourg-Saint-Andéol (Ardèche) argued that once nuns had their exams they would become "established and independent," refusing to accept the higher authority of their mother superior. AN, F[19] 6354, letter to the minister of the interior, 19 September 1819.

48. Turin, *Femmes et religieuses*, 118–22.

49. Curtis, *Educating the Faithful*, 50–51.

50. ADC, *Annales religieuses*, 16.

51. See Curtis, *Educating the Faithful*, 57; Turin, *Femmes et religieuses*, 122; Abbé N. Hamant, *Sainte-Chrétienne: Centenaire d'une congrégation religieuse à Metz* (Metz: Imprimerie Lorraine, 1923), 285.

52. Curtis, *Educating the Faithful*, 57–58.

53. Quoted in Turin, *Femmes et religieuses*, 121.

54. See Perrée, *Le tiers-ordre*, 113–38.

55. Anne Quartararo has shown that female normal schools graduates were few and far between and only a small number actually went into primary school teaching. By the 1860s, there was a total of some two hundred graduates from normal schools or courses per year, but ninety could not be placed in jobs. See Quartararo, *Women Teachers*, 73, 78–79, as well as Gontard, *La question des écoles normales primaries*, 45.

56. For an analysis of the role of the state in the rise of professions in France, see Gerald L. Geison, ed., *Professions and the French State, 1700–1900* (Philadelphia: University of Philadelphia Press, 1984).

57. Rogers, *Les demoiselles*, 169–70.

58. In 1881 the Sœurs de Saint-Joseph had 1,529 teaching sisters, of whom 430 (28.1 percent) had the brevet. See Curtis, *Educating the Faithful*, 59–60, 196.

59. These figures come from the reports on this survey in AN, F^{17} 6843–49. This source is explored in more detail in the following chapter.

60. See ASSC (Rome and Poitiers), *Lettres circulaires de notre bienheureuse Mère Madeleine Sophie Barat*, 29 December 1845.

61. The appointment of d'Avenas to this position was in part a way to remove her as headmistress of the Parisian boarding school. D'Avenas had an equivocal reputation in the Society as a journalist and a philosopher. Kilroy, *Madeleine Sophie Barat*, 394, 528.

62. Information on pedagogical training can be found in ASSC (Rome), series D-I 1b box 9, as well as C-I c3 box 8; see, as well, Margaret Williams, RSCJ, *The Society of the Sacred Heart: History of a Spirit (1800–1975)* (London: Darton, Longman, and Todd, 1978). In Lyons, juniorates, by and large, assisted in spiritual, not pedagogical, training. Curtis, *Educating the Faithful*, 112.

63. See the inspection reports AN, F^{17} 12434^B, 12434^D, and F^{19} 6247.

64. See the comments on the maîtresse générale in Aix in 1873, or the judgment concerning the teachers in Amiens in 1875. ASSC (Rome), series C-IV 1 Aix, box 5; C-IV 4 Amiens, letters, box 3.

65. Jégou and Mesnil, "Les Ursulines françaises," 164–65.

66. "Avis pour une mère principale de pensionnat," in Archives de la Congrégation de Notre-Dame, *Règles et Méthodes*.

67. ADC, *Entretiens familiers*, partie religieuse, 55.

68. For more information on Lamennais, see Philippe Boutry, "Le mouvement vers Rome et le renouveau missionnaire," in Le Goff and Rémond, *Histoire de la France religieuse*, 3:431–35. One should not confuse this female congregation with the order founded by Emmanuel d'Alzon, even though he and Milleret were close friends. D'Alzon's order, Les Pères de l'Assomption, acquired notoriety during the Dreyfus affair for their virulent campaign against the wrongfully accused Dreyfus.

69. Guy Avanzini, "La pédagogie de l'Assomption: Quelle spécificité?" in *Mère Marie-Eugénie Milleret*, 108.

70. The clientele she referred to explicitly were families of bankers, notaries, and lawyers, what she termed a "liberal aristocracy." See, as well, Mayeur, *L'éducation*, 40.

71. Avanzini, "La pédagogie de l'Assomption," 108.

72. Quoted in Mayeur, *L'éducation*, 46.

73. Louis Secondy, "L'éducation des filles en milieu catholique au XIXe siècle," *Cahiers d'histoire* 26 (1981): 339.

74. For information on how women contributed to charitable activities, see Catherine Duprat, *Usages et pratiques de la philanthropie à Paris au cours du premier XIXe siècle*, 2 vols. (Paris: CHSS, 1996–97), and Sylvie Fayet-Scribe, *Associations féminines et catholicisme: De la charité à l'action sociale, XIXe–XXe siècles* (Paris: Éditions Ouvrières, 1990).

75. For information on these new practices, see François Lebrun, ed., *Histoire des catholiques en France* (Paris: Privat, 1980), 378–81.

76. See Rogers, "Socialization of Girls," and Germaine Bourgade, *Contribution à l'étude de l'éducation féminine de 1830 à 1914* (Toulouse: Publications de l'Université de Toulouse-Le Mirail, 1979), 143–89.

77. Private collection of Alain Blond, letter of 14 March 1863. For descriptions of this rite in the nineteenth century, see Anne Martin-Fugier, "Les rites de la vie privée bourgeoise," in *Histoire de la vie privée*, vol. 4, *De la Révolution à la Grande Guerre*, ed. Michelle Perrot (Paris: Seuil, 1987), 251–55; for an analysis of the First Communion within the school setting, see Martine Sonnet, "L'éducation et la première communion au XVIIIe siècle," in *La première communion: Quatre siècles d'histoire*, ed. Jean Delumeau (Paris: Desclée de Brouwer, 1987), 115–32.

78. AMD, series J, diary of Eugénie Servant, March 1876, notebook 1, pp. 52–62.

79. Jeanne Paule Crouzet-Benaben, *Souvenirs d'une jeune fille bête: Souvenirs autobiographiques d'une des premières agrégées de France* (Paris: Nouvelles Éditions Debresse, 1971), 119.

80. Marie-Françoise Lévy notes the emergence of these sodalities at the schools of Sainte-Clotilde and the Sacré-Cœur in 1820. Lévy, *De mères en filles. L'éducation des françaises, 1850–1880* (Paris: Calmann Lévy, 1984), 59. This book offers an excellent introduction into the characteristics of girls' religious education at midcentury. At the Couvent des Oiseaux in the 1830s, the nuns created a Congrégation de Saint-Anges and a Société de l'Enfant Jésus. Victor Delaporte, *Le monastère des Oiseaux. Les origines. La Révérence Mère Marie Sophie, 1811–1863* (Paris: Victor Retaux, 1899), 230.

81. See Bourgade, *Contribution*, 62. A Congrégation du Sacré-Cœur de Jésus existed at the school run by the Sœurs de Sainte-Clotilde, while young girls at the school in Cusset directed by the Sœurs de Saint-Joseph could be admitted to a congregation of Enfants de Saint-Joseph. Archives of Sainte-Clotilde (Paris), C3, "Registre des premières communiantes, des Enfants de Marie, des élèves dans la congrégation du Sacré-Cœur de Jésus"; private collection of Georges Plaisance, diary of Marguerite Rousset (1868–70).

82. Private collection of Georges Plaisance, diary of Marguerite Rousset, 24 December 1868.

83. Stern, *Mes souvenirs*, 169. I have found no other evidence for this more negative vision of boarding-school sodalities, although Padberg notes that at Jesuit schools sodalists were considered informers. See *Colleges in Controversy*, 247. Stern's anticlericalism as an adult may explain this perception.

84. Private collection of Georges Plaisance, diary of Marguerite Rousset, 8 December 1869.

85. Ibid., 23 December 1869.

86. Jégou and Mesnil, "Les Ursulines françaises," 208.

87. Archives of Sainte-Clotilde (Paris), C4, "Registre des Enfants de Marie."

88. Gaëtan Bernoville, *Les religieuses de l'Assomption*, vol. 1, *La fondatrice Eugénie Milleret (Mère M. Eugénie de Jésus)* (Paris: Grasset, 1948), 54.

89. Letter of Sister Emmanuel Florat to the prioress de Quimperlé, 27 July 1871, in Jégou and Mesnil, "Les Ursulines françaises," 167.

90. Circular of 21 November 1876, in Jégou and Mesnil, "Les Ursulines françaises," 203.

91. Circular from the Ursuline Monastery of Boulogne-sur-Mer, 22 September 1876, in Jégou and Mesnil, "Les Ursulines françaises," 207.

92. AMD, series J, diary of Eugénie Servant, October 1880, notebook 5, pp. 33–34.

93. Christiane d'Ainval, *Le couvent des Oiseaux: Ces jeunes filles de bonne famille* (Paris: Perrin, 1991), 205.

94. ASSC (Rome), series D-I 1b, Conseil des Études, 1869, 53, The Society issued similar warnings in 1874, arguing that the multiplication of associations immunized children to their effect; the documents speak of the dangers of acquiring a "blasé" attitude.

95. Private collection of Georges Plaisance, diary of Marguerite Rousset, 23 December 1869.

96. Smith, *Ladies of the Leisure Class*, 166.

97. Clare Teresa, "Mère Marie-Eugénie et l'éducation propre à l'Assomption," in *Mère Marie-Eugénie Milleret*, 71.

98. Secondy, "L'éducation des filles," 343–44.

99. Quoted from the *Semaine Catholique de Toulouse*, 1866, in Bourgade, *Contribution*, 171.

100. See Smith, *Ladies of the Leisure Class*, chap. six.

101. ASSC (Rome), series C-IV Quimper/Tournai, box 2, visit of 1865; series C-IV Amiens, letters, box 3, inspections of February and March 1875.

102. See Harris, *Lourdes*, and Jonas, *France and the Cult of the Sacred Heart*.

103. Dupanloup, *Femmes savants et femmes studieuses*, 27, 29.

104. Jacques Gadille and Françoise Mayeur, eds., *Éducation et images de la femme chrétienne en France au début du XXe siècle* (Lyons: Éditions Hermès, 1980), 20.

105. ASSC (Poitiers), lettre circulaire de Mère Goetz, 13 May 1867.

106. ASSC (Rome), D-I 1 box 1, response of R. P. Olivaint to Mother Goetz, 8 September 1866. In 1869, pedagogical reforms introduced a course in "Christian philosophy," where students were given readings from such authors as Plato, Bossuet, Fénelon, Descartes, Pascal, Maistre, and Balmes. Conseil des Études, 1869.

107. Geneviève Nemo, "Vocation missionnaire africaine d'une congrégation féminine au XIXe siècle: Exemple de St-Joseph de Cluny," in *Femmes en Mission. Actes de la XIe session du CREDIC à Saint-Flour (août 1990)* (Lyons: Editions Lyonnaises d'Art et d'histoire, 1991), 83. Intriguingly, the founding mother of the Assomption congregation, Eugénie Milleret, saw religious engagement as a masculine endeavor. As a young women, she described admiring Lamennais, Lacordaire, and Montalembert: "I dreamed of being a man in order to be like them extremely useful." Bernoville, *Les religieuses de l'Assomption*, 37.

Chapter 6

1. Grew and Harrigan, *School, State, and Society*, 131, 251. In 1837 there were some 14,100 girls' schools, 17,900 boys' schools, and 20,900 schools that welcomed boys and girls. In 1863 these numbers were at 27,300, 23,700, and

17,800; more girls' schools than boys' schools existed by 1863. Between 1850 and 1875 the percentage of girls enrolled in Catholic schools rose from 44 to 59 percent.

2. The archives contain the results for eighty-three out of the existing eighty-nine departments. Information is missing for the following departments: the Indre, the Isère, the Ardèche, the Drome, the Hautes-Alpes, the Seine-et-Oise, and the Seine. See AN, F¹⁷ 6843–49.

3. For a comparison with girls' primary schools, see Grew and Harrigan, *School, State, and Society*, 135.

4. Beginning in the 1850s the archives are full of teachers' requests to add a "primary boarding school" to their existing day school. Inspectors frequently distinguished between these primary institutions and the more ambitious secondary institutions.

5. The trade book for 1860 indicates the presence of eighteen "pensionnats de demoiselles" for the Bas-Rhin; the survey indicates a total of twenty-eight schools for the region of Alsace, nineteen of which were run by laywomen.

6. Only one department indicated morality problems: in Nice a substitute priest at the Couvent du Bon-Pasteur was accused of kissing students; no disciplinary actions were undertaken. This would seem to confirm Jean-Claude Caron's argument about the very masculine character of the disciplinary affairs concerning sexual matters. See Caron, *À l'école de la violence*, 215–16.

7. AN, F¹⁷ 6846, general report by the rector concerning the Academy of Lyons, 23 October 1864.

8. AN, F¹⁷ 6848, Inspector Belhomme's report in 1863.

9. Compiled results of AN, F¹⁷ 6843–49.

10. AN, F¹⁷ 6843, inspector of the Basses-Alpes, n.d.

11. AN, F¹⁷ 6843, report of 25 September 1864.

12. AN, F¹⁷ 6846, Inspector Deloche's report, 20 October 1864. The Gard is also a southern department; its largest city is Nimes.

13. AN, F¹⁷ 6848, inspection report for the Maine-et-Loire, 14 October 1864; 6846, inspection report for the Rhône, 23 October 1864.

14. This needs to be correlated, however, with administrative changes in Paris and the annexation of outlying communes, which pushed the population from 1 million inhabitants prior to 1860 to 1,696,000. See Bernard Marchand, *Paris: Histoire d'une ville* (Paris: Seuil, 1993), 91.

15. AN, F¹⁷ 12434ᴮ. In 1874 the number of religious boarding schools had only increased to twenty-eight. See Langlois, *Le catholicisme*, 483. The figures concerning lay institutions come from Parisian trade books and Conseil général, *Résultats*, 1864. For primary schools, see Octave Gréard, *L'enseignement primaire à Paris et dans le département de la Seine de 1867 à 1877* (Paris: A. Chaix, 1878), 14.

16. For information on the urban changes wrought by Haussmann and their impact on schools, see Jeanne Gaillard, *Paris: La ville (1852–1870)* (Paris: L'Harmattan, 1997), 201–31. Her focus, however, is on primary education, and she scarcely mentions the presence of lay boarding schools for girls.

17. AN, F¹⁷ 12434ᴮ, *Inspection des pensionnats de filles tenus par des religieuses dans le diocèse de Paris en avril 1855*.

18. Archives de Paris, VD⁶ 159, inspection de maisons d'éducation de demoiselles (1851–62), 1ᵉʳ arrondissement. Both Coulon's and Rey's school were on the rue Faubourg Saint Honoré. These figures refer to an inspection in 1853.

19. See Rebecca Rogers, "French Education for British Girls in the Nineteenth Century," *Women's History Magazine* 42 (October 2002): 21–29.

20. The following analysis is not based on an exhaustive study of these sources, which are far from complete in departmental archives. I have consulted trade books and almanacs for twenty-five departments and have explored some fifteen departmental archives (Aude, Doubs, Eure-et-Loir, Haute-Garonne, Gers, Loire-Atlantique, Meurthe-et-Moselle, Moselle, Hautes-Pyrénées, Bas-Rhin, Haut-Rhin, Haute-Saône, Seine-et-Oise, Somme, and Vienne). I have also exploited other historians' case studies for individual departments or cities.

21. Like Briand and Chapoulie, I argue that historians of education need to be more attentive to the role of school directors who actively created their own clientele: see Jean-Pierre Briand and Jean-Michel Chapoulie, "L'institution scolaire et la scolarisation: Une perspective d'ensemble," *Revue française de sociologie* 24 (1993): 3–42. Marc Suteau's study of Nantes confirms the usefulness of this framework for understanding the growth of an educational system. See Suteau, *Une ville et ses écoles à Nantes, 1830–1940* (Rennes: Presses Universitaires de Rennes, 1999), 13.

22. Schvind, "L'éducation des demoiselles," 19–27. Strasbourg's population in 1860 was approximately 56,000.

23. It seems likely that the numerical dominance of religious schools in the national survey of 1864 stems from the presence of religious boarding schools in small towns and villages. Urban trade books consistently list more lay schools than religious schools.

24. I have focused on headmistresses rather than the buildings where schools operated. Often headmistresses ceded their buildings and clientele to a successor.

25. Schvind, "L'éducation des demoiselles," 31–32.

26. Ibid., 13–14.

27. In 1845 the Dames dites des Sacré-Cœurs de Jésus et de Marie asked 450 francs per year, without art lessons, for tuition, room, and board in their boarding school in Chatellerault. AD Vienne, 3 T 36, "Écoles de filles, 1836–1875."

28. Bourgade, *Contribution*, 148. The archives of the Sacré-Cœur reveal that boarding costs in this elitist institution generally ran between 600 and 750 francs per year; lessons in the decorative arts entailed additional costs.

29. Joseph Cahour, *Les écoles et pensionnats privés au XIX siècle* (Laval: Imprimerie Goupil, 1924), 20–38.

30. Bourgade, *Contribution*, 234.

31. Private collection of Viviane Isambert-Jamati, Dubois-Goblot correspondence, letter of 20 February 1876.

32. Louis Savès, *Les écoles du Saint-Nom de Jésus en Bigorre, 1827–1977* (Tarbes: Les Éditions du Minuit, 1977), 77. At midcentury, this institution had some two hundred students.

33. Jégou and Mesnil, "Les Ursulines françaises," 188; Notre-Dame de la Compassion in southwestern France similarly welcomed specific social groups in its different schools. See Jean-Claude Meyer, "La congrégation de Notre-Dame de la Compassion," in *L'enseignement catholique en France aux XIXe et XXe siècles*, ed. Gérard Cholvy and Nadine-Josette Chaline (Paris: Cerf, 1995), 137–38.

34. This analysis comes from Schvind, "L'éducation des demoiselles," 52, and is based on a study of the social origins of 136 students present in the school between October 1856 and December 1865.

35. See Germaine Bourgade, "Une maison d'éducation anglaise à Caen au temps de la Monarchie de Juillet: La pension Roberts, 1834–1843," *Bulletin de la Société des antiquaires de Normandie* 62 (1963): 514–23; Rogers, "French Education."

36. AD Loire Atlantique, 5T 4, état de 1861. Interestingly, Priet herself came from the working class; her father was a foreman for a printing press, but because he suffered from mental illness, his daughter was placed in boarding schools from the age of five on.

37. At the boarding school run by the Sœurs de Notre-Dame in Molsheim, half of the 220 students who attended between 1856 and 1865 were over 13.5 years old. Schvind, "L'éducation des demoiselles," 55–56.

38. D'Aubigny opened her boarding school with another woman, Aglaë Lelarge, in 1843; they remained active for the next three decades.

39. AD Aude, 1 T 23, "Situation scolaire des communes, états de 1867."

40. Private collection of Viviane Isambert-Jamati, Dubois-Goblot correspondence, letter from Augustine Goblot to Edouard Goblot in April 1848.

41. I have mainly found these advertisements in the T series of departmental archives and for Paris in the VD[6] series of the Archives de Paris. For the Ursulines, see Jégou and Mesnil, "Les Ursulines françaises." See R. Rogers, "Constructions de la féminité bourgeoise en France au XIXe siècle: Éducation, normes et pratiques," in *Lorsque l'enfant grandit: Entre dépendance et autonomie*, ed. Jean-Pierre Bardet et al. (Paris: Presses de l'Université de Paris-Sorbonne, 2002), 663–75.

42. Archives de Paris, VD[6] 158.

43. Henri Léon, *Les indiscrétions de Jehan Bomoloque à l'endroit des maîtresses de pension* (Paris: Chez l'auteur, 1855).

44. AN, F[17] 12432, "Dossier Shanahan, maîtresse anglaise à Paris."

45. AD Hautes-Pyrénées, T39, dossier Bernigole Forcade, 1841.

46. *Institution Protestante de jeunes demoiselles*; advertisement reproduced in Schvind, "L'éducation des demoiselles," 128.

47. Private archives of the Sœurs de Notre-Dame, Prospectus, rue Faubourg du Roule, n.d.

48. AN, AJ[16] 198.

49. See Suteau, *Une ville et ses écoles*, 130–35, and A. Donis, *Historique de l'enseignement primaire public à Bordeaux, 1414–1910* (Bordeaux: Imprimerie G. Delmas, 1913).

50. AD Doubs, 38V3.

51. Archives de Paris, D[2] T[1], supplément no. 120, dossier Isaac.

52. This analysis draws on some twenty speeches that have been collected for the most part in the Rp series at the Bibliothèque nationale. While I make no claim that such a limited number is in some way representative of the

thousands of such speeches that did not make their way into print, the variety of themes in this sample merits careful study on its own.

53. Abbé Bonin, *Pensionnat des dames de Saint-Maur. Discours prononcé à la distribution solennelle des prix des dames de Saint-Maur de Chalon* (1862).

54. Abbé Brière, *Discours prononcé à la distribution solennelle des prix de l'Institution de Mlles Delfeuille et Leconte à Nogent-le-Rotrou* (Eure et Loir) (Nogent-le-Rotrou, 1858).

55. Abbé Thomas-François-Olympiade Boulage, *Discours prononcé par M. Boulage, curé de Saint-Pantaléon le 17 août 1855 à la distribution des prix de la pension de Mlle Ernestine Pfeiffer à Troyes* (Troyes: Imprimerie de T. Bouquot, 1855).

56. Abbé Victor Hébert-Duperron, *Souvenirs de distribution de prix de l'année scolaire 1864–65* (Perigueux, 1865), and *Allocution prononcée . . . Prix du pensionnat de Mlle Hirche à Vesoul, le 19 août 1867* (Paris: Imprimerie de P. A. Bourdier, n.d.).

57. Bachellery, *Discours prononcé le jour de distribution des prix le 21 août 1843* and *Discours prononcé . . . le 29 août 1857*. Private collection of Viviane Isambert-Jamati, speeches of 1866 and 1868 before Dubois school in Pont Audemer.

58. Lequien, *Institution de jeunes filles dirigiées par Mlle Lequien. Discours prononcé à la distribution des prix le 28 août 1838, Poissy, 1838* (manuscript text).

59. De Loziéras, *De l'émulation. Discours prononcé à la distribution solennelle des prix fin de l'année scolaire 1851–52* (Senlis: Imprimerie Chez Duriez, 1852).

60. Viviane Isambert-Jamati, *Crises de la société. Crises de l'enseignement. Sociologie de l'enseignement secondaire français* (Paris: Presses Universitaires de France, 1970), 69–104.

61. Private collection of Viviane Isambert-Jamati, prize-giving speech by Eugénie Dubois in 1866.

62. For more information on class programs, see Rogers, *Les demoiselles*, 195–234.

63. See Jean-Marie Chapoulie, "L'enseignement primaire supérieur, de la loi Guizot aux écoles de la IIIe République," *Revue d'histoire moderne et contemporaine* 36 (July-September 1989): 413–37.

64. Archives de Paris, VD⁶ 159, inspection de maisons d'éducation de demoiselles, 1851–62; Brada [Countess Puliga], *Souvenirs d'une petite Second Empire* (Paris: Calmann-Lévy, 1921).

65. Brada, *Souvenirs*, 107.

66. *Le nouveau manuel de piété à l'usage de la jeune pensionnaire* (1865), quoted in Gibson, *Social History*, 186. For more information on the ethos of convent boarding school education, see Arnold, *Le corps et l'âme*, 94.

67. Circular from the Ursulines of Clermont-Ferrand, 21 November 1876, in Jégou and Mesnil, "Les Ursulines françaises," 95.

68. ASSC (Rome), series C-I c3 box 8, travail de la commission pour les études et le pensionnat.

69. Classroom pedagogy, in general, remained heavily structured around memorization, a common aspect of boys' education as well.

70. ASSC (Rome), series D-I 1b, Conseil des études, 1869. Bonnie Smith's analysis of Sacré-Cœur schools in Lille at the end of the century suggests that these recommendations were not universally applied. See Smith, *Ladies of the Leisure Class*, 168–76.

71. This trend is evident as well in other elite-oriented religious orders. Alice Bizot, student at the Couvent des Oiseaux in 1859, laughingly warned her mother: "To begin with, I need to warn you that when I return you will find me transformed into the consummate philosopher, because . . . recently we have been plunged in the study of logic, reasoning, syllogism, induction . . . this study interests me greatly." *Mémorial des enfants de Marie de la congrégation Prima primaria établie dans le Monastère des Religieuses de la congrégation de Notre-Dame, maison dites des Oiseaux, Paris, rue des Sèvres 86* (Paris: Pélagaud, 1864), 74.

72. Private collection of Viviane Isambert-Jamati, letter of 23 October 1874.

73. Colette Cosnier, *Le silence des filles: De l'aiguille à la plume* (Paris: Fayard, 2001), 227–32. A nice example of this can be found in Elisabeth de Bonnefonds's memoirs. After she returns home from convent school, she regrets having studied sewing, since she finds it boring; nonetheless, she thanks her mother for giving her these habits of work. Bonnefonds, *Mes souvenirs* (Paris: Lecoffre, 1869), 69–72.

74. Rogers, *Les demoiselles*, 209–11.

75. Private collection of P. Lejeune, diary of Mathilde Savarin, 25 June 1881.

76. Lemonnier, *Elisa Lemonnier*.

77. For information on the École professionnelle Drouot in Nancy, see Philippe Savoie, "Offre locale et engagement de l'État: Les enseignements technique et primaire supérieur à Nancy et les conditions de leur évolu-

tion sous la Troisième République," *Histoire de l'éducation* 66 (May 1995): 47–84. For Nantes and the creation of the École Guépin (1873), see Suteau, *Une ville et ses écoles*, 125–39. For the development of higher primary education for girls, see Emilien Constant, "Les débuts de l'enseignement secondaire (et primaire supérieur) des jeunes filles dans le Var, 1867–1925," *Historical Reflections* 7 (1980): 301–12, and Kathleen Alaimo, "Adolescence, Gender and Class in Educational Reform in France: The Development of *Enseignement Primaire Supérieur*, 1880–1910," *French Historical Studies* 18 (fall 1994): 1025–56.

78. Rogers, *Les demoiselles*, 205–8, and "Retrograde or Modern?"

79. See, in particular, Mayeur, *L'éducation*, 115.

80. Gréard, *Éducation et instruction*, 1:142.

81. Bourgade, *Contribution*, 234, and AD Vienne, 8°E 2396, distribution des prix faite le 7 août 1863.

82. AD Hautes-Pyrénées, T 39.

83. The significance of teaching diplomas can be seen in a family's decision to engrave a funerary plaque in 1865 for a young schoolgirl. The plaque depicted her portrait under a caption stating that she had obtained the *brevet de capacité*. Jean-Marc Ferrer and Philippe Grandcoing, *Des funérailles de porcelaine: L'art de la plaque funéraire en procelaine de Limoges au XIXe siècle* (Limoges: Cultures et Patrimoine en Limousin, 2000), 155.

84. Bourgade, *Contribution*, 233.

85. By 1863 there were eleven women's normal schools and fifty-seven *cours normaux* nationwide. Quartararo, *Women Teachers*, 75.

86. Anne Quartararo's study of girls' normal schools has revealed a puzzling situation for laywomen who pursued these degrees in order to teach: few actually took up the communal teaching posts for which they had ostensibly trained. In the Bouches-du-Rhône in 1863 only one out of thirteen women obtained a communal teaching post and twelve remained unemployed. Quartararo, *Women Teachers*, 86. See, as well, Gemie, *Women and Schooling*, 117–27.

87. Private collection of Viviane Isambert-Jamati, Dubois-Goblot correspondence, Augustine to Eugénie Dubois, 25 August 1872.

88. Archives de Paris, VD[6] 158.

89. Private collection of Philippe Lejeune, diary of Mathilde Savarin.

90. It is difficult to ascertain how long girls stayed in schools and whether they actually progressed through the different classes. Based on a few well-known memoirs, historians have tended to repeat that boarding schools represented a year or two of a young girl's life, I have been struck by my reading of memoirs as well as the educational itineraries headmistresses had to submit to open a school that many spent far more time. We need detailed monographs based on student registers to know more.

91. For the spatial organization of middle-class homes, see Monique Eleb and Anne Debarre, *Architectures de la vie privée: Maisons et mentalités, XVIIe–XIXe siècles* (Brussels: Archives d'architecture moderne, 1989), and *L'invention de l'habitation moderne. Paris 1880–1914* (Brussels: Hazan, 1995).

92. Henriette Picanon, *Mon frère et moi: Souvenirs de jeunesse accompagnés de poésies d'E. Berthoud* (Paris: J. Bonhoure, 1876), 21.

93. AD Loire-Atlantique, 76 T 1, maisons d'éducation de jeunes filles, 1811–57. Tautain ran this school in Nantes from approximately 1848 until the late 1870s. She received generally good marks in inspection reports although hers was not considered one of the better schools.

94. Private collection of Viviane Isambert-Jamati, Dubois-Goblot correspondence, letter of 9 May 1878; at this point they had seventy-seven students.

95. See Rogers, "Schools, Discipline, and Community: Diary-writing and Schoolgirl Culture in Late Nineteenth-Century France," *Women's History Review* 4, no. 4 (1995): 525–54.

96. Private collection of Philippe Lejeune, diary of Pauline Weill; private collection of Georges Plaisance, diary of Marguerite Rousset, 17 January 1869.

97. Brada, *Souvenirs*, 41.

98. AMD, series J, diary of Eugénie Servant, July 1875, notebook 1, p. 29.

99. Adèle Riobe, *Notice sur ma fille* (Le Mans: Imprimerie Monnoyer Frères, 1863), 121.

100. Brada, *Souvenirs*, 29–32.

101. She is one of approximately one hundred students at the convent of the Sœurs de Saint-Maur in Montluçon. Bonnefonds, *Mes souvenirs*, 58.

102. Emilie Gossot, *Un pensionnat d'autrefois: Souvenirs d'une pensionnaire* (Tours: Mame, 1900), 31.

103. AMD, series J, diary of E. Servant, 1 May 1875, notebook 1, pp. 11–12, and March 1876, notebook 1, p. 58.

104. M***, *Souvenirs de la vie d'Eléonore de Gaulmyn, élève du Sacré-Cœur*, 1848, cited in Arnold, *Le corps et l'âme*, 41.

105. See, in particular, Pauline Weill's diary, *Histoire de ma vie. Journal* (1858–59), private collection of Philippe Lejeune.

106. Juliette Lambert Adam, *Le roman de mon enfance et de ma jeunesse*, 3d ed. (Paris: A. Lemerre, 1902), 68.

107. Picanon, *Mon frère et moi*, 34–35.

108. AMD, diary of Eugénie Servant, April 1878, notebook 2, p. 14.

109. Private collection of Georges Plaisance, diary of Marguerite Rousset, January 1870.

110. For evidence that corporal punishment was more prevalent in boys' schools, see Paul Gerbod, *La vie quotidienne dans les lycées et les collèges au XIXe siècle* (Paris: Hachette, 1968), 101–6, and Caron, *À l'école de la violence*, 114–64.

111. Cited in Gemie, *Women and Schooling*, 184.

112. For an example of this sort of encouragement for self-evaluation, see Lejeune, *Le moi des demoiselles*, 353.

113. Private collection of A. Blond, letter written in 1865.

114. The nuns at the boarding school of the Sacré-Cœur also used this method to stimulate emulation. Nobécourt, "Un exemple," 228.

115. M. Lévêque, *Mathilde Salomon: Directrice du Collège Sévigné, Membre du Conseil Supérieur de l'Instruction Publique, Chevalier de la Légion d'honneur, 1837–1909* (Saint-Germain-lès-Corbeil: Imprimerie Leroy, 1909). Protestants in general appear to have had reservations about the pedagogic value of emulation.

116. Private collection of P. Lejeune, diary of M. Savarin, 18 June 1881.

117. AMD, diary of Eugénie Servant, notebook 1, p. 20. In 1870 the religious teachers of Marguerite Rousset also banned the use of the familiar *tu* between students. Private collection of Georges Plaisance, diary of Marguerite Rousset, 4 March 1870.

118. Brada, *Souvenirs*, 55.

119. See Rogers, "Schools, Discipline, and Community."

120. For a rather different focus on male and female friendships within the boarding-school setting, see Vincent-Buffault, *L'exercice de l'amitié*, 143–55. She emphasizes the medical underpinnings of these prohibitions, whereas for girls, I would argue, the moral underpinnings were more powerful. See, as well, Houbre, *La discipline de l'amour*, 192–95.

121. Picanon, *Mon frère et moi*, 13. Thirty years earlier George Sand described two contrasting models of headmistresses. Mme Héreau, with whom she first places her daughter Solange, is characterized as having a "more expansive, maternal, and indulgent familiarity." Solange was then transferred to the far stricter Mme Bascans, who frequently punished the novelist's wayward daughter. G. Sand, *Correspondance de George Sand (April 1840–December 1842)* (Paris: Éditions Garnier Frères, 1969), 5:479.

122. Private collection of Viviane Isambert-Jamati, Dubois-Goblot correspondence, letter of 23 February 1878.

123. AMD, diary of Eugénie Servant, September 1880, notebook 5, p. 26. See as well Rogers, *Les demoiselles*, 257–59.

124. On the constructed nature of British nineteenth-century family life, see Leonore Davidoff, Megan Doolittle, Janet Fink, and Katherine Holden, *The Family Story: Blood, Contract and Intimacy, 1830–1960* (London: Longman, 1999).

125. Lejeune establishes three types of diary writers that correspond to three stages in nineteenth-century girls' diary-writing: (1) the Romantic writer (roughly 1800–1850); (2) the "moral order" writer (roughly 1850–80); and (3) the "modern" writer (roughly 1880–1910). Lejeune, *Le moi des demoiselles*.

126. AMD, diary of Eugénie Servant, October 1878, notebook 2, p. 37.

127. Private collection of P. Lejeune, diary of Pauline Weill, 22 February 1859 and 22 September 1859.

128. Crouzet-Benaben, *Souvenirs*, 273–98.

129. Cited in Gemie, *Women and Schooling*, 187. The diary is located in AD Calvados, T 1537, 8 April 1883.

130. Private collection of P. Lejeune, diary of Pauline Weill, 10 February 1859.

131. Private collection of P. Lejeune, diary of M. Savarin, 23 June 1881.

132. Crouzet-Benaben, *Souvenirs*, 182; private collection of Georges Plaisance, diary of Marguerite Rousset.

133. Octave Feuillet, *Quelques années de ma vie*, 4th ed. (Paris: Calmann Lévy, 1894), 15. For more information on girls' readings practices, see Cosnier, *Le silence des filles*, 233–57, and Rogers, *Les demoiselles*, 212–24.

134. See Quartararo, *Women Teachers*, and Linda Clark, *Schooling the Daughters of Marianne: Textbooks and the Socialization of Girls in Modern French Primary Schools* (Albany: SUNY Press, 1984).

135. Christine Bellaigue, "The Development of Teaching as a Profession for Women Before 1870," *The Historical Journal* 44 (2001): 963–88; Carol Dyhouse, *Girls Growing Up in Late Victorian and Edwardian England* (London: Routledge

& Kegan Paul, 1981); Deborah Gorham, *The Victorian Girl and the Feminine Ideal* (Bloomington: Indiana University Press, 1982); Joyce Senders Pedersen, "The Reform of Women's Secondary and Higher Education: Institutional Change and Social Values in Mid and Late Victorian England, *History of Education Quarterly* 19 (spring 1979): 61–99, and *The Reform of Girls' Secondary and Higher Education in Victorian England: A Study of Elites and Educational Change* (London: Garland, 1987). For Germany, see James Albisetti, *Schooling German Girls and Women. Secondary and Higher Education in the Nineteenth Century* (Princeton: Princeton University Press, 1988).

136. Vicinus, *Independent Women*, 163–210.

137. Dyhouse, *Girls Growing Up*, 48; see, as well, Andrea Jacobs, "Les examens, la professionnalisation et les enseignantes: Les établissements féminins du secondaire en Angleterre, 1850–1900," *Histoire de l'éducation* 98 (May 2003): 87–108.

138. Bellaigue, "Development of Teaching," 970; see also Ruth Watts, who notes the influence of foreign schooling experiences on Unitarian women educationalists, in her *Gender, Power and the Unitarians in England, 1760–1860* (London: Longman, 1998), 124.

139. *Mémorial des enfants de Marie*, 32, 61.

140. Adam, *Le roman*, 371.

Part III

1. Quoted in Mayeur, *L'enseignement secondaire*, 16.

2. This sort of analysis has yet to be done for nineteenth-century France. I am influenced here by the burgeoning literature on such issues within Anglo-American historical scholarship. See Chapter 8 for specific references.

Chapter 7

1. See Philip Bertocci, *Jules Simon: Republican Anticlericalism and Cultural Politics in France, 1848–1886* (Columbia: University of Missouri Press, 1978).

2. As early as 1844 Jules Michelet argued that the clergy was dividing the family, pitting women against men; see his article in the *Revue des deux mondes* in 1844 claiming 622,000 women were raised by nuns. For more information on anticlerical debates revolving around educational issues, see Rémond, *L'anticléricalisme en France*, 69. Well before the Second Empire, religious congregations were criticized for their antiliberal attitudes, but such criticisms were not often the object of public debate.

3. Jules Ferry, speech at the Salle Molière on 10 April 1870, quoted in Mayeur, *L'éducation*, 139–40.

4. The best overall analyses of the Duruy courses can be found in Mayeur, *L'éducation*, 113–38, and in Horvath-Peterson, *Victor Duruy and French Education*. See also her "Victor Duruy and the Controversy over Secondary Education for Girls," *French Historical Studies* 9, no. 1 (1975): 83–104.

5. Quoted in Mayeur, *L'éducation*, 113. For the debates surrounding male Catholic secondary education, see Patrick Harrigan, "Social and Political Implications of Catholic Secondary Education During the Second French Empire," *Societas* 6, no. 1 (1976): 41–59, and "Church, State, and Education in France from the Falloux to the Ferry Laws: A Reassessment," *Canadian Journal of History* 36, no. 1 (2001): 51–83.

6. Napoleon III's willingness to support Duruy's initiative probably stemmed in part from the Empress Eugénie's well-known commitment to promoting girls' education. She patronized the creation in Paris of the Société libre pour l'instruction médicale des femmes and is considered responsible for authorizing women to study within French universities. See Victor Duruy, *Notes et souvenirs, 1811–1894*, 2d ed. (Paris: Hachette, 1902), 2:206–9, and Moses, *French Feminism*, 175.

7. Circular of 30 October 1867, reproduced in Félix Dupanloup, *La femme chrétienne et française; dernière réponse à M. Duruy et à ses défenseurs par Mgr l'evêque d'Orléans* (Paris: Charles Duniol, 1868).

8. Quoted in Mayeur, *L'éducation*, 15.

9. Duruy, *Notes et souvenirs*, 2:201.

10. Ibid., letter of 4 February 1866, 190.

11. AN, AJ[16] 516, report on cours secondaire in *Journal officiel de la République française*, 4 August 1879, 8094. See also Mayeur, *L'éducation*, 25.

12. She notes the presence of 29 classes in French literature, 27 in history, physics, and chemistry, 14 in natural history, 13 in cosmography, and 9 in grammar, style, or the French language; only two schools offered courses in English, five in drawing, three in domestic or political economy, and one in philosophy (in Cambrai). Mayeur, *L'éducation*, 121–22.

13. AN, F[17] 8755, rector's report for the academy of Montpellier, 9 May 1868.

14. More detailed analyses of the courses in specific cities can be found in: Raymond Oberlé, *L'enseignement à Mulhouse de 1798 à 1870* (Paris: Les Belles Lettres, 1961); Bourgade, *Contribution*, 191–242; Claude Lelièvre, "Développement et fonctionnement des enseignements post-élémentaires de la Somme, 1850–1914" (Thèse d'État, Université de Paris V, 1985), chap. 3.

15. See Bourgade, *Contribution*, 239. She notes as well that in some cities the courses were rejected despite democratic and anticlerical municipal councils, such as in Caen and in Lille.

16. AD Moselle, 2T 165, dossier on the secondary courses. All three headmistresses were decorated with medals for their activities on behalf of the courses. In Limoges, as well, a boarding-school mistress in 1868 brought five out of the seventeen students. AD Vienne, 10T 360, report of 15 December 1868.

17. AN, F[17] 8754, letter from the *proviseur* of the imperial *lycée* to the inspector on 18 November 1868. A similar attitude was noted in Besançon.

18. See Horvath-Peterson, *Victor Duruy and French Education*, 168–71; Mayeur, *L'éducation*, 113–38.

19. For an analysis town by town, see AN, F[17] 8753.

20. The most thorough analysis of this law and of the schools that were created in its wake can be found in Mayeur, *L'enseignement secondaire*.

21. Report of M. Camille Sée, in *Les lycées et collèges de jeunes filles: Documents, rapports et discours...* (Paris: Léopold Cerf, 1888), 150.

22. Mayeur, *L'enseignement secondaire*, 38.

23. Philip Nord, *The Republican Moment: Struggles for Democracy in Nineteenth-century France* (Cambridge: Harvard University Press, 1995), 220.

24. Speech by Pierre Foncin, the director of secondary education under Minister Paul Bert, for the inauguration of secondary courses for girls in Abbeville, 15 December 1880, quoted in Claude Lelièvre and Françoise Lelièvre, *L'histoire de la scolarisation des filles* (Paris: Nathan, 1991), 108.

25. Mayeur, *L'enseignement secondaire*, 41.

26. Cited in ibid., 56. For a more detailed analysis of the debates surrounding religion, morals, and philosophy, see 53–61.

27. Paul Bert's proposal was motivated in part by pragmatic reasons, since day schools were far cheaper.

28. Quoted in L.-R. Lamotte, *De l'enseignement secondaires des filles* (Paris: Delagrave, 1881), 94.

29. Quoted in Mayeur, *L'enseignement secondaire*, 47.

30. Report of M. Camille Sée, in *Les lycées et collèges*, 159. In comparison, the study of the French language occupied five hours a week in the first two years, and gymnastics an hour and a half each week.

31. The program of studies was first established in 1882 and then revised in 1897. As Claude and Françoise Lelièvre have noted, the reduced hours for girls' education reflected medical concern about the effect of intellectual study on adolescent girls going through puberty. Lelièvre and Lelièvre, *Histoire de la scolarisation*, 121. For a detailed analysis of the program of studies and its evolution that offers as well a comparative perspective with boys' education, see Mayeur, *L'enseignement secondaire*, 210–20.

32. Margadant, *Madame le Professeur*, 17.

33. Antoine Villemont, *Étude sur l'organisation, le fonctionnement et les progrès de l'enseignement secondaire des jeunes filles en France de 1879 à 1887*, quoted in Margadant, *Madame le Professeur*, 7.

34. See Mayeur, *L'enseignement secondaire*, 69–84.

35. Hubertine Auclert, *La Citoyenne*, 24 April 1881, in *La citoyenne: Articles de 1881 et 1891*, ed. Edith Taïeb (Paris: Syros, 1982). See, as well, Mayeur, *L'enseignement secondaire*, 41, and Steven Hause, *Hubertine Auclert: The French Suffragette* (New Haven: Yale University Press, 1987), 127.

36. Mayeur emphasizes that, contrary to England, feminists had little impact on the Republican decision to develop a public system of girls' secondary education. Karen Offen has argued, however, that by equating feminism with suffragism, Mayeur underestimates the extent to which feminists were active in the reform of girls' education. See Offen, "Second Sex."

37. See Laurence Klejman and Florence Rochefort, *L'égalité en marche. Le féminisme sous la Troisième République* (Paris: Presses de la Fondation National des Sciences Politiques, 1989); Moses, *French Feminism*; Karen Offen, *European Feminisms, 1700–1950: A Political History* (Stanford: Stanford University Press, 2000); Steven Hause with Ann Kenney, *Women's Suffrage and Social Politics in the French Third Republic* (Princeton: Princeton University Press, 1984); Bidelman, *Pariahs Stand Up!*; and James McMillan, *Housewife or Harlot: The Place of Women in French Society, 1870–1940* (New York: St. Martin's Press, 1981).

38. Fauvety was a prominent freemason who collaborated with Charles Lemonnier on the journal *La Revue philosophique et religieuse*. He was host to a salon that attracted both d'Héricourt and Juliette Lambert. Renouvier, a Kantian philosopher and founder of *L'année philosophique* in 1868, is the better known of the two.

39. Adam, *Le roman*, 371. See the quotation in the conclusion to Chapter 6 herein.

40. Jenny P. d'Héricourt, "De l'avenir de la femme," *La Ragione*, 10 November 1855, 59–60. Many thanks to Karen Offen for this quotation. For the impact of d'Héricourt's ideas in the United States, see Bonnie S. Anderson, *Joyous Greetings: The First International Women's Movement* (Oxford: Oxford University Press, 2000).

41. For information on d'Héricourt's life, see Karen Offen, "A Nineteenth-Century French Feminist Rediscovered: Jenny P. d'Héricourt, 1809–1875," *Signs* 13 (autumn 1987): 144–58, and Caroline Arni, "'La toute puissance de la barbe.' Jenny P. d'Héricourt et les novateurs modernes," *Clio. Histoire, Femmes et Sociétés* 13 (2001): 45–154.

42. See Moses, *French Feminism*, 179–84.

43. Maria Deraismes, *Œuvres complètes* (Paris: Félix Alcan, 1896), 90–91.

44. Maria Deraismes, "La femme dans la société," in *Eve dans l'Humanité, 1868* (Paris: Côté-femmes, 1990), 90.

45. Maria Deraismes, "La femme telle qu'elle est" (18 November 1869), in *Eve dans l'Humanité*, 149.

46. See the manifesto signed by thirty-eight women in *Le droit des femmes*, April 1869, 10.

47. Félix Hément, "Enseignement supérieur des femmes," *Le droit des femmes*, 10 April 1869. See, as well, Maria David, "De l'instruction," ibid., 12 June 1869. For a general discussion of the place of education in feminist debates during the Second Empire, see Klejman and Rochefort, *L'égalité en marche*, chap. 1.

48. *Le droit des femmes*, 10 July 1869, see as well Moses, *French Feminism*, 85.

49. Hubertine Auclert, *La citoyenne*, 10 April 1881, 1.

50. Katherine Auspitz, *The Radical Bourgeoisie: The Ligue de l'Enseignement and the Origins of the Third Republic, 1866–1885* (Cambridge: Cambridge University Press, 1982), 114.

51. For evidence of these alliances, see Nord, *Republican Moment*, 27–28 and 77. With regard to Freemasons, Nord argues that feminism was no more than a minor current but that Masonic feminists were partisans of women's education mainly to promote virtuous domesticity. Jewish republicans also promoted schools for girls.

52. Léon Richer, *La femme libre* (1877), quoted in Moses, *French Feminism*, 202.

53. Dubesset and Zancarini-Fournel, *Parcours de femmes*, 35.

54. See, for example, Mme Charles Sauvestre, *Guide pratique pour les écoles professionnelles des jeunes filles* (Paris: Hachette, 1868). For an analysis of the relationship between boys' secondary education and the professions, see Patrick Harrigan, "Secondary Education and the Professions in France During the Second Empire," *Comparative Studies in Society and History* 17, no. 3 (1975): 349–71.

55. Marc Suteau's analysis of the École Guépin in Nantes emphasizes the liberal orientation of the founder, Ange Guépin, who was also a close friend of Elisa Lemonnier. See Suteau, *Une ville et ses écoles*, 130–35. For information on the development of girls' higher primary schools, see Alaimo, "Adolescence, Gender, and Class in Educational Reform in France."

56. Léo's real name was Léodile Bera Champceix (her name is also spelled Champseix). In 1869 she published *Les femmes et les mœurs: Liberté ou monarchie*, which included a call for the right to divorce, equal access to education, and political equality.

57. Hause, *Hubertine Auclert*, 30–31. Céleste Toulmé married Pierre Hardouin, a saddle maker, and ran a boarding school in the eighteenth arrondissement from 1868 until 1903.

58. M. J. de Marchef-Girard, *Les femmes, leur passé, leur présent, leur avenir* (Paris: Louis Chappe, 1860), 499.

59. This current of opinion in favor of offering some form of professional education to middle-class women bears no comparison to the organizational successes of British women at the same time. See Vicinus, *Independent Women*; Poovey, *Uneven Developments*, 26–163; and Renton, *Tyrant or Victim?*

60. Mayeur, *L'éducation*, 82–83. For her general proposals to reform girls' education, see Mme Caubet-Darius, *Réflexions sur l'éducation et l'instruction de la femme* (Saint Gaudens: Imprimerie et libraire de Veuve Tajan, 1866).

61. The *Journal des économistes* was founded in 1842; it sought to define the terms of a new science of economics and to establish appropriate rules and good practices. This journal first published her essay "Quels moyens de subsistance ont les femmes" between 1862 and 1863 and then her essay "De l'enseignement secondaire pour les femmes." See *Journal des économistes*, June 1865, 382–402; September 1865, 384–403; and December 1865, 408–27.

62. See the preface to her text by Agnès Thiercé for more details on Daubié's life and publication as well as the special issue "Julie Daubié," *Bulletin du Centre Pierre Léon d'histoire économique et sociale* 2–3 (1993). She became progressively more radical as she gained notoriety, notably advocating women's right to vote as early as 1870. Hause notes that she founded a group variously called the Association pour le suffrage des femmes and the Association pour l'émancipation des femmes in 1871, the first French group to devote its efforts to women's suffrage. Hause, *Hubertine Auclert*, 30.

63. Daubié, *La femme pauvre*, 1:155; italics in the original.

64. Ibid., 116.

65. Julie-Victoire Daubié, "De l'enseignement secondaire pour les femmes," *Journal des économistes* 138 (June 1865): 395.

66. See Joan Wallach Scott, "'L'Ouvrière! Mot impie, sordide . . .' Women Workers in the Discourse of French Political Economy, 1840–1860," in Scott, *Gender and the Politics of History*, 39–163.

67. Daubié, *La femme pauvre*, 1:136–37.

68. Ibid., 3:42.

69. In the United States the last quarter-century spawned far more books and articles on European education than the previous seventy-five years. Stewart Fraser, "British and Continental Education: American Nineteenth-Century Notes," *Paedagogica Historica* 12 (1972): 21–32. For France, George Weisz describes how comparisons with German universities underwrote French reforms in higher education. Weisz, *The Emergence of Modern Universities in France, 1863–1914* (Princeton: Princeton University Press, 1983).

70. Comparative research on girls' education is in its infancy. The most detailed exploration of the subject can be found in the works of James Albisetti: see "American Women's Colleges Through European Eyes, 1865–1914," *History of Education Quarterly* 32 (winter 1992): 439–58; "The Feminization of Teaching"; "Catholics and Coeducation: Rhetoric and Reality in Europe before *Divini Illius Magistri*," *Paedagogica Historica* 35, no. 3 (1999): 667–96; and "The French *Lycée de jeunes filles* in International Perspective, 1878–1910," *Paedagogica Historica* 40 (April 2004): 143–56.

71. Daubié, *La femme pauvre*, 1:151.

72. Ibid., 154.

73. Mayeur, *L'éducation*, 135.

74. Célestin Hippeau, "L'éducation des femmes et des affranchis en Amérique," *Revue des deux mondes* 93 (1869): 452. Hippeau had a long-standing interest in educational matters, having founded with Bernard Jullien the journal *Enseignement, Journal mensuel d'éducation* under the auspices of the Société des méthodes d'enseignement. In 1870 he published a detailed report of his visit to the United States for the French government: *L'instruction publique aux États-Unis: Écoles publiques, collèges, universités, écoles spéciales. Rapport au ministre de l'Instruction Publique* (Paris: Didier, 1870).

75. Eugène Pelletan, *La chaine d'union* (1877), quoted in Mayeur, *L'enseignement secondaire*, 21. Pelletan associated educational reforms with political reforms, but remained relatively trapped within a Rousseauean vision of society with women exerting influence within a more egalitarian domestic sphere. See Judith F. Stone, *Sons of the Revolution: Radical Democrats in France, 1862–1914* (Baton Rouge: Lousiana State University Press, 1996), 1–59.

76. *Congrès international du droit des femmes*, quoted in Bidelman, *Pariahs Stand Up!* 102.

77. Clarisse Coignet, *Rapport présenté au nom de la commission des dames chargées d'examiner les questions relatives à la réforme de l'instruction primaire* (Paris: Imprimerie Administrative de Paul Dupont, 1871); see Barry Bergen, "Education, Equality, and Feminism: The 1870 Women's Commission on Education Reform," *Proceedings of the Annual Meeting of the Western Society for French History*, ed. Norman Ravitch, 20 (1993): 293–302.

78. The countries he described in the sixty-six pages preceding his analysis of the French situation are the United States, Switzerland, Germany, Italy, Russia, Holland, England, Scotland, Austria, Sweden, Norway, and Greece (in that order). Report of M. Camille Sée, in *Les lycées et collèges*. For a brief analysis of this aspect of his report, from which this quotation is taken, see Mayeur, *L'enseignement secondaire*, 36.

79. Other pedagogical writers would imitate Sée in the aftermath of his law. See, for example, L.-R. Lamotte, who also offered comparisons with other countries in *De l'enseignement*.

80. See Françoise Mayeur, "Les Catholiques libéraux et l'éducation des femmes," in *Les Catholiques libéraux au XIXe siècle: Actes du Colloque international d'histoire religieuse de Grenoble des 30 sept–3 octobre 1971* (Grenoble: Presses Universitaires

de Grenoble, 1974), 421–40, as well as "Les évêques français et Victor Duruy: Les cours secondaires de jeunes filles," *Revue d'histoire de l'Église de France* 62 (July–December 1971): 267–304. Mayeur emphasizes that the debate about these courses coincided with the emperor's decision to intervene in support of Italian unity. The battle of Mentena, in particular, was seen by Catholics as an about-face in the French defense of the pope's interests.

81. Dupanloup, *Femmes savantes et femmes studieuses*, 28. See also his *De la haute éducation intellectuelle* (Orléans, 1855). For an analysis of his support for education in general, see Christiane Marcilhary, *Le Diocèse d'Orléans sous l'épiscopat de Monseigneur Dupanloup, 1849–1878*. *Sociologie religieuse et mentalités collectives* (Paris: Plon, 1962).

82. See Jacques Gadille and Jean Godel, "L'héritage d'une pensée en matière d'éducation des femmes," in Gadille and Mayeur, *Éducation et image*, 15–24.

83. Auguste Cochin, a Catholic liberal, helped Dupanloup develop his arguments against Duruy; see Mayeur, "Les Catholiques libéraux," 429.

84. Félix Dupanloup, *M. Duruy et l'éducation des filles. Lettre de Mgr l'Evêque d'Orléans à un de ses collègues* (Paris: Charles Douniol, 1867), 18.

85. Ibid., 27–28. This twenty-nine page letter was followed by a second letter shortly afterward: see Félix Dupanloup, *Seconde Lettre de Mgr l'Evêque d'Orléans sur M. Duruy et l'éducation des filles* (Paris: Charles Douniol, 1867).

86. Dupanloup, *Seconde Lettre*, 9.

87. AN, F^{19} 3972.

88. Dupanloup, *La femme chrétienne*, 108.

89. AN, F^{19} 3972, *L'Univers*, 23 March 1869. For an analysis of the clerical response to Duruy's courses, see Mayeur, "Les evêques français et Victor Duruy." A more general analysis of the clerical opposition can be found in Jean Maurain, *La politique ecclésiastique du Second Empire de 1852 à 1869* (Paris: Felix Alcan, 1930), 839–55.

90. Dupanloup, *La femme chrétienne*, 108, 125.

91. Ibid., 125–38.

92. My interpretation of the impact of this reform effort differs in its emphasis from that of Horvath-Peterson. She sees Duruy's legacy as an "important precedent for the State's taking an active role in the fostering of higher education throughout the country." She then notes how his ideas and programs were borrowed in the creation of the Camille Sée law of 1800. Horvath-Peterson, *Victor Duruy and French Education*, 72–73. While accurate, this interpretation fails to consider, however, how the debates at this time reified the figure of the teaching nun, closing off other — more professional — models of women teachers.

93. Mayeur, "Les Catholiques libéraux," 430.

94. Rogers, "Le professeur a-t-il un sexe?"

95. See Margadant, *Madame le Professeur*, 37–40.

96. A series of essays begin to address this issue in Gadille and Mayeur, *Éducation et images*.

97. The Sacré-Cœur superior general Janet Erskine Stuart wrote an articulate reexamination of Catholic girls' education and its objectives just before World War I: *L'éducation des jeunes filles catholiques* (Paris: Perrin, 1914).

98. Emile Poulat, "Le rêve contrarié d'une religieuse enseignante: L'Affaire de Mère Marie du Sacré-Cœur," in Gadille and Mayeur, *Éducation et images*, 95–104.

99. Mère Marie du Sacré-Cœur, *Les religieuses enseignantes*, 5th ed. (Paris: X Rondelet, 1899), 129, 133.

100. Cited in Mayeur, *L'éducation des filles*, 163.

101. Mère Marie du Sacré-Cœur, *Les religieuses enseignantes*, 256.

102. Vicomtesse d'Adhémar, *Une religieuse réformatrice, la mère Marie du Sacré-Cœur de 1895 à 1901* (Paris: Bloud, 1908), 178. The Société générale pour l'éducation et l'enseignement was an organization that defended Catholic education.

103. Ibid., 221.

104. Quoted in ibid., 337.

105. See Curtis, *Educating the Faithful*, 146–71, and André Lanfrey, *Les Catholiques français et l'école*, 2 vols. (Paris: Cerf, 1990).

106. Quoted from Fénelon Gibon, in Mayeur, *L'enseignement secondaire*, 391.

107. For an analysis of the development of this private sector, see Henri Peretz, "La création de l'enseignement secondaire libre de jeunes filles à Paris (1905–1920)," *Revue d'histoire moderne et contemporaine*, 32 (April-June 1985): 237–75. He notes that in 1914 Mlle Desrez's report on the situation of Catholic secondary education for girls indicated the presence of twenty schools, with 2500 students over the age of twelve; of this number, some 800 were

listed as studying Latin and 10 were preparing the Latin-Greek option of the *baccalauréat* (248). See, as well, Blandine Berger, *Madeleine Daniélou, 1880–1956* (Paris: Cerf, 2002).

108. See Offen, "Second Sex." For an analysis of the relationship between university degrees, such as the *baccalauréat* and the *licence*, and professional opportunities for women, see Clark, *Rise of Professional Women*, part 2.

109. Quoted in Mayeur, *L'enseignement secondaire*, 426.

110. For a history of the slow assimilation of the male and female *agrégation*, see André Chervel, *Histoire de l'agrégation. Contribution à l'histoire de la culture scolaire* (Paris: Éditions Kimé, 1993), especially 163–68; 193–99.

111. See Mary Louise Roberts, *Civilization Without Sexes. Reconstructing Gender in Postwar France, 1917–1927* (Chicago: University of Chicago Press, 1994). She also emphasizes the contradictory discourses about women's roles in French society in the decade following the war.

112. Françoise Mayeur has noted that for those who opposed the progress in girls' education the figure of the *étudiante* had replaced that of the bluestocking. Mayeur, *L'enseignement secondaire*, 73.

113. Historians have traditionally attributed women's failure to achieve the vote after World War I at least in part to the Republican fear that women would vote on the political right with the church. See Hause and Kenney, *Women's Suffrage*. For a recent study of feminism in the interwar years, see Christine Bard, *Les filles de Marianne, histoire des féminismes, 1914–1940* (Paris: Fayard, 1995).

CHAPTER 8

1. Only the religious diaspora has received scholarly attention to date, see Elisabeth Dufourcq, *Les congrégations religieuses féminine hors d'Europe de Richelieu à nos jours. Histoire naturelle d'une diaspora*, 4 vols. (Paris: Librairie de l'Inde, 1993). See as well her *Les aventurières de Dieu. Trois siècles d'histoire missionnaire française* (Paris: Lattès, 1993). Her focus is not specifically on schooling.

2. My interests echo those of Caroline Bledsoe in "The Cultural Transformation of Western Education in Sierra Leone," in *Les Jeunes en Afrique. Evolution et rôle (XIXe–XXe siècles)*, ed. Hélène d'Almeida-Topor, Catherine Coquery-Vidrovitch, Odile Goerg, and Françoise Guitart (Paris: L'Harmattan, 1992), 1:383–406.

3. For the colonial context and an analysis that considers education, see Ann Stoler, *Carnal Knowledge and Imperial Power: Race and the Intimate in Colonial Rule* (Berkeley and Los Angeles: University of California Press, 2002).

4. Speech in a school of Saint-Joseph de Cluny in 1897, quoted in Geneviève Lecuir-Nemo, "Femmes et vocation missionnaire. Permanence des congrégations féminines au Sénégal de 1819 à 1960: Adaptation ou mutation? Impact et insertion" (Thèse d'histoire, Université Paris I, 1995), 481.

5. Sabine Méa, "La colonisation par les femmes," *Le Rappel*, 16 March 1883.

6. See, in particular, Hillary Callan and Shirley Ardener, eds., *The Incorporated Wife* (London: Croom Helm, 1984).

7. Colonial archives reveal the presence of many laywomen schoolteachers in Algeria beginning as early as the 1830s with the French occupation. Unfortunately, their motivations are far more difficult to ascertain.

8. See Patricia Lorcin, *Imperial Identities: Stereotyping, Prejudice and Race in Colonial Algeria* (New York: St. Martin's Press, 1995).

9. See William B. Cohen, *The French Encounter with Africans: White Response to Blacks, 1530–1880* (Bloomington: Indiana University Press, 2003), 120–27.

10. For the classic study of the French doctrines of assimilation and association at the end of the century, see Raymond Betts, *Assimilation and Association in French Colonial Theory, 1890–1914* (New York: Columbia University Press, 1961).

11. For theoretical insight into how assimilation operated in the colonial context, see Homi Bhabha, "Of Mimicry and Man: The Ambivalence of Colonial Discourse," *October* 28 (spring 1984): 125–33.

12. Alice Conklin, *A Mission to Civilize: The Republican Idea of Empire in France and West Africa, 1895–1930* (Stanford: Stanford University Press, 1997). Historians have yet to explore the nuances of the differences between the Catholic and Republican civilizing discourses. For a study that attends to both religious and colonial history, see Françoise Raison-Jourde, *Bible et pouvoir à Madagascar au XIX siècle. Invention d'une identité chrétienne et construction de l'État* (Paris: Karthala, 1991).

13. See Bernard Salvaing, *Les missionnaires à la rencontre de l'Afrique au XIXe siècle* (Paris: L'Harmattan, 1995).

14. See Nemo, "Vocation missionnaire africaine," 78. Yvonne Turin, in *Femmes et religieuses*, 215, similarly notes the willingness to volunteer for missionary work abroad until roughly 1870.

15. In addition to published secondary work, my research draws on the archives of the Sœurs de Saint-Joseph de Cluny, a missionary order, the Sœurs de la Doctrine Chrétienne de Nancy, and the Société du Sacré-Cœur.

16. ADC, *Entretiens familiers*, 1843–51, partie historique, 284.

17. Ibid., 44; letter written on 21 February 1841.

18. Ibid.; letter written on 5 March 1841.

19. Ibid., "Demande d'une Sœur pour la mission d'Afrique," n.d., 188.

20. Quoted in Marie-Edmonde Renson, "Les Sœurs de la Doctrine Chrétienne en Algérie: Fondation et expansion," in *Histoire des Sœurs de la Doctrine Chrétienne*, ed. Jacques Bombardier and Anne-Marie Lepage, vol. 4, *L'expansion au Luxembourg et en Algérie* (Nancy: Doctrine Chrétienne, 1999), 216.

21. Jacqueline Ravelomanana-Randrianjafinimana, *Histoire de l'éducation des jeunes filles malgaches du XVIe siècle au milieu du XXe siècle. Exemple Merina à Madagascar à la recherche du Bien-être* (Imarivolanitra: Editions Antso, 1996), 213–14; Heinrich Sébastien, *Les missionnaires oblats de Marie Immaculée et le personnel des missions sous leur juridiction en Afrique Australe de 1851 à 1910* (Mémoire de maîtrise, Université de Strasbourg II, 1995), 46.

22. Letter from the mother superior, Emilie de Vialar, to her cousin in France, 21 April 1836, cited in Esprit Darbon, *Emilie de Vialar: Fondatrice de la congrégation des Sœurs de Saint-Joseph de l'Apparition. Souvenirs et documents* (Marseille: Imprimerie de l'Oratoire Saint-Léon, 1901).

23. Draft letter to a minister, 31 October 1824, quoted in Lecuir-Nemo, "Femmes et vocation missionnaire," 170. See, as well, Geneviève Lecuir-Nemo, *Anne-Marie Javouhey: Fondatrice de la congrégation des sœurs de Saint-Joseph de Cluny (1779–1851)* (Paris: Karthala, 2001).

24. Nuns probably read primarily religious documents concerning the missionary ideal, notably internal bulletins and the *Annales de la Propagation de la Foi*.

25. Salvaing notes that male Catholic missionaries tended to view African women as a source of moral perversions. I have not encountered this attitude among women religious. Salvaing, *Les missionnaires*, 245–51. The obituary for Louise Leclerc, who eventually was in charge of all of the Algerian houses of the Sœurs de la Doctrine Chrétienne, mentions a preparation for departure that included a description of Algerian customs: "What amused them most were the explanations about the principal absurdities of Islam." ADC, *Entretiens familiers*, 1843–51, partie historique, 325.

26. Anne-Marie Javouhey, *Anne-Marie Javouhey. Fondatrice de la congrégation des sœurs de Saint-Joseph de Cluny. Lettres*, 4 vols. (Paris: Cerf, 1994), 1:112. For a general study of French attitudes toward Africans, see Cohen, *French Encounter with Africans*. He notes that, unlike scientists who increasingly drew on racist arguments to argue for African inferiority, missionaries tended to believe more in the possibility of change.

27. For an analysis of male missionary perceptions along the western coast of Africa, see Paule Brasseur, "Missions catholiques et administration française sur la côte d'Afrique de 1815 à 1870," *Revue française d'histoire d'Outre-mer* 62, no. 3 (1975): 415–66.

28. This is perhaps most evident in the actions of Monseigneur Lavigerie in Algeria. For a general overview of French missionary activities, see Salvaing, *Les missionnaires*, especially 65–79.

29. The gendered history of missions remains to be written from French sources; for suggestive approaches using English sources, see Fionie Bowie, Deborah Kirkwood, and Sherry Ardner, eds., *Women and Missions: Past and Present. Anthropological and Historical Perspectives* (Oxford: Berg, 1993); Waltraud Haas, *Mission History from the Woman's Point of View*, Texts and Documents, no. 13 (Basel: Basler Mission, 1989); and Huber and Lutkehaus, *Gendered Missions*. Although Catholic missionaries are the objects of some essays, none of them are French Catholics.

30. Centre d'Archives d'Outre Mer (hereafter "CAOM"), F[80]1746, report by Bishop Dupuch to the governor general of Algeria, 21 January 1845.

31. ADC, *Annales religieuses*, 1852–1867, notice sur Mère Thècle Braulot, 500.

32. In 1852 eight schools in the province of Algiers educated 1162 children; 1911 students attended fourteen schools in the province of Constantine. The congregation's historian, Marie-Edmonde Renson, indicates that between 1861 and 1867 they founded sixteen private schools and four boarding schools. Renson, "Les sœurs de la Doctrine Chrétienne en Algérie," in Bombardier and Lepage, *Histoire des sœurs de la Doctrine Chrétienne*, 4:268–69.

33. CAOM, F[80]1564. For more information about these early schools, see *Entretiens familiers*, vol. 1, partie historique. In eastern France, where this congregation came from, it was similarly diversified. For the history of this order, see Bombardier and Lepage, *Histoire des sœurs de la Doctrine Chrétienne*.

34. Information on this school can be found in CAOM, Gouvernement Général d'Algérie (hereafter "GGA"), 22 S2, as well as F⁸⁰1564. Hartoch received a salary of 1200 francs per year, which was considered a decent income. For more general information on French educational initiatives in the early years of the Algerian conquest, see Yvonne Turin, *Affrontements culturels dans l'Algérie coloniale: Écoles, médecine, religion, 1830–1880* (Paris: François Maspero, 1971).

35. CAOM, F⁸⁰1564, letter of 16 February 1836 from Auguste-Alexis Lepescheux, inspector of education, to the civil administrator.

36. CAOM, GGA, 22 S2, letter to the minister of education, 22 February 1846.

37. Between November 1845 and August 1850 her school took in 101 girls: 8 married "Moors from Algiers"; 9 married Arabs from the interior; 4 went into domestic service in Algiers and 23 into service elsewhere; 9 died (including the French interpreter for the mother of the Arab leader Ab-el-Kader); 17 were expelled; and 31 were written off the lists because of their absences. The girls present in the school came from ethnically mixed backgrounds that mirrored the diversity of the indigenous population in Algiers. See Pierre Boyer, *L'évolution de l'Algérie Médiane (Ancien département d'Alger) de 1830 à 1956* (Paris: Librarie d'Amérique et d'Orient, 1960).

38. Letter to M. Fouches, directeur général, 26 January 1846, quoted in Bessie Rayner Parkes, "Mme Luce of Algiers," *English Woman's Journal*, June 1861, 224.

39. Citation of the governor general, Baron Roger, 19 August 1825, in Lecuir-Nemo, "Femmes et vocation missionnaire," 128, 157. In 1835 it is estimated there were some 880 European inhabitants in Saint Louis. Because the French presence in this area known as the Four Communes dated back to the seventeenth century, a far larger population of mulatto families existed than in Algeria.

40. For studies of this school, see Lecuir-Nemo, "Femmes et vocation missionnaire," and Denise Bouche, "L'enseignement dans les territoires français de l'Afrique occidentale de 1817 à 1920" (Thèse d'État, Université de Paris I, 1974), 400–424. Similarly, in South Africa boarding schools encountered familial resistance because local families resented the domestic working orientation of this education. See Modupe Labode, "From Heathen Kraal to Christian Home: Anglican Mission Education and African Christian Girls, 1850–1900," in Bowie, Kirkwood, and Ardner, *Women and Missions*, 126–44.

41. CAOM, SEN/XVIII/25.

42. The impact of this experiment was rather limited: one women was sent back to Senegal in 1829; another was sent to Mana; and a third stayed in France to develop her musical talents, dying in Limoux in 1831. Lecuir-Nemo, "Femmes et vocation missionnaire," 169, 172. Brasseur notes that three of the African male students returned as priests in the 1840s. Brasseur, "Missions catholiques," 421.

43. In "Femmes et vocation missionaire," 416, Lecuir-Nemo offers the following estimation of student numbers: for St. Louis, 100 in 1822, 60 in 1842, and 131 in 1847; for Gorée, 64 in 1822 and 100 in 1842.

44. Quoted in ibid., 430.

45. ADC, *Annales religieuses*, 1853, 23. In Algeria orphanages were among the rare institutions where native girls received some form of education.

46. Quoted in Lecuir-Nemo, "Femmes et vocation missionnaire," 139.

47. Julia Clancy-Smith, "Islam, Gender, and Identities in the Making of French Algeria, 1830–1962," in *Domesticating the Empire: Race, Gender, and Family Life in French and Dutch Colonialism*, ed. J. Clancy-Smith and Frances Gouda (Charlottesville: University of Virginia Press, 1998), 166.

48. I am not arguing that the arrival of white women teachers in the colonies contributed to the rise of racial segregation characteristic of imperial cultures, rather that the evolving nature of the civilizing mission produced an increasingly national vision of French womanhood that made the early goals of assimilation unviable.

49. A presidential decree on 14 July 1850 created these schools.

50. See Elsa Harik and Donald Schilling, *The Politics of Education in Colonial Algeria and Kenya*, Papers in International Studies Africa Series, no. 43 (Athens: Ohio University, Center for International Studies, 1984); Turin, *Affrontements culturels*, 156–303; and Antoine Léon, *Colonisation, enseignement et éducation. Etude historique et comparative* (Paris: L'Harmattan, 1991), 122–30. By 1870 a total of thirty-nine such schools had been founded, including four for girls. At this same date, however, there were a mere 1800 students in these schools, and all but one of the girls' schools had disappeared.

51. CAOM, GGA, 22 S2, note explicative sur l'institution de Mme Allix aux membres du conseil supérieur de l'administration, 5 March 1846. Mme Allix first suggested opening a school for young Moorish girls in 1845; at the time she was living in Algiers, earning a living as a language teacher. Her educational initiatives are mentioned in Turin, *Affrontements culturels*, 52–56, 268–76.

52. CAOM, GGA, 22 S2, "Rapport sur les écoles maures-françaises," from Rector Delacroix to the governor general, 15 February 1853.

53. Ibid., "Rapport des dames inspectrices de l'école musulmane des filles," n.d. [after 1853].

54. Ibid., "Rapport du comité des dames inspectrices des écoles arabes-françaises de jeunes filles," sent to the prefect of Algiers, 7 December 1858.

55. The Arab-French schools for boys encountered difficulties as well, attracting mainly the poor.

56. CAOM, GGA, 22 S2, letter from the section leader to the director general on 8 August 1861.

57. Quoted in Turin, Affrontements culturels, 276.

58. See Stoler, Carnal Knowledge, 41–78.

59. Quoted in Léon, Colonisation, enseignement et éducation, 142.

60. Lecuir-Nemo, "Femmes et vocation missionnaire," 453. The term "assimilés" referred to the Senegalese who had assimilated French culture; they tended to be mulatto families.

61. Bouche, "L'enseignement dans les territoires," 415.

62. Lecuir-Nemo, "Femmes et vocation missionnaire," 502–6.

63. Ibid., 509–40. The Filles du Saint-Cœur de Marie were considered an affiliate of the Sœurs de Saint-Joseph de Cluny until 1904; like the latter, these African nuns spoke in French, since the rule prohibited speaking Wolof.

64. After founding the missionary order the Congrégation de Notre-Dame d'Afrique, known as the Pères Blancs, in 1868 and then the Sœurs Blanches, Monsignor Lavigerie operated a strategic reorientation of missionary impulses toward black Africa. See Georges Goyau, La femme dans les missions (Paris: Flammarion, 1933).

65. See Conklin, Mission to Civilize, 130–41.

66. It is not always easy to discern the ethnic composition of the student body; reports by the nuns often masked the fact they were mainly educating European girls. Pressures both from the home institution, which expected "results," as well as from government officials, in the case of Senegal, explain why descriptions of the schools' clientele were frequently vague.

67. See Pascale Barthélemy, "Femmes, Africaines et diplomées: Une elite auxiliaire à l'époque coloniale. Sages-femmes et institutrices en Afrique Occidentale Française (1918–1957)" (Thèse de doctorat d'histoire, Université Paris 7, 2004).

68. See Susan O'Brien, "French Nuns in Nineteenth-Century England," Past and Present 154 (February 1997): 142–80. Her focus is on sources concerning the Fidèles Campagnes de Jésus, the Sacré-Cœur, and the Sœurs de la Charité. See as well her article "Terra Incognita: The Nun in Nineteenth-Century England," Past and Present 121 (November 1985): 110–40. For a similar argument about the persistence of "Frenchness" among Catholic orders in England, see Dom Aidan Bellenger, "France and England: The English Female Religious from Reform to World War," in Catholicism in Britain and France since 1789, ed. Frank Tallett and Nicholas Atkin (London: The Hambledon Press, 1996), 3–11.

69. Patricia Byrne, "Sisters of Saint-Joseph: Americanization of a French Tradition," U.S. Catholic Historian 5 (summer/fall 1986): 241–72.

70. Quoted in Cahier, Vie de la Vénérable Mère Barat, 2:87.

71. Quoted in Phil Kilroy, Madeleine Sophie Barat, 343. The financial support of British Catholics probably also explains the preference for England over Tunisia.

72. O'Brien, "French Nuns," 154, 156. In 1870 they educated some 350,000 pupils in day schools (172). For a study of teaching orders that focuses on the schools they founded, see Reverend W. J. Battersby, FSC, "Educational Work of the Religious Orders of Women, 1850–1950," in The English Catholics, 1850–1950. Essays to Commemorate the Centenary of the Restoration of the Hierarchy of England and Wales, ed. George Andrew Beck (London: Burns Oates, 1950), 337–64.

73. Langlois, Le catholicisme, 440. For more information on this congregation, see Patricia Grogan, God's Faithful Instrument: Marie Madeleine Victoire de Bengy, Viscountess de Bonnault d'Houet, 1781–1858 (Ramsgate: privately printed, 1986).

74. French nuns, of course, were present in North America, notably in Canada, far earlier. See the study of Marie de l'Incarnation in Quebec in the seventeenth century, Natalie Zemon Davies, Women on the Margins: Three Seventeenth-Century Lives (Cambridge: Harvard University Press, 1995).

75. Cited in Carol K. Coburn and Martha Smith, Spirited Lives: How Nuns Shaped Catholic Culture and American Life, 1836–1920 (Chapel Hill: University of North Carolina Press, 1999), 38.

76. See Louise Callan, *Philippine Duchesne: Frontier Missionary of the Sacred Heart, 1769–1852* (Westminster, Md.: Newman Press, 1957); translated into French under the title *Philippine Duchesne: Une femme, une pionnière, une sainte, 1769–1852* (Clermont Ferrand: Imprimerie G. de Bussac, 1985).

77. Dufourcq, *Les congrégations religieuses féminines*, 2:343.

78. See Sister Catherine Frances, *The Convent School of French Origin in the United States, 1727 to 1843* (Philadelphia, 1936), as well as Mary Ewen, *The Role of the Nun in Nineteenth-Century America* (Minneapolis: University of Minnesota Press, 1984). I will use the American names of these French congregations when they exist.

79. See Mary J. Oates, "Catholic Female Academies on the Frontier," *U.S. Catholic Historian* 12 (1994): 121–36, and Marcel Launay, *Les Catholiques des États-Unis* (Paris: Desclée, 1990), 47–78.

80. *Annales de la Propagande de la Foi*, no. 1 (n.d.), cited in Dufourcq, *Les congrégations religieuses féminines*, 1:214.

81. The Sacred Heart arrived in Saint Louis in 1818; Philippine Duchesne only went off to found the Sugar Creek mission for the Potawatomi in 1842. For details of the Sacred Heart's American development, see Catherine Mooney, *Philippine Duchesne: A Woman with the Poor* (Mahwah, N.J.: Paulist Press, 1990).

82. The term "creole" is used in this period to designate populations of European descent born in the United States.

83. British middle- and upper-middle-class families far preferred home education with a governess if they were able, whereas the same social groups in France willingly sent their daughters to boarding schools. See Kathryn Hughes, *The Victorian Governess* (London: The Hambledon Press, 1993).

84. Letter of 29 January 1819, quoted in Callan, *Philippine Duchesne*, 287.

85. ASSC (Poitiers), *Lettres annuelles, 1841–43*, 65–79.

86. Nikola Baumgarten, "Education and Democracy in Frontier St. Louis: The Society of the Sacred Heart," *History of Education Quarterly* 34 (summer 1994): 171–92.

87. Two points nuance the "democratic" vision of education this variety might suggest. First, the orphans were used to help out with manual chores in a context where the schools were perpetually understaffed. Second, the nuns may have educated black girls but they showed no particular repugnance for the institution of slavery, having eight slaves themselves in 1834. Like the Sœurs de Saint-Joseph de Cluny in Senegal, the willingness to educate black girls did not extend to placing them beside white students on school benches. See Mooney, *Philippine Duchesne*, 132.

88. See Callan, *Philippine Duchesne*, 503.

89. Commenting on tensions within the American community of the Sacred Heart, Bishop Rosati continued, "I greatly fear this excessive desire to enlarge the house, to make it appear more like the French houses, and to put the houses here on the same footing with them. . . . In this country we have not the resources nor many wealthy Catholics." Quoted in Mooney, *Philippine Duchesne*, 203–4.

90. See Coburn and Smith, *Spirited Lives*, for the Sisters of Saint Joseph in the United States, 100–103.

91. Eileen Brewer, *Nuns and the Education of American Catholic Women, 1860–1920* (Chicago: Loyola University Press, 1987), 8–10.

92. ASSC (Rome), series C-III, USA early history, box 4, "Note pour la Supérieure seule" (ca. 1840–43), "Notes de la Mère Galitzine sur l'Amérique."

93. Prospectus of 1827 for the Young Ladies' Academy at The Convent of the Visitation, reproduced in Barbara Misner, S.C.S.C., *"Highly Respectable and Accomplished Ladies": Catholic Women Religious in America, 1790–1850* (New York: Garland Press, 1988), 273.

94. *Records of the American Catholic Historical Society* 59 (September 1848): 175.

95. Brewer has charted the growth of European Catholic academies in the United States but does not break them down by national origin: in 1847 there were 47 Catholic academies, 91 in 1850, 202 in 1860, and 511 in 1880. Brewer, *Nuns*, 15.

96. In 1834 the superior general of the Sacred Heart remonstrated her nuns in America, saying, "Banish forever . . . these odious distinctions between American and Frenchwomen." *Lettres circulaires de notre bienheureuse Mère Madeleine Sophie Barat* (Roehampton, 1917), letter of December 1836.

97. American historians of education have shown that more girls than boys attended secondary education. French Catholic academies were an important part of this phenomenon. In 1915 a report on Catholic schools revealed 557 secondary schools for girls educating 39,740 students, compared to 438 secondary schools for boys educating 34,798 students. See Coburn and Smith, *Spirited Lives*, 281.

98. ASSC (Rome), series C-III, USA early history, box 4, "Note pour la Supérieure seule" (ca. 1840–43), "Notes de la Mère Galitzine sur l'Amérique."

99. Inspection reports emphasized the need to work on students' courtesy. See the inspections reports for the different American houses in ASSC (Rome), series C-IV.

100. Historians of education have traditionally decried the quality of convent academy education, locating reform initiatives within the context of Protestant religious revivalism. See notably the excellent biography of Catherine Beecher by Kathryn Kish Sklar, *Catherine Beecher: A Study in American Domesticity* (New York: W. W. Norton, 1976). More recently, revisionist interpretations have begun to nuance this strongly negative vision of Catholic education, see Coburn and Smith, *Spirited Lives*.

101. For a comparative study of boys' and girls' education, as well as Protestant and Catholic education, see Kim Tolley, "Science for Ladies, Classics for Gentlemen: A Comparative Analysis of Scientific Subjects in the Curricular of Boys' and Girls' Secondary Schools in the United States," *History of Education Quarterly* 36, no. 2 (summer 1996): 129–53. In France the Sacré-Cœur did not introduce such subjects until 1852.

102. Coburn and Smith, *Spirited Lives*, 164–66. Sister Catherine Frances also argues for the decline of polite accomplishment and the emergence of "sterner subjects," such as the classics and mathematics. See C. Frances, *Convent School*, 221. The Sisters of Saint Joseph came from Lyons in France. The congregation split in 1860 over the issue of independence from France, and the Sisters of Saint Joseph of Carondelet became a separate, American-based community.

103. Thomas Low Nicols, *Forty Years of American Life, 1821–1861* (1937), quoted in Ewen, *Role of the Nun*, 92.

104. See O'Brien, "French Nuns," 164–67.

105. Jay Dolan, *The Immigrant Church: New York's Irish and German Catholics, 1815–1865* (Notre Dame: University of Notre Dame Press, 1983), 113.

106. In September 1860 the school moved to a new location with its 36 boarders, while the free school had 300 pupils. Mary Innocenta Montay, *The History of Catholic Secondary Education in the Archdiocese of Chicago* (Washington, D.C.: Catholic University of America Press, 1953), 43.

107. *The Chicago Times and Herald*, August 23, 1860, quoted in Montay, *History*, 392–93.

108. For examples of educational programs within these schools, see the annexes in Brewer, *Nuns*. For an analysis of the content of academy instruction, see Margaret Nash, "'Cultivating the Powers of *Human Beings*': Gendered Perspectives on Curricula and Pedagogy in Academies of the New Republic," *History of Education Quarterly* 41 (summer 2001): 239–50.

109. For an interesting study of Protestant attraction to Catholic schools and convent life, see Joseph Mannard, "Converts in Convents: Protestant Women and the Social Appeal of Catholic Religious Life in Antebellum America," *Records of the American Catholic Historical Society of Philadelphia* 104 (spring-winter 1993): 79–90.

110. Montay, *History*, 393.

111. "The Woman Question," *Catholic World*, May 1869, cited in Brewer, *Nuns*, 59–61.

112. Ewen, *Role of the Nun*, 100.

113. For a vivid description of such events, see Sister Mary Christina, "Early American Convent Schools," *The Catholic Educational Review* 39 (January-December 1941): 30–35.

114. Agnes Repplier, *In Our Convent Days* (Boston: Houghton, Mifflin, 1905), 184. Ewen also emphasizes the persistence of French pedagogical traditions in American schools. See Ewen, *Role of the Nun*, 98–99. Brewer notes, however, that the Sacred Heart, more than other institutions, fostered competition among students. Brewer, *Nuns*, 58.

115. Repplier, *In Our Convent Days*, 59–60.

116. Mary Elliott, "School Days at the Sacred Heart," *Putnam's Magazine*, March 1870, 275–86.

117. Mary McCarthy, *Memories of a Catholic Girlhood* (Harmondsworth: Penguin, 1957), 89.

118. Elliott, "School Days," 286, 285.

119. See Ann Taves, *The Household of Faith: Roman Catholic Devotions in Mid-Nineteenth Century America* (Notre Dame: University of Notre Dame Press, 1986). For an analysis of the French influences in English Catholicism, see Susan O'Brien, "Making Catholic Spaces: Women, Décor, and Devotion in the English Catholic Church, 1840–1900," in Ecclesiastical History Society, *The Church and the Arts*, ed. Diana Wood, Studies in Church History 28 (Oxford: Blackwell Publishers, 1992).

120. She has also argued, however, that German Catholic nuns clung more tightly to their ethnic identity in America than other national groups and yet they do not seem to have disseminated a specific educational vision for

girls. Margaret Susan Thompson, "Sisterhood and Power: Class, Culture, and Ethnicity in the American Convent," *Colby Library Quarterly* 25 (1989): 149–75.

121. See Anne O'Connor, "The Revolution in Girls' Secondary Education in Ireland, 1860–1910," in *Girls Don't Do Honours. Irish Women in Education in the 19th and 20th Centuries*, ed. Mary Cullen (Dublin: Women's Education Bureau, 1987), 39.

122. My thanks to Margaret MacCurtain for these references.

123. Michèle Cohen, *Fashioning Masculinity: National Identity and Language in the 18th Century* (London: Routledge, 1996), especially 87–110.

124. "Convent Boarding Schools for Young Ladies," *Fraser's Magazine*, June 1874, 784.

125. See "A Sentimental Education: Children on the Imperial Divide," in Stoler, *Carnal Knowledge*, 112–39.

126. My thinking on this subject has been much influenced by the work of Catherine Hall, see "Missionary Stories: Gender and Ethnicity in England in the 1830s and 1840s," in her collection *White, Male and Middle Class*, 205–54.

Conclusion

1. Catherine Pozzi, *Journal de jeunesse, 1893–1906* (Paris: Éditions Verdier, 1995), entry for 17 July 1900, 177–79.

2. Anne Martin-Fugier, *La bourgeoise. Femme au temps de Paul Bourget* (Paris: Grasset, 1983).

3. See Roberts, *Disruptive Acts*.

4. For the classic study of this debate, see Karen Offen, "Depopulation, Nationalism, and Feminism in Fin-de-Siècle France," *American Historical Review* 89 (1984): 648–76.

5. In addition to the diaries explored by Philippe Lejeune in *Le moi des demoiselles*, see Cosnier's analysis of women's voices in *Le silence des filles*.

6. See Anne Martin-Fugier's moving analysis of a turn-of-the-century correspondence between two bourgeois women. "Les lettres célibataires," in *La correspondance: Les usages de la lettre au XIXe siècle*, ed. Roger Chartier (Paris: Fayard, 1991). One of these women, Hélène Legros, moved from letter-writing into novel-writing.

7. For female university students, see Pierre Moulinier, *La naissance de l'étudiant moderne (XIXe siècle)* (Paris: Belin, 2002), 69–86; for the civil service, see Clark, *Rise of Professional Women*.

8. Mary Louise Roberts, "Subversive Copy: Feminist Journalism in Fin-de-Siècle France," in de la Motte and Prsyblyski, *Making the News*, 333.

9. See Robert Nye, *Masculinity and Codes of Honor in Modern France* (Berkeley and Los Angeles: University of California Press, 1998).

10. She insisted, moreover, that Protestantism had lowered the level of "bienséance" and through its principles had paved the way for the Revolution of 1789 and the Commune of Paris in 1871! Stuart, *L'éducation des jeunes filles catholiques*, 217, 235.

11. Ibid., 255, 270.

12. In 1900 in the United States alone, Dufourcq estimates there were some 2,500 French nuns; in Algeria there were 506 nuns of the Congrégation de la Doctrine Chrétienne. Dufourcq, *Les congrégations religieuses féminines*, 2:345, 421.

SELECT BIBLIOGRAPHY

ARCHIVAL SOURCES

Archives Nationales

AJ[16] 151, 157	Académie de Paris. Écoles de filles privées (1815–33, 1822–49)
AJ[16] 198–99	Académie de Paris. Écoles libres de filles de la Seine (1850–54)
AJ[16] 515	Académie de Paris. Enseignement secondaire des filles (1867–83)
AJ[16] 4698*	Registre des déclarations faites pour l'ouverture d'une école libre, filles (1850–53)
AFIV 1047	Rapport du Ministre des Cultes (1810) concernant un projet en faveur des orphelines
F[17] 6843–39	Réponses des recteurs à la circulaire de Duruy (1864)
F[17] 8753–84	Enseignement secondaires des jeunes filles: Lycées et cours secondaires (1867–97)
F[17] 12431–33	Institutions et pensions de jeunes filles (1834–91)
F[17] 12434	Pensionnats tenus par des congrégations religieuses femmes (1834–81)
F[19] 6258	Enquête sur les pensionnats des congrégations
F[19] 6343–44	Congrégations de femmes: Dossiers départementaux, Seine
F[19] 6354	Congrégations de femmes enseignantes, inspection des écoles primaires congréganistes . . . (1819–49)
156 AP II	Famille Maison: Archives Watier de Saint-Alphonse
279 AP 7–8	Famille du duc de Massa; lettres du maréchal Macdonald à sa fille Nancy
279 AP 14	Lettres de Nancy Macdonald à son père (1797–1810)

Centre d'Archives d'Outre Mer (Aix-en-Provence)

Série S Gouvernement Général d'Algérie

22S 2–3	Écoles arabes françaises (1835–76)
50S 1–2	Enseignement libre (1861–81)
Senegal /X/ 2	Sœurs de Saint-Joseph de Cluny (1815–39)
Senegal/XVIII/25	Sœurs de Saint-Joseph de Cluny personnel, 1852–94
F[80] 1561–62	Instruction publique; inspections, établissements privés; congrégations enseignantes
F[80] 1731	Instruction publique. Enseignement secondaire; collèges de jeunes filles (1862–1904)
F[80] 1746	Culte Catholique en Algérie

Archives de Paris

VD⁶   Fonds des Mairies (réglementation de l'organisation et de la surveillance des maisons d'éducation de demoiselles; inspection des pensions et institutions de demoiselles)
D²T¹   Personnel enseignant dans les écoles privées de filles (1830–49)

Archives des maisons d'éducation de la Légion d'honneur (Saint-Denis)

Student dossiers
Procès verbeaux de concours, 1828–40

Archives de la Grande Chancellerie de la Légion d'honneur (Paris)

Règlements

Archives de la Société du Sacré-Cœur (Poitiers)

Affaire d'Olivier
Règlements et cours d'études
Registre des élèves au pensionnat à Alger (1843–66)

Archives de la Société du Sacré-Cœur (Rome)

Series C-I   Central Government
Series C-III / IV   History of provinces of the Society; history of individual institutions
Series D-I   Activities of the Institute: Work of Education
                    Lettres annuelles de la Société du Sacré-Cœur
                    Lettres des supérieures générales

Archives des Sœurs de la Doctrine Chrétienne (Nancy)

Entretiens familiers des Sœurs de la Doctrine Chrétienne (Nancy, 1850)
Annales religieuses des Sœurs de la Doctrine Chrétienne, 1852–67.

Archives des Sœurs de Saint-Joseph de Cluny (Paris)

St.-Joseph Cluny Marine
5A   Pièces émanant du Ministère des Colonies
2 A G   Congrégation de Saint-Joseph à la Guadeloupe
156 API 207 Établissements de la congrégation de Saint-Joseph de Cluny dans les colonies françaises et à l'étranger

Archives de la Congrégation de la Mère de Dieu (Paris)

Série E   Noviciat, registres d'entrée, état du personnel
Série J   Les maisons de la Legion d'honneur; journal d'Eugénie Servant (1875–81)

Archives de la Congrégation de Notre Dame (Paris)

Règles et Methodes dediées aux Religieuses de Notre-Dame (Clermont Ferrand: Imprimerie de la Librairie Catholique, 1844)

Archives de l'Ardenne (Charleville-Mézières)

21 J 11   Famille Pascal-Diacre: Cahiers de classe d'Eugénie Pascal-Diacre, élève d'Ecouen sous l'Empire; correspondence reçue par elle d'une ancienne élève d'Ecouen

Departmental Archives

I have looked through the T series on secondary education for girls and private schools, as well as the V series on religion in the departments of Aude, Doubs, Eure-et-Loir, Haute-Garonne, Gers, Loire-Atlantique, Meurthe-et-Moselle, Moselle, Hautes-Pyrénées, Bas-Rhin, Haut-Rhin, Haute-Saône, Seine-et-Oise, Somme, and Vienne.

Private collections

The following persons and institutions have lent me documents: the Ursulines of Paris (Jégou et Mésnil, "Les Ursulines françaises au XIXe siècle. Documents pour une histoire"); Philippe Lejeune (diaries of Pauline Weill, 1858–59, and Mathilde Savarin, 1881–93); Viviane Isambert-Jamati (Dubois-Goblot correspondence, 1841–83); Alain Blond (correspondence of Sophie Simon, student at the Legion of Honor in the 1860s); Baron Pinoteau (correspondence for the First Empire); and Georges Plaisance (diary of Marguerite Rousset, 1868–70).

Printed Sources

Adam, Juliette Lambert. *Le roman de mon enfance et de ma jeunesse.* 3d ed. Paris: A. Lemerre, 1902.

Adhémar, Vicomtesse d'. *Une religieuse réformatrice, la mère Marie du Sacré-Cœur de 1895 à 1901.* Paris: Bloud, 1908.

Aimé-Martin, Louis. *De l'éducation des mères de famille ou de la civilisation du genre humain par les femmes.* 2 vols. Brussels: Meline, Cans, 1837.

Bachellery, Joséphine. "Comment nous comprenons l'émancipation des femmes sous la République." *La voix des femmes,* 19 April 1848; 24–25 April 1848.

———. "Lettre à M. Lévi-Alvarès, professeur d'histoire, etc., sur les Inspectrices de la ville de Paris." Paris, 1844.

———. *Lettres sur l'éducation des femmes.* Paris, 1848.

Bassanville, Comtesse de. *Les salons d'autrefois, souvenirs intimes.* 2 vols. Paris: Brunet, 1863.

Beauharnais, Hortense de. *Mémoires de la Reine Hortense.* Paris: Plon, 1927.

Bernier, Mme. *Discours qui a remporté le prix à la Société des sciences et des arts du département du Lot.* Paris, 1803.

Bonin, Abbé. *Pensionnat des dames de Saint-Maur. Discours prononcé à la distribution solennelle des prix des dames de Saint-Maur de Chalons.* Saint-Maur de Chalons, 1862.

Bonnefonds, Elisabeth de. *Mes souvenirs.* Paris: Lecoffre, 1869.

Bosquet, Amélie. "Une écolière sous la Restauration." *Revue Bleue,* 21 August 1897, 225–33.

Bouilly, Jean Nicolas. *Conseils à ma fille.* 2 vols. 2d ed. Paris: Rosa, 1812.

Boulage, Abbé Thomas François-Olympiade. *Discours prononcé par M. Boulage, curé de Saint-Pantaléon le 17 août 1855 à la distribution des prix de la pension de Mlle Ernestine Pfeiffer à Troyes.* Troyes, 1855.

Boury, Adèle. *Mémoires de Mlle Adèle Boury.* Paris: Vimont, 1833.

Brière, Abbé. *Discours prononcé à la distribution solennelle des prix de l'Institution de Mlles Delfeuille et Leconte à Nogent-le-Rotrou (Eure-et-Loir).* Nogent-le-Rotrou, 1858.

Browne, Mary. *The Diary of a Girl in France in 1821.* London: John Murray, 1905.

Brada [Comtesse Puliga]. *Souvenirs d'une petite Second Empire.* Paris: Calmann-Lévy, 1921.

Burney, Fanny. *The Journals and Letters of Fanny Burney (Madame d'Arblay).* Vol. 5, *West Humble and Paris: 1801–1803.* Edited by Joyce Hemlow et al. Oxford: Clarendon Press, 1975.

Campan, Jeanne. *Conseils aux jeunes filles; théâtre pour les jeunes personnes, quelques essais de morale.* Paris: Barrière, 1824.

———. *Correspondance inédite avec la Reine Hortense.* 2 vols. Paris: Levasseur, 1835.

———. *De l'éducation, suivi des conseils aux jeunes filles.* 3 vols. 2d ed. Paris: Baudouin Frères, 1824.

Cappelle, Marie. *Mémoires de Madame Lafarge.* Revised ed. Vol. 1. Paris: M. Lévy frères, 1867.

Carreau, Mlle [Mlle Vanhove]. *Pension de jeunes demoiselles ou nouvelles propres à éclairer les jeunes personnes dans toutes les positions où elles peuvent se trouver dans le monde à la sortie de leur pensionnat.* 2d ed. Paris: Caillot, ca. 1830.

Carroy, Julie. *Étude et récréation ou l'intérieur d'un pensionnat. Ouvrage divisé en 30 journées contenant plusieurs histoires morales et instructives.* Paris: Parmentier, 1825.

———. *Zélie ou le modèle des jeunes filles.* Paris: Caillot, ca. 1830.

Castel de Courval, Amélie. *Les jeunes orphelines ou les contes d'une grandmère.* Paris: Vernarel et Tenon, 1825.

Caubet-Darius, Mme. *Réflexions sur l'éducation et l'instruction de la femme.* Saint Gaudens: Imprimerie et libraire de Veuve Tajan, 1866.

Celnart, Elisabeth [Elisabeth Félicie Bayle-Mouillard]. *Les institutrices réunies ou dialogues sur les arts et métiers.* Paris: Locard et Davi, 1825.

———. *La sortie de pension ou la bonne tante; ouvrage destiné aux jeunes demoiselles de 15 à 16 ans.* 2 vols. Paris: Boiste fils ainé, 1825.

Coignet, Clarisse. *Rapport présenté au nom de la commission des dames chargées d'examiner les questions relatives à la réforme de l'instruction primaire.* Paris: Imprimerie Administrative de Paul Dupont, 1871.

Condorcet, Marquis de. *Premier mémoire sur l'instruction publique.* 1790. Paris: Éditions Klincksieck, 1989.

Conseil général du département de la Seine. *Résultats de l'inspection des pensionnats.* 1845–61.

Couailhac, Louis. *Physiologie du célibataire et de la vieille fille.* Paris: J. Laisné, 1841.

Cours d'études à l'usage des élèves de la Légion d'honneur (classe violet uni et liseré). Paris: Imprimerie Nationale, 1823–32.

Crouzet-Benaben, Jeanne-Paule. *Souvenirs d'une jeune fille bête. Souvenirs autobiographiques d'une des premières agrégées de France.* Paris: Nouvelles Éditions Debresse, 1971.

Daubié, Julie-Victoire. *La femme pauvre au dix-neuvième siècle.* 3 vols. Paris: Côté-femmes, 1992.

Dauriat, Louise. *Mémoire adressé à Messieurs les membres du conseil général du département de la Seine.* Paris, 1846.

Deraismes, Maria. *Eve dans l'Humanité, 1868.* Paris: Côté-femmes, 1990.

———. *Oeuvres complètes.* Paris: Félix Alcan, 1896.

Le Diable à Paris. 2 vols. Paris: Hetzel, 1845–1846.

Dupanloup, Félix. *La femme chrétienne et française; dernière réponse à M. Duruy et à ses défenseurs par Mgr l'évêque d'Orléans.* Paris: Charles Douniol, 1868.

———. *Femmes savantes et femmes studieuses.* 6th ed. Paris: Charles Douniol, 1868.

———. *M. Duruy et l'éducation des filles: Lettre de Mgr l'Évêque d'Orléans à un de ses collègues.* Paris: Charles Douniol, 1867.

———. *Seconde lettre de Mgr l'Evêque d'Orléans sur M. Duruy et l'éducation des filles.* Paris: Charles Douniol, 1867.

Durand, Sophie. *Mes souvenirs sur Napoléon, sa famille et sa cour.* Paris: Beraud, 1820.

Duruy, Victor. *Notes et souvenirs, 1811–1894.* 2d ed. 2 vols. Paris: Hachette, 1902.

Elliott, Mary. "School Days at the Sacred Heart." *Putnam's Magazine,* March 1870, 275–86.

Esquiros, Adèle. *Histoire d'une sous-maîtresse.* Paris: E. Pick, 1861.

Feuillet, Octave, Mme. *Quelques années de ma vie.* 4th ed. Paris: Calmann Lévy, 1894.

Les Français peints par eux-mêmes. 2 vols. Paris: Philipart, 1861. New edition. 2 vols. Edited by Léon Curmer. Paris: Omnibus, 2003–4.

Goblet, F.-V. *Dictionnaire administratif et topographique de Paris: Du commerce, des arts, et des produits en tous genres de l'industrie qui s'y trouve.* Paris: Allut, 1808.

Gossot, Emile. *Un pensionnat d'autrefois: Souvenirs d'une pensionnaire.* Tours: Mame, 1900.

Gréard, Octave. *Education et instruction, enseignement secondaire.* Vol. 1. Paris: Hachette, 1882.

———. *L'éducation des femmes par les femmes: Études et portraits.* Paris: Hachette, 1889.

———. *L'enseignement primaire à Paris et dans le département de la Seine de 1867 à 1877.* Paris: A. Chaix, 1878.

Guizot, Elisabeth-Charlotte-Pauline. *Éducation domestique ou Lettres de famille sur l'éducation.* 6th ed. 2 vols. Paris: Didier, 1881.

Hébert-Duperron, Victor. *Allocution prononcée . . . Prix du pensionnat de Mlle Hirche à Vesoul, le 19 août 1867.* Paris: Imprimerie de P. A. Bourdier, n.d.

———. *Souvenirs de distribution de prix de l'année scolaire, 1864–65.* Perigueux: Imprimerie de Dupont, 1865.

Hippeau, Célestin. "L'éducation des femmes et des affranchis en Amérique." *Revue des deux mondes* 93 (1869): 450–76.

———. *L'instruction publique aux États-Unis. Écoles publiques, collèges, universités, écoles spéciales. Rapport au ministre de l'Instruction Publique.* Paris: Didier, 1870.

Javouhey, Anne-Marie. *Anne-Marie Javouhey. Fondatrice de la congrégation des sœurs de Saint-Joseph de Cluny. Lettres.* 4 vols. Paris: Cerf, 1994.

Jégou, Marie Andrée, and Marie-Odile Mesnil. "Les Ursulines françaises au XIXe siècle. Documents pour une histoire." Amiens, 1985. Typescript.

Kilian, Étienne. *De l'instruction des filles à ses divers dégrés, institutions et pensions, écoles primaires supérieures et élémentairess.* Paris: Paul Dupont, 1842.

Lajolais, Nathalie de. *Le livre des mères de famille et des institutrices sur l'éducation pratique des femmes.* 2d ed. Paris: Didier, 1843.

Lamotte, L.-Rose. *De l'enseignement secondaires des filles.* Paris: Delagrave, 1881.

Lecestre, L. *Lettres inédites de Napoléon Ier (an VII-1817).* Paris: Plon, 1897.

Legouvé, Ernest. *La femme en France au XIXe siècle.* Paris: Librairie de la bibliothèque démocratique, 1875.

———. *Histoire morale des femmes.* 5th ed. Paris: Didier, 1859.

Legrand, Louis. *Le mariage et les mœurs en France.* Paris: Hachette, 1879.

Le Groing la Maisonneuve, Françoise Thérèse Antoinette. *Essai sur l'instruction des femmes.* 3d ed. Tours: Pornin, 1844.

Lemonnier, Charles. *Elisa Lemonnier: Fondatrice de la Société pour l'enseignement professionnel des femmes.* Saint-Germain: Imprimerie de L. Toinon, 1866.

Léon, Henri. *Les indiscrétions de Jehan Bomoloque à l'endroit des maîtresses de pension.* Paris, 1855.

Lequien, Mlle. *Institution de jeunes filles dirigées par Mlle Lequien: Discours prononcé à la distribution des prix le 28 août 1838.* Poissy, 1838. Manuscript.

Lévêque, M. *Mathilde Salomon: Directrice du Collège Sévigné. Membre du Conseil Supérieur de l'Instruction Publique. Chevalier de la Légion d'honneur, 1837–1909.* Saint-Germain-lès-Corbeil: Imprimerie Leroy, 1909.

Lévi-Alvarès, David. *Éducation secondaire et supérieure des jeunes filles.* Paris, [1847?].

Lievyns, A. Verdet, and P. Bégat. *Les fastes de la Légion d'honneur (1803–1804).* 5 vols. Paris: Au bureau, et chez B. Saint Edme, 1847.

Limayrac, Paulin. "Les femmes moralistes." *Revue des deux mondes* 13, no. 4 (1843): 50–70.

Longueville, Madeleine Stéphanie de. "The Great Lady of 1830." In *Pictures of the French. A Series of Literary and Graphic Delineations of French Character,* 169–76. London: Orr, 1840.

Loziéras, Mme de. *Pensionnat de jeunes demoiselles à Senlis (Oise). De l'émulation. Discours prononcé à la distribution solennelle des prix fin de l'année scolaire 1851–52.* Senlis: Imprimerie C. Duriez, 1852.

Les Lycées et collèges de jeunes filles, documents, rapports et discours. . . . Preface and foreword by Camille Sée. Paris: Léopold Cerf, 1888.

Mackau, Annette de. *Correspondance d'Annette de Mackau, comtesse de Saint-Alphonse. Dame du palais de l'Impératrice Joséphine (1790–1879).* Edited by Chantal de Tourtier-Bonnazi. Paris: SEVPEN, 1967.

Manceau, Adelaide Victoire Antoinette de Lussault. *L'ange de paix. Ouvrage dédié aux jeunes personnes.* 2 vols. Paris: Marcilly, ca. 1830.

Marchef-Girard, Marie-Joséphine de. *Les femmes, leur passé, leur présent, leur avenir.* Paris: Louis Chappe, 1860.

Marie du Sacré-Cœur. *Les religieuses enseignantes et les nécessités de l'apostolat.* 5th ed. Paris: X. Rondelet, 1899.

Martin, Thérèse Mélanie. *Souvenirs d'une ancienne élève de la Maison de la Légion d'honneur d'Ecouen: Thérèse Mélanie Martin, 1807–1815.* Edited by E. Joppé. Saint Dizier: Imprimerie de A. Brulliard, 1924.

Maze, Hippolyte. *Mme Bascans, 1801–1878.* Paris: Jouas, 1878.

Mémorial des enfants de Marie de la congrégation Prima primaria établie dans le Monastère des Religieuses de la congrégation de Notre-Dame, maison dites des Oiseaux, Paris: Rue des Sèvres 86. Paris: Pélagaud, 1864.

Mémoire en défense et expertise pour Mlle Laure Bronville (Pensionnat, demi-pensionnat et externat de demoiselles) contre la Ville de Paris. 1865.

Mongellas, Fanny de. *De l'influence des femmes sur les mœurs et les destinées des nations, sur leurs familles et la sociéte, et de l'influence des mœurs sur le bonheur de la vie.* 2d ed. 2 vols. Paris: L.-G. Michaud, 1831.

Monniot, Victorine. *Le journal de Marguerite ou les deux années préparatoires à la première communion.* 2 vols. Lyons: Périsse, 1858.

Necker de Saussure, Albertine. *L'éducation progressive ou étude du cours de la vie.* Brussels: Meline, Cans, 1840.

Paris ou le Livre des Cent-et-Un. Vol. 5. Paris: Ladvocat, 1832.

Parkes, Bessie Rayner. "Mme Luce of Algiers." *English Woman's Journal* 7 (May 1861): 157–68; (June 1861): 224–36; (July 1861): 296–307.

Picanon, Henriette. *Mon frère et moi. Souvenirs de jeunesse accompagnés de poésies d'E. Berthoud.* Paris: J. Bonhoure, 1876.

Pictures of the French. A Series of Literary and Graphic Delineations of French Character. London: Orr, 1840.

Portalis, Jeanne Etienne Marie. *Discours, rapports, et travaux inédits sur le Concordat de 1801.* Paris: Joubert, 1845.

Pozzi, Catherine. *Journal de jeunesse, 1893–1906.* Paris: Éditions Verdier, 1995.

Rémusat, Claire de. *Essai sur l'éducation des femmes.* Paris: Ladvocat, 1824.

Reboul, Ernestine. *Nouvelle réponse de Mlle Reboul, provoquée par la pétition de M. Loveday.* Paris: Chez Lamy, 1822.

Renan, Ernest. *My Sister Henriette. A Memoir.* New York: Macmillan, 1896.

Repplier, Agnes. *In Our Convent Days.* Boston: Houghton, Mifflin, 1905.

Riballier. *De l'éducation physique et morale des femmes avec une notice alphabétique de celles qui se sont distinguées dans les différentes carrières des sciences et des beaux-arts et des actions mémorables.* Paris: Chez les frères Estienne, 1790.

Riobe, Adèle. *Notice sur ma fille.* Le Mans: Imprimerie Monnoyer Frères, 1863.

Rivail, H.L.D. *Projet de réforme concernant les examens et les maisons d'éducation des jeunes personnes.* Paris, 1847.

Rousseau, Jean-Jacques. *Émile, ou de l'éducation.* Paris: Flammarion, 1966.

Rousselot, Paul. *La pédagogie féminine: Extraits des principaux écrivains qui ont traité de l'éducation des femmes depuis le XVIe siècle.* Paris: Delagrave, 1881.

Sand, George. *Correspondance de George Sand (April 1840–December 1842).* Vol. 5. Paris: Éditions Garnier Frères, 1969.

———. *Histoire de ma vie.* Paris: Flammarion, 2001.

Sincère, Marie [Marie Dubreuil de Saint-Germain Romieu]. *Les pensionnats de jeunes filles.* Paris: Desloges, 1854.

Soulié, Frédéric. *Physiologie du bas-bleu.* Paris: Aubert, 1841.

Stern, Daniel [Comtesse d'Agoult]. *Mes souvenirs.* Paris: Calmann Lévy, 1877.

Stuart, Janet Erskine. *L'éducation des jeunes filles catholiques.* Paris: Perrin, 1914.

Taïeb, Edith, ed. *La Citoyenne: Articles de 1881 et 1891.* Paris: Syros, 1982.

Taine, Hippolyte. *Notes sur l'Angleterre.* 2d ed. Paris: Hachette, 1872.
Willard, Emma. *Journals and Letters from France and Great Britain.* Troy, N.Y.: N. Tuttle, 1833.
Weiler, Amélie. *Journal d'une jeune fille mal dans son siècle, 1840–1859.* Edited by Nicolas Stoskopf. Strasbourg: La Nuée Bleue, 1994.

Journals Consulted

Le droit des femmes (1869–70)
La gazette des femmes (1836–38)
Journal des maîtres de pension (1840–42)
La mère institutrice (1834–45)
Revue de l'enseignement des femmes (1845–48)
La tribune de l'enseignement (1838–40)
La voix des femmes (1848)

Trade Books (Annuaires de commerce) Consulted

Alpes-Maritimes	Finistère	Meurthe-et-Moselle	Haut-Rhin
Aube	Haute-Garonne	Meuse	Rhône
Aude	Gers	Moselle	Haute-Saône
Calvados	Gironde	Nièvre	Seine
Côte-d'Or	Haute-Loire	Nord	Seine-et-Oise
Doubs	Hérault	Puy-de-Dome	Somme
Eure	Loire-Atlantique	Hautes-Pyrénées	Vienne
Eure-et-Loir	Maine-et-Loire	Bas-Rhin	

Secondary Sources

Adler, Laure. *A l'aube du féminisme: Les premières journalistes (1830–1850).* Paris: Payot, 1979.
Ainval, Christiane, d'. *Le couvent des Oiseaux: Ces jeunes filles de bonne famille.* Paris: Perrin, 1991.
Alaimo, Kathleen. "Adolescence, Gender and Class in Educational Reform in France: The Development of *Enseignement Primaire Supérieur,* 1880–1910." *French Historical Studies* 18 (fall 1994): 1025–56.
Albisetti, James. "American Women's Colleges Through European Eyes, 1865–1914." *History of Education Quarterly* 32 (winter 1992): 439–58.
———. "Catholics and Coeducation: Rhetoric and Reality in Europe Before *Divini Illius Magistri.*" *Paedagogica Historica* 35 (October 1999): 667–96.
———. "The Feminization of Teaching in the Nineteenth Century: A Comparative Perspective." *History of Education* 22, no. 3 (1993): 252–63.
———. "The French *Lycée de jeunes filles* in International Perspective, 1878–1910." *Paedagogica Historica* 40 (April 2004): 143–56.
———. *Schooling German Girls and Women: Secondary and Higher Education in the Nineteenth Century.* Princeton: Princeton University Press, 1988.
Allen, James Smith. *Poignant Relations: Three Modern French Women.* Baltimore: Johns Hopkins University Press, 2000.
Ariès, Philippe. *Centuries of Childhood: A Social History of Family Life.* Translated by Robert Baldick. London: Jonathan Cape, 1962.
Arnold, Odile. *Le corps et l'âme: La vie des religieuses au XIXe siècle.* Paris: Seuil, 1984.
Auslander, Leora. *Taste and Power: Furnishing Modern France.* Berkeley and Los Angeles: University of California Press, 1996.

Avanzini, Guy. "La pédagogie de l'Assomption: quelle spécificité?" In *Mère Marie-Eugénie Milleret: Milleret. Fondatrice des Religieuses de l'Assomption. Actes du Colloque du Centenaire, Cannes, 24–25 avril 1998.* Paris: Éditions Don Bosco, 1999.

Barthélemy, Pascale. "Femmes, Africaines et diplomées: Une élite auxiliaire à l'époque coloniale. Sages-femmes et institutrices en Afrique Occidentale Française (1918–1957)." Thèse de doctorat d'histoire, Université Paris 7, 2004.

Baumgarten, Nikola. "Education and Democracy in Frontier St. Louis: The Society of the Sacred Heart." *History of Education Quarterly* 34 (summer 1994): 171–92.

Bellaigue, Christine. "Behind the School Walls: The School Community in French and English Boarding Schools for Girls, 1810–1867." *Paedagogica Historica* 40 (April 2004): 107–21.

———. "The Development of Teaching as a Profession for Women Before 1870." *Historical Journal* 44 (2001): 963–88.

Bellenger, Dom Aidan. "France and England: The English Female Religious from Reform to World War." In *Catholicism in Britain and France since 1789*, ed. Frank Tallett and Nicholas Atkin, 3–11. London: The Hambledon Press, 1996.

Bergman-Carton, Janice. *The Woman of Ideas in French Art, 1830–1848.* New Haven: Yale University Press, 1995.

Bernos, Marcel. "De l'influence salutaire ou pernicieuse de la femme dans la famille et la société." *Revue d'histoire moderne et contemporaine* 29 (July–September 1982): 453–461.

Bernoville, Gaëtan. *Les religieuses de l'Assomption.* Vol. 1, *La fondatrice Eugénie Milleret (Mère M. Eugénie de Jésus).* Paris: Grasset, 1948.

Bertocci, Philip. *Jules Simon: Republican Anticlericalism and Cultural Politics in France, 1848–1886.* Columbia: University of Missouri Press, 1978.

Bhabha, Homi. "Of Mimicry and Man: The Ambivalence of Colonial Discourse." *October* 28 (spring 1984): 125–33.

Bidelman, Patrick. *Pariahs Stand Up! The Founding of the Liberal Feminist Movement in France, 1858–1889.* Westport, Conn.: Greenwood Press, 1982.

Boiraud, Henri. "La condition féminine et la scolarisation des filles en France au XIXème siècle de Guizot à Jules Ferry." Thèse d'État, Université de Caen, 1978.

Bombardier, Jacques, and Anne-Marie Lepage. *Histoire des Sœurs de la Doctrine Chrétienne.* 4 vols. Nancy: Doctrine Chrétienne, 1999.

Bouche, Denise. "L'enseignement dans les territoires français de l'Afrique occidentale de 1817 à 1920." Thèse d'État, Université de Paris I, 1974.

Bourdieu, Pierre. *Distinction: A Social Critique of the Judgment of Taste.* Translated by Richard Nice. Cambridge: Harvard University Press, 1984.

———. *Masculine Domination.* Translated by Richard Nice. Stanford: Stanford University Press, 2001.

Bourgade, Germaine. *Contribution à l'étude de l'éducation féminine de 1830 à 1914.* Toulouse: Publications de l'Université de Toulouse-Le Mirail, 1979.

Bowie, Fiona, Deborah Kirkwood, and Sherry Ardener. *Women and Missions: Past and Present. Anthropological and Historical Perspectives.* Oxford: Berg, 1993.

Brasseur, Paule. "Missions catholiques et administration française sur la côte d'Afrique de 1815 à 1870." *Revue française d'histoire d'Outre-Mer* 62, no. 3 (1975): 415–66.

Brewer, Eileen. *Nuns and the Education of American Catholic Women, 1860–1920.* Chicago: Loyola University Press, 1987.

Briand, Jean-Pierre, and Jean-Michel Chapoulie. "L'institution scolaire et la scolarisation: Une perspective d'ensemble," *Revue française de sociologie* 24 (1993): 3–42.

Bricard, Isabelle. *Saintes ou pouliches. L'éducation des jeunes filles au XIXe siècle.* Paris: Albin Michel, 1985.

Cahier, Adèle. *Vie de la Vénérable Mère Barat: Fondatrice et première supérieure générale de la Société du Sacré-Cœur de Jésus*. 2 vols. Paris: E. de Soye et fils, 1884.

Cahour, Joseph. *Les écoles et pensionnats privés au XIX siècle*. Laval: Imprimerie Goupil, 1924.

Callan, Louise. *Philippine Duchesne: Frontier Missionary of the Sacred Heart, 1769–1852*. Westminster, Md.: Newman Press, 1957.

Caron, Jean-Claude. *A l'école de la violence: Châtiments et sévices dans l'institution scolaire au XIXe siècle*. Paris: Aubier, 1999.

Caspard, Pierre, ed. *La presse d'éducation et d'enseignement, XVIIIe siècle–1940. Répertoire analytique*. 4 vols. Paris: INRP-CNRS, 1981–91.

Causse, Étienne. *Madame Necker de Saussure et l'éducation progressive*. 2 vols. Paris: Édition "je sers," 1930.

Certeau, Michel de. *The Practice of Everyday Life*. Translated by Steven Rendall. Berkeley and Los Angeles: University of California Press, 1984.

Chaline, Jean-Pierre. *Les bourgeois de Rouen: Une élite urbaine au XIXe siècle*. Paris: Presses de la Fondation Nationale des Sciences Politiques, 1982.

Chapoulie, Jean-Marie. "L'enseignement primaire supérieur, de la loi Guizot aux écoles de la IIIe République." *Revue d'histoire moderne et contemporaine* 36 (July–September 1989): 413–37.

Charle, Christophe. *La république des universitaires, 1870–1940*. Paris: Seuil, 1994.

Charry, Jeanne de. *Histoire des constitutions de la société du Sacré-Cœur*. 3 vols. Rome: General Archives of the Société du Sacré-Cœur, 1977.

———. "La Société du Sacré-Cœur: Institut Contemplatif et apostolique." In *Les religieuses enseignantes (XVI–XXe siècles), Actes de la 4e rencontre d'histoire religieuse à Fontevrault, 4 octobre 1980*. Angers: Presses Universitaires d'Angers 1981.

Chartier, Roger. *On the Edge of the Cliff: History, Language, and Practices*. Translated by Lydia Cochrane. Baltimore: Johns Hopkins University Press, 1997.

Chartier, Roger, Alain Boureau, and Cécile Dauphin, eds. *Correspondence. Models of Letter-Writing from the Middle Ages to the Nineteenth Century*. Translated by Christopher Woodal. Princeton: Princeton University Press, 1997.

Chaudhuri, Nupur, and Margaret Strobel. *Western Women and Imperialism: Complicity and Resistance*. Bloomington: Indiana University Press, 1992.

Chaussinand-Nogaret, Guy, ed. *Histoire des élites en France du XVIe au XXe siècle*. Paris: Tallandier, 1991.

Cholvy, Gérard, and Yves-Marie Hilaire. *Histoire religieuse de la France contemporaine 1800/1880*. Vol. 2. Toulouse: Privat, 1985.

Cholvy, Gérard, and Nadine-Josette Chaline, eds. *L'enseignement catholique en France aux XIXe et XXe siècles*. Paris: Cerf, 1995.

Clancy-Smith, Julia, and Frances Gouda, eds. *Domesticating the Empire: Race, Gender, and Family Life in French and Dutch Colonialism*. Charlottesville: University of Virginia Press, 1998.

Clark, Linda. *The Rise of Professional Women in France: Gender and Public Administration since 1830*. Cambridge: Cambridge University Press, 2000.

———. *Schooling the Daughters of Marianne: Textbooks and the Socialization of Girls in Modern French Primary Schools*. Albany: SUNY Press, 1984.

Coburn, Carol K., and Martha Smith. *Spirited Lives: How Nuns Shaped Catholic Culture and American Life, 1836–1920*. Chapel Hill: University of North Carolina Press, 1999.

Cohen, Michèle. *Fashioning Masculinity: National Identity and Language in the 18th Century*. London: Routledge, 1996.

Cohen, William B. *The French Encounter with Africans: White Response to Blacks, 1530–1880*. Bloomington: Indiana University Press, 2003.

Colwill, Elizabeth. "Women's Empire and the Sovereignty of Man in *La Décade Philosophique*, 1794–1807." *Eighteenth-Century Studies* 29, no. 3 (1996): 265–89.

Compère, Marie-Madeleine. *L'histoire de l'éducation en Europe: Essai comparatif sur la façon dont elle s'écrit*. Paris: INRP, 1995.

Conklin, Alice. *A Mission to Civilize: The Republican Idea of Empire in France and West Africa, 1895–1930*. Stanford: Stanford University Press, 1997.

Constant, Emilien. "Les débuts de l'enseignement secondaire (et primaire supérieur) des jeunes filles dans le Var, 1867–1925." *Historical Reflections* 7 (1980): 301–12.

Constant, Paule. *Un monde à l'usage des demoiselles*. Paris: Gallimard, 1987.

Corbin, Alain, Jacqueline Lalouette, and Michèle Riot-Sarcey, eds. *Femmes dans la Cité, 1815–1871*. Granat: Éditions Créaphis, 1997.

Corrado Pope, Barbara. "Mothers and Daughters in Early Nineteenth-Century Paris." Ph.D. diss., Columbia University, 1981.

———. "Revolution and Retreat: Upper-class French Women after 1789." In *Women, War, and Revolution*, ed. Carol R. Berkin and Clara Lovett. New York: Holmes and Meier, 1980.

Cosnier, Colette. *Le silence des filles: De l'aiguille à la plume*. Paris: Fayard, 2001.

Crubellier, Maurice. *L'enfance et la jeunesse dans la société française, 1800–1950*. Paris: Armand Colin, 1979.

Curtis, Sarah A. *Educating the Faithful: Religion, Schooling, and Society in Nineteenth-Century France*. De Kalb: Northern Illinois University Press, 2000.

———. "Lay Habits: Religious Teachers and the Secularization Crisis of 1901–1904." *French History* 9 (December 1995): 478–98.

Darbon, Esprit. *Emilie de Vialar: Fondatrice de la congrégation des Sœurs de Saint-Joseph de l'Apparition. Souvenirs et documents*. Marseille: Imprimerie de L'Oratoire Saint-Léon, 1901.

Darrow, Margaret. "French Noblewomen and the New Domesticity, 1750–1850." *Feminist Studies* 5 (spring 1979): 41–65.

Daumard, Adeline. *La bourgeoisie parisienne de 1815 à 1848*. Paris: SEVPEN, 1963.

———. *Les bourgeois de Paris au XIXe siècle*. Paris: Flammarion, 1970.

Dauphin, Cécile. "Histoire d'un stéréotype. La vieille fille." In *Madame ou Mademoiselle, Itinéraires de la solitude féminine, XVIIIe–XXe siècle*, ed. Arlette Farge and Christiane Klapisch-Zuber, 207–31. Paris: Montalba, 1984.

Dauphin, Cécile, et al. "Culture et pouvoir des femmes: Essai d'historiographie." *Annales ESC* 41, no. 2 (1986): 271–93.

Dauphin, Cécile, Pierrette Lebrun-Pézerat, and Danièle Poublan. *Ces bonnes lettre: Une correspondance familiale au XIXe siècle*. Paris: Albin Michel, 1995.

Davidoff, Leonore. *Worlds Between: Historical Perspectives on Gender and Class*. New York: Routledge, 1995.

Davidoff, Leonore, and Catherine Hall. *Family Fortunes: Men and Women of the English Middle Class, 1780–1850*. Chicago: University of Chicago Press, 1987.

Davidoff, Leonore, Megan Doolittle, Janet Fink, and Katherine Holden. *The Family Story: Blood, Contract and Intimacy, 1830–1960*. London: Longman, 1999.

Davidson, Denise. "Bonnes lectures: Improving Women and Society Through Literature in Post-Revolutionary France." In *The French Experience from Republic to Monarchy, 1792–1824. New Dawns in Politics, Knowledge and Culture*, ed. M. Cross and D. Williams, 155–71. New York: Palgrave, 2000.

———. "Constructing Order in Post-Revolutionary France: Women's Identities and Cultural Practices." Ph.D. diss., University of Pennsylvania, 1997.

Davis, Natalie Zemon. *Women on the Margins: Three Seventeenth-Century Lives*. Cambridge: Harvard University Press, 1995.

Delaporte, Victor. *Le monastère des Oiseaux. Les origines. La Révérende Mère Marie Sophie, 1811–1863*. Paris: Victor Retaux, 1899.

Desan, Suzanne. *The Family on Trial in Revolutionary France*. Berkeley and Los Angeles: University of California Press, 2004.

————. "Reconstituting the Social after the Terror: Family Property and the Law in Popular Politics." *Past and Present* 164 (August 1999): 81–12.

————. "War Between Brothers and Sisters: Inheritance Law and Gender Politics in Revolutionary France." *French Historical Studies* 20 (fall 1997): 597–634.

Dubesset, Mathilde, and Michelle Zancarini-Fournel. *Parcours de femmes. Réalités et représentations. Saint Étienne, 1880–1950.* Lyon: Presses Universitaires de Lyon, 1993.

Dufourcq, Elisabeth. *Les congrégations religieuses féminine hors d'Europe de Richelieu à nos jours: Histoire naturelle d'une diaspora.* 4 vols. Paris: Librairie de l'Inde, 1993.

Dyhouse, Carol. *Girls Growing Up in Late Victorian and Edwardian England.* London: Routledge and Kegan Paul, 1981.

Elias, Norbert. *La dynamique de l'Occident.* Paris: Calmann-Lévy, 1975.

Ewen, Mary. *The Role of the Nun in Nineteenth-Century America.* Reprint. Minneapolis: University of Minnesota Press, 1984.

Farge, Arlette, and Christiane Klapisch-Zuber, eds. *Madame ou Mademoiselle: Itinéraires de la solitude féminine, XVIIIe–XXe siècle.* Paris: Montalba, 1984.

Fayet-Scribe, Sylvie. *Associations féminines et catholicisme: De la charité à l'action sociale, XIXe–XXe siècles.* Paris: Éditions Ouvrières, 1990.

Ford, Caroline. "Private Lives and Public Order in Restoration France: The Seduction of Emily Loveday." *American Historical Review* 99 (February 1994): 21–43.

————. "Religion and the Politics of Cultural Change in Provincial France: The Resistance of 1902 in Lower Brittany." *Journal of Modern History* 62 (March 1990): 1–33.

Foucault, Michel. *Discipline and Punish: The Birth of the Prison.* Translated by Alan Sheridan. New York: Vintage Books, 1995.

Foucher, Léon. *Mme Desfontaines et la congrégation de Sainte-Clotilde de 1757 à nos jours.* Paris: Institut Sainte Clotilde, 1965.

Fraisse, Geneviève. *Les femmes et leur histoire.* Paris: Gallimard, 1998.

————. *La raison des femmes.* Paris: Plon, 1992.

————. *Reason's Muse: Sexual Difference and the Birth of Democracy.* Translated by Jane Marie Todd. Chicago: University of Chicago Press, 1994.

Fraisse, Geneviève, and Michelle Perrot, eds. *Histoire des femmes en occident.* Vol. 4, *Le XIXe siècle.* Paris: Plon, 1991. Published in English under the title, *A History of Women in the West,* vol. 4, *Emerging Feminism from Revolution to World War* (Cambridge: Belknap Press, 1993).

Frances, Sister Catherine. *The Convent School of French Origin in the United States, 1727 to 1843.* Philadelphia, 1936.

Gadille, Jacques, and Françoise Mayeur, eds. *Éducation et images de la femme chrétienne en France au début du XXe siècle.* Lyons: Éditions Hermès, 1980.

Geison, Gerald L., ed. *Professions and the French State, 1700–1900.* Philadelphia: University of Philadelphia Press, 1984.

Gemie, Sharif. "Institutional History, Social History, Women's History: A Comment on Patrick Harrigan's 'Women Teachers and the Schooling of Girls in France.'" *French Historical Studies* 22 (fall 1999): 613–23.

————. *Women and Schooling in France, 1815–1914: Gender, Authority and Identity in the Female Schooling Sector.* Keele: Keele University Press, 1995.

Gerbod, Paul. *La vie quotidienne dans les lycées et les collèges au XIXe siècle.* Paris: Hachette, 1968.

Gibson, Ralph. "Le catholicisme et les femmes en France au XIXe siècle." *Revue d'histoire de l'Église de France* 79, 202 (1993): 63–93.

————. "Female Religious Orders in 19th-Century France." In *Catholicism in Britain and France since 1789,* ed. Frank Tallett and Nicholas Atkin. London: The Hambledon Press, 1996.

————. *A Social History of French Catholicism, 1789–1914.* London: Routledge, 1989.

Gold, Carol. *Educating Middle-Class Daughters: Private Girls Schools in Copenhagen, 1790–1820*. Copenhagen: The Royal Library Museum Tusculanum Press, 1996.

Goldsmith, Elizabeth, and Dena Goodman, eds. *Going Public: Women and Publishing in Early Modern France*. Ithaca: Cornell University Press, 1995.

Gontard, Maurice. *Les écoles primaires de la France bourgeoise (1833–75)*. Toulouse: CRDP, n.d.

———. *La question des écoles normales de 1789 à nos jours*. Toulouse: CRDP, 1976.

Goodman, Dena. "Public Sphere and Private Life: Toward a Synthesis of Current Historiographical Approaches to the Old Regime." *History and Theory* 31, no. 1 (1992): 1–20.

———. ed. *Marie Antoinette: Writing on the Body of a Queen*. London: Routledge, 2003.

Gorham, Deborah. *The Victorian Girl and the Feminine Ideal*. Bloomington: Indiana University Press, 1982.

Grassi, Marie-Claire. "Le discours des 'éducatrices' en France entre 1760 et 1830." *Igitur. Gender, Letteratura, cultura* 1 (1993): 85–96.

———. "Le savoir-vivre au féminin, 1820–1920." In *Du goût, de la conversation et des femmes*, ed. Alain Montandon, 213–32. Clermont Ferrand: Association des Publications de la Faculté des Lettres et Sciences Humaines de Clermont Ferrand, 1994.

Grew, Raymond, and Patrick J. Harrigan. *Schools, State, and Society: The Growth of Elementary Schooling in Nineteenth-Century France, A Quantitative Analysis*. Ann Arbor: University of Michigan Press, 1991.

Grimaud, Louis. *Histoire de la liberté d'enseignement en France*. 5 vols. Paris: Apostolat de la Presse, 1944–54.

Hall, Catherine. *White, Male and Middle-Class: Explorations in Feminism and History*. New York: Routledge, 1992.

Harik, Elsa, and Donald Schilling. *The Politics of Education in Colonial Algeria and Kenya*. Papers in International Studies, Africa Series, no. 43. Athens: Ohio University, Center for International Studies, 1984.

Harrigan, Patrick. "Church, State, and Education in France from the Falloux to the Ferry Laws: A Reassessment." *Canadian Journal of History* 36, no. 1 (2001): 51–83.

———. "Secondary Education and the Professions in France During the Second Empire." *Comparative Studies in Society and History* 17, no. 3 (1975): 349–71.

———. "Social and Political Implications of Catholic Secondary Education During the Second French Empire." *Societas* 6, no. 1 (1976): 41–59.

———. "Women Teachers and the Schooling of Girls in France: Recent Historiographical Trends." *French Historical Studies* 21 (fall 1998): 593–610.

Harrison, Carol E. *The Bourgeois Citizen in Nineteenth-Century France: Gender, Sociability, and the Uses of Emulation*. Oxford and New York: Oxford University Press, 1999.

Harten, Elke, and Hans-Christian Harten. *Femmes, culture et Révolution*. Paris: Éditions des femmes, 1989.

Hause, Steven. *Hubertine Auclert: The French Suffragette*. New Haven: Yale University Press, 1987.

Havelange, Isabelle. "La littérature à l'usage des demoiselles, 1750–1830." Thèse de 3e cycle, École des Hautes Etudes en Sciences Sociales, 1984.

———. "1650–1830, des livres pour les demoiselles?" In *Les discours institutionnels sur la lecture des jeunes*, ed. Anne-Marie Chartier and Suzanne Pouliot, special issue, *Cahiers de la recherche en éducation* (Sherbrooke) 3 (1997): 363–76.

Havelange, Isabelle, Ségolène Le Men, and Michel Manson. *Le magasin des enfants. La littérature pour la jeunesse, 1750–1830* (catalogue de l'exposition). Alençon: Imprimerie alençonnaise, 1988.

Hecquet, Michèle, ed. *L'éducation des filles au temps de George Sand*. Arras: Artois Presses Université, 1998.

Hellerstein, Erna Olafson. "Women, Social Order, and the City: Rules for French Ladies, 1830–1870." Ph.D. diss, University of California, Berkeley, 1980.

Hesse, Carla. *The Other Enlightenment: How French Women Became Modern*. Princeton: Princeton University Press, 2001.

Horvath-Peterson, Sandra. "Victor Duruy and the Controversy over Secondary Education for Girls." *French Historical Studies* 9, no. 1 (1975): 83–104.

———. *Victor Duruy and French Education: Liberal Reform in the Second Empire*. Baton Rouge: Louisiana University Press, 1984.

Houbre, Gabrielle. *La discipline de l'amour: L'éducation sentimentale des filles et des garçons à l'âge du romantisme*. Paris: Plon, 1997.

Huber, Mary Taylor, and Nancy C. Lutkehaus, eds. *Gendered Missions: Women and Men in Missionary Discourse and Practice*. Ann Arbor: University of Michigan Press, 1999.

Hufton, Olwen. *Women and the Limits of Citizenship in the French Revolution*. Toronto: University of Toronto Press, 1992.

Hughes, Kathryn. *The Victorian Governess*. London: The Hambledon Press, 1993.

Huguet, Françoise. *Les livres pour l'enfance et la jeunesse de Gutenberg à Guizot*. Paris: INRP, Éditions Klincksieck, 1997.

Hunt, Lynn. *The Family Romance of the French Revolution*. Berkeley and Los Angeles: University of California Press, 1992.

Isambert-Jamati, Viviane. *Crises de la société. Crises de l'enseignement. Sociologie de l'enseignement secondaire français*. Paris: Presses Universitaires de France, 1970.

———. *Solidarité fraternelle et réussite sociale: La correspondance familiale des Dubois-Goblet, 1841–1882*. Paris: L'Harmattan, 1995.

Jones, Jennifer. "Repackaging Rousseau: Femininity and Fashion in Old Regime France." *French Historical Studies* 18 (fall 1994): 939–67.

Julia, Dominique. "Le choix des professeurs en France: Vocation ou concours? 1700–1850." *Paedagogica Historica* 30 (1994): 173–205.

———. *Les trois couleurs du tableau noir, la Révolution*. Paris: Belin, 1981.

Kale, Steven D. "Women, the Public Sphere, and the Persistence of Salon." *French Historical Studies* 25 (winter 2002): 115–48.

Kilroy, Phil. *Madeleine Sophie Barat (1779–1865): A Biography*. Mahwah, N.J.: Paulist Press, 2000.

Klejman, Laurence, and Florence Rochefort. *L'égalité en marche. Le féminisme sous la Troisième République*. Paris: Presses de la Fondation Nationale des Sciences Politiques, 1989.

Knibiehler, Yvonne. "Les médecins et la 'nature feminine' au temps du code civil." *Annales, E.S.C.* 31, no. 4 (1976): 824–45.

Knibiehler, Yvonne, and Régine Goutalier, *La femme au temps des colonies*. Paris: Stock, 1985.

Landes, Joan. *Women and the Public Sphere in the Age of the French Revolution*. Ithaca: Cornell University Press, 1988.

Lanfrey, André. *Les Catholiques français et l'école*. 2 vols. Paris: Cerf, 1990.

Langland, Elizabeth. *Nobody's Angels: Middle-Class Women and Domestic Ideology in Victorian Culture*. Ithaca: Cornell University Press, 1995.

Langlois, Claude. *Le catholicisme au feminine: Les congrégations françaises à supérieure générale au XIXe siècle*. Paris: Cerf, 1984.

———. "Les effectifs des congrégations féminines au XIXe siècle. De l'enquête statistique à l'histoire quantitative." *Revue d'histoire de l'Église de France* 60 (January–June 1974): 39–64.

Lassère, Madeleine. *Victorine Monniot ou l'éducation des jeunes filles au XIXe siècle: Entre exotisme et catholicisme de combat*. Paris: L'Harmattan, 1999.

Lecuir-Nemo, Geneviève. *Anne-Marie Javouhey: Fondatrice de la congrégation des sœurs de Saint-Joseph de Cluny (1779–1851)*. Paris: Karthala, 2001.

———. "Femmes et vocation missionnaire. Permanence des congrégations féminines au Sénégal de 1819 à 1960: Adaptation ou mutation? Impact et insertion." Thèse d'histoire, Université de Paris I, 1995.

Le Goff, Jacques, and René Rémond, eds. *Histoire de la France religieuse*. Vol. 3, *Du roi Très Chrétien à la laïcité républicaine (XVIIIe–XIXe siècle)*, ed. Philippe Joutard. Paris: Seuil, 1991.

Lejeune, Philippe. *Le moi des demoiselle: Enquête sur le journal de jeune fille*. Paris: Seuil, 1993.

Lelièvre, Claude. "Développement et fonctionnement des enseignements post-élémentaires de la Somme, 1850–1914." Thèse d'État, Université de Paris V, 1985.

Lelièvre, Claude, and Françoise Lelièvre. *Histoire de la scolarisation des filles*. Paris: Nathan, 1991.

Léon, Antoine. *Colonisation, enseignement et éducation. Étude historique et comparative*. Paris: L'Harmattan, 1991.

Lévy, Marie-Françoise. *De mères en filles. L'éducation des françaises, 1850–1880*. Paris: Calmann-Lévy, 1984.

———, ed. *L'enfant, la famille et la Révolution française*. Paris: O. Orban, 1990.

Lorcin, Patricia. *Imperial Identities: Stereotyping, Prejudice and Race in Colonial Algeria*. New York: St. Martin's Press, 1995.

Lougee, Carolyn. "Noblesse, Domesticity, and Social Reform: The Education of Girls by Fénelon and Saint-Cyr." *History of Education Quarterly* 14 (spring 1974): 87–113.

Luc, Jean-Noël. *L'invention du jeune enfant au XIXe siècle: De la salle d'asile à l'école maternelle*. Paris: Belin, 1997.

Magray, Mary Peckham. *The Transforming Power of the Nun: Women, Religion, and Cultural Change in Ireland, 1750–1900*. New York: Oxford University Press, 1998.

Marcus, Sharon. *Apartment Stories: City and Home in Nineteenth-Century Paris and London*. Berkeley and Los Angeles: University of California Press, 1999.

Margadant, Jo Burr. "The Duchesse de Berry and Royalist Political Culture in Postrevolutionary France." *History Workshop Journal* 43 (1997): 23–52.

———. "Gender, Vice, and the Political Imaginary in Nineteenth-Century France: Reinterpreting the Failure of the July Monarchy, 1830–1848." *American Historical Review* 104 (December 1999): 1461–96.

———. *Madame le Professeur: Women Educators in the Third Republic*. Princeton: Princeton University Press, 1990.

Martin-Fugier, Anne. *La bourgeoise. Femme au temps de Paul Bourget*. Paris: Grasset, 1983.

———. "Les lettres célibataires." In *La correspondance. Les usages de la lettre au XIXe siècle*, ed. Roger Chartier, 407–26. Paris: Fayard, 1991.

———. *La vie élégante ou la formation du Tout-Paris: 1815–1848*. Paris: Fayard, 1990.

Matlock, Jann. *Scenes of Seduction: Prostitution, Hysteria, and Reading Difference in Nineteenth-Century France*. New York: Columbia University Press, 1994.

Mayeur, Françoise. "Les Catholiques libéraux et l'éducation des femmes." In *Les Catholiques libéraux au XIXe siècle. Actes du colloque international d'histoire religieuse de Grenoble des 30 sept.–3 oct. 1971*, 421–40. Grenoble: Presses Universitaires de Grenoble, 1974.

———. *L'éducation des filles en France au XIXe siècle*. Paris: Hachette, 1979.

———. *L'enseignement secondaire des jeunes filles sous la IIIe République*. Paris: Presses de la Fondation Nationale des Sciences Politiques, 1977.

———. "Les evêques français et Victor Duruy: Les cours secondaires de jeunes filles." *Revue d'histoire de l'Église de France* 62 (July–December 1971): 267–304.

———. "La formation des institutrices femmes avant la loi Paul Bert: Les cours normaux." *Revue d'histoire de l'Église de France* 81 (January–June 1995): 121–30.

———. *Histoire générale de l'enseignement et de l'éducation en France*. Vol. 3, *De la Révolution à l'école Républicaine (1789–1930)*. Paris: Nouvelle librairie de France, 1981.

———. "Vers un enseignement secondaire catholique des jeunes filles au début du XXe siècle." *Revue d'histoire de l'Église de France* 81 (January–June 1995): 197–205.

Maza, Sarah. *The Myth of the French Bourgeoisie. An Essay on the Social Imaginary, 1750–1850*. Cambridge: Harvard University Press, 2003.

McMillan, James. *Housewife or Harlot: The Place of Women in French Society, 1870–1940.* New York: St. Martin's Press, 1981.

Meyer, Jean-Claude. "La congrégation de Notre-Dame de la Compassion." In *L'enseignement catholique en France aux XIXe et XXe siècles,* ed. Gérard Cholvy and Nadine-Josette Chaline, 131–44. Paris: Cerf, 1995.

Mère Marie-Eugénie Milleret: Fondatrice des Religieuses de l'Assomption. Actes du Colloque du Centenaire, Cannes, 24–25 avril 1998. Paris: Éditions Don Bosco, 1999.

Michaud, Stéphane. *Muse et Madone: Visages de la femme de la Révolution aux apparitions de Lourdes.* Paris: Seuil, 1985.

Mills, Hazel. "Negotiating the Divide: Women, Philanthropy and the 'Public Sphere' in Nineteenth-Century France." In *Religion, Society and Politics in France since 1789,* ed. Frank Tallett and Nicholas Atkin, 28–54. London: The Hambledon Press, 1991.

Misner, Barbara, S.C.S.C. *"Highly Respectable and Accomplished Ladies": Catholic Women Religious in America, 1790–1850.* New York: Garland Press, 1988.

Montay, Mary Innocenta. *The History of Catholic Secondary Education in the Archdiocese of Chicago.* Washington, D.C.: Catholic University of America Press, 1953.

Moody, Joseph N. *French Education since Napoleon.* Syracuse: Syracuse University Press, 1978.

Mooney, Catherine. *Philippine Duchesne: A Woman with the Poor.* New York: Paulist Press, 1990.

Moses, Claire Goldberg. *French Feminism in the Nineteenth Century.* Albany: SUNY Press, 1984.

Moses, Claire Goldberg, and Leslie Wahl Rabine. *Feminism, Socialism, and French Romanticism.* Bloomington: Indiana University Press, 1993.

Moulinier, Pierre. *La naissance de l'étudiant moderne (XIXe siècle).* Paris: Belin, 2002.

Müller, Detlef, Fritz Ringer, and Brian Simon, eds. *The Rise of the Modern Educational System: Structural Change and Social Reproduction, 1870–1920.* Cambridge: Cambridge University Press, 1987.

Nemo, Geneviève. "Vocation missionnaire africaine d'une congrégation féminine au XIXe siècle: Exemple de Saint-Joseph de Cluny." In *Femmes en Mission: Actes de la XIe session du CREDIC à Saint-Flour (août 1990),* 69–98. Lyons: Éditions Lyonnaises d'Art et d'histoire, 1991.

Nique, Christian. *Comment l'ecole devint une affaire d'État (1815–1840).* Paris: Nathan, 1990.

Nobécourt, Marie-Dominique. "Un exemple de l'éducation des filles au 19e siècle par les congrégations religieuses: Le Sacré-Cœur de Paris (1816–1874)." Thèse de l'Ecole des Chartes, 1981.

Nord, Philip. *The Republican Moment: Struggles for Democracy in Nineteenth-Century France.* Cambridge: Harvard University Press, 1995.

Oates, Mary J. "Catholic Female Academies on the Frontier." *U.S. Catholic Historian* 12 (1994): 121–36.

Oberlé, Raymond. *L'enseignement à Mulhouse de 1798 à 1870.* Paris: Les Belles Lettres, 1961.

O'Brien, Susan. "French Nuns in Nineteenth-Century England." *Past and Present* 154 (February 1997): 142–80.

———. "*Terra Incognita:* The Nun in Nineteenth-Century England." *Past and Present* 121 (November 1985): 110–40.

O'Connor, Anne. "The Revolution in Girls' Secondary Education in Ireland, 1860–1910." In *Girls Don't Do Honours: Irish Women in Education in the 19th and 20th Centuries,* ed. Mary Cullen. Dublin: Women's Education Bureau, 1987.

Offen, Karen. "Ernest Legouvé and the Doctrine of 'Equality in Difference' for Women: A Case Study of Male Feminism in Nineteenth-Century French Thought." *Journal of Modern History* 58 (June 1996): 452–84.

———. *European Feminisms, 1700–1950: A Political History.* Stanford: Stanford University Press, 2000.

———. "A Nineteenth-Century French Feminist Rediscovered: Jenny P. d'Héricourt, 1809–1875." *Signs* 31 (autumn 1987): 144–58.

———."On the French Origin of the Words Feminism and Feminist." *Feminist Issues* 8 (autumn 1988): 45–51.

———. "The Second Sex and the Baccalauréat in Republican France, 1880–1924." *French Historical Studies* 3 (fall 1983): 252–88.

Orr, Clarissa Campbell, ed. *Wollstonecraft's Daughters: Womanhood in England and France, 1780–1920*. Manchester: Manchester University Press, 1996.

Ostenc, M. "L'œuvre d'éducation de la congrégation de Sainte-Marie-des-Anges au pensionnat de l'Esvière à Angers à la fin du 19e siècle." *Annales de Bretagne et des pays de l'Ouest* 89 (1982): 87–106.

Ozouf, Mona. *Women's Words: Essay on French Singularity*. Translated by Jane Marie Todd. Chicago: University of Chicago Press, 1997.

Padberg, Joseph W. *Colleges in Controversy: The Jesuit Schools in France from Revival to Suppression, 1815–1880*. Cambridge: Harvard University Press, 1969.

Palmer, R. R. *The Improvement of Humanity: Education and the French Revolution*. Princeton: Princeton University Press, 1985.

Pedersen, Joyce Senders. *The Reform of Girls Secondary and Higher Education in Victorian England: A Study of Elites and Educational Change*. London: Garland 1987.

———."The Reform of Women's Secondary and Higher Education: Institutional Change and Social Values in Mid and Late Victorian England." *History of Education Quarterly* 19 (spring 1979): 61–99.

Peretz, Henri."La création de l'enseignement secondaire libre de jeunes filles à Paris (1905–1920)." *Revue d'histoire moderne et contemporaine* 32 (April–June 1985): 237–75.

Perrée, Thérèse. *Le tiers-ordre de Notre-Dame du Mont-Carmel d'Avranches*. Coutances: Éditions Notre-Dame, 1965.

Perrot, Michelle."De la vieille fille à la garçonne: La femme célibataire au XIXe siècle." *Autrement* 32 (June 1981): 222–31.

———. *Les femmes ou les silences de l'histoire*. Paris: Flammarion, 1998.

———. *Femmes publiques*. Paris: Textuel, 1997.

———, ed. *Histoire de la vie privée*. Vol. 4, *De la Révolution à la Grande Guerre*. Paris: Seuil, 1987.

———, ed. *Une histoire des femmes est-elle possible?* Paris: Éditions Rivages, 1984.

Planté, Christine. *La petite sœur de Balzac: Essai sur la femme auteur*. Paris: Seuil, 1989.

Plessis, Alain."Une France bourgeoise." In *Histoire de France, Les formes de la culture*, ed. André Burguière and Jacques Revel, 221–300. Paris: Seuil, 1993.

Poovey, Mary. *Uneven Developments: The Ideological Work of Gender in Mid-Victorian England*. Chicago: University of Chicago Press, 1988.

Powell, Kristen, and Elizabeth C. Childs, eds. *Femmes d'esprit: Women in Daumier's Caricature*. Hanover: University Press of New England, 1990.

Prost, Antoine. *L'enseignement en France, 1800–1967*. Paris: Armand Colin, 1968.

Py, Gilbert. *Rousseau et les éducateurs. Étude sur la fortune des idées pédagogiques de Jean-Jacques Rousseau en France et en Europe au XVIIIe siècle*. Oxford: Voltaire Foundation, 1997.

Quartararo, Anne T. *Women Teachers and Popular Education in Nineteenth-Century France: Social Values and Corporate Identity at the Normal School Institution*. Newark: University of Delaware Press, 1995.

Rauch, André. *Le premier sexe: Mutations et crise de l'identité masculine*. Paris: Hachette, 2000.

Reddy, William. *The Invisible Code: Honor and Sentiment in Postrevolutionary France, 1814–1848*. Berkeley and Los Angeles: University of California Press, 1997.

Rémond, René. *L'anticléricalisme en France: De 1815 à nos jours*. New and revised edition. Paris: Fayard, 1999.

Rencontres d'histoire religieuse. *Les religieuses enseignantes (XVIe–XXe siècles)*. Actes de la 4e rencontre d'Histoire Religieuse à Fontevraud, le 4 octobre 1980. Angers: Presses de l'Université d'Angers, 1981.

Renton, Alice. *Tyrant or Victim? A History of the British Governess*. London: Weidenfeld and Nicolson, 1991.

Renonciat, Annie, Viviane Erzaty, and Genevieve Patte, eds. *Livres d'enfance, Livres de France*. Paris: Hachette, 1998.

Riot-Sarcey, Michèle. *La democratie à l'epreuve des femmes: Trois figures critiques du pouvoir, 1830–48*. Paris: Albin Michel, 1994.

———. "Des femmes pétitionnent sous la monarchie de Juillet." In *Femmes dans la Cité, 1815–1871*, ed. Alain Corbin, Jacqueline Lalouette, and Michèle Riot-Sarcey, 389–400. Paris: Éditions Créaphis, 1997.

Roberts, Mary Louise. *Disruptive Acts: The New Woman in Fin-de-siècle France*. Chicago: University of Chicago Press, 2002.

Rogers, Rebecca. "Boarding Schools, Women Teachers and Domesticity: Reforming Girls' Secondary Education in the First Half of the Nineteenth Century." *French Historical Studies* 19 (spring 1995): 153–81.

———. "Competing Visions of Girls' Secondary Education in Post-Revolutionary France." *History of Education Quarterly* 34 (summer 1994): 156–63.

———. "Constructions de la féminité bourgeoise en France au XIXe siècle: Éducation, normes et pratiques." In *Lorsque l'enfant grandit. Entre dépendance et autonomie*, ed. Jean-Pierre Bardet et al., 663–75. Paris: Presses de l'Université de Paris-Sorbonne, 2002.

———. *Les demoiselles de la Légion d'honneur: Les maisons d'éducation de la Légion d'honneur au XIXe siècle*. Paris: Plon, 1992.

———. "L'éducation des filles à l'époque napoléonienne." In *Napoléon et les lycées: Enseignement et société en Europe au début du XIXe siècle, actes du colloque des 15 et 16 novembre 2002, organisé par l'Institut Napoléon et la Bibliothèque Marmottan à l'occasion du bicentenaire des lycées*, ed. Jacques-Olivier Boudon, 275–90. Paris: Nouveau Monde Éditions, 2004.

———. "French Education for British Girls in the Nineteenth Century." *Women's History Magazine* 42 (October 2002): 21–29.

———. "Le professeur a-t-il un sexe? Les débats autour de la présence d'hommes dans l'enseignement secondaire féminin, 1840–1880." *Clio. Histoire, Femmes, Société* (1996): 221–39.

———. "Retrograde or Modern? Unveiling the Teaching Nun in Nineteenth-Century France." *Social History* 23 (May 1998): 146–64.

———. "Schools, Discipline, and Community: Diary-writing and Schoolgirl Culture in Late Nineteenth-Century France." *Women's History Review* 4, no. 4 (1995): 525–54.

———. "The Socialization of Girls in France under the Influence of Religion and the Church." In *Erziehung der Menschen-Geschlechter. Studien zur Religion, Sozialisation und Bildung in Europa seit der Aufklärung*, ed. Margret Kraul and Christoph Luth, 139–58. Weinheim: Deutscher Studien Verlag, 1996.

———. "La sous-maîtresse au XIXe siècle: Domestique ou enseignante stagiaire?" *Histoire de l'éducation* 98 (May 2003): 37–60.

Salvaing, Bernard. *Les missionnaires à la rencontre de l'Afrique au XIXe siècle*. Paris: L'Harmattan, 1995.

Savoie, Philippe. "Offre locale et engagement de l'État: Les enseignements technique et primaire supérieur à Nancy et les conditions de leur évolution sous la Troisième République." *Histoire de l'éducation* 66 (May 1995): 47–84.

Schiebinger, Londa. *The Mind Has No Sex? Women in the Origins of Modern Science*. Cambridge: Harvard University Press, 1989.

Schvind, Muriel. "L'éducation des demoiselles de la bourgeoisie: L'exemple du Bas-Rhin (1800–1870)." Maîtrise en Sciences Historiques, Université de Strasbourg II, 1995–96.

Scott, Joan Wallach. *Gender and the Politics of History*. New York: Columbia University Press, 1988.

———. *Only Paradoxes to Offer: French Feminists and the Rights of Man*. Cambridge: Harvard University Press, 1996.

Secondy, Louis. "L'éducation des filles en milieu catholique au XIXe siècle." *Cahiers d'histoire* 26 (1981): 337–52.

———. "L'enseignement secondaire féminin public dans l'Académie de Montpellier (1867–1939)." *Études sur l'Hérault* 2 (1985): 43–50.

Skedd, Susan. "Women Teachers and the Expansion of Girls' Schooling in England c. 1760–1820." In *Gender in Eighteenth-Century England: Roles, Representations, and Responsibilities*, ed. Hannah Barker and Elaine Chalus, 101–25. London: Longman, 1997.

Smith, Bonnie. *The Gender of History: Men, Women and Historical Practice*. Cambridge: Harvard University Press, 1998.

———. *Ladies of the Leisure Class: The Bourgeoises of Northern France in the Nineteenth Century*. Princeton: Princeton University Press, 1981.

Smith-Rosenberg, Carol. "The Female World of Love and Ritual: Relations Between Women in Nineteenth-Century America." *Signs* 1 (autumn 1975): 1–29.

Sohn, Anne-Marie. *Chrysalides: Femmes de la vie privée (XIXe–XXe siècle)*. 2 vols. Paris: Publications de la Sorbonne, 1996.

Sohn, Anne-Marie, and Françoise Thélamon, eds. *L'histoire sans les femmes est-elle possible?* Paris: Perrin, 1998.

Sonnet, Martine. *L'éducation des filles au temps des Lumières*. Paris: Cerf, 1987.

Stock-Morton, Phyllis. *The Life of Marie d'Agoult: Alias Daniel Stern*. Baltimore: Johns Hopkins University Press, 2000.

Stoler, Ann. *Carnal Knowledge and Imperial Power: Race and the Intimate in Colonial Rule*. Berkeley and Los Angeles: University of California Press, 2002.

Sullerot, Évelyne. *Histoire de la presse féminine en France, des origines à 1848*. Paris: Armand Colin, 1966.

Suteau, Marc. *Une ville et ses écoles à Nantes, 1830–1940*. Rennes: Presses Universitaires de Rennes, 1999.

Thébaud, Françoise. *Écrire l'histoire des femmes*. Fontenay/Saint-Cloud: École Normale Supérieure Éditions, 1998.

Théry, Irène, and Christian Biet, eds. *La famille, la loi, l'État: De la Révolution au Code civil*. Paris: Éditions du Centre Georges Pompidou, 1989.

Thibert, Marguerite. *Le féminisme dans le socialisme français de 1830 à 1850*. Paris: Giard, 1926.

Thiercé, Agnès. *Histoire de l'adolescence (1850–1914)*. Paris: Belin, 1999.

Thomas, Edith. *Les femmes de 1848*. Paris: Presses Universitaires de France, 1948.

Thompson, Victoria. *The Virtuous Marketplace. Women and Men: Money and Politics in Paris, 1830–1870*. Baltimore: Johns Hopkins University Press, 2000.

Timmermans, Linda. *L'accès des femmes à la culture (1598–1715)*. Paris: Honoré Champion, 1993.

Turin, Yvonne. *Affrontements culturels dans l'Algérie coloniale: Écoles, médecines, religion, 1830–1880*. Paris: François Maspero, 1971.

———. *Femmes et religieuses au XIXème siècle. Le féminisme "en religion."* Paris: Nouvelle Cité, 1989.

Vicinus, Martha. *Independent Women: Work and Community for Single Women, 1850–1920*. Chicago: University of Chicago Press, 1985.

Walton, Whitney. *Eve's Proud Descendants: Four Women Writers and Republican Politics in Nineteenth-Century France*. Stanford: Stanford University Press, 2000.

Weil, Kari. "A Woman's Place in the Utopian Home: The 'New Paris' and the Saint Simoniennes." In *Home and Its Dislocations in Nineteenth Century France*, ed. Suzanne Nash, 231–46. Albany: SUNY Press, 1993.

Williams, Margaret, RSCJ. *The Society of the Sacred Heart: History of a Spirit (1800–1975)*. London, Darton, Longman, and Todd, 1978.

Zeldin, Theodore. "The Conflict of Moralities: Confession, Sin and Pleasure in the Nineteenth Century." In *Conflicts in French Society: Anticlericalism, Education and Morals in the Nineteenth Century*, ed. T. Zeldin, 13–50. London: Allen and Unwin, 1970.

INDEX

Page numbers in *italic* indicate images, maps, or tables.

Sée, Camille, 199, 205–9, 217

Sée educational law (1880), 7, 205–8, 218, 224. See also *collèges* and *lycées*

Senegal, 200, 231, 234–37, 239–41, 252

Servant, Eugénie, 154–56, 182, 187–92. *See also* Legion of Honor schools

sewing
neglected in inspections, 53
recommended by pedagogues, 28, 30–31, 33, 51, 257
gendered representations of, 99, 139
and needlework within school programs, 51, 56, 58, 66, 127, 179, 207
practice of in schools, 63, 182, 291 n. 73
representation of in children's literature, 38
in schools in Africa, 233–35

Séverine (pseudonym for Caroline Rémy), 254

Sévigné, Marie de Rabutin-Chantal, Marquise de, 9, 56

Simon, Jules, 201, 214

Simon, Sophie, 154, 189

Sirey, Madeleine, 86, 94, 278 n. 5

Smith, Bonnie, 8, 36, 79

Smith, Martha, 247

Société de la morale chrétienne, 86

Société de philosophie panécastique et d'enseignement universel, 88

Société de revendication des droits de la femme, 211, 213

Société des méthodes de l'enseignement, 86

Société générale pour l'éducation et l'enseignement, 222, 298 n. 102

Société mutuelle d'éducation des femmes, 103

Société pour l'enseignement professionnel des femmes, 104, 212–13

Sonnet, Martine, 22

Soulié, Frédéric, 96

sous-maitresse, 130–31, *See also* teachers' aides

Spiritains, 240

Staël, Germaine de, 22, 24, 254, 267 n. 11

Stern, Daniel (pseudonym of d'Agoult), 63–65, 67, 71–72, 80, 195

Stévens, Marie, 124, 282 n. 60

Stoler, Ann, 252

students, 6
age in schools, 172–74, 173, 290 n. 37
and defiance of school rules, 1, 191–94
and diary-writing, 189, 191–94, 293 n. 125
foreign students, 169, 172
length of study, 60, 292 n. 90
within Parisian schools, 169
and schooling experiences, 1, 53, 62–75. *See also* boarding schools, Legion of Honor, religious schools, Sacré-Cœur

Suard, Jean-Baptiste, 24

Stuart, Janet Erskine, 257–58

Talleyrand, Charles Maurice de, 20

talents, 28, 40–41, 46, 52, 252
within school programs, 32, 60, 62, 100–101, 111, 179, 270 n. 98. *See also* accomplishments; decorative arts; school programs: arts

teachers' aides, 48–49, 112, 118, 121, 125, 127–28. *See also* teaching examinations; teachers: laywomen

teaching examinations, 48, 115–25, 129, 167–68
content of, 49, 115, 282 n. 51
diplomas held by women, 127, 164
diplôme de maîtresse de pension, 118, 122, 131, 282 n. 49
at the Hôtel de Ville, 49
expanding interest in, 183–85, 194, 292 n. 83
nuns exempted from, 50, 115
preparation for in schools, 175, 178, 180, 183–84, 190–91
qualifications to open secondary school, 48–50
situation in the provinces, 117–18, 122–23. *See also* boarding-school headmistresses, nuns, professionalization

teachers: laywomen, 5, 12, 46, 109–34
competition from nuns, 213–14
professional identity of, 7, 80
representations of, 52, 111–13, 191
as substitute mothers, 88, 110, 175. *See also* boarding school headmistresses; *brevet de capacité*; Legion of Honor schools; normal schools; professionnalization; teaching examinations

teachers: male, 50, 53, 114, 225, 283 n. 66
within boarding schools, 90, 119, 121, 125–28, 145, 170, 174, 180–81
in Duruy courses, 204, 208, 218–19

Thompson, Margaret, 250

Tiers-Ordre de Notre-Dame du Mont-Carmel, 146, 148

training school, 50. *See also* normal schools

tribune de l'enseignement, La, 89

tribune des femmes, La, 86

Turinez, Monsignor, 222

United States, 227
American girls' education, 215–18, 222
anti-Catholicism in, 251
Catholic academies in, 303 nn. 95, 97, 304 n. 100
French model of education in, 13, 246–50, 256
French nuns in, 241, 243, 305 n. 13
French schools in, 200, 227, 244–46
as mission territory, 242–46
representations of American women, 217, 222
Sacred Heart schools in, 58, 243. *See also* Sacré-Cœur and individual religious orders

Printed in Great Britain
by Amazon

45168115R00200